SWEET

SWEET

Desserts from London's Ottolenghi

Yotam Ottolenghi
Helen Goh

with Tara Wigley

TEN SPEED PRESS
California | New York

For my three sweet treats, Karl, Max and Flynn, who always refuse to share their chocolate chip cookies with me.

——

YOTAM

For my mother, Cheng, who never fails to cook with her heart and soul; and for my sister Lily, who ignited my passion for baking and has been with me every step of the way.

——

HELEN

Preface 7

Yotam's introduction 10

Cookies 16

Mini-cakes 70

Cakes 122

Cheesecakes 198

Tarts & pies 226

Desserts 260

Confectionery 312

Baker's tips & notes 344

Ingredients:
A (selected) glossary 351

Index 357

Acknowledgments 362

Our Sugar Manifesto

There's so much sugar in this book that we thought about calling it, well, *Sugar*. There's nothing like a perfectly light sponge cake flavored with spices and citrus, for example, or a mega-crumbly confectioners' sugar–dusted cookie, straight out of the oven, to raise the spirits and create pure joy. These are the moments we rejoice in, celebrating the sweet things in life.

We say this not to be Irreverent or flippant—wo are completely aware of current concerns about the adverse effects of sugar—but we want to make it clear that this is a recipe book full of more than 110 wonderful sweet things.

In the fickle world of food fads and fashions, Public Enemy No. 1 is constantly changing: eggs, fats, carbs—we are told to restrict our intake of them one year, and then to make them a major part of our diet the next. To those who do as they're told, it's all very confusing.

In the midst of this confusion, we try to stick to the simple rule of what you see is what you get. People will make responsible choices about what and how much to eat as long as they are not consuming things without realizing it—hidden sugars, hidden salts, hidden elements with names we can't even pronounce, let alone understand what they are. There is nothing wrong with treats, as long as we know what they are and enjoy them as such.

Just as we don't hide anything, we also never "free from" anything, just for the sake of it. The decision to deny ourselves an entire food group is one we are never going to make. We're lucky to not have any food allergies and are pleased that those who really can't eat gluten have lots of "free from" choice, but "free from" cooking, for the sake of it, is just not something that excites us. If a recipe is "free from" gluten or nuts or dairy, it is the result of accident rather than design. A happy accident, certainly—we had no idea we were creating more than 20 gluten-free recipes here, and are delighted that we have!—but it's not something we specifically set out to do. To make things easier, we have added gluten-free (GF) and nut-free (NF) symbols to the recipes where this happy accident occurs.

The Ottolenghi way has always been about abundance, inclusion and celebration. It's the way we've always cooked and it's the way we've always baked. It's the way we've always eaten and the way we've always lived.

My first job in a professional kitchen was whisking egg whites. Yes, just that. It was the 1990s, and I was doing my training as a chef during the day and assisting the pastry chef in a fancy central London restaurant at night. On the dessert section, most of the work is done before service starts. Since I was so junior and tended to do the late shift, there was one job I spent a lot of time doing: beating egg whites to order for our very popular vanilla soufflés. By the end of three months, I was a bona fide expert in the right consistency of egg whites needed for the perfect soufflé.

It must be fate then, or some kind of direction from above, that I ended up making my name on egg whites, sugar and lots and lots of air. The famously giant Ottolenghi meringues, which have adorned our windows for many years, have become our trademark. I am crediting this to divine intervention, rather than all my whisking, because it would not have been my plan A for Ottolenghi to be referred to, by some, as the meringue shop. There are worse names to be called, I know, but my ambivalence toward meringues is no secret. I do actually love meringue, just not so much of it! The Louise cake on page 173, for example, wearing a white crown of meringue and gilded with flaky almonds and bits of delicious coconut, is, in fact, one of my favorite cakes in the book.

Looking beyond the Ottolenghi window, or, rather, through it, it wouldn't have been hard to spot my love for all things sweet and the fact that I eventually honed my skills as a pastry chef beyond the holy trinity of egg white, sugar and air. Sitting alongside our grilled vegetables, grain salads and the rest of the savory dishes inspired by Sami Tamimi's and my childhoods in Jerusalem were a bunch of sweet treats that were not at all fluffy or airy. Fruit galettes, little cheesecakes, Amaretti cookies, Danishes and muffins, tarts filled with citrusy curds and all manner of chocolate delights—these were rapidly rallying a crowd of lively devotees keen to augment their salad box with a little (or big) sweet finale.

In fact, it was precisely this juxtaposition of good, yet different, things—strikingly appetizing salads alongside wonderful, handcrafted sweet treats—that has come to define the Ottolenghi experience. And by *good things*, I mean anything that is freshly made, with love, a bit of flair, real ingredients and lots of attention to detail.

Helen's arrival

I assume that it is this tacit philosophy—plus the window, no doubt—that attracted Helen Goh to Ottolenghi and brought her to us as soon as she had come off the proverbial boat from Australia in 2006.

I can actually remember getting a phone call from her and then meeting her for the first time outside one of our shops, hearing her story and not quite understanding what drives such a star to leave behind a very successful career—Helen's professional history both as a pastry chef and as a psychotherapist is remarkable—in a very sunny Melbourne in favor of a rather elusive future in a rather gray London.

It took seeing Helen at work—first cooking savory food with Sami in Notting Hill and running our Kensington kitchen, later spending much of her time dreaming up pastries, cakes and all manner of sweet things for the company—for the penny to drop. I finally realized that it was Helen's restlessness and her insatiable drive for perfection that had brought her to us. What we shared, which Helen had identified right from the start and I took a bit longer to realize, was the notion that there is no upper limit to the number of times you can bake a cake or the amount of thought that can go into the components of a tart in order to get it just right; that you can discuss the minutiae of a chocolate ice cream or a nut brittle as if the fate of the entire universe rests on the conversation, without worrying for a second that this may be, just maybe, a tiny bit over the top.

This kind of intensity and commitment has been a constant throughout Helen's different roles in Ottolenghi. Over the years, she has been involved in creating canapés, testing breakfast dishes, trying out salads and offering her insights into anything, really, that appeared on our menus or was placed on our shelves and required the kind of depth and breadth of knowledge of food that she has. More than anything else, though, it is with her cakes—a term I use very loosely here, to mean anything from a dreamy chocolate chip cookie to a light-as-a-feather meringue roulade to a rum and raisin Bundt with caramel dripping down its sides—that Helen carved her inspired mark on our food.

Our tasting sessions

Forming friendships and collaborations around a spread of food is the Ottolenghi way. I bonded with Sami in this way all those years ago, then with Ramael Scully, co-author of *NOPI: The Cookbook*, who taught me to love miso and appreciate a few new cooking techniques. My friendship with Helen was mostly formed around a piece of cake.

Here is an image that I can't shake: It's a Sunday afternoon, around 4 p.m. probably; my husband, Karl, looks out the window of our first-floor West London flat, an expression of clear foreboding appears on his face and then, very quietly, he says, "Helen's here...with her cakes." Helen then walks through our front door like a gust of wind or, rather, an overzealous dusting of confectioners' sugar, carrying more brown cartons than humanly possible and, before even setting them down, begins apologizing for all the things that went wrong with her cakes. This one hasn't risen properly, the other bowed around the center, an icing has split halfway through its application, a sabayon lost its air, a sorbet failed to churn, a sugar syrup crystallized, a cookie crumbled and so on and on and on.

Helen would then open up her boxes and take out what seemed like at least three solid days' worth of standing in the kitchen and baking. In one Sunday session we could, very easily, sample three versions apiece of two cakes in progress, each with its own minuscule variation (one flavored with vanilla, for example, the other with pandan, the third with Chinese five-spice), a cookie Helen had in America, tried at home and wanted to Ottolenghify, a couple of confectionery items (say, a chocolate-nut brittle and an Italian nougat), three flavors of summer cordials, and, to round it all up nicely, she would quickly cook up a batter she'd brought with her for a new pancake or waffle to add to Islington's breakfast menus.

You'd think there's a touch of embellishment here but there really isn't, I promise. The sinking of Karl's heart was entirely justified. It had nothing to do, though, with the cakes that failed—according to Helen—or the cookies that crumbled, and everything to do with how hard it was to stop yourself from indulging in all those incredible sugary pleasures. Helen's "failures," you see, are the stuff the sweetest dreams are made of for mere mortals. Our Sunday afternoons tended to end up with all participants nearing a perfect state of sugar-induced delirium.

This book

Many of the cakes in this book are a result of those elated Sunday sessions. Items that eventually received our seal of approval, after endless tests and infinite discussions, were, if I may say so myself, pretty magnificent. Other recipes are older, going back to the early days of Ottolenghi. Those evolved organically in our stores, based on feedback from our customers and staff. Many were brought to us by a great number of talented pastry chefs who have worked with us over the years; we acknowledge them with gratitude in the introductions to the recipes. Some recipes have been developed especially for the book, when we felt we were missing a particular angle, a specific style of cake, or just something that we love to eat that happened to be sweet.

What all the recipes share is having been through the full Ottolenghi treatment, which is exactly the way I described a "good thing" earlier: they were all conceived with love and a bit of flair and made with real ingredients and lots of attention to detail. I feel confident that you'll be able to find all of these components in each of our "cakes" here.

One final note

These days, my tastings with Helen are not quite the same as they used to be. I suspect it's to do with the fact that we both became parents in recent years.

In our first meeting after Helen's Sam was born, the three-week-old was resting in his Moses basket next to us while Helen and I were debating the merits of different consistencies of marshmallow for making s'mores. To my regret, I sent an offhand tweet reporting that an infant is the third wheel in our regular tastings, only to receive a bunch of grave warnings from concerned followers about the fatal risks of feeding cakes to newborns.

Setting aside this particular mishap, Sam and his brother Jude's arrival and, later on, the birth of my boys, Max and Flynn, did slightly alter the nature of our meetings. Our attention now has to be harnessed and somewhat focused, deliberations are shorter and, unconsciously, we find our cakes a bit more child-friendly (you wouldn't know that, though, looking at the number of cakes in the book with serious quantities of booze in them). Children's birthday parties are now natural testing grounds for sponge cakes and the boys themselves are some of our fiercest critics. Just the other day I offered Max a slice of cake, to which he quickly replied "Did Helen make it?" "I am afraid not," I said. "No, then" was his resolute and final answer. What a few years back may have been a very lengthy discussion was over before it had even started. Having been put so clearly in my place, all I could do was go back to the kitchen and whip up some egg whites.

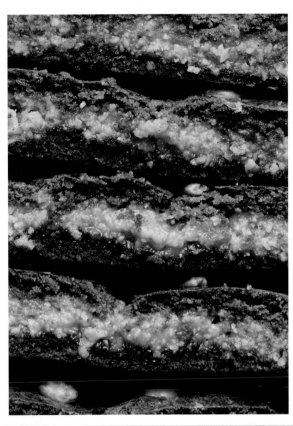

Cookies

—

Making cookies is fun, quick and easy. We'd say this about all forms of baking, of course, but cookies are particularly happy-making. This is for all sorts of reasons. Here are just a few.

EQUIPMENT-FREE › Making a batch of cookies doesn't require much equipment. Assuming that anyone with an interest in baking has baking sheets, parchment paper, measuring spoons, wooden spoons and mixing bowls, then you're pretty much ready to go. If you want to develop your interest in baking and don't already own a freestanding electric mixer, we'd highly recommend investing in one. It is a thing of great beauty! We use our electric mixer so often throughout the book that we've taken the liberty of assuming you have one. Beyond this, though, you won't need much more to open the (oven) door onto a whole world of cookies. There are occasions when a little something extra is needed—a piping bag and a nonstick silicone mat for the Cats' Tongues (see page 27) for example, or stamps and cookie cutters for the Soft Gingerbread Tiles with Rum Butter Glaze (see page 42)—but we'll suggest a shortcut or alternative where we can, so that you don't have to buy a specific piece of equipment if you don't want to.

HASSLE-FREE › The lack of equipment and general fuss makes baking cookies an ideal activity to do with kids. Baking with young ones is often, secretly, more fun in theory than in practice—the chaos! the flour! the sheer disregard for detail! With cookies, though, you really can get your mini-helpers involved in rolling, shaping and mixing without being too precious about whether the dough is slightly overmixed or the size and shape of a particular cookie is somewhat idiosyncratic. There are enough recipes in the book for which precision and timing is everything—making the Frozen Espresso Parfait for a Crowd (see page 298), for example, requires an empty kitchen and full focus—but here you really can embrace the chaos and relax in the knowledge that your dough is going to be robust enough to handle a bit of four-year-old improvisation.

RULE-FREE(ISH) › Many cookie recipes are also able to handle a bit of grown-up improvisation. Recipe writers ask something completely contradictory of their readers: at the same time as saying that baking is a science—if you don't own measuring spoons, put the book down and buy some now, please!— and that instructions need to be followed closely, we also ask you to use your initiative as to whether a little bit more or less of something is needed (time in the oven, water in the dough, whisking in the mixer). So too with ingredients: alongside the instruction to put precisely ⅛ teaspoon of something in a batter, we then blithely say, "But if you don't have it, you can use this or this as an alternative, variation or substitute." It's not meant to be a paradox: we have tested and retested these recipes until we think we have created a perfect version. Our strong advice to you—rolling pin in hand, waving it in the air for emphasis—is to do the same. Don't bake a batch of cookies once and then move on to the next recipe. Bake and rebake (or test and retest, if you like) the same recipe so that you can make all the tweaks, changes and alterations you need to create the exact amount of crisp or spice you want in your cookie. If you don't like aniseed or brandy, don't add it; if you don't have any date syrup, use corn syrup; if you like your cookies particularly crisp, give them an extra minute in the oven; if you want to jazz up a simple cookie, sandwich two together with something delicious. Bake something enough times for it to become yours. Then you can move on to the next one of ours.

FREEZER-FRIENDLY › Cookie doughs are really happy to be hidden away in the freezer for a while, ready to be popped into the oven when the moment arrives. It's one of life's great pleasures, we think, to know that, whatever else is going on in your day, you're only ever about 14 minutes away from a perfectly baked chocolate chip cookie. We generally prefer to bake from frozen (we roll the dough into balls, then freeze them), rather than baking the cookies first and freezing them after they've cooled. There are exceptions to this rule, however, which will appear alongside all the standard getting-ahead and storage notes.

FESTIVE-FRIENDLY › There is a perfect cookie for every occasion: some of our recipes are so festive, for example, that they actually look like snowballs. Whether they resemble snow—the Pecan Snowballs (see page 63) or Amaretti with Honey and Orange Blossom (see page 38)—or simply taste of the spices we associate with festive times—the Orange and Star Anise Shortbread (see page 46)—there's always something to link with a special occasion. The cranberries in the Cranberry, Oat and White Chocolate Biscuits (see page 24) for Thanksgiving, for example, or the Chocolate "O" Cookies (see page 55) for the classic kids' party.

We've been making and selling some of the cookies featured here in our shops for years. And as with all old friends, we're feeling excited (but also a little bit protective) to be sharing these. Look after them, please! Some are twists on household or childhood classics: our Garibaldis (see page 57) and Chocolate and Peanut Butter S'mores (see page 48). Some were made for the shops but didn't quite work—the Chocolate, Banana and Pecan Cookies (see page 29), which went too soft too quickly because of the banana in the mix, but which are heaven to make at home. Others were developed specifically for *Sweet*: the Soft Date and Oat Bars (see page 45) and the Speculaas Biscuits (see page 37).

And the difference between a cookie and a British biscuit for those pondering one of life's great questions? The straightforward answer is that cookies bend and biscuits snap. Cookies are softer and often thicker than biscuits. Delve a bit deeper, though, and you could say that cookies are sweet and often chunky, while biscuits can be savory and are often crisp. We can think of crisp cookies, however—and then we have our "Anzac" Biscuits (see page 52), which also go by the name of Honey, Oat and Raisin Cookies. Is it just a case of American versus British terminology? It's a can of worms we are very happy to keep closed, in return for a jar of cookies (or biscuits), which we are more than happy to keep open.

Whatever you call them and whichever recipes you choose to make your own, we hope they make you happy. A house with a full cookie jar becomes a home.

Custard Yo-Yos with roasted rhubarb icing

Yo-Yos were a staple of Helen's Antipodean childhood, ubiquitous in all the cafés where she sweetened her tooth. Their popularity with our customers shows that the old-fashioned combination of roasted rhubarb and custard takes a lot of people back to the sweet treats of their youth.

As an alternative to custard powder, you could use cornstarch. It won't have the wonderful old-school yellow of custard powder, but the Yo-Yos will still taste great; you might just want to up the amount of vanilla extract you use from ¼ to ½ teaspoon. And if you're not opposed to food coloring, a drop or two of yellow will also help to simulate the color of the custard.

MAKES 15

The icing can be made up to 2 days in advance and kept in the fridge. If your icing is a bit loose—this can happen if you overwork it—it will benefit from time in the fridge anyway, to firm up. The dough tends to go very hard if left in the fridge, so it is best to roll on the day it is made.

Once assembled, the Yo-Yos can be kept for up to 5 days in an airtight container, so long as they are not anywhere too warm (in which case the icing will soften).

RHUBARB ICING

1 small stalk of rhubarb, trimmed, washed and cut into 1-inch/ 3-cm lengths
4½ tbsp/65 g unsalted butter, at room temperature, cubed
1 cup plus 2 tbsp/130 g confectioners' sugar
½ tsp lemon juice

DOUGH

1⅓ cups plus 2 tsp/175 g all-purpose flour, plus 1 tbsp for dusting
½ cup/65 g custard powder (or cornstarch)
½ cup plus 1 tbsp/65 g confectioners' sugar
⅛ tsp salt
¾ cup/170 g unsalted butter, at room temperature, cubed
¼ tsp vanilla extract (or ½ tsp, if using cornstarch)

1   Preheat the oven to 350°F/180°C. Line a small baking sheet with parchment paper.
2   **To make the rhubarb icing,** spread the rhubarb out on the lined baking sheet and roast for 30 minutes, or until softened. Remove from the oven and allow to cool before transferring to the small bowl of a food processor. Process to a purée, then add the butter. Sift in the confectioners' sugar, add the lemon juice and continue to process for a couple of minutes; it seems like a long time, but you want it to thicken, which it will do as it's whipped. Transfer to a small bowl and chill in the fridge for a couple of hours to firm up. (You don't want the icing to be at all runny, so add a little more confectioners' sugar if necessary; it needs to hold when sandwiched between the cookies.)
3   **To make the dough,** sift the flour, custard powder (or cornstarch), confectioners' sugar and salt into the bowl of an electric mixer with the paddle attachment in place. Beat on low speed to combine. Add the butter and continue to beat on low speed until the mixture resembles breadcrumbs. Add the vanilla extract, increase the speed to medium and beat for about 30 seconds, until the dough comes together.
4   Line two baking sheets with parchment paper. ››

5   Pinch off small bits of dough and use your hands to roll them into 1⅛-inch/ 3-cm round balls; you should have enough dough for 30 balls, about ½ oz/15 g each. Place them on the lined baking sheets, spaced about 1½ inches/4 cm apart. Dip the back prongs of a small fork in the remaining 1 Tbsp flour before gently but firmly pressing down into the middle of each cookie. The balls will increase to about 1⅓ inches/3.5 cm wide, but don't press all the way to the bottom; you just want to create firm lines in the dough rather than force them to spread out.

6   Bake for 25 minutes, rotating the sheets halfway through, until the cookies are dry on the bottom but have not taken on too much color. They will be relatively fragile when warm but still firm to the touch. Set aside on the baking sheets to cool for 5 minutes before transferring to a wire rack to cool completely.

7   Sandwich pairs of cookies together with the icing, with the "forked" sides facing outward. You should use about ½ oz/15 g of icing in each cookie sandwich. It will seem like a lot, but trust us—the cookies can take it.

Peanut sandies

These are lovely as they are—simple, nutty, moreish—but can also be used as a base for other things, if you want to build them up. A layer of melted chocolate, or Nutella straight from the jar, sandwiched together and served with a spoon of ice cream, they make for a sort of scaled-down and deconstructed Snickers bar. The marshmallow filling from the Chocolate and Peanut Butter S'mores (see page 48) also works well, with a thin layer of melted chocolate or raspberry jam.

MAKES ABOUT 18 (IF USING A 3-INCH/8-CM ROUND CUTTER)

This recipe can easily be doubled if you want to make more, or freeze half the batch, rolled and all set up to be baked as and when you want.

Once baked, these will keep for up to a week in an airtight container.

½ cup plus 1 tbsp/90 g raw peanuts (skinless, unroasted and unsalted), or roasted peanuts
1 cup plus 2 tbsp/150 g all-purpose flour
½ cup plus 1 tbsp/125 g unsalted butter, at room temperature

⅓ cup plus 1 tbsp/50 g confectioners' sugar
1 tsp vanilla extract
¼ tsp salt
¼ tsp baking powder
2 tbsp demerara sugar

1   Preheat the oven to 375°F/190°C.
2   Spread the peanuts out on a baking sheet and roast for 8–10 minutes (or 3–4 minutes if using roasted) until golden brown. Set aside until completely cool, then transfer to a food processor with ⅓ cup/50 g of the flour. Process until the nuts are finely chopped, then set aside. (The oven will not be used for more than an hour so can be turned off at this point.)
3   Place the butter and confectioners' sugar in an electric mixer with the paddle attachment in place. Beat on medium-high speed for about 2 minutes, until light and fluffy. Add the vanilla extract, beat to combine, scrape down the sides of the bowl with a rubber spatula and then turn the speed to medium-low. Sift the remaining flour, the salt and baking powder into the bowl and continue to beat. Add the nuts and beat again, just to combine.
4   Tip the dough onto a clean work surface and knead gently to bring it together, then form it into a ball. Cover loosely in plastic wrap, press to form a disk, and chill in the fridge for 1 hour to firm up.
5   Preheat the oven to 375°F/190°C. Line two baking sheets with parchment paper.
6   Roll the dough between two sheets of parchment paper to just under ¼ inch/ 0.5 cm thick. Using a 3-inch/8-cm round cutter, cut out 18 circles, rerolling the scraps so that you have enough dough. Place these on the lined baking sheets, spaced about ⅓ inch/1 cm apart. Sprinkle with the demerara sugar and bake for 15 minutes, or until golden brown all over. Remove from the oven and set aside on the baking sheets to cool before serving.

Almond, pistachio and sour cherry wafers

These are lovely to snack on with tea or coffee, of course, but they also work well after a meal with a spoonful of ice cream. Don't be put off by how many slices one loaf makes: the slices are wafer thin so you can easily eat four or five at a time! Play around with the dried fruit: raisins, roughly chopped figs or apricots can be used instead of (or in combination with) the sour cherries.

Thanks to Carol Brough, previously head pastry chef at Ottolenghi, for introducing us to these.

MAKES 1 LARGE LOAF, 55–60 WAFER-THIN SLICES

At the bakery, we use a meat slicer to produce very fine, uniform slices. Using a large kitchen knife also works well, though. Freeze the dough once it's shaped into a loaf (but before it's sliced and baked), then transfer it to the fridge the night before you want to bake it, or just remove it from the freezer for a couple of hours before slicing. It is much easier to slice when not completely frozen; it should be cold but pliable when pressed.

The unbaked dough can be kept in the freezer for up to 3 months.

Once baked, the crisp wafers keep for up to a week in an airtight container.

3¼ cups/400 g all-purpose flour
1 tsp baking soda
½ tsp ground cinnamon
½ tsp salt
7 tbsp/100 g unsalted butter, cubed

1¼ packed cups/240 g dark brown sugar
¼ cup plus 1 tbsp/70 ml water
1 cup/150 g whole almonds, skin on
⅔ cup/90 g shelled pistachio kernels
½ cup/100 g dried sour cherries

1   Line the base and sides of a regular 8½ x 4½-inch/900-g loaf pan with parchment paper and set aside.
2   Sift the flour, baking soda, cinnamon and salt into a large bowl and set aside.
3   Place the butter, sugar and water in a small saucepan over medium-low heat. Cook for about 5 minutes, until the sugar has dissolved, then pour into the dry ingredients, along with the almonds, pistachios and cherries. Mix to form a smooth, glossy dough, then tip the mixture into the prepared pan, pressing down firmly. Cover the top with a piece of parchment paper and transfer to the fridge or freezer for several hours to firm up; it should be cold but pliable when pressed for ease of slicing (see Note).
4   Once the dough is firm, preheat the oven to 375°F/190°C. Line a baking sheet with parchment paper.
5   Slice the loaf as thinly as you can without the slices breaking—⅛ inch/3 mm thickness is ideal—and lay them out on the parchment-lined baking sheet; they won't spread during baking, so don't worry about spacing them apart.
6   Bake in batches for 10–14 minutes (timing will vary, depending on how thick the slices are), until golden brown. Remove from the oven and set aside until completely cool; they will be slightly soft when warm but will harden and crisp up as they cool.

Cranberry, oat and white chocolate biscuits

We first made these to sell around Thanksgiving, but our customers soon demanded them all year-round. They have enough going for them to appeal to all senses, as well as seasons: tartness from the cranberries, chewiness from the oats, nuttiness from the whole wheat flour and almonds, and a bit of sweet luxury from the white chocolate coating. Dried sour cherries can be used instead of the cranberries, if preferred.

MAKES ABOUT 30 (IF USING A 3-INCH/8-CM CUTTER)

1 cup/150 g whole almonds, skin on
1 cup plus 2 tbsp/150 g all-purpose
    flour, plus extra for dusting
½ cup/75 g whole wheat flour
1½ cups/150 g old-fashioned
    rolled oats
¼ tsp salt
1 cup/225 g unsalted butter, at
    room temperature, cut into
    1½-inch/4-cm pieces

½ cup/100 g granulated sugar
finely grated zest of 1 large
    orange (1 tbsp)
¾ cup/125 g dried cranberries,
    chopped in half (if they are not
    already chopped), soaked in
    1 tbsp plus 2 tsp/25 ml orange juice
9 oz/260 g white chocolate

These will keep for up to a week in an airtight container.

1   Preheat the oven to 350°F/180°C.

2   Spread the almonds out on a rimmed baking sheet and roast for 10 minutes. Remove from the oven and, once cool enough to handle, roughly chop into ⅓-inch/1-cm pieces. Transfer the nuts to a large bowl and add both flours, the oats and salt. Mix together and set aside.

3   Increase the oven temperature to 375°F/190°C. Line two or three baking sheets with parchment paper and set aside.

4   Place the butter, sugar and orange zest in the bowl of an electric mixer with the paddle attachment in place. Beat on medium speed for about 2 minutes, until combined and light. Add the almond-flour mixture and continue to beat on low speed until the dough just comes together. Add the cranberries and orange juice and beat for another few seconds to combine, then tip the dough onto a lightly floured work surface. Knead into a ball, sprinkling over more flour if needed to prevent it getting too sticky.

5   Cut the dough in half and roll out one half so that it's just over ¼ inch/0.5 cm thick. Use a 3-inch/8-cm cookie cutter to cut the dough into rounds. Transfer these to a lined baking sheet while you continue with the remaining dough. Bake for 18 minutes, until lightly colored all over. Remove from the oven and set aside until completely cool.

6   Meanwhile, place the white chocolate in a small heatproof bowl over a pan of gently simmering water, stirring occasionally, until melted. Do not let the base of the bowl touch the water. To coat the biscuits, use the back of a dessertspoon to spread 1 tbsp of melted chocolate over each. Set aside on a cooling rack for the chocolate to set, which can take up to an hour, before serving.

Chocolate chip and pecan cookies

Our version of this classic American cookie is a huge seller in the Ottolenghi delis. In fact, some of our customers have become such cookie connoisseurs that each store tailors its bake to their particular preference. It's true! Our Ledbury Road regulars, for example, like them crisp on the edges and soft in the center. This is achieved by cooking the rolled dough when it is fridge-cold (rather than room temperature). Our customers on Upper Street, on the other hand, prefer them crisp all the way through. To achieve this, you just flatten the balls slightly before they are baked and give them an extra minute in the oven.

The pecans can be substituted with either walnuts or hazelnuts, if you prefer. Whichever nut you choose, they'll need to be roasted. The cookies also work without any nuts at all. If you go for this option, you'll need to increase the amount of chocolate to 13 oz/370 g. It's important to start with chips or callets here, rather than chopping from a block of chocolate—see page 352.

MAKES ABOUT 36 (THE BATCH IS QUITE LARGE, BUT THE BALLS ARE SO EASY TO ROLL, FREEZE AND BAKE FROM FROZEN THAT WE HAVE NOT TRIED TO REDUCE IT)

1 cup/120 g pecan halves (or walnut halves or hazelnuts)
1 cup plus 1½ tbsp/250 g unsalted butter, at room temperature, cut into ¾-inch/2-cm cubes
1 packed cup plus 2 tbsp/200 g light brown sugar

1 cup/200 g granulated sugar
1½ tsp vanilla extract
2 large eggs
4½ cups/560 g self-rising flour
1 tsp salt
9 oz/260 g dark chocolate chips or chunks (60-70% cocoa solids)

Once the unbaked dough has been rolled into balls, they can be frozen for up to 3 months. You can also bake them from frozen; you'll just need to add an extra minute of cooking time (unless, like our Ledbury Road customers, you like a soft center).

The cookies keep well for 5 days in an airtight container.

1 Preheat the oven to 350°F/170°C.

2 Spread the pecans out on a rimmed baking sheet and roast for 10 minutes. Remove from the oven and, when cool enough to handle, roughly chop into ⅔-inch/1.5-cm pieces and set aside. (You can turn the oven off at this point, as the dough will need to chill in the fridge before baking.)

3 Place the butter and both sugars in the bowl of an electric mixer with the paddle attachment in place. Beat on high speed for about 2 minutes, until light and fluffy. With the machine still running, add the vanilla extract and eggs, one at a time, beating well after each addition. Turn the speed to low, sift in the flour and salt and continue to beat until combined. Finally, add the chocolate chips and roasted nuts, mixing until just combined. Turn off the machine and gently bring the dough together by hand; the consistency should be firm and come together easily.

4 Use your hands to form the dough into large golf-ball-sized balls, about 1⅔ oz/45 g each, and set aside in the fridge for an hour to firm up.

5 When ready to bake, preheat the oven to 400°F/200°C. Line two large baking sheets with parchment paper.

6 Spread the balls of dough out on the lined baking sheets—you'll need to bake them in two batches—spaced 2⅓ inches/6 cm apart. Bake for 12 minutes, rotating the sheets halfway through, until golden brown and slightly cracked on top. Remove from the oven and set aside to cool on the baking sheets for 10 minutes until firm, then transfer to a wire rack to cool completely.

Cats' tongues

Langues de Chat, Lenguas de Gato, Katte Tong, Cats' Tongues: whatever the name you use, these long and delicate biscuits are so light that you can nibble a load of them. We've kept the flavor deliberately simple so they can be served alongside all sorts of flavored ice creams, sorbets and puddings: the Campari and Grapefruit Sorbet (see page 304), for example, or the Yogurt Panna Cotta with Basil and Crushed Strawberries (see page 282). You can also sandwich two together with chocolate ganache, if you like, for something more substantial.

The lemon zest can be substituted with orange or lime zest, perhaps, or a pinch of spice can be added—ground cloves, ginger, cardamom or mahleb all work well.

MAKES ABOUT 36

8½ tbsp/120 g unsalted butter, at room temperature, cubed
½ cup plus 1 tbsp/120 g granulated sugar
scraped seeds of ¼ vanilla pod
finely grated zest of ½ lemon (½ tsp)

⅛ tsp salt
2⅛ oz/60 g egg whites (from 1½ large eggs)
½ cup plus 1½ tbsp/90 g all-purpose flour
a drop or two of lemon oil

1   Preheat the oven to 425°F/220°C.
2   Place the butter, sugar, vanilla seeds, lemon zest and salt in the bowl of an electric mixer with the paddle attachment in place. Beat on medium speed for about 3 minutes, until light. Turn the speed to low and gradually dribble in the egg whites, beating all the time and scraping down the bowl to ensure even mixing. Sift the flour into a separate bowl, then, with the mixer still on low speed, add the flour in three batches. When completely combined, add the lemon oil, then mix through and scrape the mixture into a piping bag fitted with a ⅓-inch/1-cm plain tip.
3   Pipe 3½-inch/9-cm fingers onto a nonstick silicone mat or a parchment-lined baking sheet, spaced about 1½ inches/4 cm apart, as they will spread during baking. Bake for 8 minutes, rotating the sheet halfway through, until the cookies are light brown around the edges. Remove from the oven and wait for a minute or two before transferring to a cooling rack. Set aside until completely cool and then store in a parchment paper-lined airtight container (the paper will prevent the delicate cookies breaking when being moved about).

Use a nonstick silicone baking mat here, if you have one, instead of regular parchment paper. It will help the delicate cookies cook more evenly. If you have only parchment paper, that's fine. Just switch the oven to conventional heat (rather than convection) to prevent the paper and light cookies fluttering around inside and becoming misshapen; the cookies might need an extra minute in the oven on this setting.

You will need a piping bag with a ⅓-inch/1-cm plain tip here. You can either invest in a piping bag that comes with a range of tips, or buy a disposable piping bag and just cut a ⅓-inch/1-cm hole in the end.

These will keep well in an airtight container for up to 5 days, or in the freezer for up to 10 days. Once baked, they're actually very good eaten frozen!

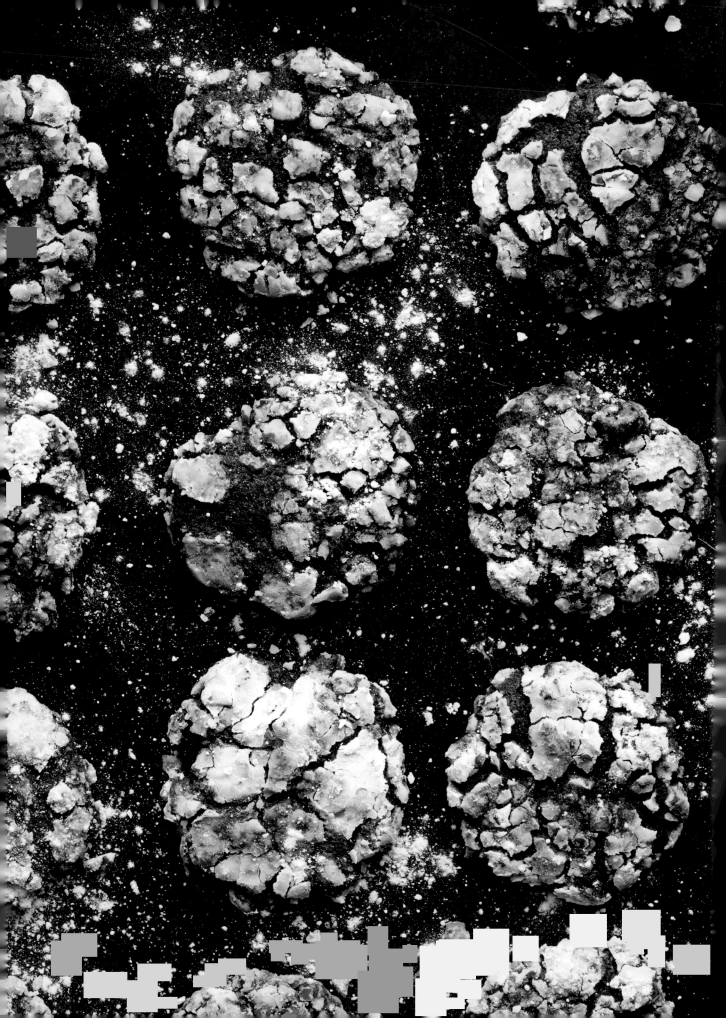

Chocolate, banana and pecan cookies

These were introduced by Jim Webb, an original member of the Ottolenghi team along with Sami, Noam and Yotam. Jim mostly worked on pastry, bringing with him some brilliant ideas, along with a serious knowledge of bread and viennoiserie. It was Jim's suggestion to add banana to the dough here, both for the moisture and distinct flavor it brings. Pecans are classic, but walnuts can be used, if you prefer.

The secret here is to slightly underbake the cookies, which keeps them soft and fudgy. It's for this reason that they've never become a feature in the shops, particularly in the summer, when they'd bend and break after an hour or two piled up in a bowl. There are worse things to happen, though, than to be told you need to eat a whole batch of cookies within a day or so of them being baked.

MAKES ABOUT 24

Once the unbaked dough has been rolled into balls, they can be kept in the fridge for up to 2 days, or frozen for up to 3 months. You can also bake them from frozen; you'll just need to add an extra minute of cooking time.

These cookies are best eaten within a day of being baked.

8 tbsp/110 g unsalted butter, at room temperature, cubed
½ cup plus 2 tsp/110 g granulated sugar
1 large egg, lightly beaten
1 cup/125 g all-purpose flour
½ tsp baking powder
3½ tbsp/20 g Dutch-processed cocoa powder
½ tsp ground cinnamon
¼ tsp salt

¾ cup/100 g dark chocolate chips (70% cocoa solids), or 3½ oz/ 100 g dark chocolate, cut into ¼-inch/0.5-cm pieces
2 oz/55 g mashed banana (about ½ small banana)
1⅓ cups/165 g pecan halves, finely chopped
¾ cup plus 1 tbsp/100 g confectioners' sugar

1   Place the butter and granulated sugar in the bowl of an electric mixer with the paddle attachment in place. Beat on medium-high speed until light and fluffy, then gradually add the egg and continue to beat until incorporated. Sift the flour, baking powder, cocoa powder, cinnamon and salt into a bowl, then add to the butter and sugar. Mix on low speed for about 15 seconds, then add the chocolate chips and banana. Beat until combined, then transfer to the fridge for 2 hours to firm up.

2   When firm, use your hands to form the dough into 1-inch/3-cm round balls, about ⅔ oz/20 g each; you might need to wash your hands once or twice when making them, if they get too sticky. Place the pecans in a medium bowl and drop the balls into the nuts as you form them, rolling them around so that they are completely coated and pressing the nuts in so that they stick.

3   Line a baking sheet with parchment paper, place the cookies onto the sheet— there is no need to space them apart—and transfer to the fridge for an hour.

4   When ready to bake, preheat the oven to 375°F/190°C. Line two baking sheets with parchment paper.

5   Place the confectioners' sugar in a bowl and roll the cookies in the confectioners' sugar, pressing it in as you go so that it sticks well. Place on the lined baking sheets, spaced 1 inch/2.5 cm apart, and flatten the cookies to ⅓ inch/1 cm thick.

6   Bake for 10 minutes. They will be soft to the touch when they come out of the oven, so allow them to cool on the baking sheet for 10 minutes before gently transferring to a wire rack. These can be served warm, when they will be a little gooey in the center, or set aside until completely cool.

Brown butter almond tuiles

These tuiles (or tiles) are, like the Cats' Tongues (see page 27), deliciously simple cookies to eat with ice cream, sorbet (they work well with the Campari and Grapefruit Sorbet, see page 304) or just with a cup of coffee. It's browning the butter that gives the tuiles their nutty caramel note. And if you've made the ice cream yourself, you'll already have the egg whites, waiting to be put to good use.

Traditionally, tuiles are cooled over a rolling pin to produce their characteristically curved shape. We tend to cool ours flat, however, as they store more easily this way and are less prone to snapping; but feel free to stick with tradition, if you prefer.

MAKES ABOUT 20

3 tbsp/40 g unsalted butter, cubed
1¼ cups/120 g sliced almonds
½ cup plus 1 tbsp/120 g
   granulated sugar

¼ cup/35 g all-purpose flour
2½ oz/70 g egg whites (from
   2 large eggs)
¼ tsp vanilla extract

Provided they are cooked through (completely crisp), they will keep for up to 10 days in an airtight container. If they do soften, you can crisp them up in the oven for 5 minutes at 350°F/180°C before setting aside to cool completely.

1   Place the butter in a small saucepan over medium heat. Once melted, continue to cook until the butter is foaming. Swirl the pan gently from time to time, to allow the solids to brown more evenly, until you see dark brown sediments begin to form on the sides and bottom of the pan. Continue to let it bubble away until it turns a rich golden brown. It will also smell heavenly, like toasted nuts and caramel. Remove the pan from the heat and let it stand for 5 minutes, to allow the burnt solids to collect at the bottom of the pan. Strain through a fine-mesh (or muslin-lined) sieve, discarding the solids. You need ¾ oz/25 g browned butter, so pour away any excess (this can be reserved for cooking), then set aside to cool to room temperature.

2   Place the sliced almonds, sugar and flour in a medium bowl and add the cooled butter. Add the egg whites and vanilla extract and mix with a wooden spoon until combined.

3   Preheat the oven to 350°F/180°C. Line a baking sheet with parchment paper.

4   Drop tablespoons of the almond mixture—about ½ oz/15 g each—onto the baking sheet, spaced about 2 inches/5 cm apart. Flatten the mixture by patting them down with moistened fingers—keep a small bowl of warm water nearby to dip into—until the almonds are just about in a single layer and each tuile is about 2⅓ inches/ 6 cm wide.

5   Bake for 18 minutes, rotating the baking sheet halfway through, until the tuiles are golden brown all over. Remove the sheet from the oven and allow them to cool for 5 minutes before gently transferring them with a small metal spatula to a wire rack (or drape them over a rolling pin, if you prefer the traditional shape) until completely cool.

Gevulde Speculaas

Speculaas are spiced shortcrust cookies, hugely popular in the Netherlands. *Gevulde* means "stuffed," which—with their almond paste filling—these certainly are. Both are eaten by the Dutch around Sinterklaas—the 5th and 6th December—when the legendary figure rides into town on his white horse, bearing presents for those who've been good. You'll worry that the dough is not going to come together when rolling it, but trust the recipe—it works!

You'll have twice as much spice mixture as you need for this recipe, but it keeps well in a sealed container, so it can be used in your next batch of Gevulde Speculaas or in the Speculaas Biscuits (see page 37)—one batch needs exactly the amount of spice mixture you'll have left over.

Thanks to Hennie Franssen for this recipe (as well as for translating all of Yotam's books into Dutch).

SERVES 12

Once baked, these will keep for up to 5 days in an airtight container.

SPICE MIX
1 tbsp ground cinnamon
1 tsp ground aniseed
¾ tsp ground white pepper
¾ tsp ground ginger
½ tsp ground coriander
1 tsp ground cardamom
¼ tsp ground nutmeg
¼ tsp ground cloves

DOUGH
7 tbsp/100 g unsalted butter, at room temperature, plus 1 tbsp/15 g, melted, for brushing
½ packed cup plus 1 tbsp/100 g dark brown sugar
1 tbsp whole milk, plus up to 1 tbsp, if the dough needs it
½ tsp baking soda
1⅓ cups plus 1 tbsp/180 g all-purpose flour, plus extra for dusting
⅓ tsp salt

ALMOND PASTE
1½ cups/200 g whole blanched almonds
¾ cup/150 g granulated sugar
1 large egg
2 tsp lemon juice, plus finely grated zest of 1 small lemon (¾ tsp)
2 oz/55 g mixed candied citrus peel (or candied orange peel), chopped

TO DECORATE
1 large egg, lightly beaten
¼ cup/30 g whole blanched almonds (about 22 almonds)

1   **To make the spice mix,** combine all the ingredients in a bowl and set aside until ready to use.

2   **To make the dough,** place the room-temperature butter in the bowl of an electric mixer with the paddle attachment in place. Add the brown sugar and milk and beat on medium speed until smooth. Sift the baking soda, 4 tsp spice mix, the flour and salt into a bowl, then add this to the dough. Continue to beat until the dough is soft and pliable, adding a little more milk if needed. Transfer the dough to your work surface and lightly knead. Cover in plastic wrap and keep in the fridge until ready to use. ››

3   To make the almond paste, place the almonds in a food processor and process for 30 seconds—you don't want the texture to be completely smooth. Add the granulated sugar, egg and lemon juice and process again, until it is slightly smoother but still grainy. Finally, add the lemon zest and candied peel and pulse once or twice, just to mix through. The paste should be sticky and softer than the dough, but still hold its shape. Transfer to a small bowl until ready to use.

4   Preheat the oven to 375°F/190°C.

5   Roll the dough out on a lightly floured 16 x 12-inch/41 x 30.5-cm sheet of parchment paper to form a 13 x 7½-inch/33 x 19-cm rectangle, just over ¼ inch/ 0.5 cm thick. Dust with more flour if needed to prevent it sticking.

6   Transfer the dough and parchment sheet to a large baking sheet and brush two-thirds of the melted butter evenly over the dough. Spoon the almond paste lengthwise down the center of the dough to form a long sausage, about 2⅓ inches/ 6 cm wide. Brush the almond paste with the remainder of the butter and then, using the parchment paper to help you, fold the left side of the dough so it's on top of the paste. Fold the right side on top of this (again, using the paper to help you) so that the two sides are slightly overlapping. Press gently to secure and carefully turn the whole thing over so that the seal is at the bottom and the paste is secured—a bit like a giant sausage roll.

7   To decorate, brush the dough evenly and lightly with some of the beaten egg, arrange the whole almonds on top—positioning as you like—and then brush again with the egg.

8   Place in the oven and bake for 30 minutes, until the dough begins to color and the almonds are golden. Don't be alarmed that the roll flattens out—this is meant to happen! Set aside on the baking sheet until completely cool, then cut into 12 slices, each about 1 inch/2.5 cm wide, and serve.

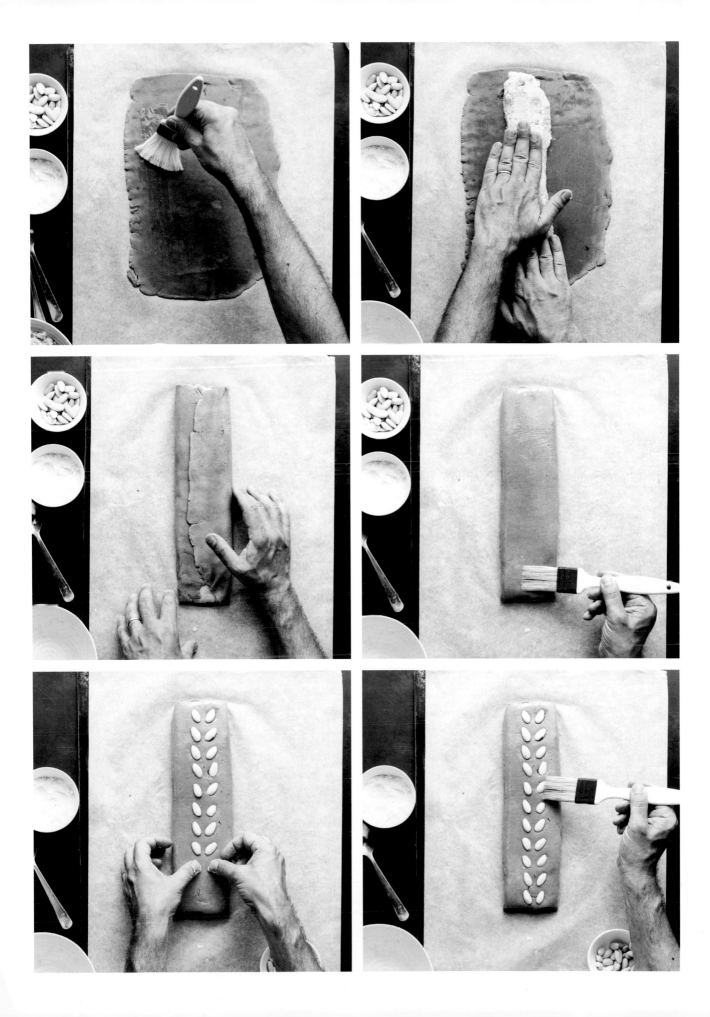

Speculaas biscuits

We originally made these crisp biscuits to use up the spice mix left over from making Gevulde Speculaas. Yet they swiftly became the very reason to make the spice mix in the first place! Either way, you're onto a festive winner. Both the Gevulde Speculaas and these biscuits are traditionally eaten in the Netherlands around Sinterklaas, during the first week of December. They're delicious all year-round, though, perfect for snacking on or for serving with ice cream.

Use any size or shape of cookie cutter you like, depending on the occasion and season. The more frilly the edge of your cutter, the more quickly your biscuit edges will cook, so keep an eye on timing as you might need to decrease it by a minute or two. Be sure not to underbake them, though; you want them to be supercrisp, and they are meant to take on a lot of color.

MAKES ABOUT 60 (IF USING A 3-INCH/8-CM ROUND CUTTER)

The dough can be frozen before or after it is rolled and shaped; if the latter, bake from frozen and increase the cooking time by 1 minute.

Once baked, these will keep for up to a week in an airtight container.

3⅔ cups/450 g all-purpose flour
about 3½ tsp spice mix (see page 33)
1 tbsp baking powder
½ tsp salt
1 cup plus 1½ tbsp/250 g unsalted
  butter, at room temperature

1¾ packed cups/330 g dark
  brown sugar
3½ tbsp/50 ml dark rum (or brandy)
1 large egg white, lightly beaten
  until frothy
1 cup/100 g sliced almonds

1   Sift the flour, spice mix, baking powder and salt into a medium bowl and set aside.

2   Place the butter and sugar in the bowl of an electric mixer with the paddle attachment in place. Beat on medium-high speed for about 3 minutes, until the mixture is light and fluffy. Add the rum (or brandy) and beat until incorporated. Finally, add the sifted ingredients and continue to beat on low speed; the dough can initially feel dry and difficult, but trust us, it will come together. Tip onto a clean work surface and knead lightly to bring together. Divide the dough into two pieces, cover each loosely in plastic wrap, then press down to form flattish disks and transfer to the fridge for 30 minutes (or freeze one of the disks if you just want to make 30 biscuits).

3   When ready to bake, preheat the oven to 400°F/200°C. Line two large baking sheets with parchment paper and set aside.

4   Roll out the dough on a lightly floured work surface until it is just under ¼ inch/0.5 cm thick. Using a 3-inch/8-cm round cutter (or whatever size or shape you like), cut out the biscuits and place them on the lined baking sheets, spaced ¾ inch/2 cm apart. Reroll the scraps to cut out more biscuits. Use a pastry brush to lightly paint a thin layer of egg white over each biscuit, then sprinkle lightly with the sliced almonds (use ½ cup/50 g if you have frozen half the dough).

5   Bake for 12 minutes, rotating the sheets halfway through, until golden brown and the almonds are toasted. Remove from the oven and set aside for 10 minutes on the baking sheets for the biscuits to cool slightly, then transfer to a wire rack to cool completely.

Amaretti with honey and orange blossom

With no flour at all, the almond meal are allowed to be the star here, so use the freshest, best-quality you can find.

MAKES 20

2 cups plus 2 tbsp/200 g almond meal
½ cup plus 2 tsp/110 g granulated sugar
finely grated zest of 1 lemon (1 tsp)
finely grated zest of 1 small orange
 (1 tsp)
⅛ tsp salt
2⅛ oz/60 g egg whites (from
 1½ large eggs)

3½ tsp/25 g honey
¼ tsp orange blossom water
⅛ tsp best-quality almond extract
1 cup/100 g sliced almonds, for rolling
3½ tbsp/25 g confectioners' sugar

The key to making these is in the timing. As with any recipe with an Italian meringue component (see page 347 for more on Italian, French and Swiss meringues), the sugar syrup—in this case, honey syrup—needs to be at exactly the right temperature just as the egg whites have formed soft peaks. The trick is to have the egg whites whipping slowly, and then be ready to increase the speed as the honey comes to a boil.

The unbaked, rolled dough can be kept in the fridge, covered in plastic wrap, for up to 2 days.

Once baked, these will keep well for up to 10 days in an airtight container.

GF

1   Combine the almond meal, sugar, lemon zest, orange zest and salt in a large bowl and set aside.

2   Place the egg whites in the bowl of an electric mixer with the whisk attachment in place and beat on medium speed. Heat the honey in a small saucepan over medium heat, and just before it comes to a boil, increase the speed of the mixer to medium-high while the honey continues to boil for 30 seconds and the egg whites form soft peaks. Remove the honey from the heat and carefully pour into the egg whites, in a continuous stream, beating all the time. When all the honey has been added, keep beating for a minute until the meringue is fully whipped and cooled. Stop the mixer, remove the whisk attachment and change to the paddle attachment.

3   Add the almond meal–sugar mixture, along with the orange blossom water and almond extract. Beat until it all comes together to form a soft, pliable paste. Transfer to a bowl, cover with plastic wrap and transfer to the fridge for 1 hour to firm.

4   Once chilled, divide the mixture into four portions of about 3 oz/85 g each. Sprinkle a quarter of the sliced almonds on a clean work surface and roll out one piece of dough to form a log 12 inches/30.5 cm long and ⅔ inch/1.5 cm wide, covered in almonds.

5   Line a baking sheet with parchment paper, and either lift the log onto the sheet by hand or roll it onto a clean ruler and use that to transfer it easily to the sheet. Continue until you have rolled all four pieces into logs, sprinkling more sliced almonds on the work surface with each batch. Place them all on the baking sheet, cover with plastic wrap, and place in the fridge for at least 2 hours or up to 2 days.

6   When ready to bake, preheat the oven to 375°F/190°C. Line a baking sheet with parchment paper.

7   Remove the baking sheet from the fridge and cut each log into five smaller logs, 2⅓ inches/6 cm long. Sift the confectioners' sugar into a bowl and roll each piece in the confectioners' sugar so that they are covered all over. Spread out on the parchment-lined baking sheet, spaced ¾ inch/2 cm apart, and bake for 13–15 minutes, rotating the sheet halfway through, until the Amaretti are golden brown but still soft. Remove from the oven and set aside on the baking sheet for 10 minutes. These can be served warm or transferred to a wire rack to cool and firm up before serving.

SOFT GINGERBREAD TILES WITH RUM BUTTER GLAZE

Soft gingerbread tiles with rum butter glaze

Helen has been slightly obsessed with these ever since she saw them on the front cover of the original *Tartine* baking book by Elisabeth M. Prueitt and Chad Robertson. In the book, they used an antique embossed rolling pin to create the imprint before cutting them into rectangles; here, we use round cookie stamps for the imprint before cutting them out with a round cookie cutter. Once the glaze is applied, they really do look like antique tiles. Try and get ahold of some stamps if you can—they're very popular in Scandinavian countries and can easily be bought online. If you can't get any, the gingerbreads can also be made as regular cookies, using round cutters, or cut into squares or rectangles with a knife.

If you want to keep the glaze booze-free, the rum in the icing can be replaced with lemon juice.

MAKES 12–14 (DEPENDING ON THE SIZE OF STAMP AND CUTTER)

—

6 tbsp/85 g unsalted butter, at
  room temperature
⅓ packed cup plus 2 tbsp/90 g dark
  brown sugar
¼ cup/100 g blackstrap molasses
1 large egg yolk
1¾ cups plus 2 tbsp/235 g all-purpose
  flour, plus extra for pressing
1 tbsp Dutch-processed cocoa powder
½ tsp baking soda
1 tsp ground ginger
½ tsp ground cinnamon
⅛ tsp ground cloves
¼ tsp salt
¼ tsp freshly ground black pepper

RUM BUTTER GLAZE
⅔ cup/80 g confectioners' sugar
⅛ tsp ground cinnamon
1 tbsp/15 g unsalted butter,
  melted and warm
1 tbsp dark rum (or lemon juice)
1 tsp warm water

—

Once the dough is made, it can be covered in plastic wrap and kept in the fridge for up to 2 days before baking.

These will keep for up to 5 days in an airtight container. The glaze will discolor and crack a little, but this will not affect how they taste.

1   Place the butter, sugar and molasses in the bowl of an electric mixer with the paddle attachment in place. Beat on medium speed until smooth and incorporated. Add the egg yolk and continue to beat until fully combined.

2   Sift the flour, cocoa powder, baking powder, ginger, cinnamon, cloves, salt and pepper into a bowl. Turn the speed of the mixer to low, and add the dry ingredients to the butter and molasses. Once the mix comes together, tip the dough onto a lightly floured work surface and knead gently. Roll out the dough so that it is about ¼ inch/ 0.5 cm thick. If the dough is very soft, you will need to chill it.

3   Preheat the oven to 375°F/190°C. Line two baking sheets with parchment paper and set aside.

4   Dip the cookie stamps in a small bowl of flour, shake off any excess and then press them firmly into the dough, one at a time, to create a deep imprint. How far you need to press to get an imprint will depend on your stamp; the patterns on some are more deeply cut than others. Bear in mind that the cookies rise a little when cooked, so any soft imprints will disappear. Using a round cookie cutter that is slightly larger than the pattern, cut out the pieces of imprinted gingerbread. Transfer the cookies to the lined baking sheets, spaced about ¾ inch/2 cm apart. Reroll the dough and continue to stamp and cut cookies until all the dough is used up.

5   Bake for 9–10 minutes, rotating the sheets halfway through, until firm to the touch. They will continue to firm up as they cool, so don't be tempted to bake them for any longer.

6   **To make the rum butter glaze** while the gingerbreads are in the oven, as the glaze needs to be brushed onto the cookies while they are still warm, sift the confectioners' sugar and cinnamon into a small bowl. Add the melted butter, rum (or lemon juice) and water and mix with a spoon until smooth. The glaze will thicken slightly if it sits around, so stir through a little more warm water if you need to—it should be the consistency of runny honey.

7   Remove the cookies from the oven, leave them to cool for 5 minutes, then brush or dab the glaze all over with a pastry brush. Transfer to a wire rack to cool completely.

Soft date and oat bars

We have decided to call these "bars," as "flapjacks" conjure up American-style pancakes to many, which these are very much not. Whatever you want to call them, these nut-and-seed-filled slices have a crunchy edge and a slightly chewy middle. It's the way we like them, but they might be a bit softer than you're used to. If you want to firm them up—so they're robust enough to cart about in Tupperware, for example—store them in the fridge.

MAKES ABOUT 14

These will keep for up to 5 days in an airtight container.

⅓ cup/50 g whole almonds, skin on
⅓ cup/50 g cashews
2 cups/200 g old-fashioned rolled oats
¼ cup/35 g pumpkin seeds
¼ cup/35 g sunflower seeds
2 tbsp sesame seeds
7–8 large Medjool dates, pitted
   (4¼ oz/120 g), halved lengthwise
   and each half cut into 3 pieces

¾ cup plus 2 tbsp/200 g unsalted
   butter, cut into 1½-inch/4-cm cubes
¾ cup/180 g demerara sugar
¼ cup/75 g date syrup (or dark
   corn syrup)
finely grated zest of 1 small orange
   (1 tsp)
2 tsp orange blossom water
1 tsp ground cinnamon
¼ tsp salt

1   Preheat the oven to 350°F/180°C. Grease a 12 x 8-inch/30.5 x 20-cm baking dish or pan and line with parchment paper, then set aside.

2   Spread the almonds and cashews out on a rimmed baking sheet and roast for 10 minutes, or until the nuts are lightly browned. Remove from the oven and allow to cool for a few minutes before chopping into roughly ⅔-inch/1.5-cm pieces. Transfer to a large mixing bowl and set aside.

3   While the nuts are in the oven, place ¾ cup/80 g of the oats in a food processor and roughly pulse, you want them to be broken into small pieces rather than turned to powder. Add the processed oats (which will help keep the bars together when baked) to the unprocessed oats in a bowl and set aside.

4   Place all the seeds in a dry frying pan and toast over medium-low heat, shaking the pan frequently, so that they toast evenly. Add the seeds to the chopped nuts along with the dates and all of the oats. Mix to combine and set aside.

5   Place the butter, sugar, date syrup (or corn syrup) and orange zest in a medium saucepan and place over medium-low heat. Stir gently until the butter has melted (don't worry if the demerara sugar has not melted, it will add to the crunch) and the mixture comes together. Remove from the heat, stir in the orange blossom water, cinnamon and salt, then pour over the oat mixture. Mix well and tip out into the lined baking dish. Use a small spatula or the back of a spoon to spread and press the mixture evenly into the lined dish.

6   Bake for about 35 minutes, or until bubbling and a dark golden color. Remove from the oven and allow to cool for about 30 minutes before cutting into squares or 3 x 1-inch/8 x 2.5-cm rectangles; however you slice them, you want to do so before they harden. Don't remove them from the baking dish until they are completely cool, however, as they will crumble and fall apart.

Orange and star anise shortbread

Using two types of flour here—the finely milled Italian "00" flour and the white rice flour—creates a shortbread with a crisp and buttery texture. For the rice flour, you need the grainy type—a brand such as Bob's Red Mill, for example—rather than the finely milled Asian variety used to make dumpling wrappers.

If you are looking for ideas for biscuits to give as gifts, these should go on the list: they're sturdy enough to be wrapped in cellophane bags, with a shelf life that allows them to be enjoyed at leisure.

MAKES ABOUT 40 (IF USING A 3-INCH/8-CM CUTTER)

———

2½ cups/360 g Italian "00" flour
⅓ cup plus 1 tbsp/70 g white grainy rice flour
¾ cup plus 1½ tbsp/165 g granulated sugar
⅛ tsp baking powder
1½ tsp ground star anise (3 whole star anise, ground in a spice grinder and passed through a fine-mesh sieve)

1 tsp flaky sea salt
finely grated zest of 1 large orange (1 tbsp)
scraped seeds of ½ vanilla pod
½ cup plus 1½ tbsp/125 g unsalted butter, fridge-cold, cut into ¾-inch/2-cm cubes
1 large egg, lightly beaten

———

1   Sift both flours, the sugar, baking powder and ground star anise into a large mixing bowl. Add the salt, orange zest and vanilla seeds and mix to combine. Add the butter and use the tips of your fingers to rub it into the dry mixture until there are no large bits of butter and the consistency is that of breadcrumbs. Add the egg and mix gradually, using your hands or a wooden spoon, until the dough comes together. Shape into a rectangle and cover tightly in plastic wrap. Set aside in the fridge for 1 hour to firm up.

2   Preheat the oven to 350°F/180°C. Line two baking sheets with parchment paper and set aside.

3   Cut the dough in half and roll out one half on a lightly floured work surface until it is just under ¼ inch/0.5 cm thick. Using a 3-inch/8-cm cutter, cut out the cookies and place them on the lined baking sheets, spaced ⅓ inch/1 cm apart. Reroll the scraps to cut out more cookies.

4   Bake for 16–17 minutes, in batches if necessary, rotating the sheets halfway through to get an even color. They should be golden brown on the edges, lightly golden in the center and have a golden brown underside. Transfer to a cooling rack until completely cool.

The dough can be made a day ahead and kept in the fridge overnight; make sure you allow it to sit at room temperature for 30 minutes before rolling, so it becomes malleable. The dough can also be frozen before or after it is rolled and shaped; if the latter, bake from frozen and increase the cooking time by 1 minute.

Once baked, these will keep well for up to 10 days in an airtight container.

Chocolate and peanut butter s'mores

This is our take on s'mores, the campfire classic of melted marshmallows and chocolate squished between two graham crackers. These are a little more elaborate, but there's got to be a scout's badge for making your own marshmallow, surely?

Helen's childhood memories of Wagon Wheels—chocolate-coated cookies with a marshmallow center—predispose her to keeping these simple, leaving out the crunchy peanut butter in the filling. Yotam, whose own childhood memories are rich in nutty tahini, prefers them with. They work both ways.

MAKES 22 (IF USING A 2½-INCH/6.5-CM CUTTER)

—

COOKIES
½ cup plus 2½ tbsp/150 g unsalted butter, at room temperature, cut into ¾-inch/2-cm cubes
⅓ cup plus 1 tsp/75 g granulated sugar
1 large egg yolk (save the egg white for the marshmallow)
2 tbsp maple syrup
⅓ cup/50 g roasted (unsalted) peanuts, finely ground in the small bowl of a food processor
2 cups plus 1 tbsp/260 g all-purpose flour
⅛ tsp salt
½ cup/140 g crunchy peanut butter, for spreading

MARSHMALLOW
1½ tsp powdered gelatin, or 1½ leaves (about 4 x 2 inch/10 x 5 cm) platinum gelatin
⅓ cup/80 ml cold water
⅓ cup plus 1 tbsp/90 g granulated sugar
1½ tsp light corn syrup
scraped seeds of ¼ vanilla pod
1 oz/30 g egg white (from 1 large egg)

TO FINISH
1½ tbsp/15 g roasted (unsalted) peanuts, roughly chopped into ¼-inch/0.5-cm pieces
¼ tsp flaky sea salt
4½ oz/125 g dark chocolate (70% cocoa solids), roughly chopped into ¼-inch/0.5-cm pieces

You will need a piping bag with a ⅓-inch/1-cm plain tip here. You can either invest in a piping bag that comes with a range of tips, or you can buy a disposable piping bag and just cut a ⅓-inch/1-cm hole in the end. You will also need a candy thermometer to make the marshmallow.

The dough for the cookies can be made a day ahead and kept in the fridge.

Once baked and filled, these will keep for 3 days in an airtight container.

—

1   **To make the cookies,** place the butter and sugar in the bowl of an electric mixer with the paddle attachment in place. Beat on medium-high speed for about 2 minutes, until light and fluffy. Add the egg yolk and, when combined, add the maple syrup and ground peanuts. Once combined, sift in the flour and salt and mix together until a dough forms. Tip onto a clean work surface and knead gently for a few seconds to bring it together. Cover the dough loosely in plastic wrap, press to form a disk, and keep in the fridge for at least 1 hour or up to overnight.

2   Preheat the oven to 375°F/190°C. Line two baking sheets with parchment paper and set aside.

3   Remove the dough from the fridge about 5 minutes before rolling, so that it has some malleability. On a lightly floured work surface, roll out the dough so that it is just under ¼ inch/0.5 cm thick; you can divide it in half before rolling, if that's easier. Using a 2½-inch/6.5-cm round cutter, cut out 44 circles and place them on the parchment-lined baking sheets. Bake for about 15 minutes, rotating the sheets halfway through, until the cookies are firm and turn a light golden color around the edges. Remove from the oven and set aside, still on the baking sheet, to cool.

4 Once cool, turn the cookies over so that the underside sits up. Spread half of the cookies with the peanut butter and set aside.

5 **To make the marshmallow,** place the gelatin sheets or powder in a small bowl. Cover with 3 tbsp/45 ml of the water and set aside.

6 Place the sugar, corn syrup, vanilla seeds and remaining water in a small saucepan and place over medium heat. Stir until the sugar has melted, then increase the heat to medium-high. Bring to a boil and simmer for 8–10 minutes, until the mixture turns a very light amber color and starts to thicken (you are looking for it to eventually reach 262°F/128°C on a thermometer).

7 Keep a close eye on the sugar as it's simmering, and when the temperature reaches about 248°F/120°C, place the egg white in the bowl of an electric mixer. Starting off with a handheld whisk (there is not enough egg in the bowl for the machine whisk to be effective at this stage), beat the egg white until stiff peaks form, then continue beating with the machine.

8 When the sugar reaches 262°F/128°C, remove it from the heat, add the softened gelatin and soaking water to the sugar mixture and stir to combine. With the electric mixer running, slowly and carefully pour the sugar syrup over the egg white and continue to beat until the mixture is glossy and thick and the bowl of the mixer is completely cool; about 15 minutes.

9 **To finish,** immediately spoon the marshmallow into a piping bag and pipe the mixture into a circular pattern over the remaining uncovered cookies, covering the whole of the base with a generous amount of the marshmallow. Sandwich a peanut butter covered cookie on top of a marshmallow-covered cookie and press gently together. Continue with the remaining cookies in the same way, then leave for about a half hour to set.

10 Combine the chopped peanuts and sea salt in a small metal bowl, rubbing the salt between your fingers to break it up. Set aside.

11 Place the chocolate in a heatproof bowl over a pan of simmering water, stirring occasionally, until melted. Do not let the base of the bowl touch the water.

12 Gently hold the peanut side of the cookie sandwich and dip the marshmallow half lightly into the melted chocolate, so that the cookie is covered. Sprinkle a pinch of the peanut-salt mix into the center of the chocolate side of the cookie and allow to set before serving.

CHOCOLATE AND PEANUT BUTTER S'MORES

"Anzac" biscuits (aka Honey, oat and raisin cookies)

Anzac biscuits—a mix of rolled oats, finely grated coconut and sugar, held together by flour, golden syrup and butter—are very popular in Australia and New Zealand. Traditionally, they are sweet, flat and crispy. Very untraditionally (as Yotam was informed in no uncertain terms by his Antipodean Instagram followers, after posting a picture of our Anzacs), ours are plump, chewy and slightly malty. Amidst outcries of "travesty," we both applauded the loyalty of the Southern Hemisphere to their baked goods while also defending our version as a twist on (rather than a cruel departure from) the original. They get their chew from the addition of the raisins and the honey, while the bran flakes give them a slight but distinctive malty flavor. They're lovely to have sitting on the kitchen counter for snacking on throughout the day.

MAKES 22

1 cup/100 g old-fashioned rolled oats
¾ cup/50 g crushed bran flakes,
    lightly crushed by hand
¾ cup/90 g finely shredded coconut
1⅓ cups plus 2 tbsp/185 g
    all-purpose flour
½ cup/100 g granulated sugar
¼ packed cup/40 g light brown sugar
⅔ cup/100 g raisins
finely grated zest of 1 lemon (1 tsp)
¾ cup plus 1 tbsp/185 g unsalted butter
3 tbsp/60 g honey
2 tbsp water
1 tsp baking soda

Once baked, don't keep these in an airtight container as they will soften very quickly. Place them in an open container, separating the layers of biscuits with parchment paper, and wrap the whole thing in aluminum foil. This way, they will keep for 3–4 days.

1   Preheat the oven to 350°F/170°C. Line two large baking sheets with parchment paper and set aside.

2   Combine the oats, bran flakes, coconut, flour, both sugars, raisins and lemon zest in a large bowl and set aside.

3   Heat the butter, honey and water in a small saucepan over low heat until the butter melts. Remove from the heat and quickly stir in the baking soda for about 15 seconds, until the mixture becomes light and frothy. Pour the mixture into the dry ingredients, mix thoroughly, then roll into golf-ball-sized balls, about 1½ oz/40 g each. Place the balls on the two baking sheets, spaced about 2 inches/5 cm apart.

4   Bake for 18–20 minutes, until the biscuits are golden brown but still slightly soft. Remove from the oven and set aside for 5 minutes on the baking sheet before transferring them to a wire rack to cool completely. They should be crispy on the outside but still retain a chew on the inside.

Chocolate "O" cookies

Helen set herself the challenge of making a cookie to rival the popularity of our chocolate chip cookie. These were the result and they've become something of a signature cookie in the shops. We find their combination of salty, sweet and spicy both delicious and intriguing.

The "O" in the name nods three ways: first to Thomas Keller, whose own version of an Oreo inspired the base for our cookie; second to their small coin shape; and third, of course, to the big round "O" in the name on the door.

MAKES 22 (IF USING A 2½-INCH/6.5-CM CUTTER)

The dough can be made in advance and kept in the fridge for up to 2 days, or frozen for future use.

Once baked and filled, these will keep for 5 days in an airtight container.

COOKIES
¾ cup plus 1½ tbsp/190 g unsalted butter, at room temperature, cubed
⅔ cup/130 g granulated sugar
½ tsp flaky sea salt
1¾ cups/220 g all-purpose flour
¾ cup/75 g Dutch-processed cocoa powder
¼ tsp baking soda

WATER GANACHE
½ cinnamon stick
shaved peel of ½ orange
¼ tsp crushed red pepper flakes
6 tbsp/90 ml boiling water
4½ oz/125 g dark chocolate (70% cocoa solids), roughly chopped into ⅓-inch/1-cm pieces
scraped seeds of ½ vanilla pod
¼ tsp flaky sea salt
¼ cup/50 g granulated sugar
2½ tbsp/50 g light corn syrup
3½ tbsp/50 g unsalted butter, cut into ¾-inch/2-cm cubes

1 **To make the cookies,** place the butter, sugar and salt in the bowl of an electric mixer with the paddle attachment in place. Beat on medium-high speed for about 3 minutes, until light and fluffy. Sift the flour, cocoa powder and baking soda into a bowl, turn the speed of the mixer to low, then add the dry ingredients in two batches until a dough forms. Tip onto a clean work surface and knead gently until smooth and uniform. Cover the dough loosely in plastic wrap, press to form a disk, and keep in the fridge for 1 hour to firm up.

2 Preheat the oven to 350°F/180°C. Line two baking sheets with parchment paper and set aside.

3 Remove the dough from the fridge about 5 minutes before rolling, so that it has some malleability. On a lightly floured work surface, roll out the dough so that it is about ⅛ inch/3 mm thick; you can divide it in half before rolling, if that's easier. Using a 2½-inch/6.5-cm round cutter, cut out 44 circles and place them on the parchment-lined baking sheets. Bake for 13–15 minutes, rotating the sheets halfway through, until firm, then remove from the oven and set aside on the sheets until completely cool.

4 **To make the ganache,** place the cinnamon, orange peel and pepper flakes in a small bowl and cover with the boiling water. Set aside to infuse for 30 minutes. ››

5   After the water has been infusing for about 20 minutes, place the chocolate, vanilla seeds and salt in a medium bowl and set aside.

6   Place the sugar and corn syrup in a small pan and warm over medium heat, stirring from time to time, until the sugar has melted. Increase the heat to medium-high and boil until the sugar caramelizes and turns a light amber color, about 5 minutes. Remove from the heat and add the infused water and aromatics. Don't worry if the sugar seizes in the pan; just return it to the heat and stir until the sugar has dissolved. Return the caramel to a boil, then strain the liquid over the chocolate and vanilla; the aromatics can be discarded. Leave for 2–3 minutes until the chocolate has melted, then mix together.

7   Add the butter, one piece at a time, stirring continuously until all the butter is incorporated and the chocolate is smooth. Place in the fridge for 30 minutes until the ganache is firm.

8   Spoon a heaped teaspoon of the ganache onto the underside of a cookie, then, using a knife or the back of a spoon, spread it evenly all over the cookie. Place another cookie, underside down, on top of the ganache and sandwich together. Set aside while you repeat with the remaining cookies and ganache.

Garibaldis

These are an altogether more decadent version of the so-called squashed fly biscuit. Where the original is dry and not too sweet, our butter-rich pastry is flaky and positively oozing with caramel. Commercial garibaldis come in strips of stuck-together cookies, which are then snapped off one at a time. Ours can also become stuck together as the caramel oozes out when the pastry is baked. Don't worry, though: once they are cool enough to handle, just cut through the caramel and neaten the pastry up with scissors. The result is quite rustic, but this is as it should be!

MAKES 20

The caramel can be made a day ahead. If it becomes too firm, warm it gently to soften; you want it to be spreadable rather than runny. The dough can also be made ahead and will keep in the fridge for 3–4 days. Once assembled, the garibaldis can be frozen before baking. When ready to eat, they can be baked from frozen; you'll just need to add an extra minute of cooking time.

Once baked, these will keep for a week in an airtight container.

FILLING
⅔ cup/120 g raisins
4 tsp sweet Marsala wine
finely grated zest of 1 small orange (1 tsp)
4 tsp orange juice

PASTRY
2 cups/250 g all-purpose flour
½ cup plus 2 tbsp/75 g confectioners' sugar
finely grated zest of ½ lemon (½ tsp)
⅛ tsp salt

½ cup plus 3 tbsp/160 g unsalted butter, fridge-cold, cut into ¾-inch/2-cm cubes
1 large egg yolk
1 tbsp cold water

CARAMEL
¼ cup/60 ml water
½ cup plus 1 tbsp/120 g granulated sugar
6 tbsp/90 ml heavy cream
¼ tsp flaky sea salt

1 large egg, lightly beaten, to glaze

1   **To make the filling,** place the raisins in a small jar or container with the Marsala, orange zest and orange juice. Cover and leave at room temperature for 6 hours (or up to 24 hours), shaking it occasionally, until all the liquid has been absorbed and the raisins are soft and plump.

2   **To make the pastry,** place the flour, confectioners' sugar, lemon zest and salt in the bowl of a food processor and process to combine. Add the butter and pulse to the consistency of breadcrumbs, making sure there are no large lumps of butter left. Add the egg yolk and water and continue to pulse until the dough just comes together. Take care not to mix any longer than necessary; the dough doesn't so much come together as hold when pressed into a ball, so don't worry if it appears slightly crumbly. (At the same time, you might need to add an extra tablespoon or two of water, if the dough needs it.)

3   Transfer the dough to a clean work surface and knead very lightly, just to shape it into a smooth ball. Cut the dough in half, cover one half with plastic wrap and place in the fridge while you roll out the other. Place a large piece of parchment paper on your work surface and lightly flour. Roll out the first piece of dough on the parchment to about 12 x 10 inches/30.5 x 25 cm and ⅛ inch/3 mm thick. Transfer the dough and parchment paper together onto a baking sheet and set aside while you roll out the second piece of dough in the same way. Place this, along with the parchment paper, on top of the first sheet of dough. Cover with plastic wrap and place the baking sheet in the freezer for 30 minutes. This allows the pastry to firm up so that it can be sandwiched together. »

4   To make the caramel, place the water and sugar in a small saucepan and place over medium heat. Stir to combine and when the sugar has dissolved, increase the heat to medium-high. Cook until the caramel is golden in color, about 6 minutes. Remove the pan from the heat and slowly pour in the heavy cream. Return to low heat, stir until completely smooth, add the sea salt and set aside to cool to room temperature.

5   Preheat the oven to 375°F/190°C. Line two baking sheets with parchment paper.

6   Remove the pastry sheets from the freezer and, moving quickly, spread a thin layer of the caramel sauce over both sheets. The caramel will start to set as soon as it touches the cold pastry, so spread a little at a time to get a thin, even layer. Sprinkle the raisin filling over the top of one of the sheets, in one even layer, then place the other sheet of pastry, caramel side down, on top of the raisins.

7   Place a sheet of parchment paper on top of the pastry and gently roll a rolling pin over it, applying a light pressure to seal the two layers. Brush the top of the pastry with the beaten egg and trim a tiny bit of the edge away—just ¼ inch/0.5 cm—to neaten. Slice the rectangle into even strips (5 strips lengthwise and 4 strips across to get 20 rectangles), then place the rectangles on the lined baking sheets, spaced well apart.

8   Bake for 22–25 minutes, or until a nice golden brown color. Remove from the oven and allow to cool for 10 minutes. If some of the caramel and raisins ooze out, you can easily pop the raisins back into the edges of the biscuits while they are still hot. Then use a thin flat spatula or offset spatula to gently transfer the garibaldis from the baking sheet to a wire rack and cool completely before eating.

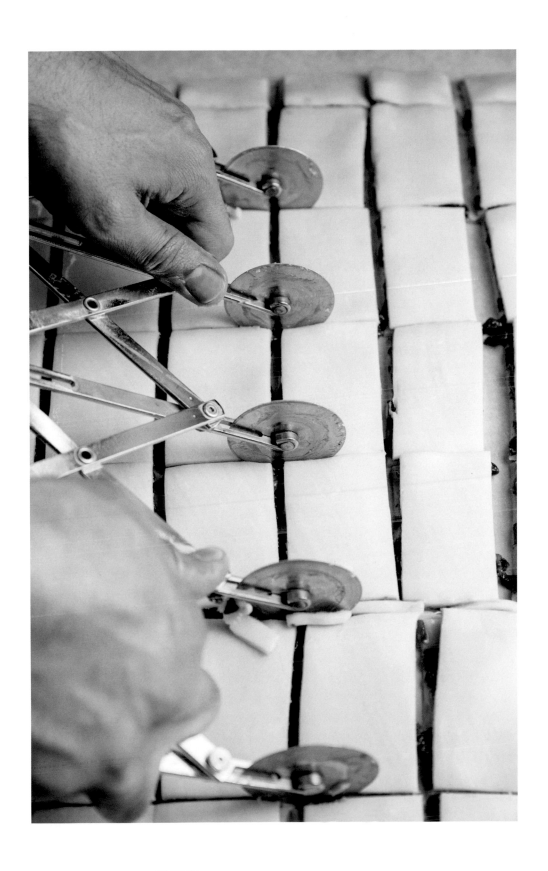

GARIBALDIS

SWEET

Pecan snowballs

Various versions of these cookies are popular throughout the world. They are sometimes called Mexican wedding cakes (even though they're a short, nutty cookie rather than a cake) and given out at festivals and celebrations. And in Greece, they're known as *kourabiedes* and made with walnuts or almonds and flavored with ouzo. We've used brandy in ours, but go with whatever bottle is open: ouzo, Pernod and rum all work well. Or you can leave out the alcohol altogether, if you prefer. For those cooking with kids (or for anyone who enjoys the bowl-and-spoon-licking stage of baking), the raw dough for these cookies is hard to resist.

Packed in cellophane bags and tied with ribbon, these make great gifts, particularly in the festive season, as they look all snowy and wintry with their thick confectioners' sugar coating.

MAKES ABOUT 21

¾ cup/90 g pecan halves
8½ tbsp/120 g unsalted butter, at room temperature, cubed
½ cup plus 1 tbsp/65 g confectioners' sugar, plus ⅓ cup plus 1 tbsp/50 g

scraped seeds of ¼ vanilla pod
¼ tsp vanilla extract
½ tsp brandy (optional)
⅛ tsp salt
1¼ cups plus 1 tbsp/165 g all-purpose flour, plus extra for dusting

These will keep well for up to 7 days in an airtight container. They also freeze well for up to a month (after baking) and are uncommonly good eaten straight from the freezer!

1   Preheat the oven to 350°F/180°C.
2   Spread the pecans out on a rimmed baking sheet and roast for 8–10 minutes, until they have taken on some color and smell nutty, then leave to cool. Transfer to a food processor, process until fine—stopping the machine before the nuts turn into an oily paste—and set aside.
3   Place the butter and confectioners' sugar in the bowl of an electric mixer with the paddle attachment in place. Beat on medium-high speed, scraping down the sides of the bowl a few times to ensure even mixing, until the mixture is light. With the machine still running, add the vanilla seeds, vanilla extract, brandy (if using), salt and ground pecans. Finally, add the flour and beat on low speed until everything comes together and there are no longer any bits of flour visible. Tip the mixture onto a clean work surface and knead gently for 30 seconds, then form into a ball. Cover loosely in plastic wrap, press to flatten into a disk and chill in the fridge for 30 minutes to firm up.
4   Increase the oven temperature to 375°F/190°C. Line a baking sheet with parchment paper.
5   Roll the dough into balls, about ⅔ oz/20 g each. Spread out on the lined baking sheet and bake for 16–18 minutes; the underside of the cookies should be firm and a light golden brown. Remove from the oven and allow to rest for 3 minutes on the baking sheet.
6   Sift the ⅓ cup plus 1 tbsp/50 g confectioners' sugar into a bowl, then, one at a time, gently roll the warm cookies in the sugar. Return them to the still-hot baking sheet to allow the confectioners' sugar to set into a thin coating. Leave for 5 minutes before coating the cookies for a second time (you may need another tablespoon or two of confectioners' sugar).

Not-quite-Bonnie's rugelach

Bonnie Stern, aka Yotam and Sami's Canadian mother, has been looking after "her boys" since they started doing book tours in Canada. As well as being told which restaurants they need to try, Sami and Yotam have come to expect a bag of Bonnie's exceptional rugelach. Filled with apricot jam, pecans and demerara sugar, they're simple, brittle and perfectly buttery.

It's the substitution of apricot jam with membrillo (quince paste) in our version that makes these Not-Quite-Bonnie's, as well as the addition of the baking powder in the dough, which makes the pastry flakier. Apricot jam still works well, though (and is more widely available than membrillo), so feel free to use the jam, if you like. We've fallen for a number of rugelach over the years, from the yeasted varieties so popular in Israel to this flakier version, preferred in North America. The yeasted variety behaves more like bread and doesn't keep as well as the flaky kind.

MAKES 24

The addition of the baking powder here—and the fact that the dough is made in a food processor with a metal blade, rather than beaten in an electric mixer—makes the pastry light and flaky. The presence of the cream cheese also makes it a dream to roll.

The pastry can be made a day ahead and kept in the fridge, or frozen for up to 3 months (remember to thaw it overnight in the fridge before using). The rolled rugelach can also be frozen (before glazing) for up to 3 months. When you are ready to bake them, brush with the glaze and bake from frozen, adding an extra minute or two to the cooking time.

These will keep for up to 4 days in an open container, separated by pieces of parchment paper, and the whole thing wrapped loosely in aluminum foil. Don't keep in an airtight container; the sugar will weep if you do and turn the rugelach soft and sticky.

PASTRY

1¼ cups/160 g all-purpose flour

⅛ tsp salt

¼ tsp baking powder

finely grated zest of 1 small lemon (¾ tsp)

scraped seeds of ¼ vanilla pod

½ cup plus 1 tbsp/125 g unsalted butter, fridge-cold, cut roughly into 1-inch/3-cm cubes

4½ oz/125 g cream cheese, fridge-cold

FILLING

⅓ cup/40 g walnut halves

½ packed cup plus 1 tbsp/100 g light brown sugar

½ tsp ground cinnamon

5¼ oz/150 g store-bought quince paste (membrillo)

1 tsp lemon juice

1 large egg, lightly beaten

1½ tbsp demerara sugar

1   **To make the pastry,** place the flour, salt, baking powder, lemon zest and vanilla seeds in a food processor and pulse for about 15 seconds to combine. Add the butter and pulse for a few seconds more, until the mixture has the texture of fresh breadcrumbs. Add the cream cheese and process just until the dough comes together in a ball around the blade; be careful not to overprocess or the pastry will be tough. Tip the dough onto a lightly floured work surface and knead for a few seconds, just to bring it together.

2   Divide the pastry in two, cover each half loosely in plastic wrap, then press to flatten into disks. Transfer to the fridge for 1 hour.

3   Preheat the oven to 350°F/180°C. Line two baking sheets with parchment paper and set aside.

4   **To make the filling,** spread the walnuts out on a rimmed baking sheet and roast for 5 minutes. Remove from the oven, set aside to cool, then chop finely and place in a small bowl with the brown sugar and cinnamon. Mix together and set aside.

5   In a separate bowl, combine the quince paste and lemon juice to form a smooth paste. (If your quince paste is very firm, warm it gently over low heat to soften [or heat for 10 seconds in a microwave], until the texture is thick like jam but spreadable, then set aside to cool before using). ››

6   Take one of the pieces of dough from the fridge and roll out on a lightly floured work surface to form a 9½-inch/24-cm circle, about ⅛ inch/3 mm thick. Use a small spatula or the back of a spoon to spread half of the quince paste evenly over the surface and then sprinkle with half of the sugar-nut mixture. Using a sharp knife or a pizza wheel, if you have one, cut the dough as though you are slicing a cake into twelve equal triangles. The best way to get even-sized triangles is to cut it first into quarters, then each quarter into thirds. One at a time, roll each wedge quite tightly, starting from the wide outside edge and working toward the point of the triangle, so that the filling is enclosed. Place them on the lined baking sheets, seam side down, spaced about 1 inch/3 cm apart. Repeat the rolling process with the remaining disk of dough and filling, then chill the rugelachs in the fridge for 30 minutes before baking.

7   Increase the oven temperature to 400°F/200°C.

8   When ready to bake, lightly brush the tops of the rugelachs with the beaten egg and sprinkle with the demerara sugar. Bake for 20–25 minutes, rotating the sheets halfway through, until golden brown all over. Don't worry if some of the filling oozes out; this will add a lovely toffee taste to the edges of the cookies. Remove from the oven and allow to rest on the sheets for 5 minutes before transferring to a wire rack to cool completely.

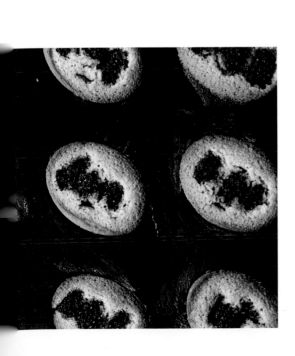

Mini-cakes

—

We love mini-cakes for lots of reasons. Being able to eat rather a lot of them is one. They also look so very lovely, all mini-me-sized and often iced in bright colors, which can't help but make you smile. And they come in all shapes, which makes them fun to make as well as to eat.

This chapter is home (sweet home) to so many of our signature cakes. Arranged in rows as neat and orderly as little soldiers, just the sight of our mini-cakes pulls hungry customers through the door. And it's not hard to see why, frankly. There's something about mini things that encourages especially big care to be taken of them, in the way they're made and displayed. There is also something about them that encourages people to make space for them, whether it's morning, noon or night.

We have syrup-soaked mini-cakes (reminiscent of Yotam's childhood), gluten-free cakes, cakes drenched in boozy caramel and cakes that have been on our shop counters since Day One—the Flourless Chocolate "Teacakes," for example (see page 108). If you want to bring out your inner cake shop, this is the chapter to start covering with specks of chocolate and flour.

THE SMALLER SOMETHING IS, THE MORE YOU CAN EAT › Some mini-cakes are so mini and light that you find yourself eating a few more than one at a time! The Baby Black and Orange Cakes (see page 94), for example, or either of our Powder Puffs (see page 82), which come as close to biting through air as we can imagine; superlight sponge cakes, held together with whipped cream and fresh strawberries; citrus-spiked cupcakes; little and light fresh madeleines—they are all bite-sized delights.

CAKES TO RELAX WITH, CAKES TO REBEL WITH › Other mini-cakes are more for the "us against the world" days, when something decadent is needed to sustain and strengthen. It's not every day that you're going to be making and eating a doughnut piped with saffron custard cream, or a brownie filled with chunks of halva and swirls of tahini. But on the days you do, you'll be guaranteed to conquer all that comes your way!

MAKE THE MINI MIGHTY › Although we tend to think of mini-cakes as something to be enjoyed throughout the day, many of them also work well when served with the sort of fanfare usually reserved for desserts. No one is ever going to feel shortchanged when presented with their very own Tahini and Halva Brownie (see page 87), for example, served with a generous scoop of vanilla ice cream, or Banana Cakes with Rum Caramel (see page 100) served with some rum and raisin ice cream. With literally a spoonful of help, mini-cakes can be made mighty.

HAVE YOUR CAKE AND EAT IT (OR NOT) › Mini-cakes love to be eaten on the day they're iced. There are always things you can do to get ahead—"teacakes" (and even a sponge cake, if you really need to) can be made a day in advance and kept in an airtight container—but always hold back on icing until the day you are planning to serve them. You don't want to keep anything iced out of the fridge for too long, and the icing will often lose its shiny gloss after a day. Don't be too precious with any leftovers, however; they'll be fine in the fridge for a day or two for you to snack on.

Even when not iced, some cakes like to be eaten on the day they are baked: the Saffron, Orange and Honey Madeleines (see page 76), or the hazelnut crumble cake (see page 90), for example. Other cakes, on the other hand, taste better the day after they're made: the flavors and texture of the Persian Love Cakes (see page 74), for example, deepen with a little bit of time.

Equipment

The fact that mini-cakes come in all shapes and sizes means, inevitably, that making them requires a wide variety of pans. We've tried not to go too far with specialized molds and pans, and we always suggest alternatives where we can so that you may improvise with what you already have. That being said, the cost of a pan or mold is often the same price as two or three store-bought cakes, so there's always that justification, if you need one, for purchasing more equipment. Home-baked Bundt cakes forever!

Following is a list of all the equipment you'd need were you to make every recipe in this chapter. Alternatives are suggested, where relevant, and instructions given in individual recipes for amending cooking times to suit the alternative pan size.

REGULAR MUFFIN PANS › These have 12 molds: 2¾ inches/7 cm wide at the top, 2 inches/5 cm wide at the bottom, and 1⅓ inches/3.5 cm deep.

LARGE (JUMBO) MUFFIN PANS › These have 6 molds: 3⅓ inches/8.5 cm wide at the top, 2⅓ inches/6 cm wide at the bottom, and 1½ inches/4 cm deep. You could use a regular muffin pan instead—you'll just make more muffins, smaller in size, and the baking time will need to be shortened.

MINI-MUFFIN PANS › These have 24 molds: about 1½ inches/4 cm wide at the top, 1 inch/3 cm wide at the bottom, and ¾ inch/2 cm deep. Again, you could use a regular muffin pan instead—you'll make fewer but larger cakes.

BOTTOMLESS CAKE RINGS › We like to make our mini Victoria sponge cakes (see page 96) in 3-inch/8-cm-wide cake rings. Alternatively, you can make one large cake instead—you'll need a 8-inch/20-cm-round springform pan and will need to increase the cooking time accordingly. We also use these small cake rings for our individual cheesecakes, so if you think you're going to be making these, too, the rings are worth having.

INDIVIDUAL BUNDT PANS › We love making our "teacakes" in individual Bundt pans, which are 4 inches/10 cm wide at the top and 2 inches/5 cm deep. They're big enough to be a real treat, but light enough to not be intimidating and exciting enough to share. And that's before the icing has been drizzled over, falling down the sides unevenly as well as through the well in the center of the cake. Alternatively, you can use one large Bundt pan: 8 inch/20 cm wide at the top, 5½ inches/14 cm wide at the bottom, and 4 inches/10 cm deep. The method will be the same, but the baking time will need to be increased. You could also use a jumbo muffin pan—the molds are not quite as big as the Bundt pans, so you'll generally make one more muffin than Bundt.

SILICONE HALF-SPHERE MOLDS › We make our Baby Black and Orange Cakes (see page 94) in these silicone trays with hole-shaped molds, 2 inches/5 cm wide at the top and 1 inch/3 cm deep. They make for very cute orb-shaped mini-cakes. Alternatively, if you have the traditional British mince pie pan that we use for the Pineapple Tartlets with Pandan and Star Anise (see page 255), you can use this instead.

SMALL RECTANGULAR SILICONE FINANCIER MOLDS › We make our Persian Love Cakes (see page 74) in small 3 x 1 x 1-inch/8 x 3 x 3-cm rectangular molds. You could also make these in a regular muffin pan, but make sure you use paper liners; the cakes won't come out if they are only greased and floured.

MADELEINE PANS › Our Saffron, Orange and Honey Madeleines (see page 76) are made in standard madeleine pans, the shell-shaped molds of which are about 3 x 2 inches/8 x 5 cm. Available in silicone or metal, we far prefer the metal—you don't get the nice crust in the silicone pan—but either is fine. You'll just need to grease and flour the metal pan before the batter is added. The pans usually have 12 molds, but because it is so very easy for one person to eat about a third of these, we would encourage you to buy two pans rather than one and make twenty-four! Madeleines are so much about their shape, but if you do need an alternative, a mini-muffin pan would work, or a domed traditional mince pie pan. In either case, you will just make more cakes that are smaller in size.

POPOVER PANS › Similar to jumbo muffin pans, with 6 large molds, but with straight sides: 2½ inches/6.5 cm wide and 2 inches/5 cm deep. We like to make our Strawberry and Vanilla Mini-Cakes (see page 95) in Popover pans, but a regular or jumbo muffin pan would also work.

MINI LOAF PANS › We make our Chocolate Guinness Cake with Baileys Irish Cream (see page 117) in mini loaf pans that are 4 x 2½ inches/10 x 6.5 cm at the top and 3 x 1½ inches/8 x 4 cm at the bottom. You can convert the recipe into one larger cake, if you like, using an 7-inch/18-cm-round springform pan. The changes you'll need to make to the recipe are all written in the Note on page 117.

NO SPECIAL PANS › If you don't want to stock your cupboards with any more equipment, that's fine—we understand! Doughnuts, brownies and powder puffs are your friends.

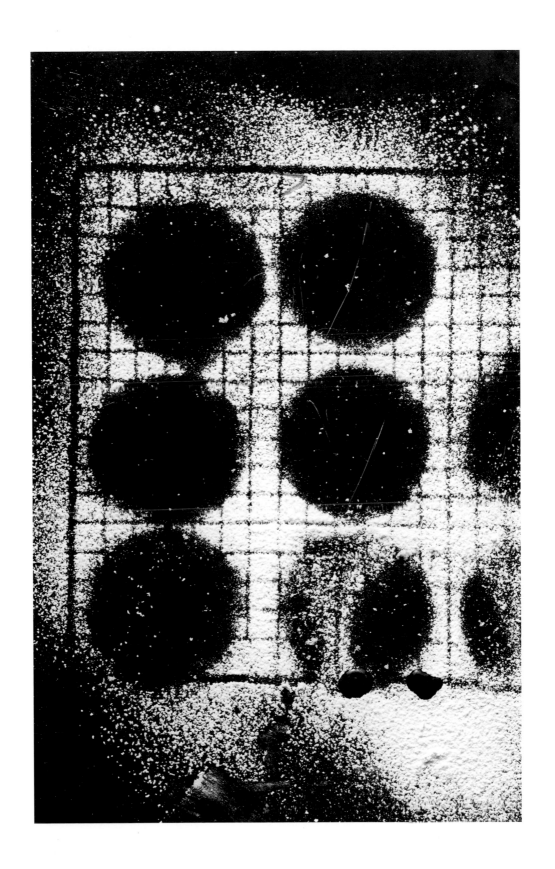

Persian love cakes

These little Persian cakes came to us by way of our Glaswegian colleague John Meechan, who adapted them from a Gerard Yaxley recipe in *Gourmet Traveller*. John's stroke of genius was to add buckwheat flour, distinctive for its nutty and slightly sour taste, and the mahleb, a spice made from grinding the seed kernel of the St. Lucie cherry. The spice is not often used outside of Greece, Turkey and the Middle East, so don't worry if you can't get ahold of any: a few drops of almond extract work well as an alternative.

The cakes can be served warm, without the mascarpone, pistachio and pomegranate seed topping, or at room temperature with all the toppings. Presentation-wise, it's a nice little trick to lay a piece of parchment paper on top of each cake, on the diagonal, hold it down flat, and sprinkle the confectioners' sugar over the exposed side of the cake.

MAKES 12

2½ cups/240 g almond meal
⅔ cup/135 g demerara sugar
⅔ packed cup/135 g light brown sugar
⅓ cup/50 g buckwheat flour
5½ tbsp/80 g unsalted butter,
    fridge-cold, cubed
¾ tsp salt
½ cup plus 2 tbsp/160 g plain
    Greek yogurt

3⅛ oz/90 g eggs (about 2½ large eggs)
1 tbsp mahleb (or ¼ tsp almond extract)
¾ tsp ground nutmeg

TO SERVE (AT ROOM TEMPERATURE)
¼ cup/60 g mascarpone
1½ tsp shelled pistachio kernels,
    slivered or finely crushed
12 pomegranate seeds (optional)
confectioners' sugar, for sprinkling

1   Preheat the oven to 350°F/180°C.
2   Place the almond meal, both sugars, flour, butter and salt in a food processor and pulse a few times, until the mixture has the consistency of breadcrumbs. Transfer two-thirds of the mix to a large bowl along with the yogurt, eggs, mahleb and nutmeg. Mix to combine and set aside.
3   Line the base of 12 financier (or muffin pan) molds with the remaining third of the crumb mix; it should come about a third of the way up the sides of the molds. Use your fingers or a teaspoon to press the mix into the base of the molds, as you would a cheesecake, so that it is compact.
4   Using two teaspoons, fill each mold to the top with the yogurt mix and level off with a small offset spatula for an even finish. Place the molds on a baking sheet and bake for 30–35 minutes, rotating the sheet halfway through, until the cakes are dark golden brown on top and a skewer inserted into the center comes out clean. The cakes will look slightly uncooked and damp inside, but this is the way they should be and is part of their charm. Allow the cakes to cool for 15–30 minutes before unmolding them. (They are delicious as is, slightly warm.)
5   **To serve,** cool before spooning a little of the mascarpone on top of each cake and topping with the pistachios and 1 pomegranate seed, if desired. Sprinkle a little confectioners' sugar on one half of each cake, at a diagonal (see introduction).

We make our cakes in small rectangular silicone financier molds, which look so elegant. Alternatively, use a regular muffin pan.

These cakes are at their best the day after they are made. They can be eaten on the day, however, and kept for up to 2 days in a sealed container (without the mascarpone topping). They don't keep for much longer than this—which is surprising, given how moist they are—because the texture becomes a bit gummy. Once the cakes have been topped with the mascarpone, they can be stored in the fridge and brought back to room temperature before serving.

Saffron, orange and honey madeleines

Traditionally, madeleines are best eaten as close to coming out of the oven as possible. The beating together of the eggs and sugar makes them superlight and fluffy, but it's all the air incorporated into them that also makes them dry out so quickly if left to sit around for too long.

Here, untraditionally, we forgo all the beating and just place the ingredients in a food processor. Mixing them this way means that the resulting madeleines won't be quite as light as those made by hand-whisking, but they're every bit as delicate and buttery as you'd hope. We do it this way to build in a little bit of robustness, which allows them to still be eaten hours (rather than minutes) after they come out of the oven.

We love the saffron here, but the spice is not to everyone's liking (particularly in a sweet context), so you can leave it out, if you prefer, and focus on the orange and honey instead.

MAKES ABOUT 22

6 tbsp plus 1 tsp/90 g unsalted butter, plus 1½ tbsp/25 g, melted, for brushing
2 tsp honey, plus 3 tbsp, for glazing
¼ tsp saffron threads (optional)
2 large eggs
⅓ cup plus 1 tsp/75 g granulated sugar
scraped seeds of ¼ vanilla pod

finely grated zest of 1 small orange (1 tsp)
½ cup plus 1½ tbsp/90 g all-purpose flour, plus extra for dusting
1 tsp baking powder
⅛ tsp salt
2½ tbsp shelled pistachio kernels, finely ground in a food processor

Ideally, use a standard madeleine pan here—metal or silicone.

These are best eaten on the day they are made, as fresh from the oven as possible. We know it's not madeleine protocol, but leftovers can be kept in an airtight container and eaten as they are (without needing to be warmed through) the following day.

1   Place the butter, honey and saffron threads (if using) in a small saucepan over low heat until the butter has melted. Remove from the heat and set aside to come to room temperature.

2   Place the eggs, sugar, vanilla seeds and orange zest in a food processor and process until smooth and combined. Sift the flour, baking powder and salt into a bowl, then add to the egg mixture. Pulse a few times, just to mix in, then add the cooled butter, honey and saffron mixture. Process once more, to combine, and then pour the batter into a small bowl. Cover with plastic wrap and allow to rest in the fridge for about an hour.

3   Preheat the oven to 400°F/200°C. If using metal madeleine pans, brush the molds with the melted butter and dust liberally with flour. Silicone pans should not need any greasing or flouring, but you can lightly brush with a little melted butter here, if you like. Tap to ensure that all the molds are dusted and then shake off the excess flour.

4   Spoon a heaped teaspoon of batter into each mold; it should rise two-thirds of the way up the sides of the molds. If you only have one madeleine pan, place the remaining batter in the fridge until you have baked the first batch. You will need to wash and dry the mold completely before greasing and flouring again and repeating with the second batch. »

5   Bake for 9–10 minutes, until the madeleines are beginning to brown around the edges and they spring back when tapped lightly in the middle. Remove the pan(s) from the oven and set aside for a minute before releasing the cakes. The best way to do this, with a metal pan, is to go around the edges of each madeleine with a small knife or offset spatula (to make sure they are not stuck) and then tap the edge of the pan on the counter until they fall out. With a silicone pan, they should just fall out of their molds. Transfer the cakes to a wire rack to cool.

6   Pile the ground pistachios onto a plate in a straight line and set aside. Melt the 3 tbsp honey in a small saucepan (a microwave is also good here) until very runny, then brush lightly over the shell-patterned side of one madeleine. With the shell side facing down toward the nuts, roll the narrower end of the madeleine along the pile of pistachios so that you have a straight ⅓ inch/1 cm strip of pistachios at the base of the madeleine. Repeat with the remaining madeleines and place on a serving platter, nut side up.

Lemon and raspberry cupcakes

The difference between a cupcake that stands the test of time and one that vanishes into obscurity is, we think, all to do with the frosting. The actual cake has to be light, tender and moist, of course, but the frosting has to be sensational. Is it not the reason, secretly, why some people choose cupcakes in the first place? Here, the simple trick of whipping the lemon curd into the mascarpone works an absolute treat. A dusting of confectioners' sugar puts these over the top.

Making your own lemon curd is satisfying and delicious, but feel free to shortcut and buy some ready-made, if you like. Since discovering a "seriously zesty" supermarket version, Helen admits that her rate of production on the homemade lemon curd front has rather reduced.

MAKES 12

The lemon curd can be made up to 3 days before frosting the cakes and then stored in the fridge. To prevent lemon zest from drying out, pop it in a ziplock bag or plastic container and freeze; it will keep for a couple of months.

Once baked, the cakes are best eaten on the same day. If not frosted, they will keep in an airtight container for a day.

LEMON CURD
1 large egg, plus 2 large egg yolks
6 tbsp/90 ml lemon juice (from
    2 lemons; the zest of these lemons
    needs to be used for the cake batter,
    so grate the zest before juicing)
⅓ cup plus 1 tbsp/90 g
    granulated sugar
5 tbsp plus 1 tsp/75 g unsalted butter,
    at room temperature, cut into
    ¾-inch/2-cm cubes

CUPCAKES
½ cup plus 1 tbsp/125 g unsalted butter,
    at room temperature
finely grated zest of 2 lemons (2 tsp)
1 cup plus 2 tbsp/225 g
    granulated sugar
3 large eggs
½ cup/120 g sour cream
1¼ cups/160 g all-purpose flour
1½ tsp baking powder
¼ tsp salt
1¼ cups/150 g fresh raspberries,
    plus 12 extra for garnish

FROSTING
1 cup/270 g lemon curd
1¼ cups/300 g mascarpone

1   **To make the lemon curd,** whisk together the whole egg and egg yolks in a bowl and set aside. Combine the lemon juice and sugar in a small saucepan and place over medium-high heat. Stir until the sugar dissolves, then, as soon as it comes to a boil, pour the syrup over the eggs, whisking the whole time. Return the mixture to the saucepan and cook over low heat for 4–5 minutes, stirring constantly with a wooden spoon until the mixture has thickened and one or two bubbles appear on the surface.
2   Remove from the heat and stir in the butter, one cube at a time, waiting until each piece melts before adding the next. When all the butter has melted and the mixture is smooth, transfer the curd to a clean container and cover the surface with plastic wrap; you want the plastic wrap to actually touch the surface to prevent it from forming a skin. Set aside to cool completely before placing in the fridge until needed. ››

3   **To make the cupcakes,** preheat the oven to 375°F/190°C and line the 12 molds of a regular muffin pan with paper liners (if you don't have liners, brush the molds and the top of the muffin pan with barely melted butter and dust all over with flour, tapping away the excess).

4   Place the butter, lemon zest and sugar in the bowl of an electric mixer with the paddle attachment in place. Beat on medium-high speed for about 3 minutes, until the mixture is light and fluffy. Add the eggs, one at a time, scraping down the paddle and sides of the bowl after each addition. Add the sour cream and beat until incorporated. Sift the flour, baking powder and salt into a bowl and add this to the mixer. Continue to mix until combined, again scraping down the paddle and sides of the bowl. Increase the speed to high and beat for another 20 seconds. Lower the speed, add the raspberries and mix for just a few seconds so that the fruit breaks up and the mixture is roughly rippled with the raspberries.

5   Spoon the batter into the paper liners—they will be nearly full—and bake for about 22 minutes, or until a skewer inserted into the center of a cake comes out clean. Set aside in the pan to cool for 5 minutes before transferring the cakes to a wire rack to cool completely.

6   **To make the frosting,** place the lemon curd and mascarpone in the bowl of an electric mixer with the whisk attachment in place. Beat on medium speed until thick, about 1 minute.

7   Use a small spatula or butterknife to frost the cupcakes. Finish with a whole raspberry in the center of each cake and serve.

Powder puffs

Helen had her first taste of powder puffs at a funeral in Victoria, Australia, more than 20 years ago. Too embarrassed to ask what they were—a funeral is no time to be sourcing recipes!—Helen wondered about the recipe for years before she came across it again thanks to Stephanie Alexander, whose insights into the magic of sifting (three times) and not overmixing allowed the penny to drop for Helen.

Looking at the cookies alone, you'd be forgiven for wondering what all the fuss is about. They're nothing more than baked sponges—a little like the Italian Savoiardi ladyfingers used to make tiramisu. It's when they're sandwiched together and left to soften for several hours, however, that they become so very light that you feel as though you're biting into thin air.

We've included two versions here: raspberry and rose for the height of summer, and chocolate and chestnut for a more autumnal feel. Strawberry jam plus the vanilla whipped cream from the chocolate and chestnut version are good alternatives to the raspberry jam and rose water, if you don't have (or like) rose water.

MAKES ABOUT 24

Raspberry and rose

3 large eggs, whites and yolks
    separated
½ tsp cream of tartar
¾ cup plus 2½ tbsp/180 g
    granulated sugar
1 tsp vanilla extract
½ cup plus 2 tsp/75 g all-purpose flour
½ cup plus 1½ tsp/70 g cornstarch
½ tsp baking soda
⅛ tsp salt

ROSE WHIPPED CREAM
1¼ cups/300 ml heavy cream
3 tbsp/20 g confectioners' sugar, sifted
1¼ tsp rose water

about ⅓ cup/130 g raspberry jam
2 tbsp confectioners' sugar, for dusting

Chocolate and chestnut

3 large eggs, whites and yolks
    separated
½ tsp cream of tartar
¾ cup plus 2½ tbsp/180 g
    granulated sugar
1 tsp vanilla extract
½ cup plus 2 tsp/75 g all-purpose flour
⅓ cup/50 g cornstarch
½ tsp baking soda
⅛ tsp salt
3 tbsp Dutch-processed
    cocoa powder

VANILLA WHIPPED CREAM
1¼ cups/300 ml heavy cream
3 tbsp/20 g confectioners' sugar, sifted
½ tsp vanilla extract
⅛ tsp salt

¾ cup/250 g sweetened
    chestnut spread
1½ tsp confectioners' sugar, for dusting
1 tbsp Dutch-processed
    cocoa powder
about 3 marron glacé in syrup,
    thinly sliced (optional)

Sift three times One of the secrets to the incredible pillowy lightness here is in the sifting of the flour three times. Though always passionate about the benefits of sifting, Helen is positively evangelical about the need to sift not once or twice but *three* times. This will create the aeration you need to produce the fluffy results.

Don't overwork the mixture Key to success, also, is not to overwork the mixture. There shouldn't be any more stirring after the flour has been folded in, otherwise air pockets will be created and the mixture will deflate.

Give them the time they need to sit around and soften It's also important to give the cakes the time they need, once sandwiched together with cream, to really soften. They are nice and soft after 5 hours, but can happily be left for up to 24 hours in the fridge.

1　Preheat the oven to 400°F/200°C. Line four baking sheets with parchment paper (or line two baking sheets and cook in batches).

2　Place the egg whites in the bowl of an electric mixer with the whisk attachment in place and beat on medium-high speed for about 1 minute, until frothy. Add the cream of tartar and continue to beat for another minute, until soft peaks form. Gradually add the sugar and keep beating for about 5 minutes, until the mixture forms a stiff and glossy meringue. Add the vanilla extract and egg yolks, one at a time, and continue to beat until just combined.

3　Place the flour, cornstarch, baking soda, and salt (and cocoa powder, if making the Chocolate Puffs) in a bowl. Sift twice before sifting for a third time into the bowl with the meringue mixture. It's vital to sift three times here to aerate the mixture as much as possible. Fold gently but thoroughly, stopping as soon as it's combined. Do not stir the mixture again after this point.

4　Use two teaspoons to drop heaped spoonfuls of the mix onto the lined sheets. They should be about 1½ inches/4 cm wide and spaced 2 inches/5 cm apart. Don't be tempted to use a piping bag here, as all the air will be knocked out. Bake for 11–12 minutes, rotating the sheets halfway through, until golden brown around the edges and starting to go crisp. Remove from the oven and set aside for about 10 minutes, until completely cool. If you need to cook them in two batches, remove the first batch with an offset spatula once cooked, then wipe down the parchment paper with a slightly damp cloth before continuing with the next batch.

5　Gently ease the cakes away from the parchment paper and separate them into similar-sized pairs.

6　**To make the rose whipped cream,** place the cream, confectioners' sugar and rose water in the bowl of an electric mixer with the whisk attachment in place. Beat on high speed for about a minute, until soft peaks form, taking care not to overbeat or it will become thick and grainy. **To make the vanilla whipped cream,** place the cream in the bowl of an electric mixer with the whisk attachment in place. Add the confectioners' sugar, vanilla extract and salt and beat on high speed for about a minute, until soft peaks form, taking care not to overbeat or it will become thick and grainy.

7　At least 5 hours (or up to 24 hours) before serving, spread 1 tbsp of the whipped cream onto the base of half of the cakes, followed by about ½ tsp of jam if making the raspberry puffs, or a heaped teaspoon of the chestnut spread if making the chocolate puffs. Sandwich together with the top cakes and place the puffs in the fridge for 4 hours—layered with parchment paper in an airtight container—until the cakes are completely softened. Remove the puffs from the fridge an hour before serving—they need to be room temperature rather than fridge-cold. If making the raspberry puffs, just dust with confectioners' sugar. If making the chocolate puffs, sift the confectioners' sugar into a bowl with the cocoa powder and sprinkle through a fine-mesh sieve over each puff. Place a piece of marron glacé on top, if desired, along with a small drizzle of the syrup. Serve immediately.

After baking, the un-assembled cakes can be stored for up to 5 days in an airtight container. They can also be frozen for up to 3 months.

Once sandwiched together, the cakes can happily be left for up to 24 hours in the fridge. Just hold back on dusting with the confectioners' sugar (if using); this needs to be sprinkled over just before serving. Remove from the fridge about an hour before serving. You want them to be room temperature, not fridge-cold.

 RASPBERRY AND ROSE ONLY

RASPBERRY AND ROSE
POWDER PUFFS

CHOCOLATE AND CHESTNUT
POWDER PUFFS

Tahini and halva brownies

The combination of tahini, halva and chocolate is so good that some members of staff (Tara, we see you!) had to put a temporary personal ban on eating these particular brownies during the making of this book. It is very hard to eat just one.

In order to achieve the perfect balance of cakey and gooey—that sweet spot that all brownies should hit—the cooking time is crucial. It will vary by a minute or so depending on where the pan is sitting in the oven, so keep a close eye on them.

MAKES 16

We made these in a 9-inch/ 23-cm-square baking pan, but a 12 x 8-inch/30.5 x 20-cm pan also works well.

These will keep well for up to 5 days in an airtight container. They also freeze well, covered in plastic wrap, for up to a month. When you take them out of the freezer, they are uncommonly good eaten at the half-frozen, half-thawed stage.

1 cup plus 1½ tbsp/250 g unsalted butter, cut into ¾-inch/2-cm cubes, plus extra for greasing
9 oz/260 g dark chocolate (70% cocoa solids), broken into 1½-inch/4-cm pieces
4 large eggs
1⅓ cups/280 g granulated sugar

¾ cup plus 3 tbsp/120 g all-purpose flour
⅓ cup/30 g Dutch-processed cocoa powder
½ tsp salt
7 oz/200 g halva, broken into ¾-inch/2-cm pieces
⅓ cup/70 g tahini paste

1   Preheat the oven to 400°F/200°C. Grease your chosen pan and line with parchment paper, then set aside.

2   Place the butter and chocolate in a heatproof bowl over a pan of simmering water, making sure that the base of the bowl is not touching the water. Leave for about 2 minutes to melt, then remove the bowl from the heat. Stir until you have a thick shiny sauce and set aside to come to room temperature.

3   Place the eggs and sugar in a large bowl and whisk until pale and creamy and a trail is left behind when you move the whisk; this will take about 3 minutes with an electric mixer, longer by hand. Add the chocolate and fold through gently with a spatula—don't overwork the mixture here.

4   Sift the flour, cocoa powder and salt into a bowl, then gently fold into the chocolate mixture. Finally, add the pieces of halva, gently fold through the mix, then pour or scrape the mixture into the lined baking pan, using a small spatula to even it out. Dollop small spoonfuls of the tahini paste into the mix in about 12 different places, then use a skewer to swirl them through to create a marbled effect, taking the marbling right to the edges of the pan.

5   Bake for about 23 minutes, until the middle has a slight wobble and it is gooey inside—they may be ready anywhere between 22 and 25 minutes. If using the 12 x 8-inch/30.5 x 20-cm pan, they will need a couple minutes less cooking time. They may seem a little undercooked at first, but they firm up once they start to cool down. If you want to serve them warmish (and gooey), set aside for just 30 minutes before cutting into 16 pieces. Otherwise, set aside for longer to cool to room temperature.

Lemon, blueberry and almond "teacakes"

We've always called these "teacakes" at Ottolenghi. There's no link to the traditional raisin-filled bready cake that's toasted and slathered with butter—it's more to do with how good they taste with a cup of tea. We make these in a muffin pan—without a paper liner, in order to keep the edges neat and straight—inverting them onto a wire rack before drizzling with icing. "Upside-down-muffins" sounds a lot less elegant than "teacakes," however, so we've taken the liberty of keeping the misnomer both here and elsewhere.

MAKES 12

¾ cup plus 1½ tbsp/190 g unsalted butter, at room temperature, cubed, plus extra for greasing

¾ cup plus 3½ tbsp/190 g granulated sugar

finely grated zest of 1 lemon (1 tsp)

4 large eggs, lightly beaten

2 cups/190 g almond meal

¼ cup plus 1 tbsp/45 g all-purpose flour, plus extra for dusting

¼ tsp baking powder

⅛ tsp salt

¼ cup/60 ml lemon juice

⅔ cup/100 g fresh blueberries, plus 36 blueberries to garnish

ICING

1⅓ cups/160 g confectioners' sugar

2½ tbsp lemon juice

Without icing, these keep well for 3 days in an airtight container. They also freeze well. Once iced, they're best stored in an airtight container in the fridge and eaten within a couple of days.

1 Preheat the oven to 350°F/180°C. Grease all 12 molds of a regular muffin pan with butter and dust lightly but thoroughly with flour. Tap away any excess flour and set aside.

2 Place the butter, granulated sugar and lemon zest in the bowl of an electric mixer with the paddle attachment in place. Beat on medium-high speed until light, then add the eggs and almond meal in three or four alternating batches. Sift the flour, baking powder and salt into a bowl, then add this to the mixer and turn the speed to low. Finally, add the lemon juice and beat until combined. Spoon the mixture into the molds and divide the ⅔ cup/100 g blueberries between the cakes: push them down slightly so that they sink into the batter. The reason we do this (rather than stirring them through the batter) is to ensure that each cake gets an equal number of blueberries.

3 Bake for 30–35 minutes, until the edges are lightly golden and a skewer inserted into the middle of a cake comes out clean. Remove from the oven to cool for 10 minutes before gently tapping the cakes out onto a cooling rack so that they are sitting upside down. Set aside until completely cool.

4 **To make the icing,** combine the confectioners' sugar and lemon juice in a bowl and stir until it has a thick pouring consistency.

5 Spoon the icing over the cakes; you want it to dribble down the sides a little without covering the cakes entirely. Dot the remaining blueberries in the center of each cake—you should have enough for 3 on top of each cake—and serve.

Hazelnut crumble cake with Gianduja (or Nutella) icing

In the shops, we use Gianduja chocolate for our icing, which we're crazy about: with its addition of hazelnut paste, it's the most wonderful match for the hazelnut crumble. You can find it in chocolate shops or online, however we've also offered a version with Nutella instead (admit it—we know you've got a jar of it somewhere).

   With thanks to Belinda Jeffery, the wonderful Australian cook whose walnut cake recipe this is adapted from.

SERVES 11 (USING INDIVIDUAL BUNDT PANS) OR 12–14 (USING ONE LARGE BUNDT PAN)

HAZELNUT CRUMBLE

2¾ oz/80 g hazelnuts, blanched or
   skin on
⅓ cup plus 2 tsp/80 g granulated sugar
1¼ tsp ground cinnamon
¼ tsp salt

CAKE

1 cup plus 2 tbsp/250 g sour cream
½ cup/130 g whole-milk plain
   Greek yogurt
1½ tsp baking soda
3 large eggs
1⅓ cups/280 g granulated sugar
1 cup plus 1½ tbsp/250 g unsalted
   butter, at room temperature,
   cut into 1-inch/3-cm cubes, plus
   extra for greasing
1 tbsp rum or brandy
2 tsp vanilla extract
3⅔ cups plus 1 tbsp/460 g all-purpose
   flour, plus extra for dusting
2 tsp baking powder
1 tsp salt

GIANDUJA GANACHE

5¼ oz/150 g Gianduja chocolate,
   chopped into ⅓-inch/1-cm pieces
6 tbsp plus 2 tsp/100 ml heavy cream

NUTELLA GANACHE

3 oz/85 g milk chocolate
   (60% cocoa solids), chopped
   into ⅓-inch/1-cm pieces
¼ cup/80 g Nutella
6 tbsp plus 2 tsp/100 ml heavy cream

about 12 hazelnuts, blanched or skin
   on, thinly sliced (use a mandoline,
   if you have one, but don't worry if
   they seem to crumble more than slice)

We've used individual Bundt pans here, but you can make it in one large Bundt pan, if you prefer. You will also need a piping bag to layer the batter in the individual pans (you can just pour it in to the large pan and use a spatula to spread it out).

The crumble mixture can be prepared up to 2 days ahead and stored in an airtight container until ready to use.

Hazelnuts behave like no other nuts, so the cakes always dry out really quickly; they are best eaten on the day they are made. They'll be fine the following day, just not at their best.

1   **To make the hazelnut crumble,** preheat the oven to 350°F/180°C. Spread the hazelnuts out on a baking sheet and roast for 12 minutes, until they begin to color and smell nutty. Remove from the oven and, if skin-on hazelnuts, place them in the middle of a clean kitchen towel, draw in the sides and rub together so that the brown papery skins fall off. If starting with blanched nuts, just set them aside to cool. Once cooled, place the nuts in a food processor, add the sugar, cinnamon and salt and process until the nuts are finely chopped. Set aside.

2   Increase the oven temperature to 400°F/200°C. Grease and flour the Bundt pans and set aside.

3   **To make the cake,** place the sour cream and yogurt in a medium bowl and whisk in the baking soda. Leave to stand for 15 minutes for the mixture to puff up and become light and airy.

4   Meanwhile, place the eggs and sugar in a food processor and process for a minute to combine. Add the butter and process for another minute. Don't worry if the mixture looks a little curdled at this point; it will come together in the end. Stir the rum or brandy and vanilla extract into the sour cream mixture and add this to the food processor. Use the pulse button to combine a few times, scraping down the sides of the bowl to ensure that the batter is evenly distributed. Tip the mixture into a large bowl. Sift the flour, baking powder and salt into a separate bowl, then stir this into the egg-butter mixture until the batter is just combined.

5   Transfer the batter to a piping bag and pipe a thin layer into the bottom of the prepared pans. Sprinkle a generous amount of the nut crumble all over: about a third (among all the pans). Continue to layer the batter and nut crumble so that you have three layers of batter, finishing with a layer of nuts. Press this last layer of nuts gently into the cake batter with a spatula (so that they don't fall out when the cakes are baked and inverted).

6   Bake for 25 minutes (or 55–60 minutes, if making one large cake), or until a skewer inserted into the center of a cake comes out clean. Set aside in the pans for 10 minutes to cool, before gently loosening the sides and inverting onto a wire rack to cool completely.

7   **To make the ganache,** place the chocolate (and Nutella, if making the Nutella version) in a bowl and set aside. Pour the cream into a small saucepan and place over medium heat. Heat for 1–2 minutes, until bubbles begin to form at the edges and the cream starts to come to a boil. Remove immediately from the heat and then pour over the chocolate. Leave for a couple of minutes, then stir the chocolate until smooth; the ganache should not be so thin that it just dribbles off the cakes, but not so thick that it doesn't dribble at all.

8   Spoon the ganache over the cooled cakes so that it drips evenly down the sides. If you are making one large cake, you can either spoon all of the ganache over the top, or spoon over about two-thirds and serve the remainder alongside each portion. Finally, sprinkle with the sliced hazelnuts and serve.

HAZELNUT CRUMBLE CAKE WITH GIANDUJA (OR NUTELLA) ICING

Baby black and orange cakes

We like to make these simple "teacakes" bite-sized, and then bag up a mix of black and orange ones to give as gifts. They're especially fun to make around Halloween, ready for sweet-toothed trick-or-treaters. We've given both versions of the cakes in one recipe, so either choose to make one or the other, or both, if you want. In this case, you'll need to double the quantity of egg whites, granulated sugar and melted butter needed. Make both batches separately, though, from beginning to end (rather than whisking up double the egg mix all together and then dividing it in two).

MAKES ABOUT 22

—

2⅛ oz/60 g egg whites (from
    1½ large eggs)
⅓ cup plus 2 tsp/80 g granulated sugar
5 tbsp/70 g unsalted butter, melted,
    plus extra for greasing

BABY ORANGE TEACAKES	**BABY BLACK TEACAKES**
3½ tbsp/30 g all-purpose flour	2½ tbsp/20 g all-purpose flour
3 tbsp/20 g almond meal	3 tbsp/20 g almond meal
3¾ tsp/10 g cornstarch	¼ cup/25 g Dutch-processed
finely grated zest of 1 orange (1½ tsp)	cocoa powder

—

We make these in silicone half-sphere molds. Alternatively, you can use a mini-muffin pan; they won't have their cute orb shape but they'll still be perfectly bite-sized.

These will keep for up to 3 days in an airtight container.

1   Preheat the oven to 375°F/190°C. Lightly grease 22 holes of your silicone mold or mini-muffin pan and set aside. It's fine to cook the mix in two batches if you need to; the batter is happy to wait.

2   Place the egg whites and sugar in the bowl of an electric mixer with the whisk attachment in place. Beat on medium-high speed for about 2 minutes, until the sugar is dissolved and the mix is thick, glossy and heavy. You can check that it is whipped enough by feeling a little of the mix between your thumb and forefinger; you should barely be able to feel the sugar granules. Keep the mixer on medium-high speed and slowly pour the melted butter down the side of the bowl. Beat until combined, scrape down the sides of the bowl and turn the speed to low.

3   **To make the baby orange teacakes,** sift the flour, almond meal and cornstarch into a bowl, then add to the mixer along with the orange zest. **To make the baby black teacakes,** sift the flour, almond meal and cocoa powder into a bowl, then add to the mixer. Mix to combine, turn off the machine and scrape down the sides of the bowl.

4   Use a piping bag (or two teaspoons) to fill the molds about three-quarters full. Bake for 12 minutes, until the center of the cakes springs back when touched. Allow to rest in the molds for 10 minutes before turning them out onto a wire rack to cool completely.

Strawberry and vanilla mini-cakes

The combination of strawberry and vanilla is another one that takes Yotam straight back to his childhood. It's a food memory so loved that he converted this mini-cake recipe to create one large number 1-shaped cake for the first birthday of his second son, Flynn. If you'd also like to do this, the method remains the same, but the baking time will need to be increased. As a guide, Yotam's great big "1" took just over 60 minutes to bake.

MAKES 12 (USING JUMBO MUFFIN PANS OR POPOVER PANS) OR 18 (USING REGULAR MUFFIN PANS)

We use Popover pans for these cakes, which are fairly large. A jumbo or regular muffin pan could be used as an alternative.

Whether iced or not, these will keep for up to 3 days in an airtight container. They don't look their best after the first day, but the taste will not be affected.

1 cup plus 1½ tbsp/250 g unsalted butter, at room temperature, plus extra for greasing
1¼ cups/250 g granulated sugar
1 tsp vanilla extract
scraped seeds of ½ vanilla pod
4 large eggs, lightly beaten
1 cup/120 g self-rising flour, plus extra for dusting
¼ tsp salt
1⅓ cups/140 g almond meal
7 oz/200 g fresh strawberries, hulled and cut into ⅓-inch/1-cm dice

STRAWBERRY ICING

2 oz/55 g fresh strawberries, hulled and roughly chopped
2½ cups/300 g confectioners' sugar
1 tbsp light corn syrup
scraped seeds of ¼ vanilla pod

6 whole strawberries (or 9 if using a regular muffin pan), cut in half lengthwise, or 2 tbsp freeze-dried chopped strawberries, to garnish (optional)

1   Preheat the oven to 400°F/200°C. Grease and flour the molds of your chosen pans.

2   Place the butter, sugar, vanilla extract and vanilla seeds in the bowl of an electric mixer with the paddle attachment in place. Beat on medium speed until light, then add the eggs, a little at a time, scraping down the sides of the bowl a few times as you go. (Adding the eggs gradually should prevent the mix from splitting, but don't worry too much if it does; it might look a bit curdled, but this will not affect the final result.) Continue to beat until fully combined. Sift the flour and salt into a bowl, then stir in the almond meal. Turn the speed of the mixer to medium-low, then add the dry ingredients in three batches and finally fold in the diced strawberries.

3   Spoon the mixture into the prepared molds—it should come about three-quarters of the way up the sides (about two-thirds in a regular muffin pan). Bake for about 22 minutes (about 20 minutes in a regular muffin pan), rotating the pan halfway through, until a skewer inserted into the middle of one of the cakes comes out clean. Remove from the oven and allow to sit for 15–20 minutes before easing the cakes out of the molds. Transfer to a wire rack to cool completely.

4   **To make the strawberry icing,** place all the icing ingredients in a food processor and process together until smooth.

5   Drizzle the tops of the upside-down cakes with the icing, allowing it to drip down the sides. If desired, garnish with half a strawberry on each cake, cut side facing up, or a sprinkle of dried strawberries.

Victoria sponge cake with strawberries and white chocolate cream

Nothing says "summer garden party" more than this: the light-as-air sponge cake, the seasonally sweet strawberries, the white chocolate cream. Add a freshly mown lawn and a cup of tea and you're there. At least that was our vision before these were photographed for the book by Peden + Munk. Taylor (the Peden side of the team) delighted in bringing a little bit of anarchy (or pileup, as he preferred to call it) to some of our more composed presentations. Perfectly organized, neat mini-cakes received the requisite Taylor treatment here, and we could not be more delighted with the results.

The secret to the sponge cake—which is as light as air, but also rich and buttery—is the reliance on the air that's whipped into the eggs, which acts as the raising agent, rather than chemical leaveners. Melted butter is then trickled into the cake batter and folded in for extra richness. All this requires a deft and light hand (and a bit of elbow grease to begin with), but the result is a deliciously versatile sponge cake for your repertoire. There's something a little bit magic about making a perfect genoise. Behind the magic, though, there's quite a lot of method. None of it is complicated; all of it is important. For more on making genoise, see page 346.

SERVES 8 (8 INDIVIDUAL CAKES OR 1 LARGE CAKE)

WHITE CHOCOLATE CREAM
2½ oz/70 g white chocolate, finely chopped
⅓ cup/80 ml heavy cream, plus ½ cup/120 ml to finish

STRAWBERRIES
9 oz/260 g hulled strawberries, roughly chopped
⅓ cup/70 g granulated sugar
1½ tsp lemon juice

SPONGE CAKE
4 large eggs
½ cup/100 g granulated sugar
scraped seeds of ½ vanilla pod (keep the pod for the strawberries)
finely grated zest of 1 lemon (1 tsp)
⅔ cup/100 g all-purpose flour
⅛ tsp salt
4 tbsp/60 g unsalted butter, melted and cooled

5½ oz/160 g hulled strawberries, sliced ¼-inch/0.5-cm thick
1 tsp confectioners' sugar, for dusting

We have used 3-inch/8-cm cake rings here. But if you don't have eight of these, make one large cake in an 8-inch/20-cm round springform cake pan instead.

The sponge is best made on the day it's served, but can be made a day ahead, if necessary, and kept in an airtight container. It can also be frozen, wrapped in plastic wrap, for up to a month.

Once assembled, the cakes should be eaten on the same day—the closer to assembly the better, as cream does not like to sit around for too long.

1   **To make the white chocolate cream,** place the chocolate in a medium bowl and set aside. Pour the ⅓ cup/80 ml cream into a small, heavy-based saucepan and place over medium-low heat. Cook until it is just starting to simmer, then pour the hot cream over the chocolate. Leave to sit for 3 minutes, for the chocolate to soften, then stir gently until the chocolate is melted and fully combined. Cover with plastic wrap and refrigerate for 1 hour until completely cold.

2   **To make the strawberries,** place the strawberries, sugar and lemon juice in a small saucepan (along with the scraped vanilla pod) and mix well. Bring to a boil over medium heat and cook for 4–5 minutes, stirring regularly, until the sugar has melted and the mixture has thickened. Remove from the heat and set aside to cool. ››

3 **To make the sponge cake,** preheat the oven to 350°F/170°C. Line a large baking sheet with parchment paper and place the eight cake rings, ungreased and unlined, on top and set aside. If making this in a 8-inch/20-cm round springform pan, you will need to line the bottom with parchment paper; you don't need the baking sheet.

4 Pour enough water into a medium saucepan so that it rises about 2 inches/ 5 cm up the sides; you want the bowl from your electric mixer to be able to fit in the saucepan and sit over the water without actually touching it. Bring the water to a boil and then lower to a simmer.

5 Place the eggs, granulated sugar, vanilla seeds and lemon zest in the bowl of an electric mixer and place the bowl on top of the saucepan of simmering water, making sure (again) that the bottom of the bowl is not touching the water. Whisk continuously by hand for about 5 minutes, until the mixture is frothy, creamy and warm. Remove the bowl and place it on the electric mixer with the whisk attachment in place. Beat on high speed until the mixture has tripled in volume and is no longer warm.

6 Combine the flour and salt in a bowl and sift it twice. When the egg mixture has tripled in volume and is no longer warm, sift half the flour (yes, a third sift!) directly over the mixture and gently fold it in with a large rubber spatula. Sift the remaining flour over the mixture and fold it in again. Now drizzle the cooled, melted butter down the sides of the bowl. Fold in gently and swiftly to incorporate.

7 Spoon the mixture into the cake rings—they should be filled two-thirds of the way up the sides. Bake for 15–18 minutes (or 25 minutes if baking one large cake), or until the cakes are a light golden brown and the sponge springs back when lightly pressed in the middle. Remove from the oven and set aside to cool for 20 minutes, in the rings, before using a small knife to remove them; take a bit of care here, to prevent the cakes tearing or sticking to the sides. Transfer to a wire rack to cool completely.

8 Place the white chocolate cream in the bowl of an electric mixer with the whisk attachment in place. Add the ½ cup/120 ml heavy cream and beat on medium-high speed for about 30 seconds, until combined and thick. It should just hold on the whisk it can overwhip very quickly, so be careful.

9 Cut the cakes horizontally and spread the cooked strawberries on the cut side of the bottom pieces (discard the vanilla pod). Spoon half of the white chocolate cream on the tops, followed by the sliced strawberries, followed by the remaining white chocolate cream. Finish with the top halves of the sponge cakes. If you have made one large cake, take care when slicing it in half; you'll need to support it underneath when lifting it back on top of the cream and strawberries. If you have a cake lifter or jumbo cookie spatula, now is the time to use it! Dust with confectioners' sugar and serve.

Banana cakes with rum caramel

Banana bread can sometimes feel like the place overripe bananas go to when no one else wants them. These decadent cakes, on the other hand, feel like the place they go to party, a bottle of rum in hand.

MAKES 6 (USING INDIVIDUAL BUNDT PANS) OR 7 (USING JUMBO MUFFIN PANS)

---

7 tbsp/100 g unsalted butter, at room
   temperature, cut into ¾-inch/
   2-cm cubes, plus extra for greasing
⅓ cup/70 g granulated sugar
⅓ packed cup/70 g light brown sugar
2 large eggs
1 tsp vanilla extract
¾ cup plus 1 tbsp/110 g self-rising flour,
   plus extra for dusting
1 cup/100 g almond meal
2 tbsp malted milk powder
   (such as Horlicks)

⅛ tsp salt
½ tsp ground cinnamon
¾ tsp baking soda
2–3 ripe bananas, peeled
   and mashed (8 oz/230 g)
⅓ cup plus 2 tbsp/100 g sour cream
2 tbsp dark rum

RUM CARAMEL

1 cup/200 g granulated sugar
½ cup/120 ml water
½ cup plus 2 tsp/130 ml heavy cream
1½ tbsp dark rum

We make these in individual Bundt pans, but you can also use a jumbo muffin pan.

Without icing, these will keep for 5 days in an airtight container. Once iced, they should be eaten within 24 hours.

---

1   Preheat the oven to 350°F/180°C. Lightly grease the bundt or muffin pans, dust with flour and set aside.

2   Place the butter and both sugars in the bowl of an electric mixer with the paddle attachment in place. Beat on medium-high speed for about 3 minutes, until light but not too fluffy. Add the eggs, one at a time, beating well after each addition, then add the vanilla extract. Beat for another minute to combine.

3   Sift the flour, almond meal, malted milk powder, salt, ground cinnamon and baking soda into a large bowl; if not all the almond meal makes it through the sieve, it's okay to tip it in. Whisk to combine and set aside.

4   Place the mashed bananas in a separate bowl with the sour cream and rum. Mix well, then add a quarter of this to the butter-sugar mixture, beating on low speed to incorporate. Add a quarter of the dry ingredients, continuing to beat, and continue in alternating batches with the remaining wet and dry ingredients until everything is combined.

5   Spoon the mixture into the prepared pans, filling them about three-quarters of the way up the sides. Bake for 25–28 minutes, or until a skewer inserted into the center of a cake comes out clean. Remove from the oven and set aside in their pans until completely cool. Once cool, place the cakes on a wire rack with a tray or sheet of parchment paper underneath.

6   **To make the rum caramel** while the cakes are in the oven, place the sugar and water in a medium saucepan and stir to combine. Bring to a boil, then simmer over medium-high heat for 8–10 minutes, until the mix begins to change color and becomes a deep amber hue. Resist the urge to stir, but gently swirl the pan from time to time to distribute the heat. Remove from the heat and carefully stir in the cream and rum. If the mixture seizes up, return the pan to a low heat and stir until smooth. Set aside for about 30 minutes in the pan

7   Drizzle the caramel liberally over the cakes, allowing it to drip unevenly down the sides, before serving.

Blackberry and star anise friands

These friands, little French cakes whose elegance and svelteness somehow betray quite how much (burnt) butter is built into their being, look splendid when iced—destined for top ranking on any tiered cake stand—but also work with no icing, in the cookie jar, for grabbing on a whim. They'll lose their slightly chewy edge after the first day or so, but still taste great. Blueberries or raspberries can be used instead of the blackberries. Don't use strawberries, though; they are too watery.

MAKES 12

We use oval molds here, but all sorts of shapes work: jumbo muffin pans, mini-muffin pans, or a regular muffin pan.

Without icing, these will keep for up to 4 days. If the weather is warm, store in the fridge and zap in the microwave for a few seconds (literally 3 seconds!) to restore their buttery moisture. They can also be frozen for up to 3 months, then thawed in the fridge and warmed in a 350°F/170°C oven for 5 minutes; this will restore their crisp edges, as well. Once iced, they're best eaten on the same day.

¾ cup plus 2 tsp/180 g unsalted butter, plus 1 tbsp/15 g, melted, for brushing
½ cup/60 g all-purpose flour, plus extra for dusting
1⅔ cups/200 g confectioners' sugar
1¼ cups/120 g almond meal
1½ tsp ground star anise (or 3 whole star anise, ground in a spice grinder and passed through a fine-mesh sieve)
⅛ tsp salt
5¼ oz/150 g egg whites (from 4 large eggs)
finely grated zest of 1 small orange (1 tsp)
18 fresh blackberries, cut in half lengthwise

ICING (OPTIONAL)
2 oz/55 g fresh blackberries, plus 24 blackberries, to garnish
¾ tbsp water
1 tsp lemon juice
1⅓ cups/160 g confectioners' sugar

1   Preheat the oven to 425°F/220°C. Brush the 12 molds in a regular muffin pan with the melted butter and dust with flour. Tap the pan gently to ensure an even coating of the flour, then turn upside down to remove the excess. Place in the fridge to chill while you make the batter.

2   Place the butter in a small saucepan and cook over medium heat until melted. Continue to cook until the butter is foaming, gently swirling the pan from time to time, to allow the solids to brown more evenly. You will see dark brown sediments begin to form on the sides and bottom of the pan. Continue to allow the butter to bubble away until it turns a rich golden brown and smells of toasted nuts and caramel. Remove the pan from the heat and let it stand for 5 minutes, to allow the burnt solids to collect a the bottom of the pan. Strain through a fine-mesh (or muslin-lined) sieve, discarding the solids. Allow the browned butter to cool slightly before using. It should still be warm when folding into the mix later. If it is too hot, it will cook the egg whites; if it is too cool, it will be difficult to incorporate into the mix. »

3   While the butter is cooling, sift the flour, confectioners' sugar, almond meal, star anise and salt into a bowl. Place the egg whites in a small bowl and use a whisk or fork to froth them up a for a few seconds—you do not need to whisk them completely. Pour the egg whites into the sifted dry ingredients and stir until they are incorporated. Add the orange zest and browned butter and mix until the batter is smooth.

4   Remove the muffin pan from the fridge and fill the molds just over two-thirds of the way up the sides. Place three halved blackberries on top, cut side down, and bake for 10 minutes. Lower the temperature to 400°F/200°C—starting with a high oven temperature and then bringing it down is the way to achieve the lovely brown crust you want—rotate the pan for even cooking and continue to bake for another 8 minutes, until the edges of the friands are golden brown and the centers have a slight peak and spring back when gently prodded. Set aside to cool before removing them from their molds; you might need to use a small knife to help you release the sides.

5   **To make the icing,** place the 2 oz/55 g blackberries in a small bowl with the water and lemon juice. Use a fork to mash them together, then pass the mixture through a fine-mesh sieve to extract as much fruit juice as possible. Sift the confectioners' sugar into a medium bowl, pour in the blackberry juice and combine to make a light purple, runny icing; it should just be thick enough to form a thin glaze on the tops of the cakes.

6   Spoon the icing over the cakes, spreading it to the edges so that it runs down the sides. Do this on a rack, if you can, as icing them on a plate or sheet of parchment paper means that the icing will pool at the bottom. Place a couple of fresh blackberries on each friand, set aside for 20–30 minutes to set, and then serve.

Coffee and walnut financiers

Financiers, like the little blocks of gold they're named after, typically come in the shape of a rectangle. We like to make them in straight, high-sided Popover pans, as we have here, so that the icing can trickle down the sides.

These pans are not widely available, however, so we have adjusted the recipe to work in either a regular muffin or mini-muffin pan. As mini-muffins, they provide the perfect end to a meal, to accompany your coffee.

Financiers are similar to friands (see page 103), and it's this "beurre noisette" that gives financiers their rich and nutty flavour.

MAKES 12 (USING A REGULAR MUFFIN PAN) OR 24 (USING A MINI-MUFFIN PAN)

The batter can be made and kept in the fridge for up to 2 days.

Once baked, financiers are best eaten on the same day, but these will keep for up to 2 days in a sealed container, even after icing. The icing will set a little but the taste won't be affected.

⅔ cup/75 g walnut halves
8½ tbsp/120 g unsalted butter, cut into ¾-inch/2-cm cubes, plus extra for greasing
1¾ cups plus 1½ tbsp/220 g confectioners' sugar
½ cup plus 1½ tbsp/90 g all-purpose flour, plus extra for dusting
1 tsp baking powder
¼ tsp salt
¾ cup/80 g almond meal
8 oz/230 g egg whites (from 6 large eggs)
1 tbsp instant coffee granules, dissolved in ⅓ cup/80 ml boiling water
1½ tsp finely ground espresso coffee (such as Lavazza)

ICING
2 cups plus 1 tbsp/250 g confectioners' sugar
2½ tsp instant coffee granules
2 tbsp hot whole milk
1½ tsp light corn syrup

12 walnut halves for finishing
confectioners' sugar for dusting
finely ground espresso powder for dusting

1   Preheat the oven to 350°F/170°C. Spread the walnuts out on a baking sheet and roast for 10 minutes. Remove from the oven and, when cool enough to handle, roughly chop them into ¼-inch/0.5-cm pieces. Set aside until ready to use.

2   Place the butter in a small saucepan and cook over medium heat until melted. Continue to cook until the butter is foaming, gently swirling the pan from time to time, to allow the solids to brown more evenly. You will see dark brown sediments begin to form on the sides and bottom of the pan. Continue to allow the butter to bubble away until it turns a rich golden brown and smells of toasted nuts and caramel. Remove the pan from the heat and let it stand for 5 minutes, to allow the burnt solids to collect at the bottom of the pan. Strain through a fine-mesh (or muslin-lined) sieve, discarding the solids. Allow the browned butter to cool slightly before using. It should still be warm when folding into the mix later. If it is too hot, it will cook the egg whites; if it is too cool, it will be difficult to incorporate into the mix. ››

SWEET

3   While the butter is cooling, sift the confectioners' sugar, flour, baking powder and salt into a medium bowl. Add the almond meal and whisk to combine. Place the egg whites in a mixing bowl and use a whisk or fork to froth them up a little—you will not need to whisk them completely. Pour the egg whites and dissolved coffee granules into the dry ingredients and stir until just combined. Add the browned butter and mix until the batter is thick, shiny and smooth. Fold in the walnuts and ground espresso, then cover with plastic wrap—making sure that it actually touches the surface of the batter—and transfer to the fridge for 2 hours.

4   Preheat the oven to 400°F/200°C. Butter the molds of your chosen muffin pan and dust with flour. Tap away any excess flour, then spoon the batter into each mold, filling them three-quarters full. Bake for about 25 minutes if using a regular muffin pan, 14 minutes for a mini-muffin pan, or until the tops are a little cracked and a skewer inserted into the center comes out clean.

5   To make the icing while the cakes are in the oven, sift the confectioners' sugar into a medium bowl and add the coffee, milk, and corn syrup. Mix until smooth and set aside; don't worry if there are undissolved coffee granules in the icing—these look good!

6   Remove the pan from the oven and set aside for 5 minutes, before gently tapping it against your work surface to encourage the cakes to fall out. If there are any stubborn bits sticking to the pan, use a butter knife to gently ease them out. Place the financiers on a wire rack to cool completely.

7   Spread the icing on top of the financiers and finish each with a walnut half and a dusting of confectioners' sugar and finely ground espresso powder before serving.

Flourless chocolate "teacakes"

Our chocolate "teacakes"—unlike the more traditional bread-like teacakes, dense with raisins—are light, airy and gluten-free. They work with a cup of afternoon tea, but are also rich enough to satisfy as a dessert, with a decorative shard of almond praline.

We were introduced to water ganache by Colleen Murphy during her many years with the company. It might sound like a contradiction in terms—a ganache? without cream?!—but it's something we're really keen on, both for its stability (it doesn't lose its shine in the way that a cream-based ganache can) and also for the hit of smooth pure chocolate it brings.

Don't be tempted to skip the resting stage before the cake is baked. It's really important to allow the almond meal to fully absorb the liquids, as this is what makes the cakes as moist as can be.

MAKES 6 TEACAKES (USING BUNDT PANS)
OR 12 REGULAR MUFFINS (USING A MUFFIN PAN)

½ cup plus 3 tbsp/160 g unsalted
 butter, cubed, plus 1½ tbsp/25 g,
 melted, for brushing
7 oz/200 g dark chocolate (70% cocoa
 solids), roughly chopped
¾ cup/150 g granulated sugar
1 tsp instant coffee granules,
 dissolved in 1 tsp boiling water
1 tbsp plus 2 tsp/25 ml Amaretto
1¾ cups/160 g almond meal
5 large eggs, whites and yolks
 separated
¼ tsp salt

ALMOND PRALINE
½ cup/50 g sliced almonds
1 tbsp water
⅓ cup/70 g granulated sugar

WATER GANACHE
3 oz/85 g dark chocolate (70% cocoa
 solids), roughly chopped into
 ¾-inch/2-cm pieces
2½ tbsp/40 g granulated sugar
1 tbsp plus 2 tsp/35 g light corn syrup
¼ cup/60 ml water
scraped seeds of ½ vanilla pod
2½ tbsp unsalted butter, at room
 temperature, cut into ¾-inch/
 2-cm cubes

You can make these in individual Bundt pans, or in a regular muffin pan.

The ganache can be kept at room temperature (covered with plastic wrap that is touching the surface of the ganache) for up to 4 days. It can also be kept in the fridge for up to 2 weeks; bring back to room temperature before spreading.

Without icing, the cakes will keep in a sealed container for up to 4 days. Once iced, they are best eaten on the day of serving, but will keep for up to 2 days: the icing will lose a bit of its sheen, but the taste will be unaffected.

1   Place the butter and chocolate in a large heatproof bowl over a pan of simmering water, making sure the base of the bowl isn't touching the water. Whisk the mixture and, when melted, remove the bowl from the heat. Add half the sugar, along with the dissolved coffee granules, Amaretto, almond meal and egg yolks. Stir to combine and then set aside.

2   Place the egg whites and salt in the bowl of an electric mixer with the whisk attachment in place. Beat on high speed for about 1 minute, until soft peaks form. Slowly add the remaining sugar and continue to beat for 3–4 minutes, until the mixture is light and dry.

3   Spoon one dollop of the egg white into the chocolate and fold to combine before gently folding in the remainder. Set aside at room temperature for an hour to rest. »

4   Preheat the oven to 350°F/180°C. Brush the base and sides of the Bundt or muffin pans liberally with melted butter, allowing the excess to drain away by placing them upside down on some paper towels.

5   Once the cake batter has rested, spoon or pipe it into the 6 molds (or 12, if making in the muffin pan), filling them three-quarters full. Place the molds on a baking sheet in the center of the oven and bake for 20–25 minutes, rotating halfway through, until the cakes are cooked and a skewer inserted into the center of a cake comes out with just a few crumbs attached (not wet batter). Remove from the oven and allow the cakes to sit for 10 minutes before inverting the molds onto a wire cooling rack. Set aside until completely cool and then gently tap out the cakes.

6   **To make the almond praline,** line two baking sheets with parchment paper. Spread the sliced almonds out on a lined baking sheet and roast for 10–12 minutes, stirring halfway through, until lightly golden brown. Remove from the oven and set aside on the baking sheet.

7   Place the water in a small pan and add the sugar. Stir with a small spoon, then place over low heat until the sugar has melted. Increase the heat to medium and gently boil the sugar, swirling the pan from time to time until the mixture turns a clear amber color. Remove from the heat and stir in the almonds. Pour the almond caramel onto the second lined baking sheet to form a thin layer. If you need to, use a wet spoon or knife to flatten it out a bit. Allow to cool until crisp, then break into as many shards as you are making cakes.

8   **To make the water ganache,** place the chocolate in a medium bowl and set aside. Put the sugar and corn syrup in a small saucepan and place over medium-low heat. Stir to combine and, when the sugar has melted, increase the heat to medium and bring to a boil, stirring gently from time to time. Continue to boil for about 7 minutes, until the color is a pale amber. Remove from the heat and carefully pour in the water. Don't worry if the mixture seizes; just return the pan to the heat. Add the scraped vanilla seeds and stir gently and continuously until it returns to a boil. Remove from the heat and wait for a minute before pouring the water-caramel over the chocolate. Allow to stand for 5 minutes, then whisk to combine. Add the butter, a couple of cubes at a time, whisking after each addition. Continue until all the butter has been added, whisking to combine until the mix is smooth and shiny.

9   Spread some water ganache over the top of each cake, allowing it to gently dribble down the sides. Set aside to cool and set, then serve with a large shard of praline inserted into the top.

Lemon and semolina syrup cakes

Syrup cakes remind Yotam of his childhood in Jerusalem, where syrup-soaked cakes—perfumed with orange blossom, rose water or a smack of citrus—were everywhere. So moist as to be positively drenched, these go very well as they are with morning coffee, afternoon tea, or served after a meal with some yogurt or crème fraîche.

The thin slice of lemon sitting on top of the cakes provides an extra citrus hit that we love, but we also know that our tolerance for eating lemon (in all forms) is higher than that of others. Some love it, some don't—a problem solved by the fact that it can easily be removed before eating, if desired.

MAKES 8

These keep well for 3 days in an airtight container.

8½ tbsp/120 g unsalted butter, at room temperature, plus extra for greasing
⅔ cup/130 g granulated sugar
1½ lemons (1 lemon is finely grated to give 1 tsp zest and squeezed to give 1½ tbsp lemon juice; the ½ lemon is very thinly sliced into 8 rounds)
1 cup/100 g almond meal
2 large eggs, lightly beaten
⅓ cup plus 1 tbsp/70 g fine semolina
½ tsp baking powder
⅛ tsp salt

SYRUP
¼ cup/60 ml lemon juice
¼ cup/50 g granulated sugar

1   Preheat the oven to 350°F/180°C. Grease 8 molds of a regular muffin pan and line each mold with squares of parchment paper so that it rises ¾ inch/2 cm above the sides.

2   Place the butter, sugar and lemon zest in an electric mixer with the paddle attachment in place. Beat on high speed for about 3 minutes, until light and fluffy, then add the almond meal. Beat for a minute before gradually adding the eggs. Turn the speed to low and add the semolina, baking powder and salt. Beat for 30 seconds, until incorporated, then pour in the lemon juice. Divide the mixture among the muffin molds and place a lemon slice on top of each cake.

3   Bake for 25–30 minutes, until the cakes are golden brown on top, the lemon slices are starting to caramelize and a skewer inserted into the center of a cake comes out clean.

4   **To make the syrup** while the cakes are baking, place the lemon juice and sugar in a small saucepan and bring to a boil over a medium-low heat. Stir to dissolve the sugar and simmer for 2–3 minutes, then remove from the heat.

5   As soon as the cakes come out of the oven, brush or spoon the syrup liberally over the tops. Set aside to cool before lifting them out of the muffin pan. Keep each cake in its parchment paper when serving, though—they look lovely as they are.

Roma's doughnuts with saffron custard cream

This recipe is adapted (so much so that it's unrecognizable from the original) from a clipping Helen's mother-in-law, Roma Kausman, tore from the *Jerusalem Post* in 1973. Roma used to make doughnuts—*sufganiyots*—at Hanukkah, but we can't think of any celebration at which a sugar-coated doughnut is not welcome, if only to remind everyone how perfectly sweet life can be.

We know you're not going to make these every day—they're a lot of work—but much of the time is spent waiting for the dough to proof. We refrigerate the dough overnight after the first proof to reduce the amount of time you'll need to wait for it to proof on the day you fry and eat the doughnuts. But all the effort you put in will be rewarded, we promise. And you'll then be able to say that you made your very own doughnuts!

Proofing the doughnuts on small squares of parchment paper is important. They will deflate if you try to lift them with your fingers, and the paper will help you transfer them to the oil without having to touch them. And yes, the paper also goes into the oil; it feels strange to do this, but trust us (or actually trust Peter Gordon, from whom we first learned the technique). Once the doughnuts start frying, the paper naturally separates and can then be fished out with tongs.

If you are looking for shortcuts, the saffron custard can be replaced by a more traditional strawberry jam. The brandy can also be skipped, if you like. It adds a lovely subtle flavor, but there's enough going on, flavor-wise, if you don't have a bottle around and open.

You will need a piping bag to pipe the custard filling.

The saffron custard cream can be made up to 2 days in advance (whip it with the cream just before serving) and kept in the fridge. The dough must be started a day in advance, as it is kept in the fridge overnight.

Once fried, the doughnuts are best eaten on the same day.

MAKES 10

DOUGHNUTS

1 cup/130 g bread flour
1 cup/125 g all-purpose flour, plus extra for dusting
2 tbsp granulated sugar
1 envelope/2¼ tsp instant yeast
¼ tsp salt
1½ tbsp/25 g unsalted butter, melted
finely grated zest of 1 small orange (1 tsp)
1 large egg yolk
⅓ cup/80 ml whole milk, warmed until tepid
⅓ cup/80 ml tepid water
1 tsp brandy (optional)

SAFFRON CUSTARD CREAM

⅔ cup/160 ml whole milk
⅛ tsp saffron threads
2 large egg yolks
¼ cup/50 g granulated sugar
3¾ tsp/10 g cornstarch
scraped seeds of ¼ vanilla pod
1½ tbsp/25 g unsalted butter, cut into small pieces
⅓ cup/80 ml heavy cream

CARDAMOM SUGAR

⅓ cup plus 2 tsp/80 g granulated sugar
1 tsp ground cardamom (see page 351)

about 4¼ cups/1 L sunflower oil, for frying

1   **To make the doughnuts,** place both flours in the bowl of an electric mixer with the sugar, yeast and salt. Use a handheld whisk to combine, then add the dough hook attachment. Add the melted butter, orange zest and egg yolk and beat on »

medium-low speed for about 30 seconds. Combine the milk, water and brandy (if using) in a small measuring cup and then, with the machine still running, gradually pour this into the flour mixture. When all the liquid has been added, increase the speed to medium-high and beat for 3–4 minutes, scraping down the sides of the bowl if you need to, until the mixture is smooth and elastic.

2   Tip the dough onto a lightly floured work surface and knead gently—adding a little more flour if necessary—until smooth and no longer sticky. Place in a lightly oiled bowl, cover with plastic wrap and set aside in a warm, draft-free place until the dough has doubled in size; this can take between 1–4 hours, depending on the temperature of your kitchen. When the dough has doubled in size, punch it down with your fist, cover with plastic wrap and place in the fridge overnight.

3   **To make the saffron custard cream,** place the milk and saffron threads in a small saucepan. Heat gently until the milk is just coming to a simmer and bubbles are beginning to form around the sides. In the meantime, combine the egg yolks with the sugar, cornstarch and vanilla seeds in a small bowl and whisk together to form a paste. When the milk is just coming to a simmer, slowly whisk half of it into the egg yolk mixture (it helps to have a damp cloth underneath the bowl to steady it while you whisk with one hand and pour with the other), before whisking this back into the remaining hot milk. Cook over medium-low heat for about 5 minutes, whisking continuously, until very thick and smooth. When you lift some of the mixture out of the pan it should hold on to the whisk for a few seconds before falling off in one big blob. Remove from the heat and whisk in the butter, one piece at a time, until fully combined and smooth. Transfer the custard to a clean bowl or jug, cover with plastic wrap—you want it to be actually touching the surface to prevent a skin from forming—and set aside in the fridge until completely chilled. The custard keeps well in the fridge for a couple of days, so it's a good idea to make this the day before the doughnuts are made.

4   Cut out ten 4-inch/10-cm squares of parchment paper and arrange on two large baking sheets. Once the dough has been in the fridge overnight, tip it onto your work surface, roll roughly into a log and then cut the log into ten pieces, each weighing approximately 1⅔ oz/45 g. Shape each into a round ball—this is best done by placing each piece on the work surface, cupping your hand over it and then applying some pressure while you roll it around into a smooth sphere. Place each ball on one square of parchment paper. Cover the sheet loosely with oiled plastic wrap and set aside somewhere warm to rise to almost double the size. Again, this can take anywhere between 45 minutes and 4 hours, depending on the temperature of the room.

5   **To make the cardamom sugar,** mix together the sugar and cardamom in a wide bowl and set aside.

6   When the doughnuts are ready to fry, fill a medium pan (about 7 inches/18 cm wide) with enough oil so that it rises 2 inches/5 cm up the sides of the pan. Heat the oil to 355°F/180°C. (To test that the oil is ready, either use a deep-fry thermometer, or drop a small piece of bread into the pan; if it rises straight to the surface and turns golden brown in about 1 minute, the oil is hot enough.)

7   Keeping the balls on the parchment paper, gently drop three balls at a time into the oil, paper side up (the paper is dropped into the oil too). Fry in batches for 3 minutes—turning over halfway through—until golden brown on both sides. As they cook, the paper will slide away and, as it does, use tongs to lift it out and discard. Use a slotted spoon to lift the doughnuts out as they finish cooking. Drain them briefly on paper towels before rolling them in the cardamom sugar. They can now either be eaten hot, as they are, or set aside until barely warm before being piped with the saffron custard cream.

8   When ready to fill the doughnuts, finish making the custard filling by placing the heavy cream in a medium bowl and, using a handheld whisk, whisk until soft peaks form. Add the cooled custard and very lightly whisk together until just combined.

9   Push a small knife through one side of the doughnut, twisting gently to create a little tunnel through the center. Fill a piping bag with the custard and pipe about a tablespoon into each one before serving.

Chocolate Guinness cake with Baileys Irish cream

The recipe in Nigella Lawson's wonderful book, *Feast*, inspired our version of these cakes. We have amplified the Irish element in her original recipe by piping Baileys-infused mascarpone cream into the middle of the cakes. Thanks to Daniel Karlsson for this idea. This is then followed by a light drizzle of chocolate ganache, followed by shavings of chocolate! It sounds extravagant, we know, but it's actually a really easy cake to make, all whisked together in one bowl.

The secret to making a really shiny chocolate ganache is to use a food processor, as we do here.

SERVES 8

We like to make these in eight mini-loaf pans, 4 x 2½ inches/10 x 6.5 cm at the top and 3 x 1½ inches/8 x 4 cm at the bottom. If you use these, you'll need a piping bag to insert the Baileys cream. Alternatively, you could use a 7-inch/18-cm round springform pan. If you do this, just line the round pan regularly (rather than allowing a ¾-inch/2-cm overhang). You'll also need to increase the baking time to 40 minutes. When the cake is cool, slice it in half, spread the Baileys cream over the bottom layer and then sandwich back together.

The ganache can be stored at room temperature, providing it's not too warm, for 3 days, or kept in the fridge for up to 2 weeks. Without the cream filling, the cakes will keep for up to 3 days in an airtight container at room temperature.

Once the cakes have been assembled, they must be kept in the fridge and eaten within a day.

(NF)

½ cup/120 ml Guinness beer
8½ tbsp/120 g unsalted butter, cubed, plus extra for greasing
⅓ cup/30 g Dutch-processed cocoa powder
1 cup/200 g granulated sugar
¼ cup/60 g sour cream
1 large egg
2 tsp vanilla extract
1 cup/125 g all-purpose flour
¼ tsp salt
1 tsp baking soda
dark chocolate (70% cocoa solids), shaved with a peeler, for garnish

BAILEYS CREAM

½ cup/120 g mascarpone
3 tbsp Baileys Irish Cream
¼ cup plus 1 tbsp/40 g confectioners' sugar, sifted

CHOCOLATE GANACHE

3½ oz/100 g dark chocolate (70% cocoa solids), chopped into ¾-inch/2-cm pieces
½ cup/120 ml heavy cream
1½ tsp light corn syrup
1½ tsp unsalted butter, at room temperature

1   Preheat the oven to 375°F/195°C. Grease eight small loaf pans and line the long side and the base of each with a strip of parchment paper. Allow a ¾-inch/2-cm overhang on each side to help you lift out the cakes later on.

2   Place the Guinness and butter in a medium saucepan over medium heat. Stir gently until the butter has melted, taking care that it does not come to a boil. Sift the cocoa powder and sugar together into the pan and whisk into the mixture, then transfer to a medium bowl.

3   In a separate bowl, whisk together the sour cream, egg and vanilla extract, then pour this into the Guinness mixture, whisking as you do so. Sift the flour, salt and baking soda together into a bowl, then whisk this into the mixture until smooth and combined. Pour the batter into the pans and bake for 20 minutes or until a skewer inserted into the center of the cake comes out clean. Remove from the oven and allow to cool for 10 minutes before gently easing them out, using the parchment paper overhang to help you. Gently run a knife around the unlined edges if they are stuck and then place on a wire rack to cool completely. ››

4   **To make the Baileys cream,** whisk together the mascarpone and Baileys using an electric mixer, if you have one, or by hand. Add the confectioners' sugar and continue to beat on low speed until the mixture is combined. Increase the speed to medium-high and beat until the cream is thick enough to spread. Keep in the fridge until ready to serve.

5   **To make the chocolate ganache,** place the chocolate pieces in a food processor, process until fine and set aside.

6   Combine the cream and corn syrup in a small pan and place over medium-high heat. As soon as bubbles begin to appear—just before it comes to a boil—remove from the heat. Get the food processor running again, with the chocolate still inside, and pour in the hot cream in a steady stream. Process for about 10 seconds, then add the butter. Continue to process until the mixture is shiny and smooth. You can also make the ganache by hand: just make sure the chocolate is chopped fairly finely before you scald the cream and corn syrup and pour it over the chocolate. Stir everything together with a wooden spoon until almost melted, then add the butter. Stir again until the ganache is smooth.

7   Use a rubber spatula to scrape the ganache into a bowl and cover with plastic wrap. Set aside until it has set to the consistency you want (if you want a thin layer to spread over the cakes, it can be poured over while still liquid so that you get an even, light and shiny coating. For a thicker ganache with a spreading consistency, leave it for about 2 hours at room temperature).

8   When the cakes are completely cool, make a cut in each cake by running a small paring knife down its center, leaving ¾ inch/2 cm uncut at either end. Transfer the cream to a piping bag fitted with a ⅔-inch/1.5-cm-wide plain tip. Gently ease the piping bag into the opening of the cut side of each cake and pipe in the cream until it starts to ooze out. Spoon about 1 tbsp ganache over each cake; you want it to cover the cut with the cream oozing out. Decorate with chocolate shavings and serve.

Cakes

—

There's something a little bit magic and a big bit satisfying about baking a cake. Starting with just a few basic building blocks—flour, eggs, butter, sugar, a leavening agent—the number of directions you can take from there is inspiring.

You'll find cakes for all occasions here: easy loaf cakes for everyday baking and cakes you'll save for special occasions; booze-filled cakes to serve to adults after supper and pink-iced cakes to make your kid's day. We have cakes you'll need to eat on the day of making and others that will be happy to stick around for the week. We have round cakes, loaf cakes, Bundt cakes, rolled cakes, long cakes, tall cakes, light cakes, dense cakes, cakes that are all (secretly) about the icing and cakes that stand alone. And we have cakes free from gluten and cakes that—though not free from sugar—are packed with lots of naturally sweet ingredients like root vegetables and tropical fruit.

That's a quick outline of the main routes we head down. Following, in more detail, are some of the attractions you'll pass on the way.

CAKES FOR EVERYDAY BAKING, CAKES FOR SPECIAL OCCASIONS › Simple loaf cakes such as our Lemon and Poppy Seed Cake (see page 187) and Tessa's Spice Cake (see page 186) are perfect for everyday baking. Eminently sliceable and in no need of elaborate icing, these are cakes that can sit around for a good few days, ready to eat alongside a cup of tea. Cakes packed with root vegetables— the Beet, Ginger and Sour Cream Cake (see page 130) and the Parsnip and Pecan Cake with Aniseed and Orange (see page 128), for example—have a similarly long shelf life. Again, they're perfect to bake for the week ahead.

Some cakes, on the other hand, are to be saved for a special occasion. Layered cakes such as the (aptly named) Celebration Cake (see page 193), the Louise Cake with Plum and Coconut (see page 173), the Pineapple and Star Anise Chiffon Cake (see page 179) and the Pistachio and Rose Water Semolina Cake (see page 165) are all, in their own way, labors of love. This is perfectly apt, though, as why would you want to make a layered cake for someone you don't adore?

CAKES FOR TEA TIME, CAKES FOR DESSERT (AND CAKES FOR BREAKFAST) › Of course, it is always possible to simplify the special, or to make the simple special—we can all scrub up for the occasion when we want to! A simple Take-Home Chocolate Cake (see page 152), for example, can be turned into an impressive dessert when served with a spoonful of espresso cinnamon mascarpone cream; and a Coconut, Almond and Blueberry Cake (see page 151), intended for teatime, can be converted into dessert when served warm with a drizzle of cream.

The opposite is also true. A showstopper such as the Pineapple and Star Anise Chiffon Cake (see page 179), adorned with pineapple "flowers" you've made yourself, will still go down very well when served unadorned; and the Pistachio and Rose Water Semolina Cake (see page 165) will still be a treat without the crystallized petals. While strewing a cake with hand-crystallized rose petals might be as close to a declaration of love as it's possible for a cake to get, no one is going to think you love them any less without the flowers.

We had lots of fun working out whether cakes made for teatime could work just as well after supper, or whether cakes made for weddings could also work on a rainy weekend. In the process, we stumbled across the fact that the Rhubarb and Strawberry Crumble Cake (see page 148)—conventionally served after a meal—also tastes uncommonly good eaten for breakfast, along with some thick Greek yogurt.

CAKES FOR BIG KIDS, CAKES FOR SMALL KIDS › The pairing of booze and fruit is one so winning that we find it hard to resist. Prunes and Armagnac, grappa and grapes, rum and raisins, wine and plums—soaking dried fruit or cooking fresh fruit with alcohol brings a depth of flavor and degree of moisture to a cake that we absolutely love. Cakes such as the Grappa Fruit Cake (see page 141) or the Rum and Raisin Cake with Rum Caramel Icing (see page 124) might not be the ones to focus on when you're baking for your child's party. And cakes with lots of coffee or distinct spices such as anise or ground cardamom—the Coffee and Cardamom Pound Cake (see page 181), for example—might also not be the stuff of six-year-old dreams. But for those to whom cake is more than just a vehicle for icing and candles, these are cakes to get seriously excited about.

Between pink-icing kiddie heaven and booze-soaked adult heaven, there are many cakes to please all. Belinda's Flourless Coconut and Chocolate Cake (see page 190) is particularly popular with all the family, as are the Louise Cake with Plum and Coconut (see page 173) and the Rhubarb and Strawberry Crumble Cake (see page 148).

Equipment

We've tried not to go too bonkers with the number of pans we use, but this also had to be balanced against the amount of fun there is to be had by baking cakes in all shapes and sizes: round, square, loaf, Bundt, chiffon, rolled into the shape of a barrel, and so on. The day that cakes are no longer fun to make, look at and eat would, we think, be a sad day indeed.

Each recipe will specify the recommended style of cake pan, and we have, where we can, suggested alternatives when a specialized pan is called for. Bundt pans can be substituted with round cake pans, for example, or round pans used instead of square. In some cases, however, the specific cake pan is really important. The Vineyard Cake (see page 134) and the Pineapple and Star Anise Chiffon Cake (see page 179), for example, must be made in a chiffon cake pan (also known as an angel food cake pan). The shape and design of the pan is not just for fun here; it affects the way the cakes are baked and cooled and the cakes don't really work without it. The same is true of springform pans. These are often called for when a cake needs to be removed from a pan without inverting it. Lots of our cakes have lovely things on top of them, and turning them out onto a rack to cool (as you'd have to do if a pan was not springform) would mean that the crumble and topping would get lost.

Rum and raisin cake with rum caramel icing

Going to the ice cream parlor is something of a tradition for Helen and her eldest son, Sam. They either share a tall sundae or go their separate ways down the cup or cone route. Sam's choice varies from week to week, but Helen always goes for a single scoop of rum raisin. This, along with her affection for the rum-soaked retro classic rum baba, was the inspiration behind this cake.

SERVES 8–10

1 cup/200 g raisins

½ cup/120 ml dark rum

2⅓ cups/300 g all-purpose flour, plus extra for dusting

1 tsp baking powder

1 tsp baking soda

½ tsp ground cinnamon

¼ tsp salt

1 cup plus 1½ tbsp/250 g unsalted butter, at room temperature, plus extra for greasing

1¼ packed cups/240 g light brown sugar

1 tsp vanilla extract

2 large eggs

¾ cup/200 g sour cream

RUM CARAMEL ICING

4 tbsp/60 g unsalted butter

⅓ packed cup plus 1 tbsp/80 g light brown sugar

3 tbsp whole milk

1 tbsp dark rum

1 cup/120 g confectioners' sugar, sifted

We make this in a 9-inch/23-cm Bundt pan. If you don't have the Bundt pan, you can use a 9-inch/23-cm round springform pan; it won't look quite as pretty, but will still work well.

The raisins need to be prepared the day before you start baking, so that they are nice and plump from soaking up all the booze.

With icing or without, this cake will keep for 1–3 days in an airtight container.

1   The day before you bake the cake, place the raisins and rum in a large container or jar for which you have a lid. Give it a good shake and set aside to macerate. Whenever you walk past the container or jar, give it a shake.

2   Preheat the oven to 375°F/190°C. Grease and flour a 9-inch/23-cm Bundt pan.

3   Sift the flour, baking powder, baking soda, cinnamon and salt together into a medium bowl and set aside.

4   Place the butter, brown sugar and vanilla extract in the bowl of an electric mixer with the paddle attachment in place. Beat on medium-high speed until smooth and lightened. Add the eggs, one a time, beating well after each addition. Turn the speed to low and, with the machine still running, add the flour mixture alternately with the sour cream, beginning and ending with the flour mixture to stabilize the mixture and prevent it from curdling. Finally, add the soaked raisins and rum and mix on low speed, just to combine. Scrape the mixture into the Bundt pan, smoothing the top, and bake for about 50 minutes, or until a skewer inserted into the center of the cake comes out clean. Remove the cake from the oven and set aside for 15 minutes in the pan before inverting onto a cooling rack to cool completely.

5   **To make the rum caramel icing** when you are ready to serve, place the butter in a small saucepan and melt over low heat. Add the brown sugar and cook for 1 minute, stirring continuously, until the mixture comes together. Add the milk, increase the heat and bring to a boil. Remove the pan from the heat, add the rum, mix well and set aside to cool to room temperature. When cool, beat in half of the confectioners' sugar using a wooden spoon. Once incorporated, add the remaining sugar and beat until thick and smooth. Spread the rum and caramel icing over the top of the cake, letting it run slowly down the sides.

Prune cake with Armagnac and walnuts

SERVES 12

This looks best made in a 9-inch/23-cm Bundt pan, but a 9-inch/23 cm round springform pan also works well. If you make it in the springform pan, you'll need a little more crumble than for the Bundt pan; we've listed both sets of quantities in the ingredient list.

The prunes need to be prepared the day before you start baking, to allow them time to soak. The crumble can be made up to 3 days in advance and stored in an airtight container.

This is at its absolute best eaten warm, fresh from the oven or on the day of making. Don't worry if you can't eat it all, though; it will keep well for up to 3 days in an airtight container. You'll just need to warm it for 5 minutes (wrapped loosely in foil) in an oven set to 350°F/180°C before serving.

1 packed cup/250 g pitted prunes, quartered
½ cup/120 ml Armagnac (or brandy)
finely grated zest of 1 orange (1½ tsp)

CRUMBLE
(THE BRACKETED WEIGHTS ARE FOR THE 9-INCH/23-CM ROUND SPRINGFORM PAN; THE SALT REMAINS THE SAME IN BOTH)
¼ packed cup/40 g light brown sugar [or ⅓ packed cup plus 1 tbsp/60 g]
2 tsp ground cinnamon [or 1 tbsp]
⅓ cup/40 g walnut halves [or ½ cup/60 g], roughly chopped into ¼-inch/0.5-cm pieces
⅛ tsp salt

2⅓ cups/300 g all-purpose flour, plus extra for dusting
1 tsp baking powder
1 tsp baking soda
½ tsp salt
¾ cup plus 2 tbsp/200 g unsalted butter, at room temperature, plus extra for greasing
1 cup/200 g granulated sugar
1 tsp vanilla extract
2 large eggs
1 cup/230 g crème fraîche, removed from the fridge 30 minutes before needed
confectioners' sugar, for dusting

1   Place the prunes in a bowl with the Armagnac (or brandy) and orange zest. Cover the bowl with plastic wrap and leave at room temperature overnight to soak, stirring a few times.

2   Preheat the oven to 400°F/200°C. Grease and flour a 9-inch/23-cm Bundt or 9-inch/23-cm round springform pan and set aside.

3   **To make the crumble,** combine the brown sugar, cinnamon, walnuts and salt in a small bowl and set aside.

4   Sift the flour, baking powder, baking soda and salt together into a bowl and set aside.

5   Place the butter and sugar in the bowl of an electric mixer with the paddle attachment in place. Beat on medium-high speed until light and fluffy. Add the vanilla extract and eggs, one at a time, beating well after each addition and scraping down the sides of the bowl to ensure even mixing. Turn the speed to low and add the flour mixture alternately with the crème fraîche, beginning and ending with the flour mixture to stabilize the mixture and prevent it from curdling. Remove the bowl from the machine and, using a rubber spatula, fold in the soaked prunes along with their syrupy alcohol.

6   Spoon half of the cake batter into the pan and sprinkle over the nut crumble. Follow this with the remaining batter. Bake for 50–55 minutes for the Bundt pan, or 60–65 minutes for the springform pan, or until a skewer inserted into the center of the cake comes out clean. Remove from the oven and allow to rest for 10 minutes in the pan. If using a Bundt pan, invert it onto a cake plate, or simply lift it out of the springform pan onto a plate. Dust with confectioners' sugar, if serving warm, or set aside to come to room temperature before dusting and serving.

RUM AND RAISIN CAKE WITH RUM CARAMEL ICING

PRUNE CAKE WITH ARMAGNAC AND WALNUTS

Parsnip and pecan cake with aniseed and orange

Yotam has always been skeptical about cakes made with root vegetables. There have been a number of attempts over the years to lure him over to the beet, parsnip and carrot side, but it wasn't until this cake that he started to see what the naturally sweet, inherently moist fuss was all about.

This cake is the happy outcome of a disagreement over what constitutes the perfect carrot cake. Yotam thinks a carrot cake should be light and fluffy, Helen thinks it should be dense and fruity. Never the twain could meet on this all-important matter, so Helen took the diplomatic route of letting the carrots be and working on a parsnip cake instead. We are both, thankfully, agreed on the suitability of this dense and fruity result.

It makes sense that parsnips work so well here, as they're from the same family as carrots: the Umbelliferae. Parsnips are at their sweetest and juiciest in the winter months—when the starch has converted to sugar—so this cake is best made then.

SERVES 8–10

—

1¼ cups/150 g pecan halves

3 large parsnips, peeled and coarsely
  grated, avoiding the core if old
  and woody (1 lb/450 g)

¾ cup/100 g dried currants

finely grated zest of 1 large orange
  (1 tbsp)

3 large eggs

1 cup plus 2 tbsp/225 g
  granulated sugar

1 cup plus 2 tbsp/270 ml sunflower oil,
  plus extra for greasing

1½ cups/190 g all-purpose flour

1 tsp ground cinnamon

1½ tsp baking powder

1½ tsp baking soda

1 tsp ground nutmeg

1 tsp ground aniseed (or 1 tsp finely
  ground fennel seeds)

¾ tsp salt

FROSTING

10½ oz/300 g cream cheese,
  at room temperature

1¼ cups/150 g confectioners' sugar,
  sifted

½ cup/120 ml heavy cream

1½ tsp ground aniseed

finely grated zest of 1 small orange
  (1 tsp)

The frosting can be made up to
2 days ahead and stored in the fridge.
You will just need to quickly beat it
again before using.

Unfrosted, the cake keeps well for
up to 3 days in an airtight container
or wrapped in aluminum foil. Once
frosted, the cake needs to be eaten
on the same day.

1   Preheat the oven to 350°F/170°C. Grease a 9-inch/23-cm round springform pan and line with parchment paper, then set aside.

2   Spread the pecans out on a baking sheet and roast for 10 minutes. Remove from the oven and, when cool enough to handle, roughly chop and place in a large bowl. Set aside until completely cool before adding the parsnips, currants and orange zest.

3   Increase the oven temperature to 400°F/200°C.

4   Place the eggs and granulated sugar in the bowl of an electric mixer with the whisk attachment in place. Beat on high speed for about 2 minutes, until thick and creamy. With the machine still running, slowly and steadily pour in the sunflower oil until it is all combined. Sift the flour, cinnamon, baking powder, baking soda, nutmeg, aniseed and salt together into a bowl, then add these to the mixer. Beat to combine, then turn off the machine before folding in the nuts, parsnips, currants and zest.

5   Pour into the pan and bake for about 60 minutes, or until a skewer inserted into the center comes out clean. Keep a close eye on it after 55 minutes or so, as the cake can go from being still wet in the center to fully cooked within just a few minutes; you might need to cover the pan with aluminum foil for the last 5–10 minutes if it is taking on too much color. Remove from the oven and set aside until completely cool before removing the cake from the pan.

6   **To make the frosting**, place the cream cheese in the bowl of an electric mixer with the paddle attachment in place. Beat on high speed for 1 minute until smooth, then add the confectioners' sugar to the mixer along with the cream. Continue to beat for 1–2 minutes, until thick, before adding the aniseed and orange zest. Beat until just combined, then transfer to the fridge until ready to use (up to 2 days).

7   On the day of serving, use an offset spatula to spread the frosting over the top of the cake, gently swirling it as you go.

Beet, ginger and sour cream cake

Esme, Yotam's test kitchen colleague, was so convinced by this particular cake that she decided to triple the recipe and slip it in as the middle tier to her wedding cake (chocolate on the bottom tier, for those interested, traditional fruit cake up top).

The addition of the vitamin C tablet helps preserve and 'set' the color of the beets in the cake. It's something Yotam does to preserve the color of quince in his savory cooking and the same method works very well here. As you slice the cake open, the streaks of magenta-colored beet will make you smile.

SERVES 6–8

⅔ cup/75 g walnut halves

1⅔ cups/200 g all-purpose flour

¾ cup/150 g granulated sugar

2 tsp baking powder

¼ tsp baking soda

¼ tsp salt

2 red beets, peeled and coarsely grated (9 oz/260 g)

finely grated zest of 1 large orange (1 tbsp)

½ cup/100 g finely chopped crystallized ginger, steeped in boiling water (see page 353) and drained

2 large eggs

¼ cup/60 g sour cream

½ cup/120 ml sunflower oil

1 large vitamin C tablet (1500 mg), crushed with a pestle and mortar or the back of a spoon to form a fine powder (optional)

FROSTING

5½ oz/160 g cream cheese, at room temperature

½ cup/60 g confectioners' sugar, sifted

⅓ cup/80 ml heavy cream

2⅓-inch/6-cm piece of fresh ginger, grated into a fine-mesh sieve placed over a bowl and the flesh squeezed to extract all the juices; reserve the juice

Use a Microplane to grate the ginger, if possible; grating the ginger so finely will really help when trying to extract the juice.

Unfrosted, the cake will keep for 3 days at room temperature in an airtight container. Once frosted, the cake is best eaten on the same day and any leftovers kept in the fridge for a couple of days. As always, bring it back to room temperature before eating.

---

1   Preheat the oven to 350°F/180°C. Grease an 8-inch/20-cm round cake pan and line with parchment paper, then set aside.

2   Spread the walnuts out on a baking sheet and roast for 10 minutes. Remove from the oven and chop into ⅓-inch/1-cm pieces, then set aside. Increase the oven temperature to 375°F/195°C.

3   Place the flour, sugar, baking powder, baking soda and salt in a large mixing bowl and whisk to combine and aerate. Add the beets, orange zest, walnuts and ginger, but do not stir.

4   Place the eggs and sour cream in another small bowl and whisk to combine. Add the oil and crushed vitamin tablet (if using) and whisk again. Pour over the beet-flour mixture and, using your hands or a large spatula, mix thoroughly to combine.

5   Pour the mixture into the cake pan and bake in the middle of the oven for 50–55 minutes, or until a skewer inserted into the center of the cake comes out clean. Remove from the oven and set aside for 30 minutes before removing from the pan and setting aside on a wire rack until completely cool. The parchment paper can be left on or removed as you like; the advantage of leaving it on is that the sides will not dry out if you are not eating it straightaway.

6   **To make the frosting,** place the cream cheese in the bowl of an electric mixer with the paddle attachment in place and beat for about 10 seconds, until smooth (the amount of time it takes to become smooth will vary, depending on the consistency of your cream cheese; see page 352). Add the confectioners' sugar and beat until well incorporated. Add the cream and beat for about 1 minute, until the frosting is thick and smooth. Add the ginger juice, beat for a final few seconds.

7   Use an offset spatula to spread over the top of the cake, and serve.

Apple and olive oil cake with maple frosting

This is such a popular staple on the Ottolenghi cake counter that we've allowed it to make a guest appearance from the pages of the first *Ottolenghi: The Cookbook*. As with all good revival tours, it's bigger and better than ever the second time around.

If you want to do without the maple frosting, you can; a dusting of confectioners' sugar also works well. Bear in mind, though, that those customers who return again and again to the same apple and olive oil cake confess that, secretly, the frosting is the reason they order it in the first place.

SERVES 10

⅔ cup/100 g golden raisins (sultanas)
1 cup/240 ml water
2⅔ cups/350 g all-purpose flour
½ tsp ground cinnamon
1½ tsp baking soda
1½ tsp baking powder
½ tsp salt
3 large Bramley or Granny Smith apples
  (1 lb 12 oz/800 g)
1 cup/200 g granulated sugar
⅔ cup/160 ml extra-virgin olive oil
2 large eggs, lightly beaten,
  plus 2 large egg whites
scraped seeds of ½ vanilla pod
finely grated zest of 1 lemon (1 tsp)

MAPLE FROSTING

7 tbsp/100 g unsalted butter, at room
  temperature, plus extra for greasing
½ packed cup plus 1 tbsp/100 g light
  brown sugar
⅓ cup/85 g maple syrup
7¾ oz/220 g cream cheese,
  at room temperature

The olive oil gives the cake a depth of flavor and moisture and also means that it lasts a long time (the flavor actually improves after a day or two). Covered in plastic wrap, the cake will keep in the fridge (unfrosted) for up to a week. Bring it back to room temperature and frost it on the day of serving.

1   Preheat the oven to 350°F/180°C. Grease the base and sides of a 9-inch/23-cm round springform pan and line with parchment paper. The paper should rise 1 inch/3 cm above the sides of the pan. Set aside.

2   Place the raisins and ⅔ cup/160 ml of the water in a medium saucepan. Simmer over low heat until all the water has been absorbed, then set aside.

3   Sift the flour, cinnamon, baking soda, baking powder and salt together into a bowl and set aside. Peel and core the apples, then cut into 1-inch/3-cm dice and set aside in a separate bowl.

4   Place the granulated sugar, olive oil, whole eggs, vanilla seeds and lemon zest in the bowl of an electric mixer with the paddle attachment in place. Beat on medium speed for 6–7 minutes, until the mixture is light in color, doubled in size and has thickened a little. Don't be tempted to increase the speed of the machine when mixing; this will create air bubbles, which you don't want. Remove the bowl from the machine and use a large spatula to fold in the apples, sultanas and the remaining ⅓ cup/80 ml water. Add the sifted dry ingredients and gently fold to combine.

5   Place the egg whites in a separate clean bowl and whisk to form soft peaks; there's only a small amount of egg white here so you might need to do this by hand. Gently but thoroughly fold the egg whites into the cake mix, then scrape the batter into the pan. Level the top with a spatula and bake for 55 minutes (slightly longer if you are using Granny Smiths, as they don't lose their shape as quickly as Bramleys), or until a skewer inserted into the center of the cake comes out clean. Remove from the oven and set aside to cool in the pan.

6   **To make the maple frosting** while the cake is cooling, place the butter, brown sugar and maple syrup in the bowl of an electric mixer with the paddle attachment in place. Beat until light and airy, then add the cream cheese, a quarter of it at a time. Continue to beat for about 2 minutes, until smooth and thick.

7   When the cake is completely cool, remove it from the pan. Use a large serrated knife to cut it in half horizontally. Spread half the frosting over the bottom layer of the cake, then place the other layer back on top. Spoon the remaining frosting on top— leave the sides unfrosted so that the frosting in the middle can be seen—and serve.

Vineyard cake (aka Cleopatra cake)

This cake originally came from Yotam's friend Kit Williams (who herself found it in *Gourmet* magazine) during her time at Baker & Spice. We then adapted it for Valentine's day and called it Cleopatra cake, on account of the large bunch of grapes needed for the recipe!

The list of ingredients may seem unlikely in a cake—the olive oil, the sweet fortified wine—but do give it a try. It's not every cake that gets a bottle of wine poured into it, and the result—with its intensity of flavor—is really rather special.

SERVES 12

—

4 cups/500 g all-purpose flour,
  plus extra for dusting
2 tsp baking powder
½ tsp baking soda
¾ tsp salt
1⅔ cups/330 g granulated sugar
¾ cup/170 g unsalted butter, at room
  temperature, plus extra for greasing
⅓ cup/80 ml extra-virgin olive oil
finely grated zest of 2 lemons (2 tsp)
finely grated zest of 1 orange (2 tsp)
scraped seeds of ½ vanilla pod

4 large eggs
1¾ cups/450 ml Carte Or Muscat
  de Beaumes de Venise wine,
  at room temperature
3½ oz/100 g seedless red grapes,
  washed and halved lengthwise

SUGAR CRUST TOPPING
5 tbsp/70 g unsalted butter,
  at room temperature
⅓ cup/70 g granulated sugar
3½ oz/100 g seedless red grapes,
  washed and halved lengthwise

This cake must be made in an angel food cake or chiffon pan. The cake is so large that it's only this kind of pan—with the hole built into the middle—that will enable an even bake. Bundt pans will not work because you want the sugar crust and grapes to remain on top when the cake is served, which would not be possible as the Bundt pan is inverted.

The cake will keep for up to 5 days in an airtight container at room temperature.

(NF)

1   Preheat the oven to 400°F/200°C. Grease and lightly flour a 10-inch/25-cm round, 4-inch/10-cm deep angel food cake or chiffon pan, tapping away any excess flour.

2   Sift the flour, baking powder, baking soda and salt together into a bowl and set aside.

3   Place the sugar in the bowl of an electric mixer with the paddle attachment in place. Add the butter, olive oil, lemon zest, orange zest and vanilla seeds and beat for 2 minutes on medium-high speed, until smooth and fluffy. Add the eggs, one at a time, beating well after each addition. Turn the speed to low and add a third of the flour mixture, followed by half of the wine. Repeat with the remaining flour and wine, finishing with the final third of flour and continuing to beat on a low speed. Once combined, pour into the prepared cake pan and scatter the grapes evenly on top. Place in the oven and bake for 20 minutes.

4   **To make the sugar crust topping** while the cake is in the oven, place the butter and sugar in a small bowl and beat with a wooden spoon to form a thick paste. When the cake has been in the oven for 20 minutes, quickly but gently remove it and dot the sugar crust evenly over the top, breaking it into small pieces as you go. Scatter the grapes evenly over the top and return it to the oven.

5   Immediately lower the oven temperature to 350°F/180°C and continue to bake for another 35–40 minutes, or until a skewer inserted into the center of the cake comes out clean. Remove from the oven and set aside to cool for 30 minutes before removing from the pan. The cake can either be served straightaway or stored in an airtight container.

Tin can cake part I
Butternut, honey and almond

Part bread, part cake, this tin can loaf is the first of what we think of as our Boy Scout or Girl Guide trilogy. We were not in the woods when they were baked and the fire was not homemade, we know, but there's something timeless and wholesome about loaves baked in a regular tin can. The end result keeps (and freezes) well, so, homemade fire or not, you can at least take it with you to sustain you on a long walk in the woods.

Traditionally, these are made in cylindrical log pans that are about 3 inches/ 8 cm wide and 6½ inches/17 cm high. They used to be more widely available than they are these days. You occasionally see them on eBay, but they're generally considered novel and difficult to come by. Our alternative—regular 14-fl-oz/400-ml tin cans—works very well. Baking in a can gives the loaves such a great shape, and they are so wonderfully sliceable into thick rounds to share, like all good scouts do.

You need to open the cans by working with the opener perpendicular to the rim so that it cuts a slice off the top without leaving a lip. Save the contents in another container for future use, then wash and dry the empty cans. Cans with a ring pull will leave a little lip, which will make it harder to slide the cake out of the can when it's baked. If you have only cans with a ring pull, that's fine; just flip them over and open them from the base with a can opener, as described. Using a can opener will make the exposed edges of the cans sharp, so take a lot of care when lining the cans with parchment paper.

MAKES 2 TIN CAN LOAVES OR 1 LARGER LOAF

—

¼ small butternut squash,
    peeled and cut into roughly
    1½-inch/4-cm pieces (3½ oz/100 g)
½ cup plus 1 tbsp/125 g unsalted butter,
    at room temperature, cubed; plus a
    little extra, melted, for brushing;
    plus extra to serve
½ cup/100 g granulated sugar
finely grated zest of 1 small orange
    (1 tsp)

1 tbsp honey
1 large egg, lightly beaten
⅔ cup/100 g raisins
½ cup/50 g toasted sliced
    almonds
1⅓ cups/160 g self-rising flour
⅛ tsp salt
¼ cup/60 ml whole milk

You'll need an extra-long wooden skewer for inserting into the center of the loaves to check they are ready. We make these cakes in 14-fl-oz/ 400-ml cans, but you can also make one larger loaf if you prefer. Use a 9 x 5-inch/23 x 13-cm loaf pan. Just make sure the parchment paper that lines the pan rises about 2 inches/ 5 cm above the rim, so that you have some leverage with which to lift it out. The batter should rise two-thirds of the way up the pan and the cake won't rise much beyond that.

1   Place the squash pieces in a small saucepan and cover with water. Bring to a simmer over medium-high heat and cook for about 10 minutes, until soft. Drain, then use a fork to mash the squash to a purée.

2   Preheat the oven to 375°F/190°C.

3   Next prepare the two empty, clean cans (see introduction). Use a brush to lightly butter the inside of the cans. Trace around the round base and cut out circles of parchment paper to fit exactly. Use the long handle of a wooden spoon to help you line the inside of the can. This sounds trickier than it is—you'll just need to take care not to cut yourself on the opened ends of the cans. To line the insides of the cans, measure the circumference and height of the can and then cut a piece of parchment paper about 2 inches/5 cm taller than the can; a slight overlap of the paper is fine.

4   Place the butter, sugar, orange zest and honey in the bowl of an electric mixer with the paddle attachment in place. Beat for about 3 minutes, until light and creamy, then slowly add the beaten egg, stopping to scrape down the sides of the bowl halfway through. The mixture may look slightly curdled at this stage, but don't worry. Add the cooled squash purée, raisins and almonds and beat on low speed to combine. Sift the flour and salt together into a bowl, then add this in batches to the squash mixture, alternating with the milk. Beat on low speed until just combined, taking care not to overmix.

5   Dollop this mixture into the cans (or loaf pan) so that it rises all the way to the top of the can; you'll need to do this by the spoonful, as the batter is quite thick and the cans are narrow. Place the filled cans on a baking sheet, sitting upright, and bake for 45–50 minutes (whether baking in the cans or in a larger loaf pan), or until a long wooden skewer inserted into the center comes out dry and clean.

6   Remove the baking sheet from the oven and set the loaves aside for 15 minutes to cool in their cans before sliding them out. This is easily done by tipping the cans on their sides (use a kitchen towel to hold them, as they will still be quite hot) and gently tugging at the overhanging parchment paper. The loaf should slide out with the parchment paper around it. Set aside until completely cool before using a serrated knife to cut them into thick slices. They are great just as they are, or toasted. Either way, spread them liberally with butter before serving.

The butternut squash can be cooked up to 2 days in advance and stored in the fridge. Cut open and clean two tin cans in preparation (see introduction).

Once made, the loaves will keep for up to 3 days, covered in plastic wrap, or frozen for up to 2 months.

Tin can cake part II
Pineapple, pecan and currant

The pineapple rings should be in their own juice for this (rather than syrup). If you can find it, start with crushed canned pineapple so you won't need to grind up the rings.

MAKES 3 TIN CAN LOAVES OR 1 LARGER LOAF

¾ cup/90 g pecan halves
8 canned pineapple rings, in juice (not syrup; from two 8-oz/227-g cans)
½ cup plus 1 tbsp/125 g unsalted butter, cubed; plus a little extra, melted, for brushing; plus extra to serve

⅔ cup/150 g demerara sugar
½ cup/75 g dried currants
2 large eggs, lightly beaten
2¾ cups/320 g self-rising flour
¼ tsp salt
¼ tsp ground cloves

We make these cakes in 14-fl-oz/400-ml cans tin cans, but you can also make one larger loaf if you prefer. Use a 9 x 5-inch/23 x 13-cm loaf pan. Just make sure the parchment paper that lines the pan rises about 2 inches/5 cm above the rim, so that you have some leverage with which to lift it out. The batter should rise three-fourths of the way up the pan and the cake won't rise much beyond that.

Cut open and clean three tin cans in preparation (see Introduction page 136).

Once made, the loaves will keep in an airtight container for up to 3 days, or covered in plastic wrap and frozen for up to 2 months. They do dry up a bit over time, so if you are eating them after the first day or so, they're best toasted.

1   Preheat the oven to 350°F/180°C.

2   Spread the pecans out on a small baking sheet and roast for 8 minutes. Remove from the oven and, once cool enough to handle, chop roughly and set aside. Increase the oven temperature to 375°F/190°C.

3   Drain the juice from the pineapple can and place in a medium saucepan. Cut each pineapple slice into four and place in a food processor. Use the pulse button so that it is chopped into fine pieces; you want it to have the consistency of crushed pineapple rather than turning it into a purée. Transfer to the saucepan with the juice, along with the butter and sugar. Place over medium-low heat until the butter and sugar have melted, then increase the heat to medium-high. Bring to a boil and simmer for 4 minutes. Remove from the heat, stir in the currants and set aside for the mixture to cool to room temperature.

4   Meanwhile, carefully line three tin cans with parchment paper (see page 137, step 3).

5   When the mixture is at room temperature, add the beaten eggs and stir to combine. Sift the flour, salt and ground cloves together into a bowl, then fold this into the pineapple mixture along with the chopped toasted pecans. Fold until just combined, taking care not to overwork the mixture.

6   Dollop the mixture into the cans (or loaf pan) so that it rises about three-fourths of the way up the sides; you'll need to do this by the spoonful, as the batter is quite thick and the cans are narrow. Place the filled cans on a baking sheet, sitting upright, and bake for about 50 minutes (whether baking in the cans or in a larger loaf pan), or until a long wooden skewer inserted into the center comes out dry and clean.

7   Remove the baking sheet from the oven and set the loaves aside for 15 minutes to cool in their cans before sliding them out. This is easily done by tipping the cans on their sides (use a kitchen towel to hold them, as they will still be quite hot) and gently tugging at the overhanging parchment paper. The loaf should slide out with the parchment paper around it. Serve warm or cold, sliced with a serrated knife into thick slices and spread liberally with butter.

Tin can cake part III
Banana, date and walnut

MAKES 3 TIN CAN LOAVES OR 1 LARGER LOAF

½ cup/60 g walnut halves

7 oz/200 g Medjool dates, pitted
and roughly chopped into
¾-inch/2-cm pieces

1 packed cup plus 2 tbsp/200 g light
brown sugar

4 tbsp/60 g unsalted butter, cubed;
plus a little extra, melted, for
brushing; plus extra to serve

¾ cup/180 ml water

½ tsp baking soda

1 large egg, lightly beaten

1 banana, peeled and mashed
(about ½ cup/100 g)

½ tsp vanilla extract

1¾ cups/200 g self-rising flour

¼ tsp salt

We make these cakes in 14-fl-oz/
400-ml tin cans, but you can also
make one larger loaf if you prefer. Use
a 9 x 5-inch/23 x 13-cm loaf pan. Just
make sure the parchment paper that
lines the pan rises about 2 inches/
5 cm above the rim of the pan, so that
you have some leverage with which to
lift it out. The batter should rise two-
thirds of the way up the pan, and the
cake won't rise much beyond that.

Cut open and clean three tin cans
in preparation (see Introduction
page 136).

1   Preheat the oven to 350°F/180°C.

2   Spread the walnuts out on a baking sheet and roast for 5 minutes. Remove from
the oven and, once cool enough to handle, chop roughly and set aside. Increase the
oven temperature to 375°F/190°C.

3   Place the dates, brown sugar, butter and water in a medium saucepan and heat
gently, stirring from time to time, until the sugar has dissolved and the butter has melted.
Increase the heat, bring the mixture to a boil, then remove from the heat straightaway.
Transfer the mixture to a large bowl and set aside to cool to room temperature.

4   Meanwhile, carefully line three tin cans with parchment paper (see page 137,
step 3).

5   Add the baking soda, egg, banana and vanilla extract to the date mixture and
beat with a wooden spoon to combine. Add the walnuts, then sift the flour and salt
together into the mix. Stir to combine thoroughly but do not overmix.

6   Dollop the mixture into the cans (or loaf pan) so that it rises about two-thirds
of the way up the sides; you'll need to do this by the spoonful, as the batter is quite
thick and the cans are narrow. Place the filled cans on a baking sheet, sitting upright,
and bake for about 35 minutes (or 40 minutes if making one large loaf), or until a long
wooden skewer inserted into the center of the cakes comes out clean.

7   Remove the baking sheet from the oven and set the loaves aside for 15 minutes
to cool in their cans before sliding them out. This is easily done by tipping the cans
on their sides (use a kitchen towel to hold them, as they will still be quite hot) and
gently tugging at the overhanging parchment paper. The loaf should slide out with
the parchment paper around it. Serve warm or cold, sliced with a serrated knife into
thick slices and spread liberally with butter.

Grappa fruit cake

The combination of the dried fruit, citrus and vanilla in this cake are reminiscent of Italian panettone. The similarity ends there, however, with the addition of the yogurt and oil, which deliver moisture, richness and a cakey texture.

Use the best grappa you can afford; some of the cheaper varieties taste a bit like paint stripper. If you can't get grappa, then brandy, Grand Marnier or Cointreau all work. If using the candied citron, vodka works well. A garnish of chopped candied peel wouldn't be unappreciated.

SERVES 10

butter, for greasing
⅓ cup/60 g golden raisins (sultanas)
⅓ cup/50 g dried currants
2 tbsp good-quality grappa
 (or Gran Marnier or Cointreau)
2½ oz/70 g eggs (about 2 large eggs),
 lightly beaten
½ cup plus 1½ tbsp/125 g
 granulated sugar
scraped seeds of ½ vanilla pod
¼ cup/60 g plain Greek yogurt
⅓ cup/80 ml sunflower oil
finely grated zest of 1 lemon (1 tsp)

¼ cup/35 g good-quality mixed
 candied peel (or candied citron
 or orange peel)
1 cup/125 g all-purpose flour, plus
 extra for dusting
½ tsp baking powder
⅛ tsp salt

ICING
1 cup/120 g confectioners' sugar, sifted
1 tbsp lemon juice
1½ tsp grappa (or Gran Marnier or
 Cointreau)

1 Preheat the oven to 375°F/195°C. Grease and flour a large brioche or square pan, or the smaller individual pans, and set aside.

2 Place the raisins and currants in a small bowl, pour in the grappa and set aside for 10 minutes.

3 Place the eggs, granulated sugar and vanilla seeds in a large bowl and whisk to combine. Add the yogurt and sunflower oil and whisk again before folding in the lemon zest, raisins, currants, grappa and candied peel.

4 Sift the flour, baking powder and salt into the egg mixture, stir through to combine, then spoon into the pan. It should rise three-quarters of the way up the sides if making it in one larger pan or about two-thirds of the way up the sides if making it in smaller pans. Bake for 55 minutes, or about 16 minutes if making in smaller pans, or until a skewer inserted into the center of the cake comes out clean. Remove from the oven and leave to cool for 30 minutes.

5 **To make the icing,** place the confectioners' sugar, lemon juice and grappa in a bowl and whisk until smooth.

6 Transfer the slightly warm cake(s) from the mold(s) onto a wire rack. Spoon the icing over the top, letting it trickle down the side(s). Serve warm, or set aside to cool and store in an airtight container.

We've made this in an 7-inch/10-cm wide brioche pan, but you can also make it in a 8-inch/20-cm square pan, if you prefer. Around Easter, we make these in individual brioche molds as an alternative to hot cross buns; a regular muffin pan also works well.

With or without icing, these keep well for up to 4 days in an airtight container. They do become denser over time, but not unpleasantly so; in fact, we actually prefer them a day or two after they are made. The icing won't look as fresh as it does on Day One—it becomes a bit wrinkly—but it tastes absolutely fine.

Lemon and blackcurrant stripe cake

We had a momentary wobble as the recipes for *Sweet* were coming together that there was not enough color. Yotam ran off to his local grocer to get as many bright berries as he could, and the refrain of the week was: color, color, color! This tall, conical showstopper of a cake is one of the happy outcomes. It starts its life, simply, as a flat sponge cake in a baking sheet. Rolled up and covered in silky buttercream, it looks rather like a barrel. Cut into it, however—revealing the stripes!—and it looks like a whole lot of vertically inclined (and very colorful) fun.

See page 349 for the importance of timing when cooking with sugar; this is useful to understand before making the buttercream.

SERVES 8–10 (IT'S NOT A WIDE CAKE—JUST 5½ INCHES/14 CM—BUT IT'S HIGH)

The buttercream can be made up to 3 days in advance and stored in the fridge or freezer. Just bring it back to room temperature and quickly whip it in the electric mixer to restore its fluffiness before spreading.

Although the cake is best eaten on the day it's made, any leftovers will be fine the following day if stored in the fridge. As always, bring it back to room temperature before serving.

8 large eggs, whites and yolks separated
⅔ cup plus 2 tbsp/140 g granulated sugar, plus 1½ tbsp
1 tbsp lemon juice, plus finely grated zest of 1 small lemon (¾ tsp)
½ cup plus 1 tbsp/80 g all-purpose flour
⅛ tsp salt
confectioners' sugar, for dusting

BLACKCURRANT (OR MIXED BERRY) PURÉE
10½ oz/300 g blackcurrants (or mixed berries), fresh or frozen and defrosted, plus 1½ oz/40 g to garnish
¼ cup/50 g granulated sugar

BLACKCURRANT (OR MIXED BERRY) BUTTERCREAM
¼ cup/85 g light corn syrup (or golden syrup)
½ cup plus 1 tbsp/120 g granulated sugar
scraped seeds of ½ vanilla pod
4 large egg yolks
1¼ cups plus 1 tbsp/300 g unsalted butter, cut into 1-inch/3-cm cubes, softened
½ cup/100 g black currant (or mixed berry) pureé

1   Preheat the oven to 400°F/200°C. Line a shallow rimmed baking sheet (approximately 15 x 12 inch/38 x 30 cm) with parchment paper and set aside.

2   Place the egg yolks in the bowl of an electric mixer with the whisk attachment in place. Add the ⅔ cup plus 2 tbsp/140 g granulated sugar and the lemon juice and beat on medium-high speed for about 3 minutes, until pale and thick. Transfer the mixture to a large mixing bowl and sift the flour and salt directly over the egg mixture in two batches, folding through the mixture with a rubber spatula after each addition. Sprinkle the lemon zest on top and set aside.

3   Place the egg whites in a clean bowl of an electric mixer with the whisk attachment in place. Whisk on medium-high speed until soft peaks form, then slowly pour in the 1½ tbsp granulated sugar. Continue to whisk until firm peaks form, then gently fold a third of the egg whites into the egg yolk mixture until incorporated. Finally, fold in the remaining egg whites until combined, then scrape the mixture into the lined baking sheet. Even the surface out with a small spatula and bake for 15 minutes, or until light golden brown and a toothpick inserted into the center comes out clean. ››

4   Remove from the oven and place on a wire rack to cool in the pan for 5 minutes before dusting the top lightly with confectioners' sugar. Place a clean kitchen towel on top of the sponge cake and then flip it over so that it is now lying on top of the kitchen towel. Carefully peel away the paper and trim the very edges of the sponge. Be careful not to cut away too much; you really just want to straighten out the edges. Starting at the shorter edge of the cake, carefully roll it up (along with the kitchen towel). This is to "train" the cake, ready for rolling up again later. After about 20 minutes, or when no longer warm, unroll the cake. With the short end facing you, measure and cut three equal strips parallel to the long edge, each about 4 inches/10 cm wide. (If you have a pizza cutter, this is a really easy way to cut the strips.) Cover with a clean kitchen towel and set aside.

5   **To make the purée,** place the blackcurrants (or berries) and granulated sugar in a medium saucepan and place over medium-low heat. Warm through for 4–5 minutes, until the blackcurrants (or berries) have softened and the sugar has dissolved. Transfer to a food processor and process to form a purée. Strain through a fine-mesh sieve set over a bowl to catch the purée; you need ⅔ cup/150 g, so save any extra in the fridge to spoon over yogurt.

6   **To make the buttercream,** place the corn syrup (or golden syrup), granulated sugar and vanilla seeds in a medium saucepan. Place over low heat and stir until all the sugar dissolves; this is your sugar syrup.

7   While the syrup is cooking, place the egg yolks in the bowl of an electric mixer with the whisk attachment in place. Beat on medium-high speed until thick and pale yellow in color. Leave the machine on while you check the sugar syrup; when all the sugar has melted, stir again, increase the heat to medium and simmer until bubbles begin to appear. Swirl the pan gently and continue to simmer until there are large bubbles all over the surface of the syrup. Remove the pan from the heat and carefully pour the hot syrup in a slow, steady stream down the edge of the mixing bowl into the beating yolks. When all the syrup has been added, increase the mixer speed to high and continue to beat the mixture for about 10 minutes, until the outside of the bowl is no longer warm. Gradually add the butter, one cube at a time, allowing it to be incorporated into the mixture before adding the next. When all the butter has been added, scrape down the bowl and continue to beat for another minute, until the buttercream is very smooth and light. Add a scant ½ cup/100 g of the blackcurrant (or mixed berry) purée and beat on medium speed until fully incorporated.

8   Spread each of the strips of sponge with about 3 oz/85 g of the buttercream; this should leave about 10½ oz/300 g to frost the top and sides of the cake. Take one strip of sponge and, starting with the short end, roll it up. Once this strip is rolled, position the exposed end at the beginning of the next strip and keep rolling. Again, once this is rolled—the cylinder will be getting wider now—position the exposed end at the beginning of the last strip and continue to roll. You now have a rolled cylindrical cake! (Imagine, for a moment, if you lined up the three strips end to end to create one very long strip. Then imagine rolling that very long strip up, from one end to the other. You should end up with a coiled barrel shape.) Turn the cylinder onto the serving plate so that it is standing on one of its flat ends.

9   Spread the remaining buttercream all over the top and sides of the cake, smoothing with a spatula to create an even surface. Dribble the remaining ¼ cup/ 50 g blackcurrant (or mixed berry) purée on top of the cake and top this with the blackcurrants (or berries) reserved for garnish. Set aside for 1 hour at room temperature (or in the fridge if it is a very warm day) before serving.

Rhubarb and strawberry crumble cake

SERVES 12

—

CRUMBLE
8½ tbsp/120 g unsalted butter, melted
¾ packed cup/150 g light brown sugar
1½ cups/190 g all-purpose flour
¼ cup/30 g finely shredded coconut
¼ tsp salt

FRUIT
9 oz/260 g rhubarb (2 or 3 medium
    stalks), cut into ⅓-inch/1-cm slices
9 oz/260 g strawberries, hulled and
    sliced ¼ inch/0.5 cm thick
2 packed tbsp light brown sugar
¼ cup/30 g tapioca flour (or
    cornstarch)
2 tsp lemon juice
scraped seeds of ½ vanilla pod
⅛ tsp salt

CAKE
1½ cups/190 g all-purpose flour
¾ tsp baking powder
¼ tsp salt
¾ cup/170 g unsalted butter,
    at room temperature, cubed
1¾ cups plus 1½ tbsp/220 g
    confectioners' sugar
3 large eggs
1 tsp vanilla extract

We make this in a 9-inch/23-cm
round springform pan, but use a
9-inch/23-cm square springform
pan if that is what you have.
Either way, just make sure it is
springform or a deep cake pan
with a removable base.

Once assembled, the cake will keep
for 2 days, covered in plastic wrap
or stored in an airtight container. The
fruits may discolor a little, but this
won't affect the taste.

—

1   Preheat the oven to 400°F/200°C. Lightly grease a 9-inch/23-cm round or square
springform pan (or deep cake pan with a removable base) and line with parchment
paper, then set aside.

2   **To make the crumble,** place all the crumble ingredients in a large bowl and use
your hands or a wooden spoon to mix; you need to work the mixture quite a lot to get
evenly moist, large crumbs. The consistency will be damper and more pebbly than
you might be expecting, but this is what you want. Set aside.

3   **To make the fruit,** place all the fruit ingredients in a medium bowl, toss gently
to combine and then set aside.

4   **To make the cake,** sift the flour, baking powder and salt together into a bowl and
set aside. Place the butter and confectioners' sugar in the bowl of an electric mixer
with the paddle attachment in place. Beat for about 3 minutes on medium-high speed,
until light and fluffy. Add the eggs, one at a time, beating well after each addition. Add
the vanilla extract, followed by the dry ingredients and beat until combined. Turn the
machine off as soon as everything is combined, then pour into the lined cake pan,
using an offset spatula or the back of a spoon to even out the surface. Next, spoon
over the fruit mixture and then sprinkle evenly with the crumble mixture.

5   Bake for about 70 minutes, until the cake is golden brown on top and a skewer
inserted into the center comes out with just a few moist crumbs attached. Have a
look at the cake 15–20 minutes before the end of cooking; if it looks like it is getting
too dark on top, cover the pan with aluminum foil for the remainder of the baking, to
prevent it taking on any more color. Set the cake aside until completely cool before
removing from the pan and transferring to a cake platter to serve.

Coconut, almond and blueberry cake

Take the word *cake* out of the title here and this pretty much reads like a list of superfoods. All food is super to us, though, particularly when *cake* is added! This is a variation of Belinda's Flourless Coconut and Chocolate Cake (see page 190), with the addition of some flour to offset the juiciness of the blueberries. It's supersimple and wonderfully moist. It's also versatile, as happy to be served warm for dessert, with some heavy cream poured over, as it is at room temperature when it's time for tea.

This will keep for up to 3 days in an airtight container or wrapped in aluminum foil. It also freezes well for up to a month.

SERVES 10–12

—

1⅔ cups/180 g almond meal
⅔ cup/60 g finely shredded coconut
1¼ cups/250 g granulated sugar
½ cup plus 1 tbsp/70 g self-rising flour
¼ tsp salt
4 large eggs
¾ cup plus 2 tbsp/200 g unsalted
    butter, melted and cooled

1½ tsp vanilla extract
finely grated zest of 2 lemons (2 tsp)
1¼ cups/200 g fresh blueberries
¼ cup/20 g sliced almonds

—

1   Preheat the oven to 350°F/180°C. Grease a 9-inch/23-cm round cake pan and line with parchment paper, then set aside.

2   Place the almond meal, coconut, sugar, flour and salt in a large mixing bowl and whisk to aerate and remove the lumps.

3   Place the eggs in a separate medium bowl and whisk lightly. Add the melted butter, vanilla extract and lemon zest and whisk again until well combined. Pour this into the dry mixture and whisk to combine. Fold in 1 cup/150 g of the blueberries, then pour the mixture into the pan. Sprinkle the last of the blueberries on top, along with the sliced almonds, and bake for 50–55 minutes, or until a skewer inserted into the center comes out clean. Keep a close eye on it toward the end of cooking; the relatively large number of eggs in the batter means that it can go from still being a little bit liquid in the center to being overcooked in just a few minutes.

4   Set aside for 30 minutes before inverting the cake out of the pan, removing the parchment paper and placing right side up on a serving plate. It can either be served warm or set aside until cool.

Take-home chocolate cake

The recipe for this first appeared in an article written about Helen when she ran her café, the Mortar & Pestle, in Melbourne. Rather intimidatingly for Helen, the headline for the article was: World's Best Chocolate Cake. Nothing like setting the bar high in terms of expectation! All these years on, though, it still stands the test of time.

It could actually be called lots of things: "world's easiest cake," possibly, requiring nothing more than one large bowl to make it all in. Or "most versatile cake," given that it can be served without icing and just a light dusting of cocoa powder, or dressed up to the nines, as we have done here, with a thin layer of chocolate ganache and served with espresso cinnamon mascarpone cream.

In the shops, however, it just goes by the name Take-Home Chocolate Cake. This is because we make it as smaller cakes (as seen in the photos) to be shared by four people after a meal. The name lives on, though, even in the recipe for our larger version here. The cake keeps so well that customers would still be able to take home a whole cake, even if there were only four people at the first sitting.

SERVES 12

1 cup plus 1½ tbsp/250 g unsalted butter, at room temperature, cut into ¾-inch/2-cm cubes, plus extra for greasing

7 oz/200 g dark chocolate (70% cocoa solids), chopped into ¾-inch/2-cm pieces

1½ tsp instant coffee granules, dissolved in 1½ cups/350 ml boiling water

1¼ cups/250 g granulated sugar

2 large eggs, lightly beaten

2 tsp vanilla extract

1¾ cups plus 2 tbsp/240 g self-rising flour

⅓ cup/30 g Dutch-processed cocoa powder, plus 1½ tsp, for dusting

¼ tsp salt

CHOCOLATE GANACHE (OPTIONAL)

7 oz/200 g dark chocolate (70% cocoa solids), broken or chopped roughly into ¾-inch/2-cm pieces

¾ cup/180 ml heavy cream

1 tbsp light corn syrup

1 tbsp unsalted butter, at room temperature

ESPRESSO CINNAMON MASCARPONE CREAM (OPTIONAL)

1½ cups plus 1 tbsp/375 ml heavy cream

¾ cup/190 g mascarpone

scraped seeds of ½ vanilla pod

2½ tsp finely ground espresso

¾ tsp ground cinnamon

2½ tbsp confectioners' sugar

The ganache can be stored at room temperature, providing it's not too warm, for 3 days or kept in the fridge for up to 2 weeks. It can also be frozen, although it will lose a bit of its shine when defrosted.

With or without icing, the cake will keep well for 4–5 days in an airtight container.

1   Preheat the oven to 350°F/170°C. Grease a 9-inch/23-cm round springform pan and line with parchment paper, then set aside.

2   Place the butter, chocolate and hot coffee in a large heatproof bowl and mix well until everything is melted, combined and smooth. Whisk in the sugar by hand until dissolved. Add the eggs and vanilla extract and whisk again until thoroughly combined and smooth. Sift the flour, cocoa powder and salt together into a bowl and whisk this into the melted chocolate mixture. The batter here is liquid, but don't think you have missed something; this is how it should be. Pour the batter into the prepared cake pan and bake for 60 minutes, or until the cake is cooked and a skewer inserted into the center comes out clean or with just a few dry crumbs attached. The top will »

form a crust and crack a little, but don't worry, this is expected. Leave the cake to cool for 20 minutes before removing from the pan, then set aside until completely cool.

3   **To make the chocolate ganache,** place the chocolate pieces in a food processor, process until fine and set aside.

4   Combine the cream and corn syrup in a small pan and place over medium-high heat. As soon as bubbles begin to appear—just before it comes to a boil—remove from the heat. Get the food processor running again, with the chocolate still inside, and pour in the hot cream in a steady stream. Process for about 10 seconds, then add the butter. Continue to process until the mixture is shiny and smooth. You can also make the ganache by hand; just make sure the chocolate is chopped fairly finely before you scald the cream and corn syrup and pour it over the chocolate. Stir everything together with a wooden spoon until almost melted, then add the butter. Stir again until the ganache is smooth.

5   Use a rubber spatula to scrape the ganache into a bowl and cover with plastic wrap, with the plastic wrap actually touching the top of the ganache. Set aside until it has set to the consistency you want. If you want a thin layer to spread over the cake, it can be poured over while liquid so that you get an even, light and shiny coating. For a thicker ganache with a spreading consistency, leave it for about 2 hours at room temperature.

6   **To make the espresso cinnamon mascarpone cream,** place all the ingredients in the bowl of an electric mixer with the whisk attachment in place. Beat for 1–2 minutes, until soft peaks form.

7   Peel the parchment from the cake and discard. Transfer to a serving platter and use a spatula or knife to spread the ganache on top of the cake. When ready to serve, slice into wedges, divide the cake among plates and spoon the mascarpone cream alongside.

Apricot and almond cake with cinnamon topping

We used apricots here, but other stone fruits—plums or peaches, for example—work well if apricots are not in season and you don't want to use canned. Just make sure the pieces of fruit are not too heavy or large, as you don't want them to sink.

The topping has a way of cooking quite irregularly—buckling here and there on top and sometimes even seeping into the batter below. Don't worry if this happens; it's all part of the cake's rustic charm.

SERVES 10

CINNAMON TOPPING
4 tbsp/60 g unsalted butter
½ cup/100 g granulated sugar
2 tsp ground cinnamon
⅛ tsp salt
2 large eggs, lightly beaten

CAKE
6 tbsp/85 g unsalted butter,
    at room temperature
1 cup/200 g granulated sugar
2 large eggs

finely grated zest of 1 small lemon
    (¾ tsp)
1 tsp vanilla extract
¼ tsp almond extract
1¾ cups plus 2 tbsp/220 g
    self-rising flour
⅛ tsp salt
⅔ cup/160 g sour cream
⅓ cup/35 g almond meal
8 large fresh apricots (1 lb 2 oz/500 g),
    halved and pitted, or 20 canned
    apricot halves (1 lb 2 oz/500 g drained
    weight)

You don't want to invert the cake here (because of the fruit baked on top) so a springform or other cake pan with a removable base is a must. We've used a round springform pan, but a square springform pan—with similar dimensions—also works well.

Once baked, the cake can be kept in an airtight container for up to 3 days. Warm it in the oven for 10–15 minutes at 400°F/200°C before serving, if desired.

1   **To make the cinnamon topping,** melt the butter in a small saucepan and add the sugar, cinnamon and salt. Stir to combine, then remove from the heat. Allow to cool for 5 minutes, stir in the beaten eggs and set aside.

2   **To make the cake,** preheat the oven to 375°F/195°C. Grease a 9-inch/23-cm round springform pan and line with parchment paper, then set aside.

3   Place the butter and sugar in the bowl of an electric mixer with the paddle attachment in place. Beat on medium-high speed until light and fluffy, then add the eggs, one at a time, beating well after each addition and scraping down the sides of the bowl a few times. Add the lemon zest, vanilla extract and almond extract and beat to combine. Sift the flour and salt into a bowl, turn the speed of the mixer to low and add the dry ingredients to the creamed mixture, alternating in batches with the sour cream, so that you begin and end with the flour. Beat to combine, then spoon or scrape the batter into the pan. Smooth the surface with a spatula or the back of a spoon and sprinkle the almond meal over the top. Arrange the apricot halves on top, cut side facing up, starting around the outside edge of the pan and working toward the center. Spoon the cinnamon topping over and around the apricots.

4   Bake for about 1 hour, or until a skewer inserted into the middle of the cake comes out clean (although the topping might still be a bit sticky). Keep an eye on it toward the end of cooking, as it can go from undercooked to overcooked very quickly. Set aside for 20 minutes in the pan to cool before removing and serving warm.

Pistachio roulade with raspberries and white chocolate

Our technique of "training" the roulade (see page 146) is a neat little trick, if you don't know it already. Once you've cracked it (or not, in the case of your sponge cake), you'll feel like a roulade-making pro.

SERVES 10

The white chocolate cream can be prepared a day in advance and kept in the fridge. Remove it from the fridge about 30 minutes before you want to use it, so that it softens up a little.

Once assembled, the cake is best eaten on the same day It's made, although any leftovers will keep in the fridge for up to a day. Allow it to rest at room temperature for 30 minutes before serving.

½ cup/70 g shelled pistachio kernels, plus 2 tbsp, roughly chopped
4 large eggs, whites and yolks separated
⅔ cup/130 g granulated sugar
2 tbsp hot water
⅔ cup/80 g self-rising flour
⅛ tsp salt
⅛ tsp almond extract
3 tbsp/20 g confectioners' sugar

WHITE CHOCOLATE CREAM
7 oz/200 g white chocolate buttons or 7-oz/200-g block of white chocolate, roughly chopped into ⅓-inch/1-cm pieces
5 tbsp/70 g unsalted butter, soft but not oily (see page 344)
10 oz/280 g cream cheese, at room temperature
1 cup plus 2 tbsp/270 ml heavy cream
⅛ tsp almond extract

2½ cups/300 g fresh raspberries

1   Preheat the oven to 400°F/200°C. Grease a 10 x 15-inch/25 x 38-cm jelly-roll pan or similar-size shallow rimmed baking sheet and line with parchment paper.
2   Place the ½ cup/70 g pistachios in the small bowl of a food processor (or use a spice grinder) and grind until fine but not oily. Don't worry if there are some medium-sized pieces in the mix; these will not affect the cake. Set aside until needed.
3   Place the egg yolks and granulated sugar in the bowl of an electric mixer with the whisk attachment in place. Beat for about 4 minutes, until thick and creamy. Transfer the mixture to a large bowl and add the hot water, dribbling it down the sides of the bowl. Sprinkle over the ground pistachios and gently fold to combine; don't worry if it's not well mixed at this stage.
4   Sift the flour and salt together into a bowl, then sift again into the egg yolk and pistachio mixture. Fold to combine.
5   Beat the egg whites in a clean bowl of an electric mixer with the whisk attachment in place. Beat to form soft peaks, then fold into the pistachio mixture, a third at a time, along with the almond extract.
6   Scrape the batter into the pan and bake for 15–18 minutes, or until the cake springs back when lightly touched in the center. Remove the cake from the oven and set aside for 5 minutes.
7   Sift half the confectioners' sugar evenly over the surface of the cake and cover with a clean kitchen towel. Place a wire rack on top and then flip the cake over, so that the wire rack is now underneath the kitchen towel and cake. Lift off the pan, carefully peel away the paper and lightly dust the top of the cake with the remaining confectioners' sugar. ››

8   With one of the short ends of the cake facing toward you, roll up the still-warm cake with the kitchen towel inside. Allow the cake to rest for 10 minutes, still rolled up in the kitchen towel (this "trains" the cake for the final roll), then unroll the cake and set aside to come to room temperature. Don't worry if the ends of the cake curl up a little or if the surface has some cracks in it; this often happens.

9   **To make the white chocolate cream** while the cake is cooling, place the chocolate in a bowl set over a pan of simmering water, making sure the base of the bowl is not touching the water. Stir from time to time until the chocolate is melted, then remove from the heat and set aside to cool slightly. Place the butter in the bowl of an electric mixer with the paddle attachment in place. Beat on medium-high speed for 30 seconds, until smooth, then add the cream cheese. Beat well to combine, then add the melted chocolate. Continue to beat until smooth before adding the heavy cream and almond extract. Beat on medium-high speed until the mixture forms soft waves.

10   Use a small spatula to spread about two-thirds of the white chocolate cream evenly over the surface of the cake. Leave a border of about ¾ inch/2 cm without any cream at the short end of the cake farthest away from you. Place all but 12 of the raspberries evenly on top of the cream and then roll the cake up as you did before, this time without the kitchen towel inside. Using a long spatula, transfer the cake to a long platter. Use a small spatula or butter knife to spread the remaining cream all over the cake, smoothing it out as you go. Place the remaining raspberries along the center of the cake, and sprinkle with the 2 tbsp pistachio nuts.

Tropical fruit cake

This is an exceptionally moist cake—almost unusually so, with its bounty of pineapple and banana and the addition of oil. It's known as a "hummingbird cake" in Australia, New Zealand and Canada and is traditionally frosted with a cream cheese frosting. We've added mango purée here. It's not that the cake needs any help—you can eat it without any frosting at all, if you like—but we love the chrome-yellow color it brings to the cake and the way it complements the tropical fruits inside. Piled high with fresh fruit on top, this is an unexpectedly refreshing cake.

Canned pineapple is a fine alternative to fresh, if you prefer. Drain your chunks or slices and proceed, as per the recipe, to chop them in the food processor.

The cream cheese frosting can be made a day ahead. In fact, it needs to be refrigerated for 2 hours to firm up before covering the cake, so it's good to prepare ahead.

Unfrosted, the cake will keep for about 3 days in an airtight container. Once frosted, it is best eaten on the same day. Leftovers can be kept in the fridge for a day or two; just bring the cake back to room temperature before serving.

SERVES 8

1 pineapple, peeled and cored.
   10½ oz/300 g of the flesh should be cut into 1-inch/3-cm chunks for the cake, 2 oz/55 g of the flesh should be cut into ¾-inch/2-cm chunks for the garnish
2 large eggs
1 tsp vanilla extract
½ packed cup plus 1 tbsp/100 g light brown sugar
½ cup/100 g granulated sugar
⅔ cup/160 ml sunflower oil
2 ripe bananas, peeled and mashed (5¼ oz/150 g)
⅓ cup/35 g finely shredded coconut
1¾ cups/220 g all-purpose flour
1 tsp baking soda
½ tsp ground cinnamon
½ tsp ground ginger
½ tsp ground cardamom
½ tsp salt

FROSTING

¼ large ripe mango, peeled and roughly chopped (2 oz/55 g)
4½ tbsp/65 g unsalted butter, at room temperature
3½ oz/100 g cream cheese, at room temperature
⅔ cup/80 g confectioners' sugar, sifted

TO SERVE

½ banana, cut into roughly ⅓-inch/1-cm pieces (2 oz/55 g)
⅓ large ripe mango, flesh cut into long, thin strips (2½ oz/70 g)
2 oz/55 g pineapple flesh (see preceding)
scooped-out seeds of 1 passion fruit
3 tbsp/20 g flaked coconut

1   Preheat the oven to 400°F/200°C. Grease the base and sides of a 9-inch/23-cm round springform pan and line with parchment paper, then set aside.

2   Place the 10½ oz/300 g pineapple flesh in a food processor and pulse to crush the fruit; it should be finely chopped but not become a purée. If starting with fresh pineapple, tip the finely chopped flesh into a medium saucepan and place over medium heat. Bring to a simmer, cook for 4–5 minutes (taking care that it does not boil vigorously, as this will cause too much of the liquid to evaporate), then transfer to a large mixing bowl (large enough to mix the whole cake in later) to cool. If you are starting with canned pineapple, you can skip this boiling stage. ››

3   Place the eggs, vanilla extract, brown sugar and granulated sugar in the bowl of an electric mixer with the whisk attachment in place. Beat for about 3 minutes, until creamy, then, with the machine on medium speed, pour in the oil in a slow and steady stream until combined. Add this to the bowl of cooled pineapple along with the mashed bananas and finely shredded coconut. Stir to combine.

4   Sift the flour, baking soda, cinnamon, ginger, cardamon and salt together into the wet mix and use a large rubber spatula to fold until just combined. Pour into the cake pan and bake for about 40 minutes, until nicely browned. Lower the oven temperature to 350°F/180°C and continue to cook for 10–15 minutes, or until a skewer inserted into the center comes out clean. Remove the cake from the oven and leave to cool in its pan on a wire rack for about an hour. Turn out onto a serving platter, carefully remove the paper, then set aside to cool completely.

5   **To make the frosting,** place the mango flesh in the small bowl of a food processor and process to form a fine purée. Tip out into a small bowl and set aside. Add the butter and cream cheese to the food processor—there is no need to wash the bowl—and process until smooth. Add the confectioners' sugar, pulse to combine, then add the mango purée. Pulse again until evenly mixed and scrape into a bowl. Keep in the fridge, covered, for 2 hours—it needs this time to thicken—before frosting the cake.

6   **To serve,** use a small spatula or knife to spread a thick layer of the mango frosting all over the top and sides of the cake. Place all the fruit in a small bowl, mix gently and then spoon it into the center of the cake; you want it to be piled up in the middle, rather than spread evenly over the top. Finish by pressing the flaked coconut into the sides of the cake.

Pistachio and rose water semolina cake

Making this cake is a labor of love, but that's only appropriate, we think, for a cake adorned with rose petals. If you want to save time, however, you can do without the petals or use store-bought dried rose petals—the cake and cream are both special enough for those you feed to know you love them. If you are going all out with the roses, red or pink petals are a matter of preference; the red petals will turn a deep purple once candied.

SERVES 10–12

___

The cake keeps well for up to 5 days in an airtight container. The rose petals should be sprinkled over just before serving.

CANDIED ROSE PETALS (IF USING)
1 large egg white
About 40 medium pesticide-free
    red or pink rose petals
2 tbsp granulated sugar

CAKE
3 cardamom pods
1 cup/150 g shelled pistachio kernels,
    plus 2 tbsp, finely chopped, to serve
1 cup/100 g almond meal
¾ cup plus 3 tbsp/170 g fine semolina
1¼ tsp baking powder
¼ tsp salt
1¼ cups plus 1 tbsp/300 g unsalted
    butter, at room temperature, cubed,
    plus extra for greasing
1⅔ cups/330 g granulated sugar
4 large eggs, lightly beaten
finely grated zest of 1 lemon (1 tsp),
    plus 1 tbsp lemon juice
2 tbsp rose water (not rose essence,
    see page 355)
½ tsp vanilla extract

ROSE CREAM
¾ cup/190 g plain Greek yogurt
¾ cup/200 g crème fraîche
1 tbsp confectioners' sugar
1 tbsp rose water

ROSE SYRUP
½ cup/120 ml lemon juice
⅓ cup/80 ml rose water
½ cup/100 g granulated sugar

___

1   Preheat the oven to 200°F/100°C. Line a baking sheet with parchment paper and grease a 9-inch/23-cm round springform pan and line with parchment paper.

2   **To make the candied rose petals,** if doing so, whisk the egg white by hand until frothy. Then, using a small pastry brush or paintbrush, very lightly paint both sides of each petal with the egg white; do this in a few small batches, brushing and then sprinkling lightly over both sides with the sugar. Shake off the excess sugar and lay the petals on the lined baking sheet. Place in the oven for 30 minutes, until dry and crunchy, then set aside to cool.

3   **To make the cake,** increase the oven temperature to 350°F/180°C. ››

4   Use the flat side of a large knife to crush the cardamom pods and place the seeds in the small bowl of a food processor. The pods can be discarded. Add the pistachios and process until the nuts are finely ground—the black cardamom seeds won't really grind down—then transfer to a bowl. Add the almond meal, semolina, baking powder and salt. Mix together and set aside.

5   Place the butter and sugar in the bowl of an electric mixer with the paddle attachment in place. Beat on medium-high speed until fully combined, but take care not to overwork it; you don't want to incorporate a lot of air into the mixture. With the machine still running, slowly add the eggs, scraping down the sides of the bowl a few times and making sure that each batch is fully incorporated before adding the next. The mixture will curdle once the eggs are added, but don't worry; this will not affect the end result.

6   Remove the bowl from the machine and add the dry ingredients, folding them in by hand and, again, taking care not to overmix. Next fold in the lemon zest, lemon juice, rose water and vanilla extract and scrape the batter into the pan. Level with an offset spatula and bake for 55–60 minutes, or until a skewer inserted into the center of the cake comes out clean but oily.

7   **To make the rose cream** while the cake is in the oven, place all the ingredients for the cream in a bowl and use a hand whisk to beat everything together for about 2 minutes, until thick. Keep in the fridge until ready to serve.

8   **To make the rose syrup,** about 10 minutes before the cake comes out of the oven (you want the syrup to be warm when the cake is ready), place all the ingredients for the syrup in a small saucepan over medium heat. Bring to a boil, stirring so that the sugar dissolves, then remove from the heat. Don't worry that the consistency is thinner than you might expect; this is how it should be.

9   As soon as the cake comes out of the oven, drizzle all of the syrup over the top. It is a lot of syrup, but don't lose your nerve—the cake can take it! Sprinkle with the finely chopped pistachios and set the cake aside in its pan to come to room temperature. Remove from the pan and scatter the rose petals over the cake. Serve immediately.

Festive fruitcake

We sell this cake at Christmas and Easter. It's also a good base for a wedding (or any other festive) cake. The very small amount of almond meal in the batter helps to bind it, as well as adding to the shelf life. The inclusion of alcohol is not traditional in an Easter cake, but we find the combination of dried fruit and booze very hard to resist. Get the best-quality dried fruit you can for this: it makes all the difference.

SERVES ABOUT 20

This can be made in either an 8-inch/ 20-cm square or round cake pan. A blowtorch is handy here, to scorch the top of the marzipan; alternatively, you can put the cake under the broiler.

The fruit needs to be macerated for 24–48 hours before baking. The cake itself needs to sit for a day before decorating and serving. The flavors will develop over time, so ideally make it a week in advance and store in an airtight container.

Once iced, the cake will keep for up to 3 months in an airtight container.

FRUIT MIX

1 cup/140 g dried currants

2½ cups/375 g raisins

⅔ cup/120 g chopped, soft dried apricots, tough stems removed

5 Medjool dates, pitted and roughly chopped (about ½ cup/75 g)

⅓ cup/80 g pitted prunes, roughly chopped

⅓ cup/75 g glacé cherries, roughly chopped

½ cup/100 g best-quality chopped mixed candied peel (or candied orange peel)

⅓ cup/80 ml dark rum

⅓ cup/80 ml brandy

CAKE

1⅔ cups/200 g all-purpose flour

2 tbsp almond meal

⅓ tsp baking soda

¾ tsp mixed spice (see page 354)

¾ tsp ground cinnamon

⅓ tsp ground nutmeg

¼ tsp salt

½ cup plus 2½ tbsp/150 g unsalted butter, at room temperature, cut into ¾-inch/2-cm cubes, plus extra for greasing

½ packed cup plus 2 tbsp/120 g dark brown sugar

finely grated zest of 1 lemon (1 tsp)

finely grated zest of 1 small orange (1 tsp)

2 tsp blackstrap molasses

1 tbsp fine-cut or no-peel orange marmalade

2 large eggs, lightly beaten, plus 1 egg, lightly beaten, for folding through at the end

2½ tbsp dark rum

2½ tbsp brandy

TOPPING

3 tbsp fine-cut or no-peel orange marmalade (if you only have thick cut, just finely chop the pieces of orange)

Confectioners' sugar, for sprinkling

10½ oz/300 g marzipan (25–30% almonds)

1   **To make the fruit mix,** place all the fruit in a large container with a lid. Pour in the rum and brandy and mix well. Cover and leave at room temperature for 24–48 hours, shaking the container every few hours. ››

2 **To make the cake,** preheat the oven to 325°F/160°C. Grease an 8-inch/20-cm square or round cake pan and line the base and sides with two layers of parchment paper. Allow for enough paper so that it rises over and above the top edge of the pan by 2 inches/5 cm. Having two layers will insulate the cake from the heat of the metal pan so that the sides don't cook too quickly. Set aside.

3 Place the flour, almond meal, baking soda, mixed spice, cinnamon, nutmeg and salt in a medium bowl. Use a hand whisk to stir until any lumps in the almond meal are broken up.

4 Place the butter, brown sugar and both zests in the bowl of an electric mixer with the paddle attachment in place. Beat on medium-high speed for 2–3 minutes, until pale and well combined. Add the molasses and marmalade and beat to combine. Add the 2 eggs gradually, beating well after each addition, until fully incorporated, scraping down the sides of the bowl. Turn the speed to low and slowly add the dry ingredients. Beat until just combined, then add the macerated fruit. Gently mix, then remove the bowl from the mixer. Use a wooden spoon to fold in the last egg.

5 Spoon the cake batter into the prepared pan and use a spatula to make a slight dip in the center of the batter to ensure an even top on the cake once it is cooked. Bake for 2–2¼ hours, or until a skewer inserted into the center of the cake comes out clean. (Cover with aluminum foil if the cake looks like it is taking on too much color.)

6 Mix together the rum and brandy in a bowl and set aside. As soon as the cake comes out of the oven, brush the alcohol over the top until it's all soaked in. Set aside until completely cool and store in an airtight container (for 1 week, ideally) before decorating.

7 **To make the topping,** spread all but ½ tsp of the marmalade over the top of the cake to form a thin layer. On a work surface that has been lightly sprinkled with confectioners' sugar, roll out the marzipan to ¼ inch/0.5 cm thick. Use the base of the cake pan to cut out a square or circle the same size as the cake and lay this on top of the cake. Gently press to seal it to the marmalade, then use the remaining marzipan to make twelve small balls, about ⅛ oz/5 g each. Dip the base of the balls in the remaining marmalade and stick them onto the cake, three balls in each corner; if you are making a round cake, put three balls in the middle of the cake and space the remaining balls around the edge.

8 If you have a blowtorch, lightly scorch the top of the cake and balls to give the marzipan some color. Alternatively, you can place the cake under the broiler for a few minutes; just keep a close eye on it so that it doesn't take on too much color.

Flourless chocolate layer cake with coffee, walnuts and rose water

This started life as a roulade. Having no flour in it, though, it was so delicate that, rather than rolling into neat layers, it kept cracking into three more-or-less even layers. It looked so great in its deconstructed form that we decided to convert it into a layer cake. Don't despair if something in the kitchen doesn't go according to plan A–plan B can be even better! The pairing of the coffee with rose water might seem a bit odd but, actually, Turkish delight is commonly eaten alongside strong black coffee.

As always with nuts—but particularly with walnuts—taste your batch before you start baking. The range in quality can be huge and will make or break the taste of the cake. You'll know by just trying one nut whether you're onto a good thing. Don't be put off by the large amount of walnuts required here; there's a lot of richness in the otherwise delicate sponge cake and cream that the nuts balance out.

SERVES 8

1 cup/120 g walnut halves

CAKE
6 large eggs, whites and yolks
   separated
1 cup plus 1 tbsp/215 g granulated sugar
7½ oz/215 g dark chocolate (70% cocoa
   solids), roughly chopped
   or broken up
2½ tsp instant coffee granules,
   dissolved in 3½ tbsp/50 ml hot water

CARAMELIZED WALNUT TOPPING
2 tbsp granulated sugar
⅓ cup/40 g roughly chopped
   walnut halves

ROSE WATER CREAM
1½ cups plus 2 tbsp/380 ml
   heavy cream
2½ tbsp confectioners' sugar
1½ tbsp rose water (not rose
   essence, see page 355)

The cake is best eaten on the day it is made. Any leftovers can be stored in the fridge, covered in plastic wrap, where it will keep for up to 2 days. Remove from the fridge 30 minutes before serving, so that it is not fridge-cold.

1   Preheat the oven to 350°F/180°C. Grease a 10 x 15-inch/25 x 38-cm jelly-roll pan and line with parchment paper, then set aside.

2   Spread the walnuts out on a rimmed baking sheet and roast for 8 minutes. Set aside to cool, then roughly chop and set aside until assembling the cake. Increase the oven temperature to 400°F/200°C.

3   **To make the cake,** place the egg yolks in the bowl of an electric mixer with the whisk attachment in place. Beat on medium-high speed and, with the machine still running, gradually add the granulated sugar. Continue to beat until the mixture is thick, lighter in color and tripled in volume.

4   While the yolks are beating, place the chocolate pieces in a large heatproof bowl set over a pan of simmering water, making sure the base of the bowl is not touching the water. Add the coffee to the chocolate and stir gently (it will seize up if you stir too often or too vigorously) until the chocolate has completely melted. Turn off the heat and fold the yolk-sugar mixture into the chocolate mixture in three batches. ››

5   Place the egg whites in a clean bowl of an electric mixer with the whisk attachment in place. Beat on high speed until stiff peaks form, then fold gently into the chocolate mix. Scrape the mixture into the pan, spreading with an offset spatula over the surface so that it is even. Bake for 20 minutes, until cooked through and a skewer inserted into the center comes out clean, then set aside to cool completely.

6   **To make the caramelized walnut topping,** line a small rimmed baking sheet with parchment paper. Place the sugar and walnuts in a small sauté or frying pan and cook over medium-high heat until the sugar begins to melt and turn a pale amber color. Use a spatula to stir the walnuts and sugar together, so that the walnuts are evenly coated. Continue to cook for another 5 minutes, until the caramel is a dark amber and the walnuts are golden brown. Remove from the heat and pour onto the lined baking sheet. Set aside to cool, then roughly break any clumps of walnuts into smaller pieces. You can make these in advance, and store in an airtight container at room temperature.

7   **To make the rose water cream,** place all the ingredients for the cream in the bowl of an electric mixer with the whisk attachment in place. Beat until soft peaks form, then set aside in the fridge until ready to assemble the cake.

8   Turn the cooled cake out onto a cutting board and remove the pan and paper. Place a second cutting board on top of the cake and flip it back over, so that the crust side of the cake is facing up. Trim about ¼ inch/0.5 cm off the short edges of the cake and then cut the sponge into three even pieces, each about 9½ x 4½ inches/24 x 10 cm. Carefully transfer one piece of cake onto a serving platter and spread one-third of the rose water cream evenly over the surface of the cake. Sprinkle half the toasted walnuts over the cream and place another layer of sponge cake on top. Repeat with the cream and remaining toasted walnuts, then place the final layer of sponge cake on top. Dollop and spread the remaining cream on top of the cake. Sprinkle the caramelized walnuts on top of the cream and serve.

Louise cake with plum and coconut

This is inspired by (but completely different to!) the Louise cake: a hugely popular teatime treat in New Zealand. More of a slice than a cake, it's traditionally made with a thin cakey bottom, a spread of raspberry jam in the middle and a thin layer of coconut meringue on top. We've kept the layers but made a lot of changes.

We sell this in our shops as a "summer slice," using the best stone fruits, from plums to peaches to apricots to cherries, depending on what's in season. Whichever fruit you use, it needs to be ripe but not too soft.

SERVES 9

Traditionally, Louise cakes are baked in rectangular pans and cut into fairly thin squares. We've made ours in a high-sided 8-inch/20-cm square pan with a removable base. The resulting slices are about three times the height of the original. We love the height—it makes everyone feel like a kid when presented with a slice—but you can also make it in a 9-inch/23-cm round springform pan instead, if necessary. Wedges are not as neat to cut as squares, but the cake will still work well.

The cake is at its best on the day it's made, but is absolutely fine kept for up to 2 days in an airtight container in the fridge. The plum juice will make the base a bit soggy after day one, but this won't affect the taste.

½ cup plus 1 tbsp/125 g unsalted butter, at room temperature, cut into ¾-inch/2-cm cubes
½ cup/100 g granulated sugar
finely grated zest of 1 lemon (1 tsp)
3 large egg yolks
1 cup/125 g all-purpose flour
1½ tsp baking powder
¼ tsp salt
3 tbsp/20 g finely shredded coconut
⅓ cup/80 ml whole milk
1 tsp vanilla extract
5 dark red plums, ripe but firm (1 lb/450 g), or peaches, apricots, cherries, and so on

MERINGUE
½ cup/50 g sliced almonds
5 oz/140 g egg whites (from 3½ large eggs)
⅛ tsp salt
¾ cup plus 3 tbsp/185 g granulated sugar
1 tsp vanilla extract
1 tsp white wine vinegar
1 tsp cornstarch

1   Preheat the oven to 350°F/170°C.

2   Spread out the sliced almonds for the meringue on a baking sheet and roast for 10 minutes, until they are a light golden brown. Remove from the oven and set aside to cool.

3   Increase the oven temperature to 375°F/185°C. Line the base and sides of a high-sided 8-inch/20-cm square or a 9-inch/23-cm round springform pan with parchment paper.

4   Place the butter, sugar and lemon zest in the bowl of an electric mixer with the paddle attachment in place. Beat on medium-high speed, until light and creamy. Add the egg yolks, one at a time, and beat until combined. Sift the flour, baking powder and salt together into a bowl. Add the coconut and stir to combine. With the machine running on a low speed, gradually add the dry ingredients to the butter mixture, alternating with the milk and vanilla extract. Scrape the batter into the prepared pan—it will rise only about a fifth of the way up the sides—and smooth the top evenly. Place in the oven and bake for 25 minutes, until the cake is fully cooked and a skewer inserted into the center comes out clean.

5   Meanwhile, slice each plum vertically in half. Discard the pits and slice each half into four segments so that you have eight segments per plum and forty segments in total. If you start with a larger quantity of smaller plums or another smaller stone fruit like cherries, then just quarter each fruit. ››

6   When the cake is cooked, remove it from the oven and lower the oven temperature to 350°F/180°C. Gently lay the plum segments on top of the cake, close together and cut side down. Don't overlap the fruit, though, as this will make the middle layer too watery.

7   **To make the meringue,** place the egg whites and salt in the clean bowl of an electric mixer with the whisk attachment in place. Beat on medium-high speed for about 1 minute until soft peaks form. Add the sugar, a tablespoon at a time, and continue to beat on high speed until the egg whites are stiff and glossy. Add the vanilla extract, vinegar and cornstarch and whisk again until combined. Finally, fold in the toasted sliced almonds.

8   Scrape the meringue into the cake pan, on top of the plums, and spread out evenly over the fruit. Swirl the meringue around so you get rough waves and peaks, then place in the oven and bake for 35 minutes, or until the meringue has formed a hard crust and is just beginning to brown. Remove from the oven and allow to cool in the cake pan for 30 minutes before pushing up the removable base (or removing the sides) to release the cake. Peel away the parchment paper, place on a platter, and serve.

Almond butter cake with cardamom and baked plums

When Helen was working as a pastry chef at Donovans restaurant in Melbourne, there was a seriously VIP reservation: Stephanie Alexander and Maggie Beer, both big names on the Australian food scene, were in for the evening, having supper together. Nervous about what to bake for such a special occasion, Helen pounced upon a fresh batch of Morello cherries, which she decided to serve along with this cake. The dish got the double thumbs-up, so a new recipe—and Helen's day—was made. Fresh Morello cherries are not always easy to come by, so we've switched to baked plums, which work wonderfully well. Use the cherries if you can find them (they also come in jars), but don't be tempted to use regular black cherries—they don't have the flavor or acidity needed for cooking. Poached quince are also lovely.

For notes on the important difference between almond paste and marzipan, see pages 351 and 354.

SERVES 8–10

———

BAKED PLUMS
1 lb 7 oz/650 g plums (8–10)
½ cup/120 ml dry white wine
⅓ cup plus 2 tsp/80 g granulated sugar
10 cardamom pods, roughly crushed
   in a pestle and mortar
¼ tsp ground cinnamon
1 long strip of orange peel
½ cup/120 ml water

CAKE
7 oz/200 g almond paste, broken into
   4 or 5 pieces
1 cup/200 g granulated sugar

1 cup plus 1½ tbsp/250 g unsalted
   butter, at room temperature
finely grated zest of 1 large orange
   (1 tbsp)
¾ tsp freshly ground cardamom
   (see page 351)
6 large eggs
⅛ tsp almond extract
1 cup plus 1 tbsp/140 g
   all-purpose flour
2 tbsp cornstarch
1½ tsp baking powder
¼ tsp salt

The plums can be baked up to 3 days in advance and warmed through (for 10 minutes at 400°F/200°C) before serving.

The cake will keep for up to 3 days, covered in plastic wrap or aluminum foil, at room temperature.

———

1   **To make the baked plums,** preheat the oven to 400°F/200°C. Place the plums in an even layer in a small 8-inch/20-cm square baking dish and set aside.

2   Place the white wine, sugar, cardamom, cinnamon, orange peel and water in a medium saucepan and bring to a boil. Remove from the heat and carefully pour over the plums. Cover the dish tightly with aluminum foil and bake for 20–40 minutes—the cooking time depends on the size and ripeness of the plums—or until they are soft but still whole. You can check their softness with a skewer. Set aside, covered, until needed. The plums can be served warm or at room temperature.

3   Lower the oven temperature to 350°F/180°C.

4   **To make the cake,** grease and flour a 9-inch/23-cm Bundt pan. Place the almond paste in the bowl of an electric mixer with the paddle attachment in place, add the sugar and beat on medium-low speed for about 3 minutes, or until the almond paste breaks up. Add the butter, orange zest and ground cardamom and continue to beat. Add the eggs, one at a time, beating well after each addition and scraping down the sides of the beater and bowl from time to time. Add the almond extract and beat to combine. Sift the flour, cornstarch, baking powder and salt together into a bowl and add this to the creamed mixture, beating on medium-low speed until just combined.

5   Scrape the mixture into the Bundt pan and bake for 50–55 minutes, or until a skewer inserted into the center of the cake comes out clean. Remove from the oven and set aside to cool in the pan for 15 minutes before inverting onto a cake platter. Serve warm or at room temperature, with the baked plums and juices alongside. Remember that the pits have not been removed from the plums—serving them as they are is part of the rustic nature of the dish—so watch out! If you do want to remove the stones, just break the plums open and do so before serving.

Pineapple and star anise chiffon cake

This cake is as light as it is large—the benefit being, of course, that everyone can have a great big slice and still be able to bounce away from the table. The light and billowy texture is a result of both the lack of butter (in the cake and the icing) and the whipped egg whites being folded (with all their aeration) into the batter just before baking.

The pineapple "flowers" look great and don't require any fancy equipment, but the cake works fine without them if it's a step too far. You've got the pineapple, though, so we encourage you to give them a try! As an alternative, some julienned strips of orange zest or whole star anise (for decoration, rather than eating) work well.

This is a cake that delivers in all areas: packed with flavor, light as a dream and a complete "wow" to look at. Get hold of your angel food cake pan, shape your pineapple slices into flowers, then get your head around the double negatives in the Note on the left. The rest is just a good old-fashioned cake.

SERVES 12

1 large pineapple (about 2 lb/900 g): peeled, cored and two-thirds of the flesh roughly chopped (14 oz/400 g) for the cake; the other third, unpeeled (7 oz/200 g), is used for the pineapple flowers

2 cups/225 g self-rising flour

1 cup plus 3 tbsp/240 g granulated sugar, plus ¼ cup/50 g for the egg whites

1½ tsp ground star anise (or 3 whole star anise, ground in a spice grinder and passed through a fine-mesh sieve)

½ tsp salt

½ cup/120 ml sunflower oil

4½ oz/130 g egg yolks and 10½ oz/300 g egg whites, separated (from 7 or 8 large eggs)

finely grated zest of 2 large oranges (2 tbsp)

scraped seeds of ½ vanilla pod

1¼ tsp cream of tartar

ICING

2½ cups/300 g confectioners' sugar (pure confectioners' sugar is best here, if you can get hold of it—see page 356) sifted

¼ cup/60 ml pineapple juice (from the large pineapple)

DRIED PINEAPPLE FLOWERS

2 tbsp granulated sugar

2 tbsp water

⅓ large pineapple, sliced widthwise as thinly as you can without tearing the slices: a serrated bread knife works well. Ideally, you'll get 10–12 slices, ⅛ inch/3 mm thick

1   Preheat the oven to 400°F/200°C.

2   Place the 14 oz/400 g chopped pineapple in a food processor and process to form a fine purée. Transfer to a medium saucepan and bring to a boil over medium-high heat. Simmer for 3 minutes, then remove from the heat. Reserve 7 oz/200 g of the purée for the cake and set aside to cool. Strain the remaining 7 oz/200 g through a fine-mesh sieve placed over a bowl to get the ¼ cup/60 ml juice you need for the icing. (If you fall short of ¼ cup/60 ml, just make it up with water or orange juice.) »

It's very important to use a 9-inch/23 cm angel food cake pan with a removable base that is not nonstick. Double negatives do funny things to the brain, we know, but it's a really vital point. Once the cake comes out of the oven, the pan is turned upside down before the cake is left to cool. If you have a nonstick pan, the cake will slip down onto the surface of the counter; you want the cake to be stuck to the pan, elevated by the legs of the angel food pan. The cake will seep down a little toward the surface. That's fine, it just needs to not be touching it. If your pan does not have little legs, raise it off the counter's surface using a few cups to rest the edge of the pan on. So, to clarify: Don't start with a nonstick pan (start with a not nonstick one!) and don't grease it. It's crucial to the success of the cake.

The pineapple "flowers" can be made a day ahead and kept in a cool, dry place until needed. Don't store in an airtight container or they will go soft.

Without icing, the cake will keep for up to 3 days, wrapped in foil or in a very large airtight container. Once iced, it's best eaten on the same day.

3   Place the flour, 1 cup plus 3 tbsp/240 g sugar, ground star anise and salt in a large mixing bowl and whisk to combine and aerate. Make a well in the center and add the 7 oz/200 g pineapple purée, sunflower oil, egg yolks, orange zest and vanilla seeds. Whisk the egg yolks and liquids together before gently drawing in the dry ingredients to form a smooth batter.

4   Place the egg whites in the bowl of an electric mixer with the whisk attachment in place. Beat on high speed for about 30 seconds, until frothy, then add the cream of tartar. Continue to beat until soft peaks form, then gradually sprinkle in the ¼ cup/ 50 g sugar. Continue to beat for about 5 minutes, until stiff, glossy peaks form. Use a large whisk or rubber spatula to gently but thoroughly fold into the batter, until the mixture is well combined and there are no streaks visible.

5   Pour the batter into the ungreased chiffon cake pan (see Note on page 179 for the importance of not greasing the pan)—the mixture should reach up to 1½ inches/ 4 cm from the top of the pan—and bake for 50 minutes, or until a skewer inserted into the center of the cake comes out clean. Cover with aluminum foil for the last 25 minutes or so, if it looks as though your cake it taking on too much color. Remove from the oven and immediately invert the pan. Don't worry if the removable base slips down a little when the cake is turned over; the cake will still stay suspended because the pan is not greased. Set aside for 1 hour, in its pan, until completely cool. Lower the oven temperature to 250°F/120°C.

6   **To make the icing,** place the sifted confectioners' sugar into a bowl and add the ¼ cup/60 ml pineapple juice. Stir with a wooden spoon until smooth. Set aside.

7   **To make the dried pineapple flowers,** place the sugar and water in a small saucepan over medium heat and cook gently until the sugar has dissolved. Increase the heat to high, boil hard for 30 seconds, then remove from the heat. Lightly brush both sides of the pineapple slices with the warm syrup, then lay them on a wire rack placed over a parchment paper–lined baking sheet. Place the baking sheet in the oven and bake for 1–2 hours (the cooking time varies hugely depending on how ripe the pineapple is), until the slices are golden and completely dry but still have some malleability.

8   Remove the baking sheet from the oven and immediately shape the slices, either over the molds of an egg carton or inside the molds of a muffin pan, to form little cups. Set aside to cool as they are—sitting on top of or inside their molds—to firm up.

9   When the cake is cooled, turn the pan the right way around again and, using a long metal spatula, loosen the cake from the sides and base of the pan, as well as the central tube (you might need a long, thin knife to help you with this). Invert the cake back onto a serving plate. Drizzle the icing over the top and sides, place the pineapple flowers randomly, then sprinkle with star anise and serve.

Coffee and cardamom pound cake

These next two (companion) recipes are adapted from the Perfect Pound Cake recipe in Rose Levy Beranbaum's *The Cake Bible*. As it really is a perfect pound cake—moist and dense—it's hard to do anything other than follow Rose's exact method. We diverge on one point, though: while Rose says that the cake doesn't work in a large pan, we find that baking it in a Bundt pan—where the tube in the middle enables the heat to distribute evenly through the cake as it bakes—works just fine.

We've gone for two versions: this one has a more adult flavor, with the coffee and cardamom, while the other, based on Neapolitan ice cream, is more family-friendly.

This is best served once completely cool, to allow the flavors to develop. In an ideal world, you'd make it in the morning and serve it six to eight hours after baking. We know that the difference between the ideal and the reality is often great, however, so don't lose sleep over a few hours here and there.

SERVES 10–12

Without icing, the cake will keep at room temperature for up to 3 days, covered in plastic wrap. It can also be frozen for up to 3 months. Once iced, it's best eaten on the same day.

(NF)

6 tbsp/90 ml whole milk, at room temperature, plus 1½ tbsp for the coffee
6 large eggs, at room temperature
2 tsp vanilla extract
1¾ cups/200 g self-rising flour
⅔ cup/100 g all-purpose flour, plus extra for dusting
½ tsp salt
1½ cups/300 g granulated sugar
1¼ cups plus 1 tbsp/300 g unsalted butter, soft but not oily (see page 344), diced, plus extra for greasing
1½ tsp freshly ground cardamom (see page 351)
1½ tbsp instant coffee granules
2 tsp Dutch-processed cocoa powder

ICING

1½ tbsp instant coffee granules
3 tbsp whole milk, warmed
2 cups/240 g confectioners' sugar
2 tbsp unsalted butter, at room temperature

1   Preheat the oven to 375°F/195°C. Grease and flour a 9-inch/23-cm Bundt pan and set aside.

2   Place the milk, eggs and vanilla extract in a medium bowl and lightly whisk, just to combine.

3   Sift both flours and the salt directly into the bowl of an electric mixer with the paddle attachment in place, then add the sugar and mix on low speed for 30 seconds. Add the butter and half the egg mixture and continue to mix until the dry ingredients are incorporated. Increase the speed to medium and beat for 1 minute. Scrape down the sides of the bowl, then gradually add the remaining egg mixture, in two batches, making sure the first batch is fully incorporated before adding the next. Don't worry if your batter looks slightly split; it's due to the large proportion of eggs in the batter, but it won't affect the final result. ››

4   Scrape down the sides of the bowl and divide the mixture among two bowls. Add the ground cardamom to one bowl and fold to combine. Warm the 1½ tbsp milk in a small saucepan, then place in a small bowl with the coffee granules and cocoa powder. Stir until the coffee dissolves and the consistency is that of thick but pourable milk. Combine this with the cake mixture in the second bowl.

5   Spoon the two mixtures into the prepared pan in four alternate blocks, two of each color. Then, use a skewer or small knife to make a zigzag-shaped swirl once through the mix to create a marble effect. Do not be tempted to overdo the swirling as you will lose the effect of the marbling.

6   Bake for 40–45 minutes, or until a skewer inserted into the center of the cake comes out clean. Remove from the oven and set aside for 10 minutes. The cake tends to dome in the oven, so if you want a perfectly flat base (the top will become the bottom once it's inverted), just slice off the top to flatten it out before turning the cake out onto a wire rack to cool completely.

7   **To make the icing,** combine the coffee and warm milk in a small mixing bowl. Add the confectioners' sugar and butter and whisk until smooth and thick.

8   Spoon the icing all over the cooled cake, so that it drips unevenly down the sides. Allow the icing to set slightly before serving.

COFFEE AND CARDAMOM POUND CAKE
AND NEAPOLITAN POUND CAKE
(FOR THE FAMILY) ›

Neapolitan pound cake (for the family)

We've gone for the classic Neapolitan colors—brown, white and pink—with a pink icing. It's basically heaven for the birthday party of a six-year-old, but a plain white or cream icing also works well if you want to tone down the pink vibe.

The degree of pinkness (or any-color-ness) will vary depending on the brand of food coloring you choose. You'll need anything from a whole tube (if you have a very basic liquid gel) to ⅛ teaspoon (if you are starting with concentrated gel). Always start with a little and take it from there; it's much easier to keep adding, rather than trying to take away (which would be impossible!).

SERVES 10

—

6 tbsp/90 ml whole milk,
    at room temperature, plus 1½ tbsp
    for the cocoa
6 large eggs, at room temperature
1 tbsp vanilla extract
1¾ cups/200 g self-rising flour
⅔ cup/100 g all-purpose flour, plus
    extra for dusting
½ tsp salt
1½ cups/300 g granulated sugar
1¼ cups plus 1 tbsp/300 g unsalted
    butter, soft but not oily (see page 344),
    diced, plus extra for greasing
2 tbsp Dutch-processed cocoa powder
a drop or two of pink or any other
    color food coloring (preferably gel
    or paste)

ICING

3 tbsp whole milk, warmed
2 cups plus 2 tbsp/260 g
    confectioners' sugar, sifted
2 tbsp unsalted butter,
    at room temperature
½ tsp vanilla extract
a drop or two of pink food coloring
    (preferably gel or paste)

Without icing, the cake will keep at room temperature for up to 3 days, covered in plastic wrap. It can also be frozen for up to 3 months. Once iced, it's best eaten on the same day.

—

1   Preheat the oven to 400°F/200°C. Grease and flour a 9-inch/23-cm Bundt pan and set aside.

2   Place the milk, eggs and vanilla extract in a medium bowl and lightly whisk, just to combine.

3   Sift both flours and the salt directly into the bowl of an electric mixer with the paddle attachment in place, then add the sugar and mix on low speed for 30 seconds. Add the butter and half the egg mixture and continue to mix until the dry ingredients are incorporated. Increase the speed to medium and beat for 1 minute. Scrape down the sides of the bowl, then gradually add the remaining egg mixture, in two batches, making sure the first batch is fully incorporated before adding the next. Scrape down the sides of the bowl, then divide the batter equally among three small bowls.

4   Warm the 1½ tbsp milk in a small saucepan, then place in a small bowl with the cocoa powder. Stir to form a smooth and very thick paste, then combine this into one of the bowls of cake batter and set aside. Tint the second bowl of cake batter with

the pink food coloring, adding a drop or two at a time until it is the color you want. Leave the third and remaining bowl of batter as it is.

5 Spoon the three mixtures into the prepared pan in six alternate blocks, two of each color, then use a skewer or small knife to make a zigzag-shaped swirl once through the mix to create a marble effect. Don't be tempted to overdo the swirling as you will lose the effect of the marbling.

6 Bake for 40–45 minutes, or until a skewer inserted into the center of the cake comes out clean. Remove from the oven and set aside for 10 minutes (the cake will start to shrink from the sides only after it's removed from the oven). The cake tends to dome in the oven, so if you want a perfectly flat base (the top will become the bottom once it's inverted), just slice off the top to flatten it out before turning the cake out onto a wire rack to cool completely.

7 **To make the icing,** combine the warm milk and confectioners' sugar in a small mixing bowl. Add the butter and vanilla extract and whisk until smooth, then add the pink food coloring (depending on how bright you want to go) and mix well.

8 Spoon the icing all over the cooled cake, so that it drips unevenly down the sides. Allow the icing to set for a few minutes before serving.

Tessa's spice cake

This is a simple spiced pound cake, but one that is seriously moist, with a lovely fine crumb. There's enough going on, spicewise, that we've restrained ourselves when it comes to icing and left it unadorned. The loaf's straight sides and the sprinkle of confectioners' sugar—all part of accentuating its simplicity—make a slice the perfect accompaniment to a cup of tea.

Mixed spice is not hard to get hold of in the United Kingdom, but pumpkin pie spice or quatre épices are both good substitutes, if you're looking for an alternative. Quatre épices is a little bit hotter and less sweet than the others, so you might want to use a pinch less. Tessa's original recipe called for Chinese five-spice powder, which is even stronger and more savory than the quatre épices. Basically, the cake is something of a blank canvas, there for you to heighten or soften the spices as you like.

With thanks to Tessa Faulkner for this recipe.

SERVES 10–12

¾ cup plus 2 tsp/180 g unsalted butter, at room temperature

¾ packed cup plus 1 tbsp/160 g dark brown sugar

¾ packed cup plus 1 tbsp/160 g light brown sugar

finely grated zest of 1 large orange (1 tbsp)

3 large eggs

½ cup/120 g sour cream

1 tbsp vanilla extract

1 tsp mixed spice (or pumpkin pie spice)

1¾ cups/220 g all-purpose flour

¾ tsp salt

½ tsp baking soda

1 tsp malt vinegar (or apple cider vinegar)

confectioners' sugar, for dusting

The cake will keep well for up to 5 days in an airtight container.

(NF)

1 Preheat the oven to 375°F/190°C. Grease a standard 8½ x 4½-inch/900-g loaf pan and line with parchment paper, then set aside.

2 Place the butter, both brown sugars and orange zest in the bowl of an electric mixer with the paddle attachment in place. Beat until lightened and smooth but not too fluffy; you don't want to aerate the cake too much.

3 In a separate bowl, whisk together the eggs by hand. Add the sour cream and vanilla extract and whisk again until smooth.

4 Sift the mixed spice, flour and salt together into a separate bowl and set aside.

5 In alternating batches and with the machine on medium-low speed, add a third of the egg–sour cream mixture to the creamed mixture, followed by a third of the sifted dry ingredients. Continue with the second and third batch, continuing to beat until combined. Stir the baking soda with the vinegar in a small bowl; it will fizz up a little, but that's fine. Add this to the mixture and as soon as everything is combined, turn off the machine. Don't worry if the mixture starts to split at this point; it will still cook up well. Scrape the mixture into the loaf pan and bake for 50–55 minutes, or until a skewer inserted into the center of the cake comes out clean.

6 Transfer the cake to a wire rack for about 15 minutes to cool slightly before inverting onto a cake plate. Set aside until completely cool, then dust with confectioners' sugar. This cake is best served at room temperature, as the flavor of the spice becomes more pronounced.

Lemon and poppy seed cake (National Trust version)

However ambitious and discerning Helen's palate, this light lemon cake is the one she'd take with her to a desert island if she could only choose one. It's much simpler than many of the other cakes she loves, but it's the one she returns to again and again. There's something safe and reassuring about it, which would comfort as the waves came crashing down around the island.

It's why we've called it, affectionately, our National Trust cake. However unpredictable the weather, however disastrous the outing, however much fun has not really been had on the family-day out, there's something wonderfully reassuring about the predictability of the cake you'll have in the café, along with a cup of tea. It's one of life's great certainties.

SERVES 8 (USING A STANDARD LOAF PAN) OR 9 (USING MINI-LOAF PANS)

You can make this in a standard 8½ x 4⅓-inch/900-g loaf pan, as we do here, or, if you have them, nine mini-loaf pans (3½ x 2⅓ x 1½ inches/ 9 x 6 x 4 cm) also work well. If you are making the mini loaves, shorten the baking time to 25 minutes.

This will keep for 3 days in an airtight container.

3 large eggs
1 cup plus 2 tbsp/225 g
    granulated sugar
½ cup/120 ml heavy cream
5 tbsp/70 g unsalted butter, cubed,
    plus extra for greasing
1 tbsp poppy seeds

finely grated zest of 3 lemons (1 tbsp)
1⅓ cups/170 g all-purpose flour
1¼ tsp baking powder
¼ tsp salt

GLAZE
¾ cup/90 g confectioners' sugar, sifted
2 tbsp lemon juice

1   Preheat the oven to 350°F/180°C. Grease the loaf pan(s) and line with parchment paper, then set aside.

2   Place the eggs and granulated sugar in the bowl of an electric mixer with the paddle attachment in place and beat on medium-high speed for about 2 minutes, until pale and frothy. Add the cream and continue to beat for about 2 minutes, until the mixture has combined, thickened a little and turned pale.

3   In the meantime, melt the butter in a small saucepan over low heat, stir in the poppy seeds and lemon zest and set aside.

4   Sift the flour, baking powder and salt together into a bowl, then use a rubber spatula to fold this into the egg mixture before folding in the butter, poppy seeds and zest.

5   Spoon the mixture into the loaf pan(s) so that it rises three-quarters of the way up the sides. Place on a baking sheet and bake for about 50 minutes, or until a skewer inserted into the center of the cake comes out clean.

6   **To make the glaze,** whisk the confectioners' sugar with the lemon juice in a bowl.

7   Pour the glaze over the top of the cake as soon as it comes out of the oven, spreading it over the top so that it sinks in and creates a nice coating. Set aside to cool for 30 minutes before removing from the pan. Leave to come to room temperature before serving.

TESSA'S SPICE CAKE

LEMON AND POPPY SEED CAKE (NATIONAL TRUST VERSION)

Belinda's flourless coconut and chocolate cake

Every month or so, we gather in the test kitchen with our pastry chefs. It's an open forum, with the chefs presenting their offerings, which we then taste and discuss. It's always exciting, as ideas are constantly being improved and implemented. This cake was a product of one of those meetings, brought to the table by Franceska Venzon, herself inspired by Belinda Jeffery's version of the cake. We've played around with the shape—baking it in a loaf pan—and added a chocolate ganache, but the base is all Belinda's.

There's something about a cake showcasing its flourlessness or gluten-free nature that can often make it sound a little bit lacking. Unfairly so, in a case like this, where the feeling of eating it is the very opposite of "free from"; it's utterly buttery and decadent.

SERVES 8

—

¾ cup plus 2 tbsp/200 g unsalted butter, at room temperature, plus extra for greasing
1¼ cups/250 g granulated sugar
⅔ cup/60 g finely shredded coconut
scraped seeds of 1 vanilla pod
¼ tsp salt
4 large eggs
1⅔ cups/180 g almond meal

WATER GANACHE
2 oz/55 g dark chocolate (70% cocoa solids), roughly chopped into ⅓-inch/1-cm pieces
2 tbsp granulated sugar
1 tbsp light corn syrup
3 tbsp water
scraped seeds of ¼ vanilla pod
1½ tbsp unsalted butter, at room temperature, cut into ¾-inch/2-cm cubes

This can be made in a standard 8½ x 4½-inch/900-g loaf pan or in a 9-inch/23-cm round springform pan.

This will keep well for up to 5 days in an airtight container. It can be eaten on the day of making, but we think it tastes even better served at room temperature the following day.

1   Preheat the oven to 350°F/180°C. Grease the base and sides of a standard 8½ x 4½-inch/900-g loaf pan or a 9-inch/23-cm round springform pan and line with parchment paper, then set aside.

2   Place the butter, sugar, coconut, vanilla seeds and salt in an electric mixer with the paddle attachment in place. Beat on medium-high speed, until pale and fluffy, about 3 minutes. Add the eggs, one at a time, beating well after each addition. Turn the speed to low, add the almond meal and mix until just combined.

3   Scrape the mixture into the pan and bake for 40 minutes if using the loaf pan or 50 minutes if using the round pan, or until the cake is golden brown on top and a skewer inserted into the middle comes out clean. Remove the cake from the oven and set aside to cool in the pan before inverting onto a serving plate. Set aside until completely cool.

4 **To make the water ganache** when you are ready to serve, place the chocolate in a medium bowl and set aside. Put the sugar and corn syrup in a small saucepan and place over medium-low heat. Stir to combine and, when the sugar has melted, increase the heat to medium and bring to a boil, stirring gently from time to time. Continue to boil for about 7 minutes, until the color is a pale amber. Remove from the heat and carefully pour in the water. Don't worry if the mix seizes; just return the pan to the heat, add the vanilla seeds and stir gently and continuously until it returns to a boil and the sugar has melted again. Remove from the heat and wait for a minute before pouring the water-caramel over the chocolate. Allow to stand for about 3 minutes, then whisk to combine. Add the butter, a couple of cubes at a time, whisking after each addition. Continue until all the butter has been added, whisking to combine until the consistency is that of thick syrup.

5 Spread the ganache over the top of the cake, letting it run down the sides a little, and serve.

Celebration cake

All cakes are cause for a certain degree of celebration, but certain celebrations are cause for a cake with layers! This is the cake we make for our customers' big parties: birthday parties, wedding celebrations, anniversaries and all sorts. It's enormous, it's delicious, and it's great for parties as you prepare everything well in advance. It's also, incidentally, gluten-free, held together not by flour, not even by ground nuts, but by the magic of beaten egg whites, sabayon and the chilling effect of the freezer.

Decorate it as you like: we tend to go for a bit of restraint in our presentation, smoothing out the icing with an offset spatula and adding some confectioners' sugar–dusted fruit to each corner of the cake. It's a blank canvas for you to do what you like with, though; more fruit or some nuts, for example, always look good.

SERVES 20–25 (IT'S NOT CALLED A CELEBRATION CAKE FOR NOTHING!)

15½ oz/440 g dark chocolate (70% cocoa solids), broken into ¾-inch/2-cm pieces
2 cups plus 2 tbsp/440 g granulated sugar
9 oz/260 g egg yolks (from 12 or 13 large eggs)
14 oz/400 g egg whites (from 10 large eggs)
1 tbsp brandy

GANACHE
10½ oz/300 g white chocolate, broken into ¾-inch/2-cm pieces
1¼ cups/300 ml heavy cream

2 cups plus 1 tbsp/500 ml heavy cream
7 oz/200 g fresh blueberries, plus 8 to garnish
7 oz/200 g fresh blackberries, plus 12 to garnish
7 oz/200 g fresh strawberries, hulled and thinly sliced lengthwise, plus a few extra slices to garnish
7 oz/200 g fresh raspberries, plus 8 to garnish
confectioners' sugar, for dusting (optional)

We use three 10 x 15-inch/25 x 38-cm jelly-roll pans for this cake, but it's fine to use one. You'll just need to bake the sponge layer in three separate batches—the mixture is happy to sit around and wait. If you have three shallow rimmed baking pans with slightly different dimensions, this is also fine; the individual layers can be trimmed to size once they're out of the freezer.

Both the sponge cake and ganache need to be made at least a day ahead for the sponge cake to freeze and the ganache to set. The sponge cake can be made and frozen up to 2 weeks before assembling. The ganache is fine for up to 3 days in the fridge, then gently warmed over a pot of simmering water to soften before using.

Ideally, the cake should be eaten on the day it is assembled. Leftovers are delicious the next day; they just don't look all that great. If assembling a few hours in advance, keep the cake in the fridge and bring it out a half hour before serving, to come to room temperature.

1   Preheat the oven to 375°F/190°C. Grease three 10 x 15-inch/25 x 38-cm jelly-roll pans and line with parchment paper (or just one, see Note), then set aside.

2   Place the chocolate in a large heatproof bowl set over a pan of simmering water, making sure the base of the bowl is not touching the water. Stir occasionally until melted, then remove from the heat and set aside to cool slightly.

3   Place the granulated sugar and egg yolks in the bowl of an electric mixer with the whisk attachment in place. Beat for about 3 minutes, until thick and pale, then gently fold into the melted chocolate. Stir until almost combined and set aside.

4   Place the egg whites in a clean bowl of an electric mixer with the whisk attachment in place. Beat on high speed, until soft peaks form, then gently fold into the chocolate. Lastly, fold in the brandy, then divide the mixture among the three jelly-roll pans (or pour a third of the batter into your one pan, if you're cooking in three batches). Use a spatula to even out the top(s) and place in the oven. Bake for 15 minutes, until firm to touch and a skewer inserted into the sponge cake comes out clean. Set aside to cool. ››

5 Once all the cakes are cooled, place a baking sheet or cutting board (that fits in your freezer and that you won't mind being without for 24 hours) over one of the pans and flip the whole thing over, so the board is now sitting underneath the cake. Remove the pan and the paper—do this carefully, to prevent the cake sticking to the paper and tearing—and place a clean sheet of parchment paper on top of the cake. Flip the second layer of cake so that it is sitting on top of the first, and then again, carefully remove the paper before replacing it with a clean layer of parchment. Repeat with the third layer, then cover the whole thing—baking sheet or cutting board and all—firmly in plastic wrap. Freeze for 24 hours.

6 **To make the ganache,** place the white chocolate in a medium bowl and set aside. Add the cream to a heavy saucepan and place over medium-low heat. Cook until just starting to simmer, then pour over the chocolate. Allow to sit for 3 minutes, for the chocolate to soften, then gently stir until the chocolate is melted and fully combined. Cover with plastic wrap and refrigerate overnight (or up to 3 days).

7 Assemble the cake on the day it is going to be eaten. Place the ganache in the bowl of an electric mixer with the whisk attachment in place. Add the heavy cream and beat on medium-high speed for about 30 seconds, until thick and only just pourable; it shouldn't go quite as far as whipped cream, as it will firm up as you spread it. Keep a close eye on it, as it can overwhip very quickly.

8 Mix the berries, apart from those for the garnish, in a large bowl and set aside.

9 Just before assembling the cake—you need to do this at the very last minute, as the layers need to be frozen stiff to work with—remove the layers from the freezer. If you have worked with shallow rimmed baking pans with slightly different dimensions, now is the time to trim them so that they are all the same size. Do this one layer at a time (rather than attempting to cut them all at once, stacked on top of one another).

10 Place one layer of sponge on your serving platter and spread a third of the ganache on top, taking it right up to the edges. Scatter half the berries on top, again taking them right to the edges of the cake. Place the second layer of sponge on top of the first and repeat with the cream and fruit. Top the cake with the final layer of sponge and spread the remaining cream on top, either smoothed out with an offset spatula or in a wavy pattern. Scatter the reserved fruit in each corner of the cake and dust the fruit lightly with confectioners' sugar, if desired. From here you can either add some more garnish, if you like, or perhaps a piped message of celebration on top of the ganache.

Cheesecakes

—

We often talk about breaking recipes down to their component parts to help with getting organized and getting ahead. Nowhere is this more applicable than in the making of cheesecakes, whose layers are so completely distinct: the base (which can always be made well in advance), the filling (which often needs to be made in advance so that it has time to chill and set), and the topping (which is the one thing that usually has to be kept on the to-do list until the day of serving). Within these three parallel objectives, there's a lot of room for play.

THE BASE › Most of our cheesecake bases are graham cracker–oriented and crunchy; the contrast between this and the chilled, set, creamy filling is always a winning formula. A couple of the cakes follow a different path, however: the Roasted Strawberry and Lime Cheesecake (see page 221) is sponge-soft and the Baked Ricotta and Hazelnut Cheesecakes (see page 209) has no base at all.

THE FILLING › The filling for every cheesecake will always be, well, rich. Cream cheese often plays a starring role, of course, but surprise yourself with our Baked Ricotta and Hazelnut Cheesecakes (see page 209). They are very different—completely opposite, in fact—to what you might be expecting, served warm from the oven rather than set and chilled from the fridge.

THE TOPPING › This is where you can really go to town. We've had our own fun with all sorts of options, such as crunchy coconut, meringue kisses, and a great big bunch of fruit options—cranberry compote, baked apricots, roasted strawberries and caramelized pineapple—to cut through the richness of the filling. Play around and try things out here; your cakes will work with all sorts of alternatives.

OUR PANS, TIPS AND TRICKS › We often prefer to make lots of small cheesecakes rather than one large one. The inherent decadence of cheesecake is somehow heightened when you have an entire (mini) cake to yourself. To make the Passion Fruit Cheesecakes with Spiced Pineapple (see page 207), Lime Meringue Cheesecakes (see page 201) and the Baked Ricotta and Hazelnut Cheesecakes (see page 209), you'll need a set of 3-inch/8-cm round, bottomless rings. A muffin pan will also work for the ricotta cakes, if you are looking for an alternative. Otherwise, a 9-inch/23-cm round springform cake pan (or other pan with a removable base) is used for many of the larger cakes.

Timingwise, don't cut corners. Cheesecakes need to bake for a long time in a low oven. They need a long time to cool and they often need a long time to set. The reason they're so precious is that they don't respond well to swift changes in temperature. If you were to try and speed up the cooling process by taking the cheesecake out of the oven and transferring it to the fridge, for example, it would quite literally fall apart at the seams and develop a big crack. This need not be a disaster—it won't affect the taste and you can often cover the crack with a topping—but it's always pleasing to bake a crack-free cake. Start with room-temperature ingredients and follow our cake-cooling instructions exactly; we leave the cake in the oven once it's baked, propping the oven door slightly open with a wooden spoon.

Although a lot of people bake their cheesecakes in a water bath (bain-marie)—where the individual cake or cakes sit in a larger pan that is filled with warm water before going into the oven—this is not a technique we're huge fans of. The rationale behind the water bath is that because the temperature of the water cannot rise above 212°F/100°C, the cheesecake will cook evenly, resulting in a smooth, creamy texture. While this makes sense in theory, we find that it can be rather messy and sometimes even dangerous (try carrying a pan full of hot water across the kitchen and discovering—d'oh!—you've forgotten to leave the oven door open). And however much we've mummified our pans in foil, we also find that, more often than not, the water will somehow seep in and result in a disappointingly soggy crust. The long, slow bake and the long, slow cooling period is the method we prefer

Lime meringue cheesecakes

Part lime meringue pie, part classic cheesecake, these make for an impressive dessert. It's one to save for a special occasion—there is a fair bit of work—but, as with lots of cakes with more than one layer, they are not quite as epic a feat as they first seem. Being able to make two out of the three layers the day before you are serving—the base layer and the cheesecake—helps, leaving just the meringue to make on the day itself. Decadent and rich, but light in texture, these are a big hit with citrus fans.

We use a Swiss meringue for these cheesecakes (as opposed to French or Italian meringue, see page 347), so the texture is chewy and marshmallow-like. Beyond the heat treatment the egg whites and sugar receive before they are whipped, there's no extra baking, so it's important to ensure they are very warm, ideally reaching the temperature of 160°F/71°C on a candy thermometer.

MAKES 8

In addition to the candy thermometer, you would ideally use a blowtorch to brown the meringue, as this produces the best results. If you don't have one, place the cakes under the broiler until browned. We like to make these as individual cakes, in 3-inch/8-cm round cake rings. Slightly smaller rings are fine if that's what you have (you'll just make an extra cake as a result), but don't be tempted to use larger rings: part of the attractiveness of these cakes is their height, and you will lose this if they are too wide. You will also need a piping bag with a ⅓-inch/1-cm plain tip for piping the meringue kisses.

The base can be made a day in advance and stored in the fridge. The cheesecakes (without the meringue topping) can be made a day in advance and refrigerated overnight. The nut topping can be made up to 5 days in advance and stored in an airtight container.

Once the meringues have been browned, they are best eaten within 3 or 4 hours. Any leftover cakes can be kept in the fridge for a day; the meringue will have softened, but they'll still taste good.

BASE

2 oz/55 g Brazil nuts
5 oz/140 g graham crackers (about 9 sheets), roughly broken
3 tbsp/20 g finely shredded coconut
5 tbsp/70 g unsalted butter, melted, plus extra for greasing

FILLING

10 oz/280 g cream cheese
one 14-oz/410-g can sweetened condensed milk
4¼ oz/120 g egg yolks (from 6 large eggs)
¾ cup/180 ml lime juice (you'll need the zest from 2 of the limes before juicing)
finely grated zest of 2 limes (2 tsp)

TOPPING (OPTIONAL)

¼ cup/15 g flaked coconut
¾ oz/25 g Brazil nuts, thinly sliced (don't worry if they break up a bit when sliced; they'll still be fine)
1½ tbsp dark brown sugar
½ tsp lime juice

MERINGUE

3½ oz/100 g egg whites (from about 2½ large eggs)
¾ cup plus 2½ tbsp/180 g granulated sugar
⅛ tsp salt

1   **To make the base,** preheat the oven to 350°F/170°C. Lightly grease the sides of eight individual 3-inch/8-cm round cake rings and line the sides with parchment paper—you want the paper to rise 1½ inches/4 cm above the top of the ring—then place on a large baking sheet that is also lined with parchment paper.

2   Spread the Brazil nuts out on a baking sheet and roast for about 12 minutes, until lightly golden. Set aside to cool before placing in the small bowl of a food processor. Process until finely chopped, then add the graham crackers to the food processor. Process to form fine crumbs and tip into a small bowl. Add the coconut and melted butter and use your hands to mix well. Place two heaped tablespoons of crumbs in the base of each ring, using your hands to press them into the base. Even out the crust with the back of a spoon or the bottom of a glass and set aside in the fridge. ››

3   **To make the filling,** place the cream cheese in the bowl of an electric mixer with the paddle attachment in place. Beat on medium-low speed until creamy, then add the condensed milk and egg yolks. Continue to beat until smooth, scraping down the sides occasionally, before adding the lime juice. Mix to incorporate, then transfer the mixture into a large measuring cup. Stir in the lime zest.

4   Pour the mixture into the prepared rings so that it rises three-quarters of the way up the sides. Bake for 20 minutes, until the cheesecakes have just set. Remove from the oven and allow to cool completely before covering lightly with plastic wrap and placing in the fridge for at least 4 hours or up to overnight.

5   **To make the topping,** put the flaked coconut and Brazil nuts in a small saucepan and place over medium heat. Toast for about 3 minutes, stirring frequently, until light golden brown. Add the brown sugar and lime juice and cook for 1 minute, until melted and well combined. Tip onto a parchment-lined baking sheet and set aside to cool.

6   **To make the meringue** on the day of serving, using a pan large enough to allow the bowl of your electric mixer to sit on top, pour enough water into the pan so that it rises a quarter of the way up the sides. Bring to a boil. Place the egg whites, granulated sugar and salt in the bowl of the electric mixer with the whisk attachment in place and whisk to combine. Lower the heat so that the water is just simmering, then place the bowl on the pan, making sure the water doesn't touch the base of the bowl. Whisk the whites continuously for 5 minutes by hand, until they are very warm (you want the whites to reach a temperature of 160°F/71°C on a thermometer—see introduction), then transfer back to the electric mixer. Beat for about 5 minutes on high speed, until the meringue is stiff and cool. Transfer the meringue to a piping bag fitted with a ⅓-inch/1-cm plain tip.

7   Carefully remove the rings and paper collars from the cheesecakes, then pipe meringue "kisses" on top. You will have more meringue to play with than you need here, but it's better to have extra, in this instance, than go without your kisses.

8   Using a kitchen blowtorch, heat the meringue so that parts of it turn a golden brown. Alternatively, place the baking sheet of cheesecakes under the broiler for 1–2 minutes; you'll need to watch them constantly to make sure they don't burn. Sprinkle with the coconut topping—you might have a couple of tablespoons left over to snack on—and serve.

White chocolate cheesecake with cranberry compote

All the sweetness comes from the white chocolate here, so use the best-quality chocolate you can find; you'll really taste the difference. The cranberry compote, spooned on top, provides a sharp and welcome counterpoint, but the cake also works without it if you are looking for a shortcut. Some fresh berries served alongside—strawberries, raspberries or blackberries—would be perfect.

SERVES 10–12

The compote will keep for up to 5 days in the fridge and also freezes well. The cheesecake must be made at least the day before you plan to serve it and kept in the fridge.

Once assembled, the cake will keep well for 3–4 days in the fridge.

BASE

2½ oz/70 g whole raw almonds, skin on
6½ oz/180 g graham crackers (about 12 sheets), roughly broken
7 tbsp/100 g unsalted butter, melted, plus extra for greasing

FILLING

1 lb 5 oz/600 g good-quality white chocolate: 1 lb 2 oz/500 g roughly broken; 3½ oz/100 g chopped into ⅓-inch/1-cm pieces (or use white chocolate chips)
1 lb 2 oz/500 g cream cheese, at room temperature
4 large eggs, lightly beaten
1⅓ cups/300 g sour cream
finely grated zest of 1 small orange (1 tsp)
scraped seeds of ½ vanilla pod

CRANBERRY COMPOTE

1¼ cups/150 g fresh (or frozen and defrosted) raspberries
1⅓ cups/180 g fresh (or frozen and defrosted) cranberries
½ cup/100 g granulated sugar
¼ cup/60 ml orange juice

1   **To make the base,** preheat the oven to 350°F/180°C. Lightly grease the base and sides of a 9-inch/23-cm round springform pan and line with parchment paper.

2   Spread the almonds out on a baking sheet and roast for 10 minutes, then set aside to cool. Transfer to a food processor and pulse just a few times—you want the almonds to be in roughly ¼-inch/0.5-cm pieces rather than turning to powder—then transfer to a separate bowl.

3   Put the graham crackers into the food processor and process until fine; you want the consistency to be that of dried breadcrumbs. Add to the bowl of almonds, along with the melted butter, and use your hands or a wooden spoon to combine. Spoon the crumbs into the pan, pressing them firmly into the base. Even out the crust with the back of a spoon or the bottom of a glass and set aside in the fridge.

4   **To make the filling,** place the roughly broken white chocolate in a heatproof bowl set over a pan of simmering water (make sure the base of the bowl is not touching the water), stirring from time to time. Once the chocolate has melted, turn off the heat, remove the bowl from the pan of hot water and set aside for 5 minutes to cool slightly, stirring occasionally. ››

5   Place the cream cheese in the bowl of an electric mixer with the paddle attachment in place. Beat on medium-high speed until smooth. Turn the speed to medium-low and gradually add the eggs, followed by the sour cream, orange zest and vanilla seeds. Add the melted chocolate—it should be tepid rather than warm, as you don't want the chopped white chocolate to melt when it is added later—and beat on a medium-low speed until combined. Finally, stir in the chopped white chocolate (or white chocolate chips).

6   Pour the mixture into the chilled base. Smooth over the top and place on a baking sheet. Bake for about 1 hour, or until the middle of the cheesecake has a slight wobble when you gently shake the pan. Turn off the oven but leave the cheesecake inside for an hour, with the oven door propped open with a wooden spoon. Remove from the oven and cool completely before covering in plastic wrap and chilling in the fridge for at least 4 hours, or preferably overnight, until the cheesecake is cold and firm.

7   **To make the cranberry compote,** place the raspberries in the small bowl of a food processor and process to form a liquid—don't use a blender here as it will pulverize the seeds as well as the fruit and give the purée a slightly bitter taste. Pass through a fine-mesh (or muslin-lined) sieve to remove the seeds, which can be discarded. You should have around ⅓ cup/80 ml purée.

8   Stir together the cranberries, sugar and orange juice in a medium saucepan. Place on medium-low heat until the sugar has dissolved. Increase the heat and gently boil for 8–10 minutes, until most of the cranberries have burst and the mixture is thick. Remove the pan from the heat and stir in the raspberry purée. Transfer to a bowl, place some plastic wrap directly on top of the compote and set aside to cool. The compote will thicken to an almost jelly-like consistency but will break up readily when stirred before you spoon it on top of the cake.

9   When ready to serve, release the springform pan and remove the parchment paper. Slide the cheesecake on to a serving plate and spoon over the cranberry compote. Use a warm knife (dip the blade in hot water and wipe dry before using) to cut slices and serve at once.

Passion fruit cheesecakes with spiced pineapple

When we have our regular kitchen meetings, all our pastry chefs—there are about fifteen—come bearing their sweet offerings, which are then passed around the table and closely scrutinized. This cheesecake was brought to one of those meetings by Céline Lecoeur, and it received unanimous praise from everyone at the table. And our customers—who made it an instant best seller—agreed.

For details on where to get hold of strained passion fruit pulp, see page 355. The alternative is to scoop out the pulp from about a dozen passion fruit, place it in a food processor and process to a purée. Don't worry about the numerous seeds releasing their bitter flavors as they're crushed; they're so slippery that they just whizz around and around the processor rather than breaking down.

SERVES 8 (8 INDIVIDUAL CAKES OR 1 LARGE CAKE)

We like to make these as individual cakes, in 3-inch/8-cm round cake rings. Alternatively, you could make one large cake in a 9-inch/23-cm round springform pan. Baking and resting times in the oven are listed in the recipe for both options.

The cheesecakes must be made a day before serving, to allow the filling to set overnight (the pineapple topping is best made and added on the day of serving).

Once assembled, the cakes are best eaten on the same day. Leftovers will keep for up to 2 days in the fridge; they just won't look as perfect as on Day One.

BASE

⅓ cup/40 g sliced almonds, lightly crushed in your hand
4½ oz/125 g graham crackers (about 9 sheets), roughly broken
½ tsp ground cinnamon
½ tsp ground star anise (or 2 whole star anise, ground in a spice grinder and passed through a fine-mesh sieve)
6 tbsp/85 g unsalted butter, melted, plus extra for greasing

FILLING

⅔ cup/140 g strained passion fruit pulp, or the puréed pulp of about 12 passion fruit (see introduction)
1 lb 10 oz/750 g cream cheese
1 cup/200 g granulated sugar
⅓ cup/80 g sour cream
3 large eggs, plus 3 large egg yolks, lightly beaten

SPICED PINEAPPLE

1 small pineapple (1 lb 9 oz/700 g), peeled, core removed and flesh cut into roughly ⅔-inch/1.5-cm cubes
¼ tsp ground cinnamon
¼ tsp ground star anise (or 1 whole star anise, ground in a spice grinder and passed through a fine-mesh sieve)
½ vanilla pod, sliced in half lengthwise and seeds scraped
¼ cup plus 1 tbsp/60 g granulated sugar
1 tbsp lemon juice
1 tbsp water

pulp and seeds from 2 passion fruit

1   **To make the base,** preheat the oven to 350°F/170°C. Lightly grease the sides of eight individual 3-inch/8-cm round cake rings, and line the sides with parchment paper—you want the paper to rise ⅓ inch/1 cm above the top of the ring—then place on a large parchment-lined baking sheet. If using a large springform pan, grease and line the base and sides—again, the paper should rise ⅓ inch/1 cm above the sides of the pan—place the pan on a baking sheet and set aside.

2   Place the almonds on a parchment-lined baking sheet and roast for 6 minutes, until golden. Remove from the oven and set aside to cool. ››

3   Place the graham crackers in a food processor and process to form fine crumbs; the consistency should be that of dried breadcrumbs. Tip into a medium bowl and add the almonds, ground cinnamon and ground star anise. Add the melted butter and stir well to combine. Spoon the crumbs into the pans, using your hands to press them into the base. Even out the crust with the back of a spoon or the bottom of a glass and set aside in the fridge for around 30 minutes to chill.

4   **To make the filling,** if using puréed passion fruit pulp, strain through a fine-mesh (or muslin-lined) sieve, discarding the seeds. Set the juice aside.

5   Place the cream cheese and sugar in the bowl of an electric mixer with the paddle attachment in place. Beat on medium speed until smooth, then add the sour cream and mix until just combined. Turn the speed to medium-low and, with the machine still running, pour in the whisked eggs and yolks in a steady stream. Beat thoroughly, then add the passion fruit juice and gently combine.

6   Pour the filling into the chilled crumb-lined cake pans; it should rise to the top of the rings or about ¾ inch/2 cm from the top if making one large cake. Bake for 25 minutes, or 55–60 minutes if making one large cake, until the edges are set but the center remains slightly wobbly when the baking sheet is gently shaken. Turn off the oven but leave the cheesecakes inside for 30 minutes, or 1 hour for the large cake, with the door propped open with a wooden spoon. Remove from the oven and set aside to cool completely, before covering the baking sheet in plastic wrap and refrigerating overnight; the cheesecake is very soft so will not cut without chilling.

7   **To make the spiced pineapple,** on the day of serving, preheat the oven to 400°F/200°C. Place the pineapple cubes in a medium bowl with the cinnamon, star anise and vanilla pod and seeds. Toss well and spread out on a parchment-lined baking sheet. Bake in the oven for 15 minutes, until lightly roasted, then set aside.

8   Place the sugar in a medium sauté pan over medium-high heat. It will seem as though nothing is happening until suddenly a small section around the edge will begin to melt and turn brown. It may even smoke a little, but don't worry and don't stir; continue to heat, tilting the pan often and swirling gently so that the sugar continues to melt and brown evenly until the caramel is golden in color. As soon as the caramel is ready, remove the pan from the heat and carefully pour in the lemon juice and water. It will splutter and spit, so take care. Swirl again over the heat to melt the caramel if the addition of the lemon juice has hardened it. Bring to a boil, stir and reduce for 30–60 seconds to form a thick syrup, then add the pineapple cubes. Stir to combine and set aside to cool.

9   When ready to serve, run a small knife around the base of the pans, releasing the graham cracker base, and gently push the cheesecakes up and out of their molds. Remove the paper and transfer to a serving platter. Spoon the caramelized pineapple and syrup onto the center of the cheesecakes, then spoon the passion fruit pulp and seeds on top of that. Serve immediately.

Baked ricotta and hazelnut cheesecakes

Unlike most other cheesecakes, this doesn't need to be made ahead of time in order to chill and set. In fact, it tastes best served a little warm. It's not what people expect from a cheesecake—there's no crunchy base and it's served warm from the oven—but in Italy, where they certainly know how to "do" ricotta, nearly all cheesecakes are more of a warm, moist cake like this (although you can serve it from the fridge, if you like).

    With thanks to Laura Jane Stewart, pastry chef at our Ledbury shop, for this recipe.

MAKES 10 (USING 3-INCH/8-CM RINGS), 18 (USING A REGULAR MUFFIN PAN) OR 1 LARGE CAKE

We like to make these as individual cakes, in 3-inch/8-cm round cake rings. Alternatively, you could use a regular muffin pan, or you could make one large cake in a 9-inch/23-cm round springform pan. Instructions for all options are listed in the recipe.

The ganache can be made in advance and kept at room temperature for up to 4 days or in the fridge for up to 2 weeks. If keeping it in the fridge, you'll need to warm it over a pan of simmering water to return it to a spreadable glaze.

Without icing, these will keep for 3 days in an airtight container in the fridge. You'll need to take the chill off them, so take them out a good 30 minutes or so before serving. Once iced, they are best eaten straightaway.

2¼ cups/300 g blanched hazelnuts
3½ tbsp all-purpose flour
5½ oz/160 g chocolate (70% cocoa solids), roughly chopped
1 cup/100 g almond meal
1 cup/225 g unsalted butter, at room temperature, roughly cubed, plus extra for greasing
1¼ cups/250 g granulated sugar
6 large eggs, whites and yolks separated
1½ cups/400 g ricotta cheese
2 tsp vanilla extract
¼ tsp salt

WATER GANACHE
3½ oz/100 g dark chocolate (70% cocoa solids), roughly chopped into ¾-inch/2-cm pieces
3 tbsp granulated sugar
2½ tbsp light corn syrup
⅓ cup/80 ml water
scraped seeds of ¼ vanilla pod
3 tbsp/40 g unsalted butter, at room temperature, cut into ¾-inch/2-cm cubes

1   Preheat the oven to 350°F/180°C.

2   Lightly grease the sides of ten individual 3-inch/8-cm round cake rings and line the sides with parchment paper—you want the paper to rise ¾ inch/2 cm above the top of the ring—then place on a large baking sheet that is also lined with parchment paper. (Once the rings have been filled with the cake mixture, they cannot be moved, so arrange them on the baking sheet as you want them to be baked.) If using a muffin pan, line the base of the molds with a circle of parchment paper and grease the sides. If using a 9-inch/23-cm springform pan, grease and line the base and sides—again, the paper should rise ¾ inch/2 cm above the sides of the pan—place the pan on a baking sheet and set aside.

3   Spread the hazelnuts out on a rimmed baking sheet and roast for 10 minutes, until they have taken on just a little bit of color. Remove from the oven and set aside until completely cool (if you process them when they are warm, they will turn to an oily paste). Roughly chop ⅓ cup/50 g of the cooled nuts (it's okay if a few remain whole) and set aside—they will be used to garnish—and place the remainder in the bowl of a food processor, along with the flour. Process until fine, then tip into a medium bowl. Place the chocolate in the food processor, pulse to form large crumbs and add these to the hazelnuts and flour. Add the almond meal, mix together and set aside; the texture is a bit rustic here, which is what you want. ››

4   Increase the oven temperature to 375°F/190°C.

5   Place the butter and sugar in the bowl of an electric mixer with the paddle attachment in place. Beat on medium-high speed for about 3 minutes, until light and creamy. Add the egg yolks, one at a time, beating well after each addition. Turn the speed to low, add the chocolate-nut-flour mixture and continue to mix until just combined. Remove the bowl from the machine and stir in the ricotta, vanilla extract and salt. Transfer the cake mixture to a separate large bowl and set aside.

6   Wash and dry the bowl of the electric mixer very well before adding the egg whites to it. Beat the whites on medium-high speed until stiff, then use a large spatula to fold the egg whites, in two or three batches, into the cake mixture. Scrape the mixture into the pans, filling them to the top of each ring. Bake for 30–35 minutes if using the individual cake rings, 20 minutes if using a muffin pan, or about 60 minutes if making it in one large pan, rotating the baking sheet halfway through, until golden brown and a skewer inserted into the middle comes out more or less clean; it might have a few crumbs attached but should not be wet. Remove from the oven and set aside to cool completely. Remove the cakes from their pans, peel away the paper and set aside. If you are making one large cake and it is a bit cracked on top, don't worry; rustic is fine here and the chocolate ganache will cover it completely.

7   **To make the water ganache,** place the chocolate in a medium bowl and set aside. Put the sugar and corn syrup in a small saucepan and place over medium-low heat. Stir to combine and, when the sugar has melted, increase the heat to medium and bring to a boil, stirring gently from time to time. Continue to boil for about 5 minutes, until the color is a pale amber. Remove from the heat and carefully pour in the water; don't worry if the mixture seizes. Return the pan to the heat, add the scraped vanilla seeds and stir gently and continuously until it returns to a boil. Remove from the heat and wait for a minute before pouring the water-caramel over the chocolate. Allow to stand for 5 minutes, then whisk to combine. Add the butter, a couple of cubes at a time, whisking after each addition. Continue until all the butter has been added, whisking to combine until the mix is smooth and shiny. Remove from the heat.

8   Spoon the ganache over the cakes, letting it drip down the sides. Sprinkle with the reserved hazelnuts and serve.

Fig, orange and mascarpone cheesecake

Recipes are like stories, passed on from one person to another. The details and emphases change, but tribute should always be paid to the original source. Ever-mindful of paying tribute where it's due, Helen thought she'd first seen a version of this cake years ago in *The Australian Women's Weekly* magazine. Not content to simply acknowledge the publication and move on, Helen bought no less than five old *Women's Weekly* books and magazines before she finally tracked down the original reference. Hat tipped, we were then happy to take hold of the recipe and retell it in our own way.

This is a rich cheesecake, but one with a lighter texture than most, thanks to the whisked-up, air-filled egg whites that are folded through the mixture just before baking. It will rise up a little like a soufflé, then deflate when cooled.

We like to serve the cake as it is, simple and unadorned, but you can play around with the decoration, if you like. Finely julienned strips of orange zest look great on top of the cheesecake and echo the juice within; or if you can get hold of any large fig leaves, these are also fun to sit the cake on top of when serving.

SERVES 12

BASE

3½ oz/100 g graham crackers (about
    6½ sheets), roughly broken
¾ cup/80 g walnut halves, finely
    chopped
4 tbsp/60 g unsalted butter, melted,
    plus extra for greasing
9 oz/260 g soft dried figs, tough
    stems removed, sliced into
    ¼-inch/0.5-cm strips
1 cup plus 1 tbsp/250 ml orange juice
1 cinnamon stick
⅛ tsp ground cloves

FILLING

1 lb 2 oz/500 g cream cheese,
    at room temperature
1 lb 2 oz/500 g mascarpone
1¼ cups/250 g granulated sugar
finely grated zest of 1 large orange
    (1 tbsp)
4 large eggs, whites and yolks
    separated
2 tsp vanilla extract

The base can be made 2 days in advance and stored in the fridge.

The cheesecake can be assembled up to 2 days in advance and stored in the fridge.

1   **To make the base,** grease the base and sides of a 9-inch/23-cm round springform pan and line with parchment paper, making sure that the paper rises at least 2 inches/5 cm above the rim; the cake rises a lot in the oven.

2   Place the graham crackers in a food processor and process to form fine crumbs; the consistency should be that of dried breadcrumbs. Place in a medium bowl and add the walnuts and melted butter. Use your hands or a large spoon to combine; the mixture should be the consistency of wet sand. Spoon the crumbs into the pan, using your hands to press them into the base, then place in the fridge for 20 minutes to firm up.

3   Place the figs, orange juice, cinnamon stick and ground cloves in a medium saucepan over a medium heat. Bring to a simmer and cook for 15–20 minutes,

until most of the liquid has evaporated but the mixture is still moist. Set aside to cool, remove the cinnamon stick, then spread over the base. Return to the fridge.

4   Preheat the oven to 350°F/180°C.

5   **To make the filling,** place the cream cheese in the bowl of an electric mixer with the paddle attachment in place. Beat on medium speed for 1 minute, until smooth, before adding the mascarpone, sugar, orange zest, egg yolks and vanilla extract. Continue to beat until all of the ingredients are incorporated and the mixture looks smooth and creamy, scraping down the paddle and sides of the bowl from time to time, if you need to.

6   Place the egg whites in a separate clean bowl and whisk (either by hand or with an electric mixer) until firm peaks form. Fold a third into the cream cheese mixture, followed by the remaining two-thirds.

7   Pour the filling over the chilled fig and graham cracker base. Place on a baking sheet and bake for 75–80 minutes, until the cheesecake is a light golden brown at the edges and the center is only just firm. Turn off the oven but leave the cheesecake inside for an hour or so, with the door propped open with a wooden spoon. Allow it to come to room temperature before covering in plastic wrap and keeping in the fridge for 4 hours.

8   When ready to serve, release the springform pan, remove the parchment paper and transfer to a cake platter. The cheesecake is best served chilled, straight from the fridge, and cut with a warm knife (dip the blade in hot water and wipe dry before using).

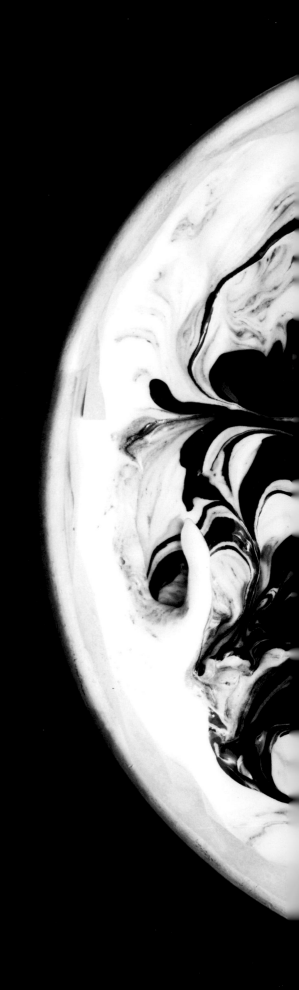

CHOCOLATE BANANA RIPPLE CHEESECAKE

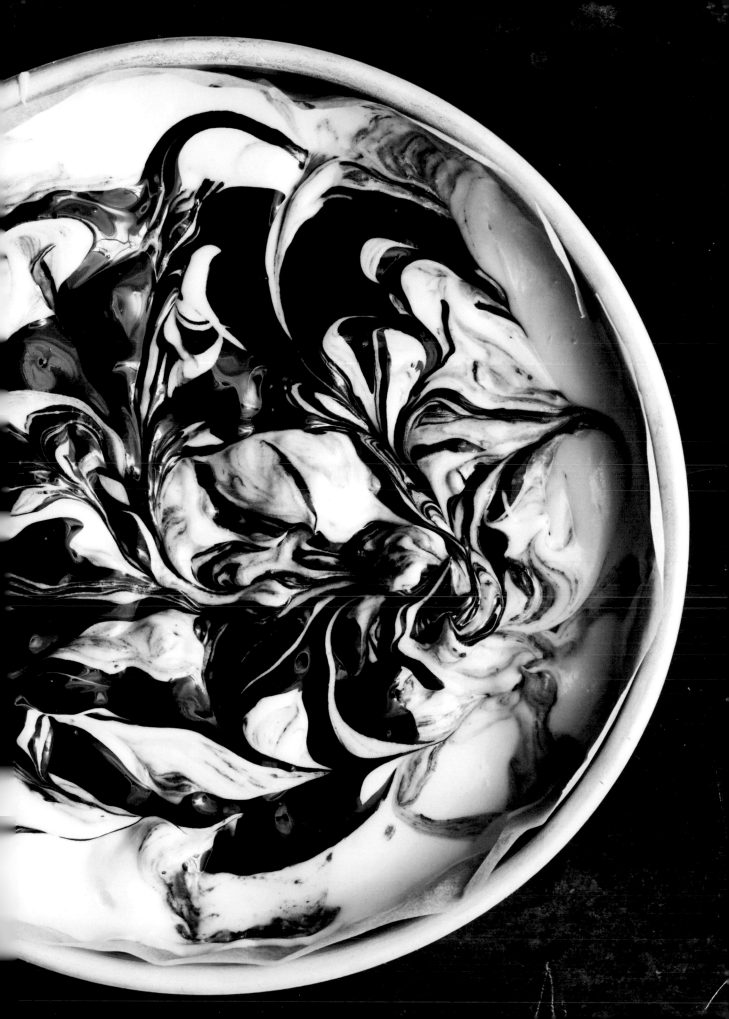

Chocolate banana ripple cheesecake

If you are going to do it, you might as well do it. Take even a couple of the words in this recipe's name and you have something approximating a dessert. Take all four and you have yourself about as serious a teatime or end-of-meal treat as you can imagine.

SERVES 10–12

BASE

¼ cup/30 g walnut halves

7 oz/200 g graham crackers (about 13 sheets), roughly broken

2 tbsp Dutch-processed cocoa powder

¼ cup/50 g demerara sugar

7 tbsp/100 g unsalted butter, melted, plus extra for greasing

2–3 large ripe bananas, peeled and sliced on the diagonal into ⅓-inch/1-cm-thick pieces (9 oz/260 g)

BANANA GANACHE

4½ oz/125 g dark chocolate (70% cocoa solids), roughly chopped into ⅓-inch/1-cm pieces

5 tsp/25 ml whole milk

3½ tbsp/50 ml heavy cream

1 large ripe banana, peeled and mashed (3½ oz/100 g)

FILLING

2 cups/375 g white chocolate chips (or 13¼ oz/375 g white chocolate, roughly chopped into ⅓-inch/1-cm pieces)

13¼ oz/375 g cream cheese, at room temperature

3 large eggs, lightly beaten

1 cup/220 g sour cream

1 tsp vanilla extract

The crumb base can be made and pressed into the cake pan up to 2 days in advance and stored in the fridge. The ganache can also be made 2–3 days in advance, stored in the fridge, and gently warmed over a pot of simmering water to soften before swirling. The whole cake needs to be made at least 4 hours before serving and then kept in the fridge to firm up. Ideally, make it the day before you are going to serve it so that it can chill overnight.

Once assembled, the cake is best stored in the fridge and eaten within 3 days.

---

1   **To make the base,** preheat the oven to 350°F/180°C. Grease the base and sides of a 9-inch/23-cm round springform pan and line with parchment paper.

2   Spread the walnuts out on a rimmed baking sheet and roast in the oven for 6 minutes. Set aside to cool, then chop roughly into ¼-inch/0.5-cm pieces.

3   Place the graham crackers in a food processor and process to form fine crumbs. Tip into a medium bowl and add the cocoa powder, sugar and chopped walnuts. Add the melted butter and stir well to combine. Spoon the crumbs into the pan, using your hands to press them into the base. Even out the crust with the back of a spoon or the bottom of a glass and set aside in the fridge.

4   **To make the banana ganache,** place the chopped dark chocolate in a medium heatproof bowl. Heat the milk and cream in a small pan, and just as it comes to a boil, pour it over the chocolate. Allow to stand for 1 minute before stirring gently with a rubber spatula so that the chocolate melts; you might need to heat it a little more if it hasn't all melted. Stir in the mashed banana and set aside to cool.

5   **To make the filling,** place the chopped white chocolate in a small heatproof bowl set over a pan of simmering water (make sure the base of the bowl is not touching the water), stirring from time to time. Once the chocolate has melted, turn off the heat, remove the bowl from the pan and set aside to cool slightly, stirring occasionally.

6   Place the cream cheese in the bowl of an electric mixer with the paddle attachment in place. Beat on medium-high speed until smooth, then turn the speed to medium. Gradually add the eggs, scraping down the sides of the bowl once or twice, followed by the sour cream and vanilla extract. Add the melted white chocolate—don't worry if it's slightly tepid rather than completely cool—and beat on medium-low speed until combined.

7   Arrange the sliced bananas evenly over the crumb base so that they form a single layer. Pour the filling carefully over the bananas, then, using a small spoon, gently dollop the banana ganache on top of the filling. Using a knife (like a butter knife), gently swirl the ganache and filling together by repeatedly drawing a figure 8 through the mixture to create a marbled look. Place the cheesecake on a baking sheet and bake for 60–70 minutes, until the outside is set but the center is still slightly soft to the touch. Turn off the oven but leave the cheesecake inside, with the door closed, for 1 hour. Remove from the oven and set aside until completely cool, then cover the whole thing carefully in plastic wrap and chill in the fridge for at least 4 hours or preferably overnight, until the cheesecake is completely firm.

8   When ready to serve, release the springform pan, remove the parchment paper and transfer to a cake platter. Set aside for 15 minutes before slicing.

Apricot and Amaretto cheesecake

This is the cheesecake to round off a dinner party. Some will have this instead of a glass of Amaretto; others will see it as the perfect excuse to bring the bottle to the table. Whichever way the party goes, there's built-in synergy here, with the sweet Amaretto liqueur (made from a base of apricot kernels and bitter almonds) complementing the roasted apricots and flaked roasted almonds.

SERVES 10–12

The crumb base can be made and pressed into the cake pan up to 2 days in advance and stored in the fridge. The cheesecake can be made up to 3 days in advance and stored in the fridge (the topping should only be added on the day of serving).

Once assembled, the cake is best eaten on the same day. Leftovers will keep for up to 2 days in the fridge; they just won't look as perfect as on Day One.

BASE

6½ oz/180 g graham crackers (about 12 sheets), roughly broken
⅔ cup/70 g sliced almonds, toasted
7 tbsp/100 g unsalted butter, melted
12 oz/350 g fresh apricots, halved and pitted

FILLING

1 lb 14 oz/840 g cream cheese, at room temperature
¾ cup plus 2 tbsp/170 g granulated sugar
scraped seeds of ½ vanilla pod
finely grated zest of 1 large orange (1 tbsp)
5 large eggs, lightly beaten
⅓ cup/80 g sour cream
⅓ cup/80 ml Amaretto

TOPPING

14 oz/400 g fresh apricots, halved and pitted
1 tbsp granulated sugar
1 tbsp water
1 tbsp Amaretto

3 tbsp/15 g sliced almonds, toasted

---

1   **To make the base,** preheat the oven to 400°F/200°C. Lightly grease the base and sides of a 9-inch/23-cm round springform pan and line with parchment paper.

2   Place the graham crackers in a food processor and process to form fine crumbs; the consistency should be that of dried breadcrumbs. Tip into a medium bowl and add the almonds and melted butter. Use your hands or a large spoon to combine: the mixture should be the consistency of wet sand. Spoon the crumbs into the pan, using your hands to press them into the base. Even out the crust with the back of a spoon or the bottom of a glass and set aside in the fridge.

3   Spread the apricots for the base out on a baking sheet, cut side up, and roast in the oven for 25 minutes (or a little longer, if they were very firm to begin with), until they are soft but still holding their shape. Set aside to cool.

4   Lower the oven temperature to 350°F/170°C. ››

5   **To make the filling,** place the cream cheese, sugar, vanilla seeds and orange zest in the bowl of an electric mixer with the paddle attachment in place. Beat on medium speed until smooth. Gradually add the eggs, followed by the sour cream, and beat until combined; you might need to scrape down the sides of the bowl once or twice. Finally, add the Amaretto and mix until combined.

6   Remove the base from the fridge and arrange the roasted apricots evenly over the bottom, cut side down. The apricots should fit quite snugly without overlapping or leaving gaps. Gently pour the filling over the apricots and then place on a baking sheet. Bake for 1 hour, or until the sides of the cheesecake are set but the middle has a wobble when shaken very gently. Turn off the oven but leave the cheesecake inside for another hour, with the door propped open with a wooden spoon, before placing in the fridge for at least 3 hours or up to overnight to chill and set completely.

7   **To make the topping,** on the day of serving, preheat the oven to 400°F/200°C. Spread the apricots out on a baking sheet, cut side up, and roast for 25 minutes (or a little longer, if they were very firm to begin with), until they are soft but still holding their shape. Sprinkle the apricots with the sugar, water and Amaretto. Return to the oven and bake for another 10 minutes, until the apricots are moist and syrupy. Remove from the oven and set aside to cool.

8   When ready to serve, release the springform pan, remove the parchment paper and transfer to a cake platter. Spoon the roasted syrupy apricots into the center of the cake and sprinkle over the toasted almonds before slicing.

Roasted strawberry and lime cheesecake

The sponge-cake base of this cheesecake was inspired by (and adapted from) a recipe used by the legendary Junior's Cheesecake in Brooklyn. It's a natural partner to the strawberries and a welcome change from the graham cracker base more commonly associated with cheesecakes. The sponge cake is twice baked: first by itself, as a very shallow cake, and again when the cream cheese mixture goes on top. We love this base, but alternatives work just as well, if you'd prefer something nutty and crunchy and quick to prepare; try the base from the Apricot and Amaretto Cheesecake (see page 219), with or without the sliced almonds.

SERVES 12–16

The cheesecake can be made up to 3 days in advance and kept in the fridge (the strawberries should only be roasted and added on the day of serving).

Once assembled, the cake is best eaten on the same day. Leftovers will keep for up to 3 days in the fridge, but they won't look as perfect, as the strawberries will leak.

BASE
½ cup/60 g all-purpose flour
1 tbsp cornstarch
¾ tsp baking powder
⅛ tsp salt
2 large eggs, whites and yolks separated
½ cup/100 g granulated sugar, plus 2 tbsp
scraped seeds of ¼ vanilla pod
finely grated zest of 1 lime (1 tsp), plus 1 tsp lime juice
2 tbsp/30 g unsalted butter, melted
¼ tsp cream of tartar

FILLING
2 lb/900 g cream cheese, at room temperature
¾ cup plus 2½ tbsp/180 g granulated sugar
scraped seeds of ½ vanilla pod
5 large eggs (10¼ oz/290 g), lightly beaten (the weight is important here, and as eggs vary in size, you might need slightly more or less than 5)
⅓ cup plus 1 tbsp/90 g sour cream
finely grated zest of 3 limes (1 tbsp), plus 1 tbsp lime juice

TOPPING
about 30 large strawberries, hulled (1 lb 5 oz/600 g)
3 tbsp/20 g confectioners' sugar, plus 1 tsp, for dusting

1   **To make the base,** preheat the oven to 375°F/190°C. Grease the base and sides of a 9-inch/23-cm round springform cake pan and line with parchment paper.
2   Place the flour, cornstarch, baking powder and salt in a small bowl and set aside. Put the egg yolks in the bowl of an electric mixer with the whisk attachment in place and add the ½ cup/100 g sugar and vanilla seeds. Beat on high speed until pale and thickened. Remove the bowl from the mixer and sift the dry ingredients directly onto the eggs. Fold to combine, then add the lime zest, lime juice and melted butter and mix to incorporate. Transfer to a large bowl and set aside.
3   Wash and dry the bowl for the electric mixer very well and return it to the machine with the whisk attachment in place. Add the egg whites and beat on high speed until frothy. Add the cream of tartar and continue to beat until soft peaks form, then gradually sprinkle in the 2 tbsp granulated sugar. Continue to beat until firm peaks form. ››

4   Fold a third of the egg whites into the cake mixture to lighten it, before folding in the rest until fully combined. Scrape the mixture into the prepared pan, smooth the top with a small spatula and place in the oven for about 12 minutes, or until the sponge cake is pale golden and the center springs back when touched lightly. Remove from the oven and set aside to cool.

5   Lower the oven temperature to 350°F/170°C.

6   **To make the filling,** place the cream cheese, granulated sugar and vanilla seeds in an electric mixer with the paddle attachment in place. Beat until smooth, then gradually add the eggs, beating all the time. Add the sour cream, lime zest and lime juice and continue to beat until combined. At this point the mixture will be quite runny, so remove the paddle attachment and finish whisking with a large hand whisk until completely smooth.

7   Sit the cake pan on top of a parchment-lined baking sheet (to protect against any spillage from the base) and pour the filling over the base; the filling will rise close to the top of the pan, but that's fine. Bake for 55 minutes; the center will still be wobbly but, as long as the sides of the cheesecake are firm, this is how it should be. (Don't worry if a crack has formed on the surface of the cake; this can often result from a long cooking time and will be hidden by the strawberries piled on top.) Turn off the oven, but leave the cheesecake inside for an hour or so, with the oven door propped open with a wooden spoon. Remove from the oven and leave to cool to room temperature before transferring to the fridge for 4 hours, uncovered, or until completely chilled. Don't be tempted to cover the cake with plastic wrap, as this will cause condensation.

8   **To make the topping,** on the day you plan to serve the cheesecake, preheat the oven to 475°F/250°C.

9   Sit the strawberries on a wire rack, tip end pointing up, and place the wire rack on a parchment-lined baking sheet. Raising them above the baking sheet allows the strawberries to roast rather than stew. Dust with the 3 tbsp/20 g confectioners' sugar and roast for 15 minutes, until the tips of the strawberries have slightly blackened; not all of the confectioners' sugar needs to have melted. Remove from the oven and set aside.

10   When the strawberries are cool, place them in the center of the cake, tip pointing up. Drizzle the cooking juices over the strawberries and dust with the remaining 1 tsp confectioners' sugar. If not serving straightaway, return the cake to the fridge; you want to serve this fridge-cold.

Tarts & pies

—

Tarts and pies have a real sense of occasion about them. Which occasion it is will determine which tart or pie is brought to the table. Homely weekend lunches need Walnut and Black Treacle Tarts (see page 245), while more exotic feasts might require Pineapple Tartlets with Pandan and Star Anise (see page 255) or those filled with fig and frangipane (see page 247). Classic chocolate tarts are for the smart and well-heeled event, while those baking for a more free-form, rustic occasion might prefer an open galette. The choice is entirely yours: as with all dress codes, guidance is there for those who want it rather than to be followed to the letter. Anything goes, really.

We use four different types of pastry in our tarts and pies: sweet shortcrust (pâte sucrée), flaky (pâte brisée), polenta and cream cheese.

SWEET SHORTCRUST (PÂTE SUCRÉE) PASTRY › Yotam first worked with this pastry during his time at Baker & Spice and it's been with us ever since. It's unusual in that it has both a delicate snap, yet is robust enough to contain all sorts of fillings. When blind-baked it becomes very light and crisp; when baked directly with the filling it becomes short and buttery. The pastry itself tastes so delicious—with a hint of lemon—that it could pass as a simple cookie. As long as you chill and rest it properly, it's also very easy to work with.

Most of our recipes use only a half batch of sweet shortcrust pastry, the exception being the Fig and Pistachio Frangipane Tartlets (see page 247), which use about two-thirds. This is because one batch uses one egg yolk, so rather than mucking about with half an egg yolk, we find it preferable to make a full batch and freeze the half we do not use. If you find this annoying, you obviously haven't tried to split an egg yolk in two!

FLAKY PASTRY (PÂTE BRISÉE) › This recipe for this crisp and light pastry comes from Australia's Bourke Street Bakery, always Yotam's first stop when he's visiting Sydney. The dough has a high proportion of water—3 tbsp/45 ml—so it shrinks (as the water evaporates) during baking. This makes it superlight and crisp and is also, because of the flakiness, what leads to the slightly uneven or rustic look on the baked shell. This is fine—we like rustic!—but take care not to overwork or stretch the dough when you're lining a pan because you don't want to encourage too much shrinkage.

CREAM CHEESE PASTRY › This version is from *The Pie and Pastry Bible* by Rose Levy Beranbaum. In her introduction, Rose says of "her favorite pie crust" that it took her several years and more than fifty attempts to get right. Thank you, Rose, your hard work was not in vain! It's full of flavor, thanks to the cream cheese, turns a lovely golden brown when baked, and manages to be both tender and flaky at once. The flakiness of the pastry is attributed to the freezing of the butter and flour (for between 30 and 60 minutes), so don't be tempted to skimp on this stage. The cream cheese in the mixture also makes it wonderfully pliable and a dream to roll. It makes for a very soft dough, though, so you might need to return it regularly to the fridge while rolling if the day is particularly warm. We have used regular all-purpose flour in our version (rather than the pastry flour that—due to its lower protein content—Rose recommends), as this is the flour more widely available to us.

The consistency of cream cheese can vary hugely (according to its water content) from one brand or from one country to another (see page 352). This can have a bearing on the making of the pastry. In America, for example, cream cheese is very firm, which means that the ingredients for the pastry won't come together in a food processor and the dough needs to be kneaded. In the United Kingdom, on the other hand, the cream cheese is more watery and soft, so the ingredients come together very quickly in the food processor. Our instructions are for the cream cheese we have worked with—the soft and spreadable kind—so this is something to be mindful of if your cream cheese is very firm.

POLENTA PASTRY › This was developed in the early days of Ottolenghi, when we needed a gritty texture to stand against the creaminess of various curds and creams in some of our tarts or fruity galettes. We use it here in our apricot and thyme galettes (see page 253).

Our pans, tips and tricks

If you really want to stock up and be able to bake all our tarts and pies, you'll need the following. Don't worry if you don't have them all, however, as alternatives are suggested.

MINI-FLUTED TART PANS › A set of eight (or even twelve) mini-fluted tart pans, 3½ inches/9 cm wide and 1 inch/3 cm deep, are needed to make the Walnut and Black Treacle Tarts (see page 245), the Mont Blanc Tarts (see page 235) and the Chai Brûlée Tarts (see page 239). The reality of our kitchen is that we have a selection of very similar but slightly different mini-tart pans: some are 3 inches/8 cm wide and 1 inch/3 cm deep; some are 3½ inches/9 cm wide and ¾ inch/2 cm deep; and some are 4 inches/10 cm wide and either ¾ or 1 inch/2 or 3 cm deep. When writing *Sweet*, we spent some time obsessing about the difference between one pan and another, and an equal amount of time feeling very relaxed about the fact that whichever pan you use (even within our obsessive margins!), all will be fine. You might make one additional or fewer tart than a recipe states, but worse things happen at sea. Whatever the exact dimensions of your pans, make sure they have removable bases.

LARGE FLUTED TART PANS › The Chocolate Tart with Hazelnut, Rosemary and Orange (see page 241) is made in a large (10-inch/25-cm) fluted tart pan with a removable base. In addition, if you don't have a set of mini-fluted pans, you can make the Walnut and Black Treacle Tarts (see page 245) and the Mont Blanc Tarts (see page 235) in a large fluted pan. The walnut tart will bake and slice as neatly large as it does in mini form. The Mont Blanc tart, on the other hand, is less neat and tidy when baked whole—it will still taste delicious, but will shatter when sliced. The Chai Brûlée Tarts (see page 239) only work in mini form.

REGULAR MUFFIN PANS › These have 12 molds: 2¾ inches/7 cm wide at the top, 2 inches/5 cm wide at the bottom, and 1⅓ inches/3.5 cm deep. A regular muffin pan is used for the Fig and Pistachio Frangipane Tartlets (see page 247) and little baked chocolate tarts (see page 232) and is also a suitable alternative to the traditional mince pie pan (see following).

TRADITIONAL MINCE PIE PANS › These have 12 molds with curved bottoms: just less than 2 inches/ 5 cm at the top and ⅔ inch/1.5 cm deep. They are used for the pineapple tartlets (see page 255).

COOKIE CUTTERS › You can't get a 4⅓-inch/11-cm round cookie cutter, we know, so you can either use a 4-inch/10-cm round cutter or, as we do, improvise with whatever you can find that is round and 4⅓ inches/11 cm wide: a lid or a bowl works well. Baking is a science, of course, but necessity can also be the mother of invention when you're trying to create the perfect round of pastry to fit the ideal muffin mold.

TRIMMING PASTRY › Whether you trim your pastry edges before or after baking (if they need trimming) is a matter of personal preference. If there's an overhang, some prefer to trim before baking, others like to trim after the tart is baked so that any shrinkage has been accounted for. We find the second option creates a bit too many crumbs, so tend to trim things up before the tart goes in the oven. It's entirely up to you.

DOCKING THE PASTRY › Whether you dock the pastry—pricking it in a few places with the tines of a fork once the pan has been lined and before it is baked—is something we also leave up to you. The reason for docking is to prevent the pastry from rising and baking unevenly in the oven. It's not something we tend to do, regardless of whether the pie shells are being blind-baked or going straight in the oven with their filling, but if you were always taught to dock your pastry, there is no downside to doing so.

Working with pastry requires you to feel confident about assessing what you are creating and then making a call. If you've rolled your pastry a bit thinner than suggested, for example, it will need a minute or two less in the oven; thicker pastry will need a minute longer. The difference between the ideal slight wobble of a filling and a filling that is so unset as to still be liquid is something you need to be able to recognize. As we've said before, the best way to become a really confident baker is to make the same thing more than once—bake and rebake the same recipe until you can read it like an old friend. You'll soon know it better than it knows itself.

RHUBARB AND BLUEBERRY GALETTE

Rhubarb and blueberry galette

The rhubarb and blueberry are so good together here, but do play around with the fruits, if you like; figs and raspberries also pair nicely. If you'd prefer to use just one fruit, some thinly sliced peaches, apricots or apples work well. Serve this with whipped cream or vanilla ice cream alongside.

   The Amaretti cookies are useful for soaking up the excess liquid from the fruits. You want the dry, crumbly variety, not the soft and chewy ones. They're not hard to get hold of, but if you find yourself without, crushed ladyfingers or ground almonds can be used instead. They won't provide the flavor hit of the Amaretti, but will be fine.

SERVES 8

CREAM CHEESE PASTRY
8½ tbsp/120 g unsalted butter, fridge-
   cold, cut into ¾-inch/2-cm cubes
1⅓ cups plus 2 tbsp/185 g all-purpose
   flour, plus extra for dusting
¼ tsp salt
⅛ tsp baking powder
3 oz/85 g cream cheese
2–3 tbsp heavy cream
2 tsp cider vinegar

BASE
2 oz/55 g Amaretti cookies
3 tbsp/45 g granulated sugar
1 tbsp all-purpose flour
1 tsp ground cinnamon

FILLING
8 oz/230 g rhubarb, trimmed and
   washed, halved lengthwise, if thick,
   and cut into 2-inch/5-cm lengths
¾ cup/120 g fresh blueberries
½ cup/100 g granulated sugar
1 tbsp tapioca flour (or cornstarch)
finely grated zest of 1 small orange
   (1 tsp)
⅛ tsp salt

GLAZE
1 large egg
2 tsp water
1 tbsp demerara sugar

The pastry can be made 2 days in advance (it will last longer, but the cream cheese will make it discolor) and kept in the fridge, covered in plastic wrap. It can also be frozen, again covered in plastic wrap, for up to 2 months.

Once baked, this will keep for 1 day at room temperature.

1   **To make the cream cheese pastry,** cover the cubes of butter in plastic wrap and place in the freezer for about an hour to freeze solid. Place the flour, salt and baking powder in a resealable freezer bag and freeze for 30 minutes.

2   Tip the flour mixture into the bowl of a food processor and process for about 30 seconds to combine. Add the cream cheese and process for another 20 seconds, or until the mixture has the consistency of coarse breadcrumbs. Add the frozen butter cubes and pulse to form crumbs. They'll be uneven in size—some the size of peas and some a bit larger—but that's fine.

3   Add 2 Tbsp of the heavy cream and the vinegar and pulse until the dough starts to hold together; add the remaining 1 Tbsp cream if the dough needs it. Tip onto a clean work surface and use your hands and knuckles to press the mixture until it holds together in one piece. Cover the pastry loosely in plastic wrap (or put it in the bag you used to chill the flour) and press to flatten it into a disk. Place in the fridge for 45 minutes (or up to 2 days).

4   Preheat the oven to 400°F/200°C.

5   **To make the base,** roughly crush the Amaretti cookies in a small bowl. Add the granulated sugar, flour and cinnamon and set aside.

6   **To make the filling,** place all the filling ingredients in a medium bowl, toss gently to combine and then set aside.

7   Remove the disk of pastry from the fridge 10 minutes before you want to roll it, so that it has some malleability. Place it on a large sheet of parchment paper that has been lightly dusted with flour. Roll out evenly into a large circle, about 15 inches/38 cm wide and ⅛ inch/3 mm thick. Trim the edges to create a rough circle, then transfer it, along with the parchment paper (it is too soft to transfer alone), onto a large baking sheet. Sprinkle the base in a 10-inch/25-cm circle over the middle of the pastry. Spoon the fruit filling on top of the crumbs and then carefully draw the pastry border up and over the fruit, roughly pleating it as you go and leaving a small area of the fruit-filled center of the galette exposed. If the pastry has become too soft or warm during this process, place the galette in the fridge to chill for up to 1 hour before baking.

8   **To make the glaze,** beat the egg with the water in a bowl and brush all over the outside of the pastry, then sprinkle with the sugar.

9   Bake for about 40 minutes, rotating the baking sheet halfway through, or until the galette is golden. Remove from the oven and set aside on a wire rack to cool before serving.

Little baked chocolate tarts with tahini and sesame brittle (or marmalade)

Rather than making one large chocolate tart to serve after a meal (see Chocolate Tart with Hazelnut, Rosemary and Orange, page 241), it's sometimes fun to make lots of individual tarts. Chocolate mousse pairs so well with so many flavors that you can fill the base of these tarts with pretty much anything you like. We've given two options here—tahini and marmalade—but you can play around with other fillings, such as a teaspoon of crumbled halva, mint icing, some chopped nuts, a slice of banana, the brittle used in the large chocolate tart, a teaspoon of jam—they all work well. It's fun, if serving them as canapés, to have a mix of fillings, so that people have a pop of surprise. If you want to give a clue as to what's inside, you can do so with the garnish. A shard of Sesame Brittle (see page 334), works well on top of the tahini tarts (as pictured opposite), or a thin slice of candied orange peel on those with the marmalade filling.

We've included enough of the marmalade filling to fill one whole batch of tarts. If you want to do half and half, you'll just need to reduce the amount of filling you make.

MAKES 12
—

SWEET SHORTCRUST PASTRY
(YOU WILL NEED ONLY ⅔ QUANTITY)
2⅓ cups/300 g all-purpose flour, plus extra for dusting
¾ cup/90 g confectioners' sugar
¼ tsp salt
¾ cup plus 2 tbsp/200 g unsalted butter, fridge-cold, cut into cubes, plus 1 tbsp, melted, for brushing
finely grated zest of 1 lemon (1 tsp)
1 large egg yolk
4 tsp water

CHOCOLATE MOUSSE
7 oz/200 g chocolate (70% cocoa solids), roughly chopped
½ cup plus 2½ tbsp/150 g unsalted butter, roughly cut into ¾-inch/ 2-cm cubes
3 large eggs
¼ cup/50 g granulated sugar

TAHINI FILLING
⅔ cup plus 1 tbsp/180 g tahini paste
3 tbsp/60 g honey

MARMALADE FILLING
(HALVE THE QUANTITIES IF YOU ARE DOING ½ BATCH WITH MARMALADE AND ½ WITH TAHINI)
½ cup/180 g fine-cut or no-peel Seville marmalade

Dutch-processed cocoa powder, for dusting
½ cup/120 g mascarpone

The pastry will make more than you'll need. It keeps well in the fridge, covered in plastic wrap, for up to 3 days. It also freezes well, covered first in plastic wrap and then aluminum foil, for up to 2 months. If freezing the dough, do so in disk form or, if planning to make individual tarts, roll it out and cut it to size so that you're all set for your next bake.

Once baked, any uneaten tarts may be kept at room temperature or in the fridge for up to 2 days. If kept in the fridge, just bring them back to room temperature before serving.

1   **To make the sweet shortcrust pastry,** sift together the flour, confectioners' sugar and salt and place in a food processor. Add the butter and lemon zest and pulse a few times, until the mixture has the consistency of fresh breadcrumbs. Lightly whisk together the egg yolk and water and add this to the mix; the dough will feel quite wet, but this is as it should be. Process once more, just until the dough comes together, ›

then tip onto a clean, lightly floured work surface. Lightly knead the dough into a ball. Cover loosely in plastic wrap and press gently to form a flattish disk. The pastry is very soft, so keep it in the fridge for 1 hour (or up to 3 days).

2   Lightly brush the molds of a regular muffin pan with the melted butter and dust with flour, tapping away the excess.

3   When ready to roll out, allow the pastry to rest at room temperature for 30 minutes (if it has been in the fridge for more than a few hours) and place on a lightly floured work surface. Tap all over with a rolling pin to soften slightly before rolling out to ⅛ inch/ 3 mm thick. Using a 4-inch/10-cm round cookie cutter (or alternative, see page 228), cut out twelve circles and gently ease these into the muffin molds, pressing down to fill the molds. Reroll the scraps if necessary, until you get twelve circles. Refrigerate for 1 hour before blind-baking the cases. The remaining third of the dough can be frozen for future use.

4   Preheat the oven to 350°F/180°C.

5   Line the pastry shells in the muffin molds with squares of parchment paper or paper muffin liners. Fill with rice or dried beans. Bake for 20–25 minutes, or until the tart shells are a light golden brown around the edges. Remove the rice and paper and return the shells to the oven for another 3 minutes. Set the pastry shells aside (still in their molds) to cool down.

6   **To make the chocolate mousse,** place the chocolate and butter in a large heatproof bowl over a pan of simmering water, making sure the base of the bowl is not touching the water. Stir occasionally until melted, then remove from the heat and set aside to cool for about 10 minutes.

7   Place the eggs and sugar in the bowl of an electric mixer with the whisk attachment in place. Beat on high speed for 10 minutes, until the mixture is extremely pale, thick and foamy and has tripled in volume. Remove the bowl from the machine and, using a large slotted spoon or hand whisk, gently fold a third of the mixture into the melted chocolate and butter. Gently but thoroughly fold in the rest of the egg-sugar mixture until well combined.

8   Increase the oven temperature to 400°F/200°C.

9   **To make the tahini filling,** place the tahini and honey in the bowl of the electric mixer with the whisk attachment in place and beat until thickened, about 3 minutes. Spoon 1 tbsp into the base of each tart shell and set aside. **If using the marmalade filling,** spoon 1 tbsp into the base of each shell and set aside.

10   Pipe or spoon the mousse over the tahini or marmalade filling, right up to and over the rim. Be confident here; you want the mousse to rise up and form a dome shape. Bake for 9–10 minutes, until a crust has formed on top but the center is still gooey. Set aside to cool completely in the pan—the tarts are too molten to be served warm. When cool, use the tip of a small knife to pry the tarts out of their molds. Dust lightly with cocoa powder and use two small teaspoons to form quenelles of mascarpone to top each tart before serving.

Mont Blanc tarts

Named after the snowy mountain they resemble, Mont Blanc tarts—with their white meringue, whipped cream and tan-colored chestnut purée—can often taste more fabulous than they look, with all that beige and white. We wanted to see if we could improve their visual appeal—bring in some more contrast by playing around with the colors, for example—but after various experiments (dark chocolate pastry, a lighter-colored purée), we were beginning to think that the timetested route up this particular mountain was the only winning one.

It was a moment of pure synchronicity, then, that at one of our weekly pastry meetings there were various things lying around that came together in a flash: empty tart shells, candied pecans, an open can of chestnut spread. At the same time, Helen and Yotam both grabbed an empty shell, filled it with the chestnut spread, spooned over smooth whipped cream and added the element that had been missing—the candied pecans—which brought the crunch and the look needed. There's a metaphor in there, we're sure, about climbing mountains, not giving up and things tasting all the sweeter when you've had to work just a little bit harder to earn them.

MAKES 8

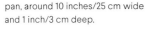

You will need eight mini fluted tart pans, about 3½ inch/9 cm wide and 1 inch/3 cm deep. Alternatively, you can make this in one large fluted tart pan, around 10 inches/25 cm wide and 1 inch/3 cm deep.

The pastry can be made up to 3 days ahead and kept in the fridge (covered in plastic wrap) until ready to roll. It can also be frozen for up to 2 months. The candied pecans can be made up to 5 days in advance and kept in an airtight container.

Once assembled, the tarts are best eaten on the day they are baked.

FLAKY PASTRY
1⅔ cups/200 g all-purpose flour
8½ tbsp/120 g unsalted butter, fridge-cold, cut into ⅓-inch/1-cm cubes, plus extra, melted, for brushing
2 tbsp granulated sugar
¼ tsp salt
½ tsp white wine vinegar
3 tbsp ice-cold water

CANDIED PECANS
1 tbsp maple syrup
1 tbsp light corn syrup
1 tbsp granulated sugar
1 cup/120 g pecan halves
⅛ tsp flaky sea salt

FILLING
2 oz/55 g dark chocolate (70% cocoa solids)
1 cup/320 g sweetened chestnut spread (we use Clement Faugier; whichever brand you use, just make sure that it is not the unsweetened variety)

VANILLA WHIPPED CREAM
1¼ cups/300 ml heavy cream
1 tbsp confectioners' sugar
1 tsp vanilla extract
½ tsp brandy

1   **To make the flaky pastry,** place the flour, butter, sugar and salt in the bowl of a food processor. Pulse a few times, until it is the consistency of fine breadcrumbs, then add the vinegar and water. Continue to pulse for a few seconds, then transfer to a work surface. Shape into a ball and flatten into a disk, cover in plastic wrap and set aside in the fridge for 1 hour (or up to 3 days).

2   Preheat the oven to 400°F/200°C.

3   When ready to roll out, allow the pastry to rest at room temperature for 30 minutes (if it has been in the fridge for more than a few hours) and place on a lightly floured work surface. Roll out the dough to about ⅛ inch/3 mm thick and cut out eight circles, 5½ inches/14 cm wide. Reroll the dough, if necessary, to get eight circles. **»**

4   Transfer one circle at a time to the 3½-inch/9-cm-wide and 1-inch/3-cm-deep fluted tart pans and gently press the pastry into the corners of the pan; you want it to fit snugly and for there to be a decent amount of pastry hanging over the edge of the pan, as the pastry can shrink a little when baked. Place in the fridge for 30 minutes to rest.

5   Line the pastry shells in the pans with parchment paper or paper liners and fill with rice or dried beans. Bake for 18 minutes, until the pastry is golden brown at the edges. Remove the rice and paper and bake for another 8 minutes, or until the shell is golden brown. Remove from the oven and set aside to cool completely on the baking sheet. Once cool, trim the shell (so that it can be removed from the pans) and set aside until ready to fill.

6   Line a rimmed baking sheet with parchment paper and set aside.

7   **To make the candied pecans,** combine the maple syrup, corn syrup and granulated sugar in a small saucepan and place over a low heat. Stir gently until the sugar has melted, then add the pecans and salt. Stir so that the nuts are coated in the syrup, then tip the nuts onto the lined baking sheet. Place in the oven for about 0 minutes, or until the syrup is bubbling around the nuts. Remove the baking sheet from the oven and set aside until completely cooled. When the nuts are cooled, the glaze should be completely crisp; if not, return them to the oven for a few minutes more. Once cooled, break or roughly chop the nuts into ¼-inch/0.5-cm pieces and set aside until ready to use.

8   **To make the filling,** place the chocolate in a heatproof bowl over a pan of simmering water, making sure that the base of the bowl is not touching the water. Stir occasionally until melted, then use a pastry brush to coat the inside of each tart shell with the chocolate. Set aside for about 30 minutes, to set, then fill with enough chestnut spread so that it rises about halfway up the sides of the tart shells.

9   **To make the vanilla whipped cream,** pour the cream into the bowl of an electric mixer with the whisk attachment in place. Add the confectioners' sugar, vanilla extract and brandy and beat on high speed for 1 minute, or until medium-soft peaks form.

10   Divide the whipped cream among the tarts, so that it is slightly domed on top of the chestnut spread. Sprinkle the candied pecans generously on top—you might have a tablespoon or two left over, but these can be saved to munch on, to sprinkle over your next bowl of breakfast granola or porridge, or to use in the Knickerbocker Glory (see page 293)—and serve.

Chai brûlée tarts

We've taken our inspiration for these from Sydney's Bourke Street Bakery, where Yotam had his first bite of their brûlée tarts. We've ramped up and chai-i-fied the spices, and we bake our custard in the oven (rather than on the stove top, as they do), so it is set. A layer of skin can develop on the surface of the custard, but don't worry; once it's spooned into the tart shells and the tops are sugared and burnt, the skin won't be noticed, so don't be tempted to take it off. Hold your nerve when caramelizing the custard: the darker you can take it the better, in terms of flavor, contrast and looks.

MAKES 8–12

We use twelve fluted tart pans, 3½ inches/9 cm wide and 1 inch/3 cm deep. If you have 4-inch/10-cm round tart pans, that's also fine; you'll just make eight tarts rather than twelve. You will also need a blowtorch to caramelize the custard (don't place them under a broiler, as the pastry will burn). You don't need anything industrial or expensive; there are lots of smaller ones around that do the job well.

The pastry can be made up to 3 days ahead and kept in the fridge (covered in plastic wrap) until ready to roll. It can also be frozen for up to 2 months. You need to start preparing the custard a day ahead to allow the flavors to infuse.

Once assembled, the tartlets are best eaten on the day they are baked.

CUSTARD

2⅓ cups/560 ml heavy cream
2⅓-inch/6-cm piece of fresh ginger (1⅔ oz/45 g), peeled and coarsely grated
7 cardamom pods, crushed, so that the seeds are released
3 large cinnamon sticks, broken in half
1 English breakfast tea bag
3 bay leaves
½ tsp whole black peppercorns
1 whole nutmeg
¼ cup plus 1 tbsp/60 g granulated sugar, plus ⅓ cup plus 2 tsp/80 g for the caramelized topping
6 oz/165 g egg yolks (from 8 large eggs) (the whites can be frozen for future use)

FLAKY PASTRY

1⅔ cups/200 g all-purpose flour
8½ tbsp/120 g unsalted butter, fridge-cold, cut into ⅓-inch/1-cm dice, plus extra, melted, for brushing
2 tbsp granulated sugar
¼ tsp salt
½ tsp white wine vinegar
3 tbsp ice-cold water

1 **To make the custard,** place the cream in a large, heavy pan and add the ginger, cardamom pods and seeds, cinnamon sticks, tea bag, bay leaves, peppercorns, nutmeg and ¼ cup plus 1 tbsp/60 g sugar. Bring slowly to a boil, then remove from the heat straightaway. Set aside to cool and then refrigerate, covered, overnight.

2 The following day, preheat the oven to 350°F/180°C.

3 Gently warm the infused cream over medium heat before straining through a fine-mesh sieve into a bowl and discarding the spices and tea bag. Place the egg yolks in a large clean bowl and whisk to combine. Slowly pour the cream over the eggs, whisking the whole time so that the eggs don't curdle. Transfer the mixture to an 8-inch/20-cm square glass or ceramic ovenproof dish and place this inside a larger baking pan. Place the pan in the oven before filling it with enough boiling water (poured straight from a just-boiled kettle) so that it rises halfway up the sides of the baking dish filled with the custard. Bake for 15–20 minutes, until just cooked; the middle will be a bit wobbly but the edges will have set completely. Lift the custard dish out of the water bath and set aside to cool before covering and chilling for about an hour, or until ready to use. Don't worry if a skin forms on top (see introduction). ››

4   **To make the flaky pastry,** place the flour, butter, sugar and salt in the bowl of a food processor. Pulse a few times, until it's the consistency of fine breadcrumbs, then add the vinegar and water. Continue to pulse for a few seconds, then transfer to your work surface. Shape into a ball and flatten into a disk, cover in plastic wrap and set aside in the fridge for 1 hour (or up to 3 days).

5   Lightly brush twelve fluted tart pans, 3⅓ inches/9 cm wide and 1 inch/3 cm deep, with melted butter. When ready to roll out, allow the dough to rest at room temperature for 30 minutes (if it has been in the fridge for more than a few hours) and place on a lightly floured work surface. Roll out the dough until it is just ⅛ inch/ 3 mm thick, then cut out twelve circles, 5 inches/13 cm wide. Reroll the scraps, if necessary, to get twelve circles. Gently press the dough into the corners of the tart pans so that it fits snugly; if there is any pastry hanging over the edges, trim this now. Place in the fridge for 30 minutes to allow the pastry to rest.

6   Preheat the oven to 400°F/200°C.

7   Place the tart pans on a baking sheet, then line the pastry in the pans with squares of parchment paper or paper muffin liners and fill with rice or dried beans. Bake for 18 minutes, until the shells are golden brown at the edges. Remove the rice and paper and bake for another 9–10 minutes, until golden brown. Don't worry if your pastry shrinks a bit during cooking; you actually want a little bit of shrinkage to ensure the perfect ratio of custard to pastry. Don't worry, also, if the edges become a little uneven; once the tarts are filled with custard and the surface has been blowtorched, this will not be noticeable. Remove from the oven and set aside to cool.

8   Just before serving, remove the pastry shells from the pans. Carefully spoon the custard into the shells, filling them all the way to the top. Use an offset spatula to even them off—not worrying, again, if the edges are uneven at this stage—then sprinkle the remaining sugar liberally on top of each one. Using a kitchen blowtorch, melt the sugar to create a crisp, dark golden caramel, and serve.

Chocolate tart with hazelnut, rosemary and orange

This rich and decadent tart is essentially a baked chocolate mousse. On its own, it is smooth and rich and really rather good. Coupled with the hazelnut crunch on the crust—which is similar to a brittle but easier to make, as you don't have to make a caramel—it's the high point on which to end a meal, alongside some lightly whipped cream to offset the richness.

SERVES 8–10

The pastry makes more than you'll need. It keeps well in the fridge, covered in plastic wrap, for up to 3 days. It also freezes well, covered first in plastic wrap and then aluminum foil, for up to 2 months. If freezing the dough, do so in disk form. The crunch can be made up to 5 days in advance and kept in an airtight container at room temperature, or frozen for up to 1 month. Don't keep it in the fridge, where it will weep. The infused cream can be prepared up to 1 day ahead and kept in the fridge. The crystallized rosemary sprigs can be made a day in advance and left at room temperature, uncovered, until ready to serve.

This can be made in a 9- or 10-inch/ 23- or 25-cm fluted tart pan with a removable base.

Once assembled, the tart is best eaten on the day it is baked but will keep for up to 2 days, stored in an airtight container.

CRYSTALLIZED ROSEMARY SPRIG GARNISH (OPTIONAL)
1–2 sprigs rosemary (⅛ oz/5 g)
½ large egg white, lightly beaten
1½ tbsp granulated sugar

FILLING
½ cup/120 ml heavy cream
6 tbsp/85 g unsalted butter, cubed
3 sprigs of rosemary (¼ oz/10 g)
shaved peel of 1 orange (avoiding the bitter white pith)
9 oz/260 g dark chocolate (70% cocoa solids), finely chopped
1 large egg, plus 3 large egg yolks
⅓ cup plus 1 tbsp/90 g granulated sugar
2 tbsp Dutch-processed cocoa powder, to serve

HAZELNUT CRUNCH
2 tbsp light corn syrup
2 tbsp maple syrup (or honey)
2 tbsp granulated sugar
⅛ tsp salt
¾ cup/100 g chopped toasted hazelnuts

SWEET SHORTCRUST PASTRY
(YOU WILL NEED ONLY ½ QUANTITY)
2⅔ cups/300 g all-purpose flour, plus extra for dusting
¾ cup/90 g confectioners' sugar
¼ tsp salt
¾ cup plus 2 tbsp/200 g unsalted butter, fridge-cold, cut into cubes, plus 1 tbsp, melted, for brushing
finely grated zest of 1 lemon (1 tsp)
1 large egg yolk
4 tsp water

1   **To make the crystallized rosemary sprigs,** lay the sprigs flat on a cutting board and, one at a time, lightly brush each side with the egg white. Sprinkle the sugar evenly and lightly over both sides of the leaves, then set aside in a cool, dry place on a wire rack for about 8 hours, until crisp.

2   **To make the filling,** place the cream, butter, rosemary and orange peel in a small saucepan and set over low heat. When the mixture is just coming to a simmer and the butter has melted, turn off the heat and refrigerate for an hour or two, or overnight, to infuse.

3   **To make the hazelnut crunch,** preheat the oven to 425°F/220°C. Place the corn syrup, maple syrup, sugar and salt in a small saucepan over low heat and stir until the sugar has dissolved. Add the hazelnuts and stir until the nuts are evenly coated, then transfer the mixture to a small parchment paper–lined baking sheet and spread the nuts out with a spoon. Bake for 7–8 minutes, until the mixture is golden brown and bubbling, then remove from the oven and allow to cool completely before roughly chopping into ¼-inch/0.5-cm pieces. Set aside until ready to use and turn off the oven. ››

4   **To make the sweet shortcrust pastry,** sift together the flour, confectioners' sugar and salt and place in a food processor. Add the butter and lemon zest and pulse a few times, until the mixture has the consistency of fresh breadcrumbs. Lightly whisk together the egg yolk and water and add this to the mix; the dough will feel quite wet, but this is as it should be. Process once more, just until the dough comes together, then tip onto a clean, lightly floured work surface. Lightly knead the dough into a ball and divide into two equal halves. Cover each half loosely in plastic wrap and press gently to form two flattish disks. The pastry is very soft, so you need to set it aside in the fridge for 1 hour (or up to 3 days).

5   Lightly grease your chosen tart pan, see Note on page 241. When ready to roll out, allow the pastry to rest at room temperature for 30 minutes (if it has been in the fridge for more than a few hours) and place on a lightly floured work surface. Tap all over with a rolling pin to soften slightly before rolling out, until it's about 13 inches/ 33 cm wide and ⅛ inch/3 mm thick. Drape the pastry over the pan and gently press it into place, filling any cracks that you have with a little extra pastry. Trim if desired, then place the pastry in the fridge for 30 minutes to rest and chill. The remaining pastry can be frozen for future use.

6   Preheat the oven to 400°F/200°C.

7   Line the pastry in the pan with a large piece of parchment paper, covering the base and sides and fill with rice or dried beans. Bake for 20 minutes. Remove the rice and paper and bake uncovered, for another 6–7 minutes, or until lightly golden and dry. Remove from the oven and allow to cool for 10 minutes before sprinkling the chopped hazelnut crunch all over the bottom of the shell. Set aside until needed.

8   Place the chocolate for the filling in a heatproof bowl set over a pan of simmering water, making sure the base of the bowl isn't touching the water. Return the infused cream to low heat and stir gently until hot. Strain the cream over the chocolate (the rosemary and orange peel can be discarded), then stir the chocolate (still over the pan of simmering water) until melted and smooth. Remove the bowl from the pan and set aside.

9   In the meantime, place the egg, yolks and sugar in the bowl of an electric mixer with the whisk attachment in place. Beat on medium-high speed for about 4 minutes, until light and thick. Fold about a third of this mixture into the melted chocolate, then gently transfer the lightened chocolate mixture back into the mixer bowl. Fold to fully combine.

10   Scrape the chocolate filling into the tart shell, over the hazelnut crunch and gently smooth out the top. Bake for 12 minutes, then remove from the oven and set aside for 20 minutes or so to cool. Using a tea strainer or small sieve, sift the cocoa powder over the tart and place the crystallized rosemary on top, if desired, just before serving.

Walnut and black treacle tarts with crystallized sage

To say this is a very treacly tart might seem like tautology, but, in the world of treacle tarts, it's an especially soft and gooey offering. True British treacle is hard to come by in the United States, so you can substitute molasses—although we're still calling it a "treacle" tart. As well as being rich and sweet, this version's got an edge of malty crispness from the addition of the bran flakes.

The crystallized sage leaves look great here but they can be replaced with fresh sage leaves, if you like. Alternatively, you can serve the tarts without any garnish at all, with just a generous amount of crème fraîche or some vanilla ice cream.

SERVES 8

You will need eight mini fluted tart pans, 3½ inches/9 cm wide and 1 inch/3 cm deep. Alternatively, you can make this in one large fluted tart pan, 10 inches/25 cm wide and 1 inch/3 cm deep.

The pastry can be made up to 3 days ahead and kept in the fridge (covered in plastic wrap) until ready to roll. It can also be frozen for up to 2 months. The sage leaves need to be made in advance in order to dry, and should be left at room temperature, uncovered, until ready to serve. They can be made a day in advance.

Once assembled, the tarts are best eaten on the day they are baked. They still taste great for 2–3 days afterward, they'll just lose their crispness.

CRYSTALLIZED SAGE LEAF GARNISH (OPTIONAL)
8 nice flat fresh sage leaves
1 large egg white, lightly beaten
2 tbsp granulated sugar

FLAKY PASTRY
1⅔ cups/200 g all-purpose flour
8½ tbsp/120 g unsalted butter, fridge-cold, cut into ⅓-inch/1-cm cubes, plus extra, melted, for brushing
2 tbsp granulated sugar
¼ tsp salt
½ tsp white wine vinegar
3 tbsp ice-cold water

FILLING
1½ cups/180 g walnut halves
4 oz/110 g whole wheat sourdough bread (crusts removed), roughly torn
1 cup/50 g bran flakes
finely grated zest from 1 small orange (1 tsp)
¼ cup/100 g blackstrap molasses (or black treacle)
⅔ cup plus 2 tsp/220 g dark corn syrup (or golden syrup)
2 tbsp/30 g unsalted butter
6 tbsp plus 2 tsp/100 ml heavy cream
2 large eggs, lightly beaten

1 **To make the crystallized sage leaves,** lay the leaves on a cutting board. One at a time, brush each side lightly with the egg white. Sprinkle the sugar evenly and lightly over both sides and set on a wire rack in a cool, dry place for 8 hours, until crisp.

2 **To make the flaky pastry,** place the flour, butter, sugar and salt in the bowl of a food processor. Pulse a few times, until it is the consistency of fine breadcrumbs, then add the vinegar and water. Continue to pulse for a few seconds, then transfer to your work surface. Shape into a ball and flatten into a disk, cover in plastic wrap and set aside in the fridge for 1 hour (or up to 3 days).

3 Lightly brush eight fluted tart pans, 3½ inches/9 cm wide and ¾ inch/2 cm deep (or one larger pan; see Note), with melted butter. When ready to roll out, allow the pastry to rest at room temperature for 30 minutes (if it has been in the fridge for more than a few hours) and place on a lightly floured work surface. Roll out until just under ¼ inch/0.5 cm thick, then cut out eight circles, 5½ inches/14 cm wide, and transfer to the tart pans. Reroll the scraps, if necessary, to get eight circles. If you are making one large tart, roll out the dough to form a 13-inch/33-cm circle. Gently press the pastry into the corners of the tart pans so that it fits snugly. There will be some pastry hanging over the sides of the pans, but don't trim it at this stage. Place in the fridge for 30 minutes to allow the pastry to rest. »

4   Preheat the oven to 350°F/180°C. Spread the walnuts out on a rimmed baking sheet and roast in the oven for 10 minutes, until golden brown. Set aside to cool and then increase the oven temperature to 400°F/200°C.

5   Line the pastry in the pans with squares of parchment paper or paper liners and fill with rice or beans. Bake for 18–20 minutes (or 25 minutes for the larger tart), until the pastry is golden brown at the edges. Remove the rice and paper and bake for another 10 minutes, or 12 minutes for the larger tart, until the base is golden brown. Remove from the oven and set aside to cool.

6   **To make the filling,** place the bread and bran flakes in the small bowl of a food processor and process to form fine crumbs. Transfer to a large bowl and then process two-thirds of the walnuts to fine crumbs in the food processor. Add these to the breadcrumb mixture along with the orange zest. Roughly chop the remaining walnuts and add to the bowl. Mix to combine and set aside.

7   Put the blackstrap molasses, dark corn syrup and butter in a small saucepan and place over high heat. Cook for 2–3 minutes, stirring frequently, until the butter has melted and the syrup is runny. Pour into the bowl with the breadcrumb mixture, combine well and stir in the cream and eggs.

8   Pour the molasses mixture into the tart shells and bake for 17 minutes (the larger tart will need a minute or two longer), until just set. Remove from the oven and set aside to cool for about 20 minutes before trimming the pastry edges; this can be done by snapping off the overhanging edges with your fingers or by running a small knife around the outside of the pan. Remove from the pans and serve warm or at room temperature with a crispy sage leaf on top, if desired.

Fig and pistachio frangipane tartlets

These received an official thumbs-up when Yotam posted a picture of them online from the display of our Belgravia shop. The stunningly Instagrammable picture—with the cut side of the figs facing up in the tarts—was flooded with thousands of likes. They are lovely as they are, or served with a spoonful of vanilla ice cream or crème fraîche alongside.

If you can't get large figs, use six smaller ones sliced in half (rather than quarters). Alternatively, raspberries work just as well; place three large raspberries in the center of each tart and bake as usual.

As with many of our recipes that call for a nip of brandy, don't worry if you don't have an open bottle on hand. It's not there for its own flavor so much as to draw out the subtle flavor of the pistachios, but the tartlets work fine without it.

MAKES 12

The pastry makes more than you'll need. It keeps well in the fridge, covered in plastic wrap, for up to 3 days. It also freezes well, covered first in plastic wrap and then aluminum foil, for up to 2 months. If freezing the dough, do so in disk form or, if planning to make individual tarts, roll it out and cut it to size so that you're all set for your next bake. The frangipane cream can be made up to 2 days in advance and kept in the fridge until ready to use. It will set reasonably firm, so remove it from the fridge 30 minutes before you want to fill the tarts.

Once assembled, these are best eaten on the day they are baked. They will keep for up to 2 days, stored in an airtight container. You can eat them at room temperature or heat them through for 5 minutes before serving.

SWEET SHORTCRUST PASTRY
(YOU WILL NEED ONLY ⅔ QUANTITY)
2⅓ cups/300 g all-purpose flour, plus extra for dusting
¾ cup/90 g confectioners' sugar
¼ tsp salt
¾ cup plus 2 tbsp/200 g unsalted butter, fridge-cold, cut into cubes, plus 1 tbsp, melted, for brushing
finely grated zest of 1 lemon (1 tsp)
1 large egg yolk
4 tsp water

PISTACHIO FRANGIPANE CREAM
⅔ cup/90 g shelled pistachio kernels, plus more, blitzed in a food processor, for sprinkling (optional)
⅓ cup/35 g almond meal
¼ cup/35 g all-purpose flour
⅛ tsp salt
½ cup plus 1 tbsp/125 g unsalted butter, at room temperature
½ cup plus 1 tbsp/120 g granulated sugar
finely grated zest of 1 lemon (1 tsp)
2 large eggs, lightly beaten
1 tbsp brandy (optional)
3 large ripe figs, quartered, or 6 smaller figs, halved (6½ oz/180 g)

1   **To make the sweet shortcrust pastry,** sift together the flour, confectioners' sugar and salt and place in a food processor. Add the butter and lemon zest and pulse a few times, until the mixture has the consistency of fresh breadcrumbs. Lightly whisk together the egg yolk and water and add this to the mixture; the dough will feel quite wet, but this is as it should be. Process once more, just until the dough comes together, then tip onto a clean, lightly floured work surface. Lightly knead the dough into a ball, cover loosely in plastic wrap and press gently to form a flattish disk. The pastry is very soft, so you need to keep it in the fridge for 1 hour (or up to 3 days).
2   Lightly brush the molds of a regular muffin pan with the melted butter and dust with flour, tapping away the excess. ››

3   When ready to roll out, allow the pastry to rest at room temperature for 30 minutes (if it has been in the fridge for more than a few hours) and place on a lightly floured work surface. Tap all over with a rolling pin to soften slightly before rolling out until ⅛ inch/ 3 mm thick. Using a 4-inch/10-cm round cookie cutter (or alternative, see page 228), cut out twelve circles and gently ease these into the muffin molds, pressing down to fill the molds. Reroll the scraps, if necessary, until you get twelve circles. Refrigerate for 1 hour before blind-baking shells. The remaining third of the dough can be frozen for future use.

4   Preheat the oven to 350°F/180°C.

5   Line the pastry in the muffin molds with parchment paper or paper muffin liners and fill with rice or dried beans. Bake for 25–30 minutes, or until the pastry shells are a light golden brown around the edges. Remove the rice and paper and set the shells aside to cool in the pan.

6   **To make the pistachio frangipane cream,** place the pistachios in the small bowl of a food processor and grind until fine but not oily. Transfer to a small bowl, mix in the almond meal, flour and salt and set aside.

7   Place the butter, sugar and lemon zest in the bowl of an electric mixer with the paddle attachment in place. Beat on medium speed for 1–2 minutes, until light but not too fluffy. Turn the speed to low and gradually add the beaten eggs. Don't worry if the mixture curdles a bit at this stage; it will be brought back together later. Add the flour mixture, beat on low speed until combined and, finally, add the brandy (if using).

8   Increase the oven temperature to 400°F/200°C.

9   When ready to bake, use a piping bag or two tablespoons to fill the baked tart shells (still in the muffin pan) with the frangipane; it should rise about two-thirds of the way up the sides of the shells. Place a quarter (or half) of a fig in the middle of each tart, cut side facing up, pressing down very lightly so that it's slightly embedded in the mixture. Bake the tarts for about 20 minutes, until the frangipane starts to brown at the edges but the middle remains slightly soft. Set aside to cool in the pan for 10 minutes before easing the tarts out of the molds and placing on a wire rack. The tarts can either be served warm or left to come to room temperature and sprinkled with blitzed pistachios, if desired.

Schiacciata with grapes and fennel seeds

This is neither a tart nor a pie, we know. But in the absence of a bread or yeasted chapter, temporary lodgings have been found here for the schiacciata. It's a delicious alternative to bread at breakfast, but great as a snack or before a meal at any time of the day. It's basically a very thin focaccia with—thanks to the oil—a nice crisp bottom. We use normal black grapes here, as they are easy to come by. If you can find Italian strawberry grapes (uva fragola) or muscat grapes, you'll get an extra layer of sweet flavor. Making your own bread is always rewarding, but when the rewards are coupled with very little effort, as is the case here, it feels like a double win.

SERVES 4–6

2⅔ cups/330 g bread flour, plus extra
   for dusting
¾ tsp active dry yeast
¾ cup plus 2 tbsp/200 ml lukewarm
   water (about 105°F/40°C)
about ½ cup/120 ml olive oil
1 large egg yolk

3½ tbsp dark muscovado sugar
2 tsp flaky sea salt
9 oz/260 g seedless black grapes,
   halved lengthwise
1 tbsp fennel seeds, lightly crushed
   in a pestle and mortar
2 tsp polenta

You will need a large baking dish, about 15 x 11 inches/38 x 28 cm.

The bread is best eaten while still warm and crunchy, but any leftovers will keep for up to a day.

1   Place half the flour in the bowl of an electric mixer and add the yeast. Pour in the water and stir well to form a wet dough. Cover with plastic wrap and set aside for 1 hour, in a warm and draft-free place, for the dough to rise slightly.

2   Transfer the bowl of dough to the mixer with the dough hook attachment in place. Add the remaining flour, 1 tbsp of the olive oil, the egg yolk, 1½ tsp of the sugar and 1 tsp of the salt. Beat on medium-low speed for 6 minutes, until the dough comes together into a sticky ball. Transfer to a large bowl that has been brushed with 1 tbsp oil, cover with plastic wrap and set aside for 1 hour until doubled in size.

3   Place the grapes in a small bowl with the fennel seeds and 2 tbsp sugar. Mix together and set aside in a warm place for 1 hour.

4   Preheat the oven to 475°F/250°C.

5   Tip the dough onto a lightly floured work surface and pull into a large 15 x 11-inch/38 x 28-cm rectangle—either stretch it by hand or use a rolling pin, if that helps. Brush a 15 x 11-inch/38 x 28-cm baking sheet (or similar size) with 3 tbsp oil and sprinkle evenly with the polenta. Transfer the dough onto the baking sheet, stretching out the edges if necessary to fit snugly. Brush with the remaining 2 tbsp oil, then spoon over the grape mixture, mashing some of the grapes with your fingers as you go. Sprinkle the final 1 tbsp sugar and remaining 1 tsp salt evenly over the dough and leave to rest for 10 minutes.

6   Bake for 12–14 minutes, rotating the baking sheet halfway through, until the dough is crisp and a deep golden brown. Remove from the oven and cool for 10–15 minutes before serving warm.

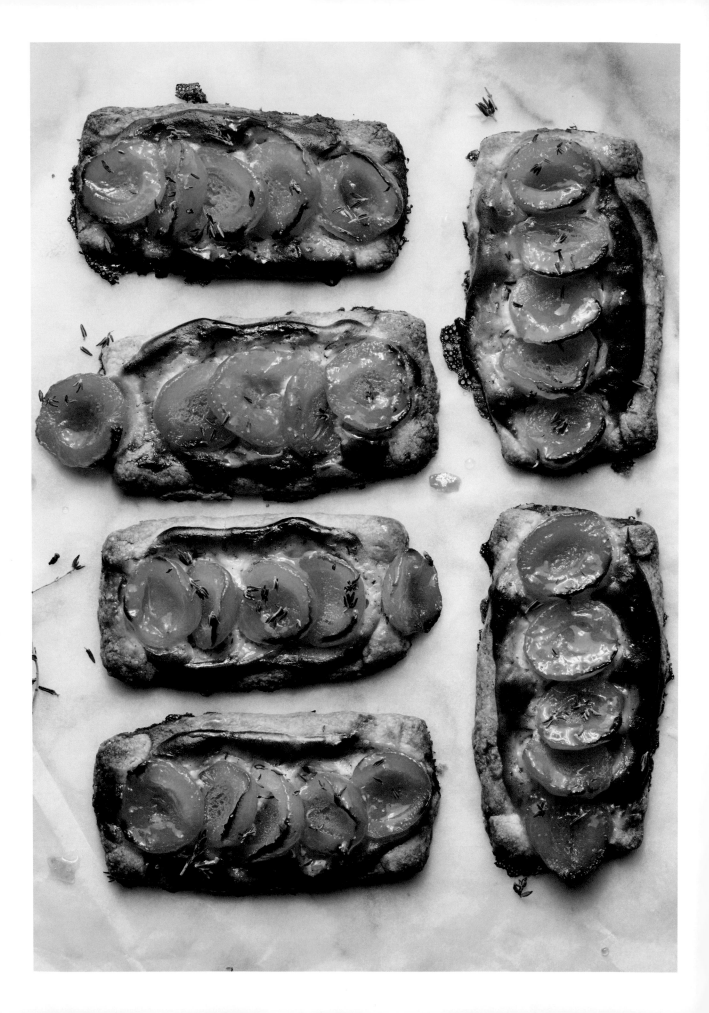

Apricot and thyme galettes with polenta pastry

We're so used to using fresh fruit for the cakes and pastries in our shops that it's easy to become a bit snobby about canned fruit. When a fruit has a very short season, such as apricots, however, the canned version can be a great option. It means that they are available year-round and that the quality is consistently high. Canned peaches also work well—if you want to play around. Mixing some polenta into the dough here is what gives the baked pastry its wonderful crunch.

MAKES 6

The pastry can be made up to a week in advance, covered in plastic wrap and kept in the fridge, or kept in the freezer for up to a month. The pastry cream can be made 2 days in advance and stored in an airtight container in the fridge.

Once assembled, these are best eaten on the day they are baked. They're still fine the following day, stored in the fridge overnight; either bring them back to room temperature before eating or, better still, warm them gently in the oven.

POLENTA PASTRY
½ cup plus 1½ tbsp/90 g
   all-purpose flour
¼ cup/45 g quick-cook polenta
2 tbsp granulated sugar
6 tbsp/85 g unsalted butter, fridge-
   cold, cut into ⅓-inch/1-cm pieces
⅛ tsp salt
1 tbsp cold water

PASTRY CREAM
6 tbsp plus 2 tsp/100 ml whole milk
scraped seeds of ¼ vanilla pod
1 tsp thyme leaves, finely chopped,
   plus 1 tsp leaves, to garnish
2 tsp unsalted butter
1½ tbsp granulated sugar
1 large egg yolk
1½ tsp cornstarch
1 tsp all-purpose flour

two 15-oz/425-g cans of apricot halves,
   in syrup, or 9–12 fresh apricots
   (depending on size), halved
2 tbsp honey, slightly warm
2 tbsp apricot jam, to glaze
1½ tbsp water

1   To make the polenta pastry, place the flour, polenta, sugar, butter and salt in a food processor and process until the mixture has the consistency of breadcrumbs. Add the water and continue to process, just until the dough comes together. Tip the dough onto a clean work surface and knead gently; you just want to bring the pastry together without overworking it. Cover loosely in plastic wrap, flatten into a rectangle and store in the fridge for about 1 hour.

2   **To make the pastry cream,** place the milk, vanilla seeds, thyme, butter and half the sugar in a small saucepan. Heat gently until the milk is just coming to a simmer and bubbles are beginning to form around the sides.

3   In the meantime, combine the egg yolk with the remaining sugar, cornstarch and flour in a medium bowl and whisk together to form a paste. Just as the milk is coming to a simmer, slowly whisk half of it into the egg yolk mixture. (It helps to have a damp cloth underneath the bowl to steady it while you whisk with one hand and pour with the other.) Once combined, whisk this back into the remaining hot milk and cook over medium-low heat for 3–5 minutes, until very thick and smooth. Check it is ready by lifting some of the mixture out of the pan on the whisk; it should slowly drop off. ››

4   Transfer the pastry cream to a clean bowl or measuring cup, cover with plastic wrap—you want it to be actually touching the surface of the custard to prevent it forming a skin—and set aside in the fridge until completely cool.

5   Remove the pastry from the fridge a few minutes before rolling it out, so that it becomes malleable. Line a baking sheet (that will fit in your fridge) with parchment paper.

6   Roll out the pastry on a lightly floured surface to form a 17 x 6-inch/43 x 15-cm rectangle, ¼ inch/0.5 cm thick. Trim the edges so that it is approximately 16 x 5 inches/41 x 13 cm and cut this into six smaller rectangles, each about 2 x 5 inches/5 x 13 cm. Place on the lined baking sheet and, one rectangle at a time, fold in all the sides by ⅓ inch/1 cm to form a second layer that will hold in the pastry cream and fruit; it will look quite rustic but this is as it should be. Place in the fridge to chill for about 30 minutes.

7   Preheat the oven to 400°F/200°C. Spread the pastry cream evenly over the pastry base. Place the drained apricots in a medium bowl and pour the honey over the top. Mix well, then lay four or five apricot halves on top of the pastry cream in one long line, cut side up and tightly overlapping by ¼ inch/0.5 cm. Place the baking sheet with the tarts in the oven and bake for about 35 minutes, or until the pastry is dark golden brown around the edges, golden brown underneath and the apricots are nicely colored around the edges. Remove from the oven and set aside to cool for 15 minutes before transferring to a wire rack to cool completely.

8   While the galettes are still slightly warm, place the apricot jam and water in a small saucepan over medium-high heat. Stir until the apricot jam has dissolved, then allow the mixture to boil for about 1 minute, stirring continuously, until thick. Immediately brush over the top of the apricots and pastry and sprinkle with the 1 tsp thyme leaves. Set aside until ready to serve.

Pineapple tartlets with pandan and star anise

Around Chinese New Year, pineapple tarts are to Malaysia and Singapore what mince pies are to the United Kingdom and Australia around Christmas. People vote and argue about where to find the best one or who has the perfect recipe. Our version uses the sweet shortcrust pastry we use for a lot of pies and tarts; it's buttery and slightly crumbly in the mouth, but sturdy enough to hold the sticky pineapple jam. In other words, delicious. Speaking of mince pies, the jam can be replaced by store-bought mincemeat, if you like; the pastry shell makes a very good mince pie base.

MAKES 18

We use traditional mince pie pans to bake these. Ideally you'd have two sets for this recipe, but don't worry if you only have one; you can just bake the tarts in two batches. They also work well in a standard muffin pan.

The pastry makes more than you'll need. It keeps well in the fridge, covered in plastic wrap, for up to 3 days. It also freezes well, covered first in plastic wrap and then aluminum foil, for up to 2 months. If freezing the dough, do so in disk form or, if planning to make individual tarts, roll it out and cut it to size so that you're all set for your next bake. The pineapple jam can be made up to 2 weeks in advance and kept in the fridge. Make double the quantity of jam, if you like, so that you always have a batch at the ready to spread on toast or pancakes, to swirl into yogurt, or to use as part of a marinade for chicken or pork.

Once assembled, the tarts will keep for up to 4 days, stored in an airtight container. The jammy filling just means they will get a bit softer over time.

PINEAPPLE JAM
2 pineapples (6 lb 3 oz/2.8 kg), peeled, cored and flesh roughly chopped into 2-inch/5-cm cubes
1¾ cups/360 g granulated sugar
6 pandan leaves, bruised with the back of a knife and tied together in a knot (or ¼ vanilla pod, sliced in half lengthwise and seeds scraped)
6 whole star anise

SWEET SHORTCRUST PASTRY
(YOU WILL NEED ONLY ½ QUANTITY)
2⅓ cups/300 g all purpose flour, plus extra for dusting
¾ cup/90 g confectioners' sugar
¼ tsp salt
¾ cup plus 2 tbsp/200 g unsalted butter, fridge-cold, cut into cubes, plus 1 tbsp, melted, for brushing
finely grated zest of 1 lemon (1 tsp)
1 large egg yolk, plus 1 large egg, lightly beaten, to glaze
4 tsp water

18 whole cloves, for studding the tarts

1   **To make the pineapple jam,** place the pineapples in a food processor (in batches) and pulse to form a coarse purée. Strain through a fine-mesh sieve into a bowl. Don't actually press down on the purée; you just want to strain out the excess juice rather than extract more from the pineapple flesh. The strained juice (about 1 cup/240 ml) can be used to make popsicles or as a refreshing drink over ice.

2   Place the pineapple purée in a large saucepan. Add the sugar, pandan leaves (or vanilla pod and scraped seeds) and star anise. Place over medium-low heat and stir just until the sugar has dissolved. Increase the heat to medium, bring to a boil and cook for about 1 hour, stirring with a wooden spoon every 5–10 minutes, until the mixture thickens. Take care as it may splutter and spit, and keep a close eye on it as it thickens; you might need to lower the heat halfway through the cooking time and stir more frequently, to prevent it sticking on the bottom of the pan. You want to take it further than regular jam; it will be ready when it is a thick golden paste and holds its shape when spooned onto a plate. Remove from the heat and allow to cool in the pan for a half hour before transferring to a bowl (or an airtight container, if making in advance). Set aside until completely cool before removing the pandan leaves (or vanilla pod) and star anise. Keep in the fridge until ready to assemble the tartlets. ››

3   **To make the sweet shortcrust pastry,** sift together the flour, confectioners' sugar and salt and place in a food processor. Add the butter and lemon zest and pulse a few times, until the mixture has the consistency of fresh breadcrumbs. Lightly whisk together the egg yolk and water and add this to the mixture; the dough will feel quite wet, but this is as it should be. Process once more, just until the pastry comes together, then tip onto a clean, lightly floured work surface. Press or pat gently to form a ball, then divide the pastry in two. Cover each half loosely in plastic wrap and press gently to form two flattish disks. The pastry is very soft, so you need to keep it in the fridge for 1 hour (or up to 3 days).

4   Brush the molds of the mince pie pan or standard muffin pan (see Note, page 255) with melted butter and set aside.

5   When ready to bake, allow the pastry to rest at room temperature for 30 minutes (if it has been in the fridge for more than a few hours) and place on a lightly floured work surface, working with one disk of pastry at a time. Tap all over with a rolling pin to soften slightly before rolling out until ⅛ inch/3 mm thick. Using a 2¾-inch/7-cm cookie cutter, stamp out eighteen circles and place one in each greased mold. Reroll the scraps, if necessary, until you get eighteen circles. Set aside in the fridge to rest.

6   Press the remaining pastry scraps together and roll into a rough rectangle, about ⅛ inch/3 mm thick. Cut the pastry into strips, about 2 x ¼ inches/5 x 0.5 cm (these will form the lattice to decorate the tarts). Transfer to a baking sheet and keep in the fridge until ready to use.

7   Preheat the oven to 400°F/200°C.

8   Spoon a heaped tablespoon of the pineapple jam—about 1 oz/30 g—into each pastry shell (don't think you've missed a step here; the shells are not blind-baked) and level the surface with the back of a teaspoon. If the kitchen is warm and the pastry is softening, return the baking sheets to the fridge for a few minutes. Place the strips of pastry on top of the tarts to form a lattice shape. The easiest way to do this is to first lay two or three strips parallel to each other and then lay another two or three on top. Trim the ends with a paring knife to fit and press the ends into the edge of the pastry.

9   Brush the beaten egg over the lattice, push a whole clove into the center of each tartlet and bake for about 20 minutes, or until the pastry is golden brown all over. Remove from the oven and allow to cool on the baking sheet for 10 minutes before transferring to a wire rack to cool completely. Remove the cloves before eating!

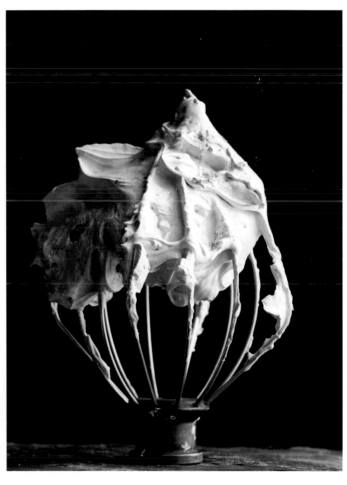

Desserts

—

You're sometimes unaware of a bias until the stats are laid out. With almost twenty desserts here, there are no less than thirteen with fruit and five with a splash of booze. The evidence is clear: We like our fruit, we like our booze, and we *very* much like our desserts.

FRUIT › We like fruit in our desserts for all sorts of reasons. Not only does it lend a bright splash of color to the end of a meal, it also has the ability to cut through and lighten an otherwise rich or creamy dessert. Orange cape gooseberries, purple blackberries, dark pink raspberries—all have the color you want and the tartness a dessert often needs. The citrus from the zest of a lime will lighten things up in a rich chocolate pudding; raspberries or blackberries will cut through the whipped cream in a pavlova; while fresh cubes of papaya are just what a rich little posset needs. Always feel free to play around with the fruit in a dessert, depending on what's in season. Just make sure that it's perfectly ripe and ready; comparing a ripe mango or papaya with an unripe mango or papaya is, well, like comparing apples and pears.

BOOZE › We like booze in our desserts for all sorts of reasons too. One, of course, is that it's just a nice way to keep the party going. However, the presence of a nip of brandy in our desserts is often there not so much for the sake of celebration but because of the way it draws out the other flavors. Soaking raisins or apples in brandy, for example, does more to heighten the inherent flavor of the raisins or apples than to showcase the flavor of the brandy. Don't open a bottle just for the sake of a couple of teaspoons or tablespoons, though. There are some recipes here that need the alcohol—the Campari and Grapefruit Sorbet (see page 304), for example—but a lot of the others—the sauce for the Chocolate, Rose and Walnut Ice Cream (see page 308) or the caramel sauce for the Frozen Espresso Parfait for a Crowd (see page 298)—still taste absolutely delicious without it. Some desserts are for all of the kids, big and small; others just reserved for the big kids among us.

A SMALL NOTE ON EPICNESS › *Epic* feels like a word that, being over the age of twelve, we shouldn't really be using, but there's a handful of desserts here that are, well, just pretty epic. Epic as in you have to get a little bit organized to make them; epic as in you'll be high-fiving the air when you've made it for the first time; epic as in you're guaranteed a wow-eeeeee when you bring it to the table. Not, however, epic as in "don't try this one at home."

One of the biggest secrets behind some of the most involved recipes is that they're often some of the easiest to make. This is because of how much can be prepared in advance. Some things *can* be made in advance—meringues can be baked, nuts can be caramelized, sponge cakes can be cooked. Some things *need* to be made in advance—the Ginger Crème Caramel (see page 279) and Kaffir lime leaf posset (see page 283) both need to set overnight in the fridge. Others are a nice combination of most of the components being made in advance, leaving just the whipping of cream and the assembling of the dessert before serving. And that's the fun bit, really—making everything look pretty.

Whatever the reason and whatever the season, there's always a dessert to fit: epic or easy, boozy or not, comforting or hearty, zesty or light. But fruity, very nearly *always* fruity.

Equipment

An ice cream maker is the obvious one here, if you are planning on making ice cream regularly. They are quite an investment, we know, but one that can bring a lot of pleasure over the years. Although some of the ice creams need an ice cream maker—the Saffron and Almond Ice Cream Sandwich (see page 301) and Chocolate, Rose and Walnut Ice Cream (see page 308). Others are semifreddos—the raspberry semifreddo for the Knickerbocker Glory (see page 293), for example—which means that whipped cream is folded in (rather than churned in an ice cream maker). If you want to make ice cream and don't have an ice cream maker, that's fine; you can churn it yourself, stirring the mix every few hours to break up the formation of ice crystals before returning it to the freezer. This process is stretched over a few hours, but the actual consumption of your time is very little.

Otherwise, the equipment we recommend is useful, though not essential: a piping bag for the Cape Gooseberry Pavlova (see page 274) and Frozen Espresso Parfait for a Crowd (see page 298); an 8-inch/20-cm square pan with removable bottom for the gingerbread (see page 266) and Frozen Espresso Parfait; a 10-inch/25-cm round fluted quiche dish for the Ginger Crème Caramel (see page 279); little glass ramekins or dariole molds for the Hot Chocolate and Lime Puddings (see page 278); and a nonstick crêpe pan to make you look the part when preparing the Ricotta Crêpes with Figs, Honey and Pistachio (see page 268). We know that the ideal world is far removed from the reality of our drawers and cupboards, however, which do well if they have matching Tupperware bases and lids, so feel free to either beg, borrow or improvise. And don't forget to make a note—on your birthday or Christmas wishlist—of the equipment you'd like in that ideal kitchen of yours. As ever, we've made alternative equipment suggestions in the recipes where we can.

Rolled pavlova with peaches and blackberries

This is the showstopper to serve as part of a big summer meal—a real statement!—huge and divine. Don't be put off by its size, though; the larger pavlovas are actually easier to roll than the smaller ones. There's always a moment when rolling a pavlova when you think, "It's not going to come together!" But hold your nerve and trust in the recipe; it's actually very forgiving.

We pair late-summer peaches with the blackberries of early autumn, but meringue is so versatile that you can add whatever fruit filling you like, depending on what's in season. Fresh raspberries, strawberries or blueberries, slow-cooked quince or plums—they all work well. You can also play around with fillings. Try vanilla and chopped pistachios with strawberry (or mixed berries); and mango, lime and passion fruit works well with whipped cream flavored with finely grated lime zest.

SERVES 10–12

The meringue base (unfilled) can be prepared up to a day ahead. Leave it in the pan and drape with a kitchen towel until needed. You are then ready to fill it with the fruit and cream up to 4 hours before (but ideally as close as possible to) serving.

This should be eaten on the day it is assembled and served, although leftovers can be stored in the fridge and eaten cold.

MERINGUE BASE
8¾ oz/250 g egg whites (from about 7 large eggs), at room temperature (they whisk better if not fridge-cold)
1¾ cups plus 2 tbsp/375 g granulated sugar
2 tsp vanilla extract
2 tsp white wine vinegar
2 tsp cornstarch

FILLING
1⅔ cups/400 ml heavy cream
1 tsp vanilla extract
3 tbsp confectioners' sugar, sifted, plus extra to dust
5 large, ripe peaches, washed but unpeeled, pitted and cut into ¼-inch/0.5-cm-wide segments (1 lb 5 oz/600 g)
10½ oz/300 g fresh blackberries
½ cup/50 g toasted sliced almonds

1   **To make the meringue base,** preheat the oven to 425°F/220°C. Line a 15 x 10-inch/38 x 25-cm jelly-roll pan or similar size shallow baking pan with parchment paper, so the paper rises ¾ inch/2 cm over the sides of the pan.

2   Place the egg whites in the bowl of an electric mixer with the whisk attachment in place and beat on medium-high speed for about 1 minute, until soft peaks form. Gradually add the sugar, 1 tbsp at a time, beating all the time for 5 minutes, until the mixture turns into a thick and glossy meringue. Turn the speed to low and add the vanilla extract, vinegar and cornstarch. Increase the speed to medium and beat for a minute, until fully combined.

3   Spoon the meringue into the lined pan and use a spatula to spread it out evenly. Place in the preheated oven and immediately lower the temperature to 400°F/200°C; the contrast in temperature helps create the crisp outside along with the gooey marshmallow-like inside. Bake for about 35 minutes, until the meringue is pale beige in color and crusty on top. Remove from the oven and set aside in the pan until completely cool. The meringue will have puffed up in the oven but will deflate slightly when cooled. If keeping until the next day, the meringue can be covered with a kitchen towel and set aside at room temperature. ››

4   **To make the filling,** using an electric mixer with the whisk attachment on medium-high speed, beat the cream until very soft peaks form—this should take about 1 minute, longer if whisking by hand. Add the vanilla extract and confectioners' sugar and whisk to incorporate.

5   Place a clean kitchen towel flat on top of the meringue (or use the one that is already there, if you've made this the day before) and quickly but carefully invert it onto the work surface, so that the crisp top of the meringue is now facing down and sitting on top of the kitchen towel. Lift the pan off and carefully peel away the parchment paper before spreading the meringue evenly with two-thirds of the whipped cream. Cover generously with 1 lb 2 oz/500 g of the peaches and 7 oz/200 g of the blackberries, and sprinkle with ⅓ cup/40 g of the almonds.

6   Starting with the longest side closest to you, and using the kitchen towel to assist, roll the meringue up and over, so that the edges come together to form a log. Gently pull away the kitchen towel as you roll, then slide the meringue onto a long tray or platter, seam side facing down. Don't worry if the meringue loses its shape a bit or some of the fruit spills out; just hold your nerve and use your hands to pat it back into the shape of the log.

7   Pipe or spoon the remaining whipped cream down the length of the log. Top with the remaining fruit and almonds, dust with confectioners' sugar and serve.

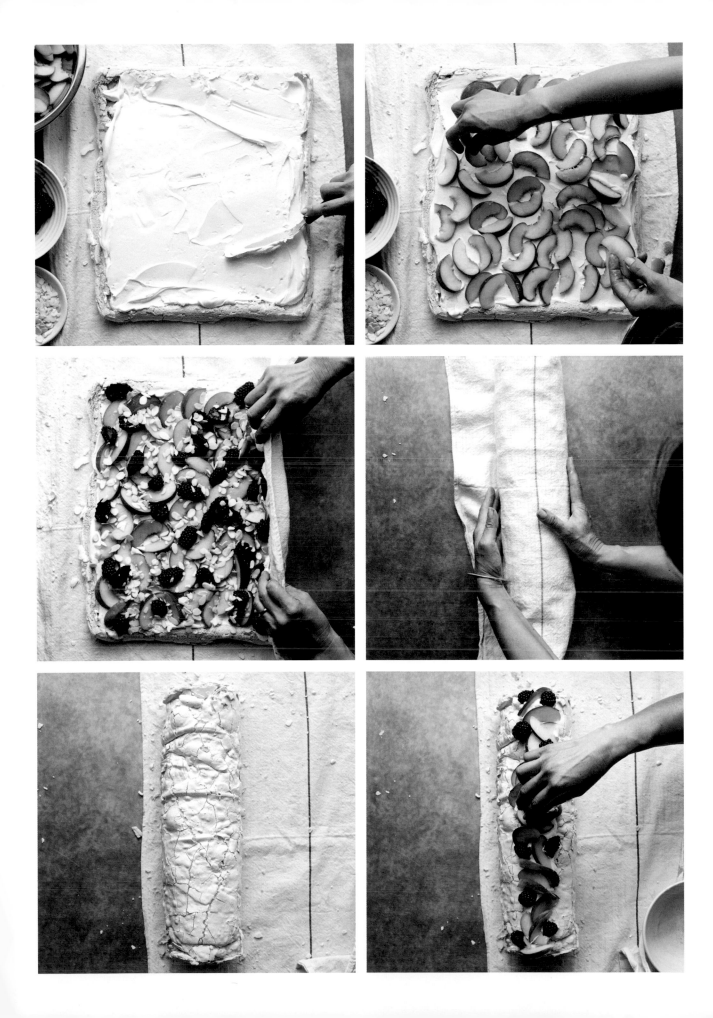

Gingerbread with brandy apples and crème fraîche

This can be served warm, as a dessert, with the sautéed apples and crème fraîche, or on its own at room temperature, with a cup of tea. We find that we can eat more of the cake when it's warm, which is why the same amount of cake serves a different number of people depending on whether it is eaten at room temperature or not. Paradoxically, it's the addition of the extras—the slightly tangy crème fraîche cutting through the sweetness of the molasses and the apples—that enables a bigger portion to be served!

SERVES 9 (WARM, AS A DESSERT) OR ABOUT 12 (AT ROOM TEMPERATURE)

Scant 1 cup/300 g blackstrap molasses (or black treacle)
½ packed cup plus 1 tbsp/100 g light brown sugar
½ cup plus 1 tbsp/120 g granulated sugar
1 cup/225 g unsalted butter, melted and cooled slightly
3 large eggs
finely grated zest of 1 orange (1½ tsp)
3¼ cups/400 g all-purpose flour
1 tbsp baking soda
1 tbsp ground ginger
2 tsp ground cinnamon
½ tsp salt
1¼ cups/300 ml just-boiled water
½ cup/100 g finely chopped crystallized ginger, steeped in boiling water (see page 353) and drained, or stem ginger

BRANDY APPLES
5 Golden Delicious or Pink Lady apples (1 lb 9 oz/700 g)
3½ tbsp/50 g unsalted butter
½ cup plus 1 tbsp/120 g granulated sugar
½ vanilla pod, sliced open lengthwise
strips of peel of 1 large lemon
3½ tbsp/50 ml brandy
3½ tbsp/50 ml lemon juice
⅛ tsp salt

1½ cups/400 g crème fraîche, if serving as a dessert (see introduction)

This is best made in a high-sided (4-inch/10-cm high) 8-inch/20-cm square springform pan, but if you don't have one of these then use a 9-inch/23-cm round springform pan instead. If you go for the round option, you'll make eight large slices or twelve regular slices. It also looks great made in a 9-inch/23-cm Bundt pan.

The cake can be made up to 3 days in advance and kept at room temperature in an airtight container. If you're serving it as a dessert, just warm it through in the oven, covered with aluminum foil. The apples are best made on the day of serving.

1   Preheat the oven to 400°F/200°C. Grease a high-sided 8-inch/20-cm square (or 9-inch/23-cm round) springform pan and line with parchment paper, leaving an overhang at the sides to help you remove the cake from the pan later on.

2   Place the molasses, brown sugar, granulated sugar, butter, eggs and orange zest in a medium bowl and whisk together by hand, or using a handheld electric mixer, until combined.

3   Sift the flour, baking soda, ginger, cinnamon and salt together into a separate larger bowl, then pour in the molasses mixture. Stir to combine and add the just-boiled water, whisking immediately to combine. Stir in the crystallized ginger, then pour the mixture into the cake pan. Bake for 50 minutes, or until a skewer inserted into the center comes out clean. Remove from the oven and set aside on a wire rack to cool for 10 minutes before removing from the pan and transferring the cake to a serving platter.

4   **To make the brandy apples** while the cake is cooling, peel and core the apples and cut into ⅔-inch/1.5-cm slices. Place a large nonstick sauté pan over high heat and, once hot, add about half of the apples (depending on the size of your pan; you don't want them to be overcrowded, as this will prevent them becoming golden). Sear for 2 minutes, turning regularly, until they are a nice golden color. Remove from the pan, wipe it clean and repeat with the remaining apples. Add these to the first batch and return the pan to medium heat. Place the butter in the pan and, once melted, add the sugar, vanilla pod and lemon peel. Return the apples to the pan, stir well to coat and cook for 5 minutes, until the apples are soft but still holding their shape. Pour in the brandy, lemon juice and salt and reduce for 3 minutes over medium-high heat, until the sauce is thick but not caramelized.

5   If serving warm, spoon some of the warmed apples on top of each portion of gingerbread and add a spoonful of crème fraîche alongside.

Ricotta crêpes with figs, honey and pistachio

These crêpes are a serious way to end a meal, but also work well for brunch, if you want to get the day off to a flying start. We've made a little bit more batter than you need for twelve crêpes; the tendency, we find, is that the first two or three crêpes don't work quite as well as those that follow, once the pan has warmed up and you know what's what, so we've built in this safety net. If you're very clever and manage to make them work from the start, you'll just have two or three extra to play around with. The crêpes are great just as they are, if you like, served with some lemon juice and sprinkled sugar.

Play around with the filling, as well, depending on what you have and what's in season. Strawberries are a good alternative to the figs, for example. Hull them, then macerate them with a little bit of orange juice, a tablespoon of brandy and a drop of orange blossom water. Walnuts also work well instead of the pistachios, if that's what you have on hand.

MAKES 12 (PERFECT) CRÊPES

FILLING
½ cup/75 g dried currants
2 tbsp brandy
5¼ oz/150 g cream cheese
1 cup plus 2 tbsp/300 g ricotta cheese
¼ cup plus 1½ tbsp/60 g
   granulated sugar
scraped seeds of ¼ vanilla pod
1½ tsp orange blossom water
finely grated zest of 1 large orange
   (1 tbsp)
2 large egg yolks
⅛ tsp salt

CRÊPES
1⅓ cups/170 g all-purpose flour
⅓ tsp salt
3 large eggs
1¼ cups/300 ml whole milk
1½ tbsp/25 g unsalted butter, melted,
   plus 5½ tbsp/80 g, melted, for
   cooking and brushing
finely grated zest of 1 large orange
   (1 tbsp)
6 fresh figs (Black Mission, if possible,
   or another ripe variety), halved,
   or quartered if large (9 oz/260 g)

HONEY SYRUP
3 tbsp/60 g honey
¼ tsp orange blossom water
1 tsp lemon juice

2 tbsp shelled pistachio kernels,
   roughly chopped

A proper nonstick crêpe pan, with shallow sides, is such a treat. It makes the cooking of crêpes easy and fun (and at the same time, crucially, allows you to look like a pro). Alternatively, use a shallow 7-inch/18-cm sauté pan.

You can make the whole dish up to the point at which it's ready to go into the oven, then store in the fridge, covered, for up to 24 hours. Simply follow the cooking instructions before serving.

1   **To make the filling,** place the currants and brandy in a small saucepan over medium heat. Warm gently for a minute and then set aside for the currants to plump up and cool.

2   Place the cream cheese in a medium bowl and beat with a wooden spoon or spatula until smooth. Add the ricotta, sugar, vanilla seeds, orange blossom water, orange zest, egg yolks and salt and beat to incorporate; the mixture should be well combined but not completely smooth. Finally, drain the currants—there won't be much liquid left but it's still useful to do—and stir them through the ricotta mixture. Set aside in the fridge until ready to use.

3   **To make the crêpes,** sift the flour and salt into a medium bowl and make a well in the center. Crack the eggs into the well and add the milk, whisking as you pour and gradually drawing in the flour until the batter is smooth. Finally, whisk in the melted butter until combined. Strain through a fine-mesh sieve—you need to do this to make sure there are no unwhisked eggs or lumps—into a clean container. Whisk in the orange zest and then refrigerate, covered, for at least 1 hour or up to overnight.

4   Place a 7-inch/18-cm sauté pan (or crêpe pan, if you have one) over medium heat and, once hot, brush lightly but thoroughly with melted butter. Add 3 tbsp of batter and swirl the pan around to ensure that the batter spreads thinly and evenly over the surface. Cook for about 1 minute, or until the bottom is golden brown, then use a spatula (or your fingers, if you're careful) to turn it over. Cook for another 30 seconds or so, until golden brown. Repeat until you have used up all of the batter, brushing the pan with additional butter between each crêpe; you should have twelve perfect crêpes. Stack them up on a plate and cover in plastic wrap or drape a clean kitchen towel over them—this prevents them drying out and cracking at the edges—until ready to fill.

5   When ready to assemble the crêpes, on a clean work surface, spoon 2 tbsp of the ricotta filling—about 1 oz/30 g—into the top quarter of one crêpe. Fold the bottom half of the crêpe up and over the filling (it looks like a semicircle at this stage) and then fold it in half again, left to right, over the filling, to form a quarter-circle.

6   Brush a 11 x 7-inch/28 x 18-cm ceramic or Pyrex baking dish with 1 tbsp of the melted butter and place the crêpes in the dish in snug rows and slightly overlapping. Brush with another 1 tbsp butter and dot the figs on top. The crêpes can be kept in the fridge at this point until ready to cook (up to 24 hours).

7   Preheat the oven to 400°F/200°C.

8   Place the crêpes in the oven and bake for 30 minutes.

9   **To make the honey syrup,** 2 minutes before the crêpes are ready, warm the honey in a saucepan over medium heat. Remove from the heat and stir in the orange blossom water and lemon juice.

10   Brush the honey syrup over the crêpes and figs as soon as they come out of the oven. Place two crêpes on each plate and spoon two fig halves alongside. Drizzle with any remaining syrup, sprinkle with the pistachios and serve.

RICOTTA CRÊPES WITH FIGS,
HONEY AND PISTACHIO

Rice pudding with roasted rhubarb and tarragon

This is as sweet and comforting as you want a rice pudding to be, but with a welcome savory note too, from the tarragon and bay leaves. This is as delicious for breakfast as it is after lunch or supper.

SERVES 6

1 cup/100 g short-grain white rice
3 cups/720 ml whole milk
shaved peel of 1 medium orange
3 large fresh bay leaves, torn in half
1 large cinnamon stick
⅛ tsp salt
1 lb 3 oz/530 g rhubarb (about
    9 thin stalks), cut into 2-inch/
    5-cm segments

⅓ cup/70 g granulated sugar
about 6 sprigs tarragon, half the sprigs
    left whole, the remaining leaves
    removed and roughly chopped
1 vanilla pod, sliced in half lengthwise
    and seeds scraped
1 tbsp water
6 tbsp plus 2 tsp/100 ml heavy cream
¼ cup/30 g confectioners' sugar, sifted
⅓ cup/100 g plain Greek yogurt

You can make the rice pudding (up to the stage before the cream is folded in) and roasted fruit the day before serving. You can then either serve it straight from the fridge (folding in the cream will bring it to room temperature) or warm it in the oven, adding the cream just before serving, if you prefer.

1   Preheat the oven to 350°F/170°C.

2   Place the rice, milk, orange peel, bay leaves, cinnamon and salt in a 11 x 7-inch/ 28 x 18-cm baking dish and bake for 70 minutes, uncovered, stirring halfway through, until the rice is cooked but still holds its shape and most of the milk is absorbed. Remove from the oven and set aside to cool before removing the orange peel, bay leaves and cinnamon stick. Transfer to a medium bowl, let cool completely, and then cover and keep in the fridge until needed.

3   Increase the oven temperature to 475°F/250°C. Place the rhubarb in a clean 11 x 7-inch/28 x 18-cm baking dish along with the granulated sugar, the whole tarragon sprigs and vanilla pod and seeds. Add the water, toss together and roast for 15–20 minutes, until the rhubarb has completely softened. Remove from the oven and set aside to cool. Remove the tarragon sprigs and vanilla pod; the tarragon can be discarded, but the pod is worth saving to flavor granulated sugar.

4   While the rhubarb is cooking, place the cream in a bowl and add the confectioners' sugar. Whisk until the cream thickens and holds its shape. Fold the cream into the cold rice, followed by the yogurt, and return to the fridge.

5   When ready to serve, divide the rice pudding among six bowls and spoon a generous amount of rhubarb on top, along with some of the juices. Serve with a final sprinkle of the tarragon leaves.

Cape gooseberry pavlova

Cape gooseberries are so lovely to look at—with their glossy yellow skin and papery husks—that they can often be used as just an exotic garnish rather than as an ingredient in their own right. They're not to be underrated, though, with their distinct taste: slightly citrusy with tones of strawberry and honey. They pair really well with the honey-spiked yogurt cream here.

SERVES 8

MERINGUES

4½ oz/125 g egg whites (from
    3 large eggs)
⅛ tsp salt
¼ tsp cream of tartar
1¼ cups/250 g granulated sugar
14 oz/400 g Cape gooseberries,
    husked and halved

TOFFEE CAPE GOOSEBERRIES

8 Cape gooseberries,
    papery husks intact
¼ cup plus 1 tbsp/60 g granulated sugar

YOGURT CREAM

⅔ cup/200 g plain Greek yogurt
¾ cup plus 2 tbsp/200 ml heavy cream
scraped seeds of ¼ vanilla pod
1½ tbsp honey
2½ tbsp confectioners' sugar

confectioners' sugar for dusting

A piping bag with a ⅓-inch/1-cm plain tip is useful for piping out the meringues, but is not essential.

The meringue can be made up to 3 days ahead and stored in an airtight container, layered between sheets of parchment paper. The yogurt cream and toffee Cape gooseberries are best prepared no more than a couple of hours before serving; the toffee tends to become sticky and will weep if made too far in advance.

---

1   To make the meringues, preheat the oven to 275°F/140°C and line two baking sheets with parchment paper. Trace or draw eight circles—each about 3 inches/8 cm wide—on each of the parchment sheets so that you have sixteen circles in total. Turn the paper over so the drawn-on side is facedown but still visible.

2   Place the egg whites and salt in the bowl of an electric mixer with the whisk attachment in place. Beat on medium-high speed until frothy, then add the cream of tartar. Continue to beat until soft peaks form, the add the sugar, a tablespoon at a time. Keep beating until the mixture is thick and glossy.

3   Spoon the mixture into a piping bag (if you have one) with a ⅓-inch/1-cm plain tip in place. Using the circles you have traced as your guide, pipe a layer of meringue onto each of the circles; they should be just under ⅓ inch/1 cm thick. Use a small spatula or the back of a spoon to smooth the tops. If you don't have a piping bag, simply dollop a large spoonful of the meringue mixture onto each circle and smooth it out with the spatula; again, they should be just under ⅓ inch/1 cm thick.

4   Place the baking sheets in the oven and bake for 2 hours, or until the meringues are dry. Switch off the oven but leave the meringues inside until they are completely cool. Once cool, remove from the oven and set aside.

5   **To make the toffee Cape gooseberries,** peel back the papery husk from the fruit but leave it attached and then set aside. Put the sugar into a small saucepan and place over medium-high heat. Cook the sugar, without stirring, until it melts and begins to brown around the edges of the pan. Tilt and swirl the pan so that the sugar melts evenly into a toffee and turns amber. Remove from the heat and, moving quickly but carefully, tilt the pan so that the toffee pools in one corner. Pick up a Cape gooseberry by the husk and carefully dip the entire fruit (not the husk) into the toffee. Hold for a few seconds over the pan to let any excess to drip away, then place on a parchment-lined baking sheet or plate. Continue with the remaining fruit and toffee and set the dipped fruit aside.

6   **To make the yogurt cream,** whisk together all the cream ingredients by hand, or using a handheld electric mixer, until soft peaks form. Keep in the fridge until needed.

7   Place a small dollop of the yogurt cream onto each serving plate (this will hold the meringues in place) and place a meringue on top of the cream, flat side down. Dollop a few tablespoons of the yogurt cream (about 1½ oz/40 g) in the center of each meringue and use the back of a spoon to smooth out the entire surface. Spoon the halved Cape gooseberries over the cream—it will seem like a lot, but they can handle it!—then spread the flat side of the remaining meringues with the remaining yogurt cream. Sit them on top of the fruit, cream side down. Dust the tops of the meringues lightly with confectioners' sugar and place a toffee-coated Cape gooseberry in the center of each. Serve as close to assembling as you can—within 1 hour—as the thin meringues will soften from the fruit and the cream.

CAPE GOOSEBERRY PAVLOVA

Hot chocolate and lime puddings

These puddings, gently baked in a bain-marie, deliver the lightness of a soufflé without any of the anxiety often associated with baking them. A portion of pudding baked in a 4-inch/10-cm ramekin dish might sound like rather a lot (particularly when you see them rise in the oven), but don't be intimidated. They are as light as they are large and, anyway, they soon deflate to a far more reasonable size.

There is just a suggestion of lime from the zest of the fruit, but feel free to substitute with orange zest if the combination of chocolate and orange appeals more.

SERVES 6

---

1 tbsp unsalted butter, at room temperature, for greasing
7 oz/200 g dark chocolate (70% cocoa solids), roughly chopped
3½ oz/100 g milk chocolate (37% cocoa solids), roughly chopped

finely grated zest of 3 limes (1 tbsp)
4 large eggs, at room temperature
¼ cup/50 g granulated sugar, plus 2 tbsp for preparing the molds
½ cup/120 ml heavy cream
¾ cup/200 g crème fraîche, to serve

---

1 Preheat the oven to 400°F/200°C. Brush the ramekins or dariole molds (see Note) with the butter, then sprinkle with a little granulated sugar to evenly coat, tapping away the excess, and set aside.

2 Place both chocolates in a medium heatproof bowl set over a pan of simmering water, making sure the base of the bowl isn't touching the water. Stir gently with a spatula from time to time to ensure that the chocolate melts evenly. Once melted, remove the bowl from the heat, stir in the lime zest and set aside to cool for 10 minutes, until tepid.

3 Place the eggs and sugar in the bowl of an electric mixer with the whisk attachment in place and beat on high speed for about 6 minutes, until the mixture is very light and fluffy and has tripled in volume. Meanwhile, place the cream in a separate medium bowl and whisk by hand or with a handheld electric mixer until very soft peaks form.

4 Remove the egg and sugar bowl from the electric mixer and add the melted chocolate in two batches, gently folding through by hand. When almost combined—there will still be some streaks—fold in the whipped cream until thoroughly combined. It will lose a little volume, so be careful not to overmix.

5 Spoon the mixture into the prepared ramekins or molds, filling them three-quarters of the way up the sides. Place the ramekins or molds in a large, deep baking dish, transfer to the oven and pour boiling water into the dish so that it rises a third of the way up the sides of the ramekins. Bake for 20–22 minutes, or until the puddings are softly set in the middle; check they are ready by gently tapping the center of the puddings with your finger. Carefully remove the baking dish from the oven and, using oven mitts, transfer the ramekins onto serving plates. Alternatively, you could unmold the puddings by setting aside for 10 minutes before inverting onto a plate. Serve with a little of the crème fraîche spooned alongside.

These can be made in ceramic or glass ¾-cup/200-ml ramekins (ours are 4 inches/10 cm wide). Alternatively, use ¾-cup/200-ml dariole molds.

These are best served warm, but will keep for a day or two at room temperature (don't keep them in the fridge or the soft inside will set). Their texture will be a little denser, but they will still taste great as they are. You can also warm them through in the oven or microwave.

Ginger crème caramel

Crème caramel can often be a rather heavy end to a meal, but ours is unexpectedly light, which we prefer. This is due to a higher ratio of milk to cream than is traditional, and also because the milk and cream are not heated before being whisked into the eggs. Helen, who cooks a lot of Chinese food, says that this is one of the few Western desserts that does not taste out of place after a Chinese meal. It's particularly perfect after a main of steamed fish.

Thanks to Suzy Zail for sharing this recipe.

SERVES 8–10

We like to make this in a 10-inch/ 25-cm round ceramic or glass baking dish with a fluted edge—like a quiche plate. A metal pan (so long as it is water-tight and does not have a removable base) will also be fine. You could also make small individual flans, but the sense of turning out a whole flan onto your serving platter, with the caramel glistening on top, is great.

The fresh ginger in the custard is wonderful, but you can skip this stage if you are looking for a shortcut and don't want to infuse the custard the day before baking it. You will still need to bake the dish at least a day before serving as, once out of the oven, the whole thing needs to be chilled in the fridge overnight.

Once made, this will keep in the fridge for up to 3 days.

3¼ cups/780 ml whole milk
½ cup/120 ml heavy cream
2¾-inch/7-cm piece of fresh ginger (2 oz/55 g), peeled and coarsely grated

½ vanilla pod, sliced in half lengthwise and seeds scraped
2 cups/400 g granulated sugar
6 large eggs
1 tsp vanilla extract

1   If infusing the custard with the ginger, you will need to start 2 days before you want to serve the dish. Place the milk, cream, ginger and vanilla pod and seeds in a medium bowl or measuring cup and whisk to combine. Cover with plastic wrap and keep in the fridge for at least 6 hours, or ideally up to 24 hours, to infuse.

2   When you are ready to make the crème caramel, preheat the oven to 350°F/ 170°C. Place the baking dish in the oven to keep warm until needed; heating the dish will make it easier to coat it with the hot caramel.

3   Add 1 cup/200 g of the sugar to a large sauté pan or skillet and place over medium heat. Cook for about 5 minutes, resisting the urge to stir but tilting and swirling the pan instead, until the sugar has melted and begins to brown around the edges. You will need to do this slowly and continually until the sugar has turned into a dark amber caramel. Remove the hot baking dish from the oven and immediately pour in the caramel, using a kitchen towel to protect your hands. Tilt the dish around so that the caramel coats the entire base and rises halfway up the sides of the dish. Place the dish in a high-sided baking pan and set aside for 15 minutes; the caramel does not need to set rock hard, but it should be firm enough that pouring the custard over the top will not disturb it in any way.

4   Place the eggs in a large bowl with the remaining 1 cup/200 g sugar and the vanilla extract. Whisk until smooth, then strain the infused milk-cream mixture into the eggs through a fine-mesh sieve—it's okay that it's fridge-cold—pressing the ginger against the mesh to extract as much flavor as you can. Discard the ginger and whisk the mixture until thoroughly combined, but not too frothy. »

5   Pour the mixture into the caramel-coated dish and place the baking pan (with the crème caramel dish inside) in the oven. Pour some recently boiled water into the baking pan so that it comes about halfway up the sides of the inside dish. Bake for about 90 minutes; the crème caramel should still have a wobble in the middle but a skewer inserted into the center should come out clean. The wobble is as it should be—it will firm up in the fridge—but cooking time can vary, depending on the size of your pan and what it is made from (glass, metal, and so on); it can take up to 2 hours.

6   Remove the baking pan from the oven and carefully transfer the crème caramel to a wire rack. Set aside until completely cool, then cover with plastic wrap and keep in the fridge overnight (or for up to 3 days) to allow the caramel to melt and the custard to firm up.

7   After refrigerating, if the custard part of the crème caramel is stuck to the sides of the dish, carefully run a small knife along the edge to release it. Then place a large plate (larger than your baking dish, and with a rim to catch the liquid caramel) on top of the crème caramel. Grasping the dish and the plate together, quickly flip the whole thing over. Gently lift off the dish to reveal the set crème caramel. Slice with a large kitchen knife, and serve—you'll be amazed at how easily and perfectly it slices as well.

Yogurt panna cotta with basil and crushed strawberries

Panna cotta is usually made with cream—the name itself means "cooked cream." Our version, however, is made with milk and yogurt and has a texture more like that of a set milk pudding. It's not set very firmly, though, so you'll still get the reassuring wobble you want. If you want to turn your panna cottas out well before they're served, that's fine; just keep them in the fridge so that they stay set. Alternatively, you can make and serve these in individual glasses, in which case they won't need turning out at all.

MAKES 6 (USING ¾-CUP/180-ML MOLDS) OR 8 (USING ⅔-CUP/160-ML MOLDS)

2¾ cups/660 ml whole milk
2½ tsp (1 envelope) powdered gelatin, or 4 leaves (about 4 x 2 inch/ 10 x 5 cm) platinum gelatin
¾ cup/150 g granulated sugar
shaved peel of 2 lemons, avoiding the bitter white pith
1 oz/30 g fresh basil leaves, plus 10 leaves for the strawberries

sunflower oil (or another flavorless oil), for greasing
1⅓ cups/350 g plain Greek yogurt
¼ cup/60 ml lemon juice
10½ oz/300 g strawberries
2 tbsp confectioners' sugar

We use six ¾-cup/180-ml dariole molds here; you could use ⅔-cup/ 160-ml molds instead—you'll just end up with a couple of extra—or use similar-sized custard cups.

These can be made up to 2 days in advance and kept in the fridge until serving. The strawberries must be prepared just before serving.

1   Place ¼ cup/60 ml of the milk in a small bowl and sprinkle the powdered gelatin over it. Set aside until needed.

2   Combine the remaining 2½ cups/600 ml milk, sugar and lemon peel in a medium saucepan and place over low heat. Stir until the sugar has dissolved, then increase the heat to medium-high. As soon as it comes to a boil, remove the pan from the heat. Roughly tear the basil leaves and drop them into the hot milk.

3   Stir the gelatin mixture into the warm milk mixture. Whisk gently, until the gelatin dissolves, then set aside to cool until tepid. Prepare the six ¾-cup/180-ml or eight ⅔-cup/160-ml dariole molds or custard cups by brushing very lightly with the oil.

4   When the milk is ready, place the yogurt in a large bowl or measuring cup and whisk lightly. Strain the milk mixture into the yogurt through a fine-mesh sieve, pressing on the basil and lemon peel to extract as much of their essence as possible. Whisk to just combine—you don't want to whisk so vigorously that air bubbles are created—then add the lemon juice. Stir, pour into the molds and place on a baking sheet that will fit in the fridge. Cover with plastic wrap and place in the fridge for 6 hours (or up to 2 days).

5   An hour or so before serving, hull the strawberries and roughly chop them. Place the strawberries in a small bowl, sprinkle with the confectioners' sugar and stir. Julienne the remaining 10 basil leaves by rolling them up as a bunch into a tight cigar shape and slicing them finely. Add to the strawberries and set aside to infuse.

6   Gently insert a knife to loosen the edges of the panna cottas, then turn them upside down over individual plates. Hold down the mold with one hand, grab the plate with the other and give it a shake to release the panna cotta. Spoon the strawberries and basil over the top and serve at once.

SWEET

Kaffir lime leaf posset with fresh papaya

Possets have been enjoyed for centuries. Traditionally served as a warm drink to the wealthy—and said to help people if they were feeling ill, much as a cup of cocoa would be offered today—they are now chilled until set and served as a custard-like pudding.

The dominance of the cream explains why it is so often paired with clean citrus flavors to cut through all the heavenly richness. Other tropical fruit can be used instead of (or alongside) the papaya—slices of mango or banana, chunks of pineapple, passion fruit pulp—just make sure the fruit you choose is nice and ripe.

Use fresh kaffir limes leaves for this; the dried variety just won't be the same. You can buy them frozen in large bags from Asian grocers, and they'll continue to freeze well at home, so you won't have to worry about racing through a whole bag.

SERVES 6

We make these in six ⅔-cup/160-ml ramekins or bowls, but any similar-sized dishes will work just as well.

These should be made the day before serving, if you can. They need at least 6 hours in the fridge to set, so it's best to just leave them overnight.

Once made, the possets can be kept in the fridge for 2 days.

2½ cups/600 ml heavy cream
12 fresh kaffir lime leaves, bruised
  with a rolling pin or pestle
  and mortar
4 strips of shaved lime zest, plus
  ¾ tsp finely grated zest, to serve

⅔ cup/130 g granulated sugar
⅛ tsp salt
3 tbsp lime juice
½ small ripe papaya, peeled,
  seeded and cut into long,
  thin slices (5¼ oz/150 g)

1   Place the cream in a medium saucepan, add the kaffir lime leaves and shaved lime zest and bring to a very gentle simmer over medium-high heat. Then, remove from the heat and set aside for 30 minutes to infuse.

2   Add the sugar to the cream along with the salt and return to medium-high heat. Bring to a boil, stirring frequently, and cook for 1–2 minutes, continuing to stir, until the cream rises to the top of the pan; watch it carefully so it doesn't boil over. Strain through a fine-mesh sieve into a large measuring cup, stir in 1 tbsp of the lime juice—the cream will thicken quickly at this stage—then pour into six ramekins (or bowls). The mixture should rise three-quarters of the way up the sides. Keep in the fridge for at least 6 hours, or overnight, to set.

3   When ready to serve, spoon the papaya on top of the possets and sprinkle with grated lime zest. Finish with 1 tsp lime juice per portion and serve.

YOGURT PANNA COTTA WITH BASIL
AND CRUSHED STRAWBERRIES

Sticky fig pudding with salted caramel and coconut topping

A variation of this cake, using dates instead of figs, was all the rage in cafés throughout Australia and New Zealand when Helen was working and baking there. It's hardly ever seen these days, which is a mystery, really, as it's so delicious: moist and fruity with a crunchy caramelized topping. We serve this warm, with some thick heavy cream.

MAKES 8

We make these in eight 3-inch/ 8-cm bottomless round cake rings, 1½ inches/4 cm high. You can also make them in a standard muffin pan; the result is not quite as elegant, but they still work very well.

These will keep for up to 2 days at room temperature (or in the fridge, if it's particularly warm) in an airtight container. Serve them as they are, or warm them through for 5 minutes in an oven set to 400°F/200°C.

2 Granny Smith apples
7 oz/200 g soft dried figs, tough stems removed, roughly chopped
1 tsp baking soda
1 cup plus 1 tbsp/250 ml water
1⅔ cups/200 g all-purpose flour
2 tsp baking powder
¼ tsp salt
½ cup plus 1 tbsp/125 g unsalted butter, at room temperature, plus extra for greasing

1 cup/200 g granulated sugar
1 large egg
1 tsp vanilla extract

SALTED CARAMEL COCONUT TOPPING
5 tbsp/70 g unsalted butter
½ packed cup/95 g light brown sugar
¼ cup/60 ml heavy cream
1 cup/95 g unsweetened flaked coconut, or finely shredded coconut
¼ tsp salt

1   Peel and core the apples and cut into roughly ⅓-inch/1-cm pieces. Place the apples, figs, baking soda and water in a saucepan. Bring to a boil, then simmer over medium heat for about 5 minutes, stirring from time to time, until the figs start to break down. Remove from the heat and set aside until cool.

2   Preheat the oven to 400°F/200°C. If using the bottomless cake rings, line a baking sheet with parchment paper, then lightly butter the rings and place on the sheet. Cut strips of parchment paper, large enough to rise 1 inches/3 cm above the cake rings, and place them around the inside of each ring; the base of the ring should be exposed when it's placed on the baking sheet. If using the muffin pan, line eight molds with paper tulip liners—or any liners—that rise about 2¾ inches/7 cm high.

3   Sift the flour, baking powder and salt together into a bowl and set aside. Place the butter and sugar in the bowl of an electric mixer with the paddle attachment in place and beat on medium-high speed for about 2 minutes, until light and fluffy. Add the egg and vanilla extract and beat until combined. Turn the speed to low and, in alternate batches, fold in the fig-apple mixture and the sifted dry ingredients.

4   Divide the batter among the rings (or muffin liners) and bake for about 25 minutes, or until a skewer inserted into the center comes out clean.

5   **To make the salted caramel coconut topping** while the cake is baking, place all the topping ingredients in a saucepan and stir over low heat until the butter is melted and everything is combined.

6   Remove the cakes from the oven and spoon 1½ tbsp of the topping over each; it should rise about ⅓ inch/1 cm. Bake for another 12 minutes, until the topping is golden.

7   Remove from the oven and leave to cool for 10 minutes, or until they come to room temperature, before removing the rings and paper; use a knife if you need to here, to help release the cake. If making in the muffin pan, let cool in the pan for 10 minutes before transferring to a wire rack to cool. Serve warm.

Pot barley pudding with roasted apples and date syrup

Think of this as a Middle Eastern rice pudding. It is either a hearty end to an autumnal Sunday lunch or wonderful eaten at breakfast to fuel you for the day ahead. The two options are not mutually exclusive, though: make it first for lunch and then eat the leftovers the following day.

Use pearl barley in place of pot barley, if necessary. It won't have quite the bite of the pot barley (because the hull and bran layers have been removed), but it will still work well.

SERVES 6

6¼ cups/1.5 L water, or as needed

1 cup/200 g pot barley (or pearl barley), rinsed

3 tbsp date syrup (or date molasses), plus 4 tbsp to drizzle

3 small cinnamon sticks

shaved peel of 1 lemon, plus 1 tbsp lemon juice

1 tsp ground nutmeg

¼ tsp salt

2 large Pink Lady apples

2 large Bramley or Granny Smith apples

¼ cup/50 g demerara sugar

3½ tbsp/50 g unsalted butter, melted

1 vanilla pod, sliced in half lengthwise and seeds scraped out

⅔ cup/200 g plain whole-milk yogurt

You can make this a day in advance, if you like. Just keep it in the fridge until ready to serve, then warm through on the stove, adding a couple of tablespoons of water to the pot to help it loosen up. The roasted apples can also be made a day or two in advance and stored in the fridge; again, just warm them through before serving.

1   Pour the water into a medium saucepan and place over high heat with the barley, date syrup, cinnamon, lemon peel, nutmeg and salt. Once boiling, turn the heat to medium and simmer for 1 hour, or 30–35 minutes if using pearl barley. Stir from time to time, until the consistency is that of rice pudding but the barley still retains a bite. If using the pearl barley, keep an eye on water levels toward the end of cooking; you might need to add another ½ cup/120 ml or so to make sure it doesn't boil dry before cooking through. Remove and discard the lemon peel and cinnamon sticks and keep the barley somewhere warm until ready to serve.

2   Halfway through cooking the pot barley, or at the start of the pearl barley cooking time, preheat the oven to 400°F/200°C. Line a rimmed baking sheet with parchment paper.

3   Peel and core all the apples and cut into 1-inch/3-cm slices (you should have about 1 lb 7 oz/650 g), then place the slices in a medium bowl with the lemon juice, sugar, butter and vanilla pod and seeds. Mix well and spread out on the lined baking sheet. Bake for 30–45 minutes, until the apples are cooked, soft and nicely colored. Remove from the oven, discard the vanilla pod and stir the apples gently to combine—the Bramley apples and Granny Smiths will be completely soft, but the Pink Lady apples will retain their shape—and set aside somewhere warm.

4   If the barley has set, add a couple of tablespoons of warm water to the pan and gently warm over medium heat. Divide the warm barley among six bowls and spoon the apples on top. Top with about 2 tbsp of yogurt per portion, drizzle with the 4 tbsp date syrup and serve.

Cinnamon pavlova, praline cream and fresh figs

This is a stunning dessert for a special occasion. It also has a nice element of surprise, as the meringue base is not quite what you might expect: gooey—almost toffee-like— rather than dry and crispy. This is due to the brown sugar in the mix. Combined with the praline cream and fresh figs, it's absolutely delicious. Pavlova is the dessert to make when you have a bit of time and are feeding people you adore. This recipe calls for sliced almonds, but you can easily substitute chopped pistachios (as pictured opposite)

SERVES 10–12 (IT'S QUITE RICH, SO THE SLICES ARE NOT TOO BIG)
——

The praline (after pulverizing but before it's mixed with the cream) can be made up to 3 days in advance and stored in an airtight container. The meringue needs to be made in advance—it takes 3 hours to cook, 2 hours to cool in the oven, and another 2 hours to set, so you're forced to get ahead by at least this much— but it will also keep for up to 3 days wrapped loosely in aluminum foil.

Once assembled, the pavlova should be eaten as soon as possible. It will hold for a couple of hours, but it won't look as good after that.

MERINGUE
4½ oz/125 g egg whites (from 3 large eggs)
½ cup plus 1½ tbsp/125 g granulated sugar
½ packed cup plus 1 tbsp/100 g dark brown sugar
1½ tsp ground cinnamon
2 oz/55 g dark chocolate (70% cocoa solids), finely chopped

PRALINE CREAM
½ cup/50 g sliced almonds
⅓ cup plus 2 tsp/80 g granulated sugar
2 tbsp water
¾ cup plus 2 tbsp/200 ml heavy cream
1⅔ cups/400 g mascarpone

1 lb 5 oz/600 g fresh figs, cut into ⅓-inch/1-cm disks
3 tbsp honey
¼ cup/20 g sliced almonds or shelled pistachio kernels

——

1   Preheat the oven to 350°F/170°C.

2   Spread out all the almonds (for the praline and finishing) on a rimmed baking sheet and roast for 7–8 minutes, until golden brown. Remove from the oven, divide into two piles (½ cup/50 g for the praline cream, ¼ cup/20 g for finishing,) and set aside to cool. Alternatively, if using pistachios for the meringue, roast the nuts for the meringue and praline separately.

3   **To make the meringue,** lower the oven temperature to 250°F/120°C. Cover a large baking sheet with parchment paper and trace a circle, about 9 inches/23 cm in diameter, onto the paper. Turn the paper over so the drawn-on side is facing down but still visible.

4   Pour enough water into a medium saucepan so that it rises a quarter of the way up the sides; you want the bowl from your electric mixer to be able to sit over the saucepan without touching the water. Bring the water to a boil. Place the egg whites and both sugars in the bowl of an electric mixer and whisk by hand to combine. Lower the heat under the saucepan so that the water is just simmering, then set the mixer bowl over the pan, making sure the water doesn't touch the base of the bowl. Whisk the egg whites continuously by hand until they are warm, frothy and the sugar is melted, about 4 minutes, then transfer back to the electric mixer with the whisk attachment in place and beat on high speed for about 5 minutes, until the meringue is cool, stiff and glossy. Add the cinnamon and beat to combine. ››

5   Spread the meringue inside the drawn circle, creating a nest by making the sides a little higher than the center. Place in the oven and bake for 3 hours, then switch off the oven but leave the meringues inside until they are completely cool; this will take about 2 hours. Once cool, remove from the oven and set aside.

6   Place the chocolate into a small heatproof bowl and set it over a small saucepan of simmering water, making sure the base of the bowl is not touching the water. Stir occasionally until melted. Let cool slightly, then brush the chocolate inside the meringue nest, leaving the top and sides bare. Do this gently, as the meringue is fairly delicate. Leave to set for about 2 hours.

7   **To make the praline cream,** place the ½ cup/50 g toasted almonds on a parchment-lined rimmed baking sheet and set aside. Put the granulated sugar and water into a small saucepan and place over medium-low heat, stirring until the sugar has melted. Cook, swirling the pan occasionally, until it turns into a dark golden brown caramel. Pour the caramel over the nuts (don't worry if they're not all covered) and leave until completely cool and set. Once cool, transfer the praline to the small bowl of a food processor and process until fine.

8   Place the cream, mascarpone and pulverized praline into a large bowl and whisk for about 1 minute, until stiff peaks form. Be careful not to overwhip here—it doesn't take much to thicken up—or it will split. (If this begins to happen, use a spatula to fold a little more cream into the mix to bring it back together.) Refrigerate until needed.

9   Spoon the cream into the center of the meringue and top with the figs. Warm the honey in a small saucepan and stir in the ¼ cup/20 g almonds or pistachios. Drizzle these over the figs and serve.

Knickerbocker glory

This is our go-to happy-making dessert. The color, the connotations, the conical glasses, the distinctive long-handled spoons you eat it with—it's just the definition of good old-fashioned fun. Happiness should not be dependent upon props, however, so don't worry if you don't have the traditional sundae glasses or long-handled spoons. Any other tall glass (or, indeed, spoon) will work fine. We like to pop our glasses in the freezer until ready to use, as this gives them a frosted look and also helps to keep the ice cream chilled after serving.

The ice cream here is a semifreddo, which does not need churning—good news for those who don't have an ice cream maker. Fresh raspberries are lovely, of course, but frozen also work really well in the semifreddo. In fact, the liquid exuded when frozen raspberries defrost gives the purée a lovely consistency.

The candied pecans can be made up to 5 days ahead and kept in an airtight container. The semifreddo needs to be made 12 hours in advance. You'll have about a third of the semifreddo left over, and this will keep in the freezer for 1 month.

SERVES 6

SEMIFREDDO
5 cups/600 g raspberries, fresh, or frozen and defrosted
2 tbsp confectioners' sugar
¾ cup plus 2 tbsp/ 200 ml heavy cream
1 large egg, plus 2 large egg yolks
1 tsp lemon juice
¾ cup plus 2½ tbsp/180 g granulated sugar
⅛ tsp salt

CANDIED PECANS
1 tbsp maple syrup
1 tbsp light corn syrup
1 tbsp granulated sugar
1 cup/120 g pecan halves
⅛ tsp flaky sea salt

CHANTILLY CREAM
1¼ cups/300 ml heavy cream
2 tbsp confectioners' sugar, sifted
1 tsp vanilla extract

about 5 red plums, pitted, chopped into 1-inch/3-cm chunks (10½ oz/300 g)

1 **To make the semifreddo,** place the raspberries in a food processor and process to a purée, then pass them through a fine-mesh sieve set over a bowl to remove the seeds. You may need to do this in batches, using a large spoon to scrape the purée through the sieve. Measure out 1 cup/240 ml of the purée and set aside. Sift the confectioners' sugar into the remaining purée and then decant it into a measuring cup. Set aside in the fridge until ready to use.

2 Place the heavy cream in the bowl of an electric mixer with the whisk attachment in place. Beat until soft peaks form, then scrape into a bowl. Set aside in the fridge until ready to use.

3 Pour enough water into a medium saucepan so that it rises ¾ inch/2 cm up the sides; you want the bowl from your electric mixer to be able to sit over the saucepan without touching the water. Bring the water to a boil, then lower to a low simmer. ››

4   In the meantime, whisk together the egg, egg yolks, lemon juice, granulated sugar and salt in a clean bowl of an electric mixer. Place the bowl over the simmering water and whisk continuously for about 5 minutes, until the sugar has dissolved and the mixture is very warm. Transfer the bowl back to the electric mixer with the whisk attachment in place and beat on medium-high speed until the mixture is thick and cool; it will thicken quite quickly but takes about 10 minutes or so to cool. Add the reserved 1 cup/240 ml purée and beat on low speed until combined. Scrape down the sides of the bowl and continue to beat until thoroughly combined. Remove the whipped cream from the fridge and fold in until incorporated. Scrape the mixture into a large freezer container, cover the top with plastic wrap and freeze for 12 hours.

5   **To make the candied pecans,** preheat the oven to 400°F/200°C. Line a rimmed baking sheet with parchment paper and set aside.

6   Put the maple syrup, corn syrup and sugar in a small saucepan and place over low heat. Stir gently until the sugar has melted, then add the pecans and salt. Stir so that the nuts are coated in the syrup, then tip the nuts onto the lined baking sheet. Place in the oven for about 8 minutes, or until the syrup is bubbling around the nuts. Remove the baking sheet from the oven and set aside until cool. When the nuts are cool, the glaze should be completely crisp; if not, return the sheet to the oven for a few minutes more. Once cooled, break or roughly chop the nuts into ¼-inch/0.5-cm pieces and set aside until ready to use.

7   **To make the chantilly cream,** place the heavy cream in the clean bowl of an electric mixer with the whisk attachment in place. Add the confectioners' sugar and vanilla extract and beat until soft peaks form. Transfer to a bowl or container and keep in the fridge until ready to assemble.

8   About 10 minutes before serving, remove the semifreddo from the freezer so that it is soft enough to scoop. Then, remove the glasses from the freezer and divide the chopped plums among them. Drizzle a generous ½ tbsp of the reserved sweetened raspberry purée, add 1 tbsp pecans and then a large scoop of the semifreddo on top. Drizzle with the remaining sauce—½ tbsp per glass—followed by 1 tbsp pecans and a couple large dollops of the chantilly cream. Finish with a final sprinkle of the chopped nuts and serve at once.

Frozen espresso parfait for a crowd

This is, in effect, an over-sized ice cream sandwich—what Helen would have called an Eskimo Pie when growing up in Australia. There are various components to this crowd-pleasing dessert, but the whole thing can be made well in advance and kept in the freezer to prevent any on-the-day meltdowns. However much work is involved, it is worth it: people cry with joy when they have this!

If you want to lose one element, you can do without the caramel sauce (which would also make the whole thing booze-free). We love it, but the parfait still works well without this sweet and final "ta da."

SERVES 12–16 (IT IS RICH, SO SLICES NEED NOT BE LARGE)

———

COFFEE PRALINE
½ cup plus 1½ tbsp/125 g
   granulated sugar
2 tbsp water
1½ tsp finely ground espresso coffee
   (such as Lavazza)

MERINGUE BASES
½ cup/75 g whole blanched hazelnuts
⅔ cup/80 g confectioners' sugar
3½ tbsp/20 g Dutch-processed
   cocoa powder
4½ oz/125 g egg whites (from
   3 large eggs—the yolks are
   used in the parfait)
⅛ tsp salt
⅛ tsp cream of tartar
½ cup/100 g granulated sugar
7 oz/200 g dark chocolate
   (70% cocoa solids), roughly
   chopped into ⅓-inch/1-cm pieces

ESPRESSO PARFAIT
1½ cups/350 ml heavy cream
6 large egg yolks (you will have
   3 from the meringues)
1 cup/240 ml espresso coffee
1 cup/200 g granulated sugar
2 tsp coffee extract (we use
   Trablit Liquid Coffee Extract,
   but any brand is fine)

CARAMEL SAUCE
1⅔ cups/330 g granulated sugar
⅓ cup/80 ml water
⅔ cup/160 ml heavy cream
⅓ cup/80 ml whiskey

———

1   **To make the coffee praline,** combine the sugar and water in a small saucepan and place over low heat. Stir to combine until the sugar has melted. Increase the heat to medium and simmer for about 5 minutes, until the sugar begins to brown at the edges. Gently swirl the pan, resisting the urge to stir, so that the sugar cooks evenly into a caramel. When the caramel has turned a clear amber—about 1 minute—remove from the heat and pour onto a small parchment-lined rimmed baking sheet. Tilt the sheet as it sets to get a thin layer of caramel. Sprinkle all over with the ground coffee, then set aside until completely cool and hard. Once cool, transfer to a food processor and process until coarsely ground; pieces will range in size from powdery to about ¼ inch/0.5 cm wide. Set aside until ready to use.

We like to make this in an 8-inch/ 20-cm square cake pan with a removable base. The removable base makes things easier, but it's not strictly necessary. So long as it's lined, you'll be fine to use any similar-sized pan. You will also need a candy thermometer for the parfait.

The caramel sauce can be made up to a week ahead and stored in the fridge; reheat in a pan over low heat just before serving. The coffee praline can be made up to 2 weeks in advance and stored in an airtight container in the freezer (not in the fridge; where the sugar will weep) until ready to use. You can also make the meringue bases in advance (before spreading with the melted chocolate and praline); they keep well in an airtight container for 3 days. However much you decide to get done ahead, the parfait needs freezing for 12 hours once assembled, so you are forced to get ahead this much at least!

2   **To make the meringue bases,** preheat the oven to 350°F/180°C and position two racks in the oven: one in the middle and one at the bottom. Cut two sheets of parchment paper to fit two large baking sheets. Using the base of the pan in which you are going to freeze the parfait (we use an 8-inch/20-cm square pan, but other pans work; see Note), trace around the base onto each sheet of parchment. Turn the paper over and place on the baking sheets so that the side you have drawn on is facing down but still visible. Set aside; this will be the template for the meringue bases.

3   Spread the whole hazelnuts out on a baking sheet and roast for about 15 minutes, or until the nuts are lightly brown. Remove from the oven and, once cool enough to handle, chop them finely into ¼-inch/0.5-cm pieces. Set aside until completely cool.

4   Sift the confectioners' sugar and cocoa powder together into a bowl and set aside. Place the egg whites in the bowl of an electric mixer with the whisk attachment in place. Add the salt and cream of tartar and beat on medium-high speed for about 2 minutes, until soft peaks form. Gradually add the granulated sugar—1 tbsp at a time—and continue to beat for 2–3 minutes, until very stiff. Gently fold in the sifted confectioners' sugar and cocoa powder and the hazelnuts.

5   Divide the meringue mixture in two and dollop onto the two traced sheets, smoothing it out with a small metal spatula to fit the traced shapes. It will spread slightly, but you can later trim it back so it fits the pan snugly.

6   Place the baking sheets onto the prepared oven racks and bake for about 1 hour, or until the meringues are crisp and dry (the inside will still be a little bit soft). Check the meringues halfway through the cooking time, rotating the sheets and swapping them between the racks if one is taking on more color than the other. Remove from the oven and set aside to cool. Once the meringues are cool, trim the edges so that they fit neatly into the pan in which the parfait will be frozen. If the pan has a removable base, use this to help you trim the meringue bases.

7   Place the chocolate in a small heatproof bowl and set it over a small saucepan of simmering water, making sure the base of the bowl is not touching the water. Stir occasionally until the chocolate melts, then set aside to cool slightly. Brush the flat side of each of the meringue bases with the melted chocolate and immediately sprinkle the coffee praline all over the chocolate so that it has time to adhere to the chocolate before it sets. Set aside to dry while you make the parfait.

8   **To make the espresso parfait,** place the cream in the bowl of an electric mixer with the whisk attachment in place. Beat until soft peaks form, then transfer to a container and store in the fridge until ready to use.

9   Place the egg yolks in a clean bowl of an electric mixer with the whisk attachment in place, in preparation for the next step. ››

The parfait can be assembled and stored in the freezer for up to 1 week, ideally, but it will keep well in the freezer for up to 1 month.

If making the meringue bases the day before the parfait, reserve the egg yolks for the parfait. Store the yolks in a small bowl, add 1 tsp water directly on top, wrap the bowl in plastic wrap and place in the fridge.

10   Put the espresso coffee and sugar in a medium saucepan and place over low heat, stirring until the sugar has dissolved. Increase the heat to medium-high and simmer the coffee syrup. In the meantime, begin whisking the egg yolks on medium-high speed. Keep checking the coffee syrup with a sugar thermometer and when it has reached 245°F/118°C (soft-ball stage), pour the hot coffee syrup slowly down the rim of the bowl onto the beating yolks, which should be thick and creamy by now. Continue to beat at medium-high speed until the bowl is no longer warm to the touch—10–15 minutes—then add the coffee extract. Whisk to combine, then turn off the mixer.

11   While the yolks are whipping and cooling, line the sides and base of your chosen pan with parchment paper, making sure there is an overhang on all sides. Place one of the meringue bases on the bottom, chocolate side down. It should fit neatly, with no large gaps around the sides.

12   When the yolk mixture is cool, remove the bowl from the mixer and use a large rubber spatula to fold in the whipped cream in three batches. Do not overmix, as you want to keep the parfait light and airy, but do make sure that there are no big lumps of cream. Pour the parfait over the meringue base and use a small spatula to smooth and even it out. Carefully place the second meringue sheet over the top of the parfait, chocolate side up. Press gently to ensure the meringue is completely in contact with the parfait. Cover with plastic wrap and place in the freezer for 12 hours, or until completely firm.

13   **To make the caramel sauce,** combine the sugar and water in a medium saucepan and place over low heat. Cook until the sugar has dissolved, stirring occasionally, then increase the heat to high. Do not stir beyond this point. Cook until the caramel is a deep amber color, then remove from the heat. Carefully add the cream—stand back here, as the mixture will bubble and splutter—and return the pan to a low heat. Stir until the caramel is smooth, add the whiskey and decant into a measuring cup.

14   When ready to serve, remove the frozen parfait from the freezer and, using the overhanging paper, gently pull the whole thing out. If your pan has a removable base, push the parfait up from underneath. Slice into small squares or rectangles with a warm knife, drizzle with the caramel sauce, and serve.

Saffron and almond ice cream sandwich

This is an ice cream sandwich for grown-ups. The appeal is timeless—Ice cream! In a sandwich! Made with cookies!—but the flavor of the saffron makes this one a treat for the big kids. Don't be put off by all the different stages here; it looks like a lot of work, but the joy of an ice cream maker is that a lot of the work is done for you.

MAKES 12

Ideally, an ice cream maker is needed to churn the ice cream. If you don't have one, you can churn it yourself, stirring the mix every few hours to break up the formation of ice crystals before returning it to the freezer.

Both the cookies and nuts can be made 3–4 days ahead and kept, separately, in airtight containers.

Once assembled, the sandwiches will keep in the freezer for up to 1 month.

¾ cup/120 g whole almonds, skin on
1⅔ cups/200 g all-purpose flour, plus
    extra for dusting
⅔ cup/55 g Dutch-processed
    cocoa powder
½ tsp baking powder
½ tsp salt
7 tbsp/100 g unsalted butter,
    at room temperature
¾ packed cup plus 1 tbsp/160 g light
    brown sugar
½ tsp vanilla extract
¼ cup/60 ml whole milk

ICE CREAM

4 large egg yolks
½ cup/100 g granulated sugar
1⅓ cups/320 ml whole milk
1¼ cups/300 ml heavy cream
½ vanilla pod, sliced in half
    lengthwise and seeds scraped
¼ tsp saffron threads

1   Preheat the oven to 350°F/180°C.

2   Spread the almonds out on a baking sheet and bake for 8 minutes. Set aside to cool, then pulse in a food processor into roughly ¼-inch/0.5-cm pieces. Store in an airtight container until needed.

3   Increase the oven temperature to 400°F/200°C. Line two baking sheets with parchment paper.

4   Sift the flour, cocoa, baking powder and salt together into a bowl and set aside.

5   Put the butter and brown sugar into the bowl of an electric mixer with the paddle attachment in place. Beat on high speed for about 3 minutes, until pale, then add the vanilla extract. Mix to incorporate, turn the speed to low and add a third of the flour mixture. Continue to incorporate, then add half the milk. Mix to combine, then repeat with another third of the flour, the remaining milk, and finish with the flour. Mix until just combined; the dough will be soft but not sticky.

6   Transfer the dough to a lightly floured work surface and knead until smooth. Divide into two and set one half aside. Roll the dough to ⅛-inch/3-mm thick and use an 3-inch/8-cm round cookie cutter to cut out disks. Arrange the disks on a baking sheet, separating the layers with parchment paper so they don't stick to each other, then repeat the process with the second piece of dough. Reroll any scraps to make twenty-four cookies in total. Place in the freezer for 15 minutes.

7   When ready to bake, arrange the disks on the lined baking sheets and bake for 6–8 minutes, until firm on the outside but still a little soft in the center. Remove from the oven and set aside to cool for 5 minutes before transferring to a wire rack to cool completely. Place the cookies in an airtight container until ready to use. ››

8   **To make the ice cream,** place the egg yolks and granulated sugar in a medium bowl, whisk to combine and set aside. Combine the milk, cream, vanilla pod and seeds and saffron in a medium saucepan and place over medium heat. Warm through for 3–4 minutes, until little bubbles start forming. Slowly pour half the hot milk into the yolk mixture, whisking constantly until smooth, then pour all the yolk mixture back into the saucepan with the remaining milk. Return to medium-low heat and cook for 8–10 minutes, stirring constantly, until the mixture coats the back of a spoon. Remove from the heat, discard the vanilla pod, transfer to a bowl and set aside to cool completely; the best way to do this is to chill the mixture over an ice bath or in the fridge before churning. When cold, place in an ice cream maker and churn until firm waves appear.

9   Before assembling, place a baking sheet (or any other tray) in your freezer. This is to put the ice cream sandwiches on as soon as they are assembled. When assembling the sandwiches, keep the ice cream churning (to prevent it from melting).

10   Spoon about two heaping tablespoonfuls of ice cream on the underside of one cookie and place another cookie on top, smooth side up. Gently squeeze the cookies together so that the ice cream just comes to the edge of the cookies. Run the tip of a teaspoon between the two cookies to remove any excess ice cream and to create a smooth finish. Give the cookies one final gentle squeeze together so that the ice cream sits evenly with the cookies. Place each sandwich on the baking sheet in the freezer as soon as it is assembled, before starting on the next. Once they are all together, freeze for 6 hours before serving.

11   Remove the ice cream sandwiches from the freezer to allow the edges of the ice cream to soften slightly. Spread the chopped almonds out on a flat plate, roll the exposed ice cream in the nuts, and serve.

Campari and grapefruit sorbet

This is so refreshing and party-like that it can be served at pretty much any point during a meal. Before you start eating, for example, with a splash of prosecco on top; as a palate-cleanser between courses; or for dessert in frosted martini glasses with a Cats' Tongue (see page 27) alongside and possibly also a naughty extra glug of Campari.

Don't be tempted to use pale yellow grapefruit here: you really want the ruby red variety, as it provides both the shock of color and the sweetness you want to bring to the party.

Once you've made the sorbet, you're all set to make the Chocolate-Coated Ruby Red Grapefruit Peel (see page 326), if you like, as you'll have the peel all ready to go. If you don't want to do this straightaway, collect the peel in a ziplock bag and store it in the fridge for up to 3 days.

SERVES 6 (AT THE END OF A MEAL), 12 (IN THE MIDDLE) OR MORE (AT THE START OF A MEAL)

---

2 cups/480 ml ruby red grapefruit juice (from 2–5 grapefruit, depending on their size and juiciness)
¼ cup/60 ml lemon juice
½ cup/120 ml orange juice
1 cup/200 g granulated sugar
⅓ cup/80 ml Campari

---

1   Combine the grapefruit juice, lemon juice and orange juice and mix together. Pour 1 cup/240 ml of this into a small saucepan with the sugar and set the remaining juice aside. Heat the pan over low heat, stirring until the sugar is dissolved, then set aside for 10 minutes to cool. Pour this into the remaining juice, add the Campari and chill completely by setting it over an ice bath or placing it in the fridge.

2   Once chilled, transfer to an ice cream maker and churn until soft waves form. Transfer the sorbet to a container, cover with plastic wrap—so that the plastic wrap is actually touching the surface of the sorbet, to prevent ice particles from forming—and seal the container. Freeze until firm enough to scoop into glasses and serve.

Ideally, an ice cream maker is needed to churn the sorbet. If you don't have one, you can churn it yourself, stirring the mix every few hours to break up the formation of ice crystals before returning it to the freezer.

Once churned, the sorbet will keep in the freezer for about 1 week.

Chocolate, rose and walnut ice cream

Something's a bit Arabian nights about these ingredients, with the Turkish delight and rose water, which is key—start with good-quality rose water, preferably Lebanese.

Thanks to Caroline Liddell and Robin Weir's *Ices: The Definitive Guide* for the technique of "cooking out" the cocoa powder in the recipe for the chocolate base, in the same way that you cook out the flour when making a béchamel.

SERVES 6–8

½ cup/60 g walnut halves
1½ cups/350 ml whole milk
1¼ cups/300 ml heavy cream
3½ tbsp/20 g Dutch-processed
   cocoa powder
3 large egg yolks
½ cup/100 g granulated sugar
3½ oz/100 g dark chocolate
   (70% cocoa solids), chopped
1 tsp instant coffee granules
about 1 tbsp rose water
3 graham cracker sheets, broken into
   ⅓-inch/1-cm pieces

CHOCOLATE SAUCE
2 oz/55 g dark chocolate
   (70% cocoa solids), finely chopped
½ cup/120 ml heavy cream
¼ tsp brandy (optional)

4¼ oz/120 g rose-flavored Turkish
   delight, cut into ⅓-inch/1-cm cubes
1 tsp dried rose petals (optional)

Ideally, an ice cream maker is needed to churn the ice cream. If you don't have one, you can churn it yourself, stirring the mix every few hours to break up the formation of ice crystals before returning it to the freezer.

The ice cream can be churned a day in advance and stored in the freezer: remove from the freezer 20 minutes before serving.

1   Preheat the oven to 350°F/180°C. Spread the walnuts out on a rimmed baking sheet and roast for 7 minutes. Remove from the oven and, once cool enough to handle, chop into ⅓-inch/1-cm pieces. Set aside.

2   Pour the milk and cream into a medium saucepan and place over medium heat. Cook for 3–4 minutes, until it starts to simmer. Pour about ⅓ cup/80 ml into a small bowl, add the cocoa powder and whisk until combined. Return the mixture to the pan, stir, turn the heat to medium-low and cook gently for another 6–7 minutes, stirring often, to "cook out" the cocoa. Remove from the heat and set aside.

3   Place the egg yolks and sugar in a medium bowl and whisk until pale. Slowly pour in about ½ cup/120 ml of the hot chocolate cream and continue to whisk. Return everything to the saucepan, along with the chocolate and instant coffee, stir to melt, then cook gently over medium heat for another 10 minutes, stirring regularly, for the custard to thicken slightly. Set aside to cool completely; you can do this by either setting it over an ice bath or chilling it in the fridge (for a few hours or overnight). Starting off with properly chilled custard is important, as it won't overwork the ice cream machine. Once chilled, gradually add the rose water (don't add it all at once; taste to make sure the rose flavor doesn't take over).

4   Transfer to an ice cream maker and churn until soft waves form, then spoon into a plastic container with a lid. Stir in the walnuts and graham crackers and freeze, covered, for 1 hour (or overnight).

5   **To make the chocolate sauce,** put the chocolate in a bowl. Place the cream in a saucepan over medium heat. As soon as it starts to boil, pour it over the chocolate and stir until melted. Stir in the brandy (if using). Spoon the ice cream into bowls, drizzle with the sauce, sprinkle with the Turkish delight and rose petals, if desired, and serve.

Confectionery

—

People love to have treats baked for them and people love to receive gifts. Combine the two and all your Christmases have, quite literally, come at once.

Christmas is a big time for confectionery in our shops: our displays are piled high with festive treats. Some things taste like Christmas—the Chocolate Panforte with Oranges and Figs (see page 332), for example, with all those winter spices. Some things look like Christmas—the little log-shaped Pecan and Prosecco Truffles (see page 324)—while others manage to both taste and look like Christmas, in the case of the oversized Spiced Praline Meringues (see page 323), which can be hung from your tree before being eaten.

The long shelf life, general robustness and abundant yield of many of the recipes in this chapter allow you to be very generous. A batch of Almond and Aniseed Nougat (see page 328) or Chocolate Panforte with Oranges and Figs (see page 332) will enable you to cross off all the cousins on your Christmas list in one go, should you so choose. Cut, slice and wrap as you like, depending on who you are making them for and how big you want your slices to be. The Pecan and Prosecco Truffles (see page 324) and the Chocolate-Coated Ruby Red Grapefruit Peel (see page 326) make well over twenty pieces each. Arrange a handful of these in individual parchment-lined boxes, and happiness is guaranteed. The bright-red Raspberry Lollipops (see page 318) look great packaged in individual see-through bags, as do the Woodland Meringues (see page 319) in packs of about ten.

Confectionery is for life, though, not just for Christmas. Valentine's day, Mother's Day, Father's Day, Hanukkah, Chinese New Year, a friend's birthday, Easter, Thanksgiving, Eid . . . whatever the occasion, there's nothing more satisfying than turning up at a friend's house with a little bag, box or stick of something, and being able to slip in the fact that you made them. "You made them?!" It's a real ta-da! moment: the celebration of small and sweet things.

The satisfaction of giving is second only, perhaps, to the satisfaction you get when you crack the making of a confectionery recipe for the first time. Quite literally in the case of the Raspberry Lollipops (see page 318), as it does take practice to get them to their perfectly brittle state. Working with sugar—making nougat, making caramel—also takes practice. It's not that it's particularly complicated, it just requires you to be on top of the timing and to know sugar well enough to gauge what's going on in the pan. A candy thermometer will be your best friend at this stage, taking the guesswork out of the equation and allowing you to relax in the knowledge that, so long as you do exactly as you are told in terms of timing and temperatures, Willy Wonka will be proud.

Equipment

As we say, a candy thermometer is a big must: you won't be able to make many of the recipes in this chapter successfully without one. A piping bag is also needed for a couple of recipes; you can either invest in a piping bag that comes with a range of tips, or you can buy disposable piping bags and cut holes in the ends. Of course, if you don't have either of these things but would like them, they are your answer to the inevitable question—"But what would you like for Christmas?"—from all those who are so grateful for the confectionery gifts you have just given them.

A note on the weather

Although the confectionery in this chapter should be enough to cheer everyone up whatever the weather, the weather is actually something you need to be mindful of when working with sugar. If it's particularly humid or muggy, it can cause problems with the setting of the caramels or lollipops, for example. The former can end up weeping and the latter can end up bendy. This is not to put you off making either of these if it is warm, but to explain why things may not be going to plan. Even the patience of Sarah Joseph—known to be neither weepy nor flaky—was tested through the re-creation of both of these recipes during a particularly humid July. Sarah worked closely with us on the making of *Sweet*, testing every recipe to make sure that what works in our shops and bakery also works at home. When you crack your first lollipop—"It works! It cracks! It's not bendy!"—spare a smile for Sarah: things cracking when they're meant to and not cracking when they shouldn't is in no small part due to all her hard work.

Saffron and pistachio brittle

Helen was inspired to create this after her first visit, with her good friend Goli, to the annual Persian market held in the run-up to Nowruz—Persian New Year—in the heart of London's Marylebone. Crowded with savvy and purposeful Iranian women getting hold of the goods they needed for their New Year preparations, Helen—not entirely sure what she was preparing for—returned home with a cashmere scarf, a ceramic replica of a pomegranate, a box of chickpea halva, two goldfish (real ones), jars of carrot jam and vegetable pickles, a dozen hyacinth bulbs and, crucially, some wonderful saffron nut brittle known as Sohan Asali.

Our version departs from the Sohan Asali she bought, but mention needs to be made of how strongly the lady who sold it to Helen felt about her using Persian saffron in the first instance. "Anything else," said Mimi, "is inferior." The same could also be said of Iranian pistachios—they are long and elegant and a vibrant green (and even better, do not need to be chopped)—but regular pistachios are also fine.

MAKES 12 PIECES (OR MORE OR LESS, DEPENDING ON SIZE)

If the brittle sticks to the saucepan so much that it's hard to clean, add a bit boiling water to the pan and return it to the heat for a minute: the brittle will quickly loosen.

A candy thermometer is a must here.

The brittle will keep for about 10 days in an airtight container. Don't be tempted to store it in the fridge, as it will weep.

(GF)

1½ cups/150 g sliced almonds
1⅓ packed cups/270 g light brown sugar
8½ tbsp/120 g unsalted butter
2 tbsp boiling water

½ tsp saffron threads, steeped in 2 tsp boiling water
¼ tsp flaky sea salt
½ tsp baking soda
2½ tbsp/20 g shelled pistachio kernels, roughly chopped

1   Preheat the oven to 350°F/180°C. Spread the almonds out on a rimmed baking sheet and roast for about 7 minutes, or until light golden brown. Turn off the oven but leave the nuts inside so that they stay warm (so that the brittle won't harden as quickly when the nuts are added).

2   Line a 11 x 9-inch/28 x 23-cm (or similar size) rimmed baking sheet with parchment paper and set aside.

3   Combine the brown sugar, butter and boiling water in a medium saucepan and place over low heat. Stir until the sugar has melted. Increase the heat to medium and stop stirring. Simmer until the temperature reaches between 284°F/140°C and 289°F/143°C on a candy thermometer ("soft crack" stage). Turn off the heat but leave the pan on the stove top. Carefully add the saffron threads with the steeping water and flaky sea salt; it will bubble up a bit, so be careful. Stir very gently to combine, then add the baking soda and warm almonds. Stir again until the mixture froths up and is evenly mixed.

4   Working quickly, pour the mixture all over the lined baking sheet and carefully tilt the baking sheet until it is evenly spread. Do not use any utensils to do this, as the consistency of the caramel will be changed. Sprinkle the chopped pistachios all over the top and press lightly with a spatula or the back of a spoon so they stick to the caramel. Set aside to cool completely—this will take about 45 minutes—before breaking into smaller pieces to serve.

RASPBERRY LOLLIPOPS

Raspberry lollipops

We make these in heart shapes around Valentine's Day, but they're a wonderful way to make loved ones smile all year-round—in a round shape! You can either shape them by hand or, if you're after perfection, use bottomless cake rings as your mold: 2¾-inch/7-cm rings are good for regular round lollipops, but there are all sorts of shapes you can play with, such as hearts, stars, and so forth.

Whether you are shaping them by hand or using a cake ring, don't make these on a rainy or humid day: the caramel will weep and you'll end up with bendy lollipops (which will not be so smile-inducing).

MAKES 12

⅔ cup/60 g fresh raspberries (about 12)
1¼ cups/250 g granulated sugar
¾ cup/250 g light corn syrup
2 tbsp plus 2 tsp/40 ml water

⅔ oz/20 g freeze-dried raspberries, half left whole and half lightly crushed

A candy thermometer is a must here, along with twelve lollipop sticks. The metal cake rings are optional.

These will keep for up to a week in an airtight container, stored between layers of parchment paper.

1　Line three baking sheets with parchment paper, then lay twelve lollipop sticks out flat on the lined sheets—the lollipops are large so they require some space—and set aside.

2　Process the fresh raspberries in the small bowl of a food processor, then strain through a fine-mesh sieve placed over a bowl; you should end up with about 2 tbsp of seedless purée. Set aside.

3　Put the sugar and corn syrup into a medium saucepan and stir in the water. Place over medium heat and cook for about 3 minutes, stirring, until the sugar melts. Increase the heat to medium-high and boil for about 10 minutes, until it reaches 297°F/147°C on a candy thermometer. Precision is key here, but it is better to be 1 degree hotter than 1 degree below. Remove from the heat and add the raspberry purée; take care here, as the sugar will be bubbling. Stir slowly and gently with a metal spoon until combined, taking care not to mix too quickly, as this will create air bubbles that will stay in the lollipops. Once fully combined, lightly stir in the whole and lightly crushed dried raspberries, again taking care as you do so. The caramel should have stopped bubbling by this time.

4　Immediately spoon 3 tbsp of the mixture onto the top one-third of each of the lollipop sticks. Use the spoon to create a circle if shaping by hand. You'll need to work fast here, as the sugar mixture will thicken quickly. Divide the freeze-dried raspberries equally among the lollipops. If you are using cake rings (see introduction), place them over the top third of the lollipop sticks and pour in 3 tbsp of the mixture.

5　Loosely lay a sheet of parchment paper over the top of the lollipops to stop them from sweating. Set aside until completely cool and set; this should take about a half hour. Once cool and set, remove the cake rings (if using) from the lollipops and serve.

Woodland meringues

Helen was inspired to create these after a walk around Kew Gardens with her young sons. It was autumn and the ground was covered in conkers (horse chestnuts). Delighting in her boys delight at the little fallen treats, Helen then had to be the one to inform them that, no, eating conkers was really not such a good idea. Their look of collective bafflement was so great that Helen's imagination set out to create something that both looks like it has fallen from a tree and, crucially, is eminently edible. These woodland meringues are the result.

We've included two versions here—dark chocolate with hazelnuts and white chocolate with freeze-dried strawberries. You can make one or the other or a combination of both. We sell them in the shops in little see-through bags, for people to take home or to buy as a gift. They're a lovely bite-sized way to end a meal or party.

MAKES ABOUT 70

When melted and used as a coating, dark chocolate can develop white streaks after a day or so. This won't affect the taste but can be avoided by tempering the chocolate (see page 345). Tempering the chocolate is optional here, however, as the chocolate is covered by the chopped hazelnuts so any white streaks won't really be seen.

You will need a piping bag with a ⅔-inch/1.5-cm tip. You can also buy disposable piping bags, if you prefer.

These will keep for up to 10 days, stored in an airtight container.

MERINGUE
4½ oz/125 g egg whites (from 3 large eggs)
½ tsp cream of tartar
1 cup plus 3 tbsp/240 g granulated sugar
¾ tsp cornstarch
⅛ tsp baking powder
½ tsp vanilla extract

DARK CHOCOLATE COATING
(HALVE THE QUANTITIES IF YOU ARE DOING A MIX OF DARK AND WHITE CHOCOLATE)
1⅓ cups/200 g hazelnuts
3½ oz/100 g dark chocolate (70% cocoa solids), chopped into ¾-inch/2-cm pieces
1½ oz/40 g milk chocolate, chopped into ¾-inch/2-cm pieces

WHITE CHOCOLATE COATING
(HALVE THE QUANTITIES IF YOU ARE DOING A MIX OF DARK AND WHITE CHOCOLATE)
5 oz/140 g white chocolate, chopped into ¾-inch/2-cm pieces
2 oz/55 g freeze-dried strawberries, finely chopped

1 Preheat the oven to 350°F/180°C. If making the dark chocolate coating, spread the hazelnuts out on a small rimmed baking sheet and roast for 10 minutes. Transfer to a clean kitchen towel, draw in the sides and then rub together to remove some of the skins. Chop the nuts very finely—it's better to do this by hand, rather than in a food processor, where the nuts will become dusty—then set aside in a bowl.

2 **To make the meringue,** lower the oven temperature to 275°F/140°C.

3 Place the egg whites in the bowl of an electric mixer with the whisk attachment in place. Beat on medium-high speed for about 2 minutes, until they appear foamy. Add the cream of tartar and continue to beat until they are stiff but not dry or crumbly, about 30 seconds. Place the sugar in a bowl, add the cornstarch and baking powder (adding both ensures a completely dry and crisp meringue), and gradually— a tablespoon at a time—add the sugar to the egg whites. Continue to beat for about 3 minutes, until the mixture is thick and glossy. Beat in the vanilla extract, then spoon into a piping bag with a ⅔-inch/1.5-cm tip in place. »

4   Line two large baking sheets with parchment paper (sticking each piece of parchment firmly to the baking sheet with a bit of the meringue mix). Pipe small droplets—or kisses—onto each lined baking sheet; the base of each droplet should be about 1 inch/3 cm wide. Raise the piping bag as you pipe, so that they are about 2 inches/5 cm high and you create a fine tip at the top. Once all the meringues have been piped, place both baking sheets in the oven at once. Immediately lower the oven temperature to 250°F/120°C—you want it to be slightly hotter when they go in, to give the meringues a crunch—and bake for 2½ hours. The meringues are done when they look dry and sound hollow when tapped gently underneath. Turn off the oven but leave the meringues inside until they are cool, propping the door open with a wooden spoon.

5   **To make the dark chocolate coating,** place the dark and milk chocolate in a medium heatproof bowl over a pan of simmering water, making sure the base of the bowl is not touching the water. Stir occasionally until melted. One at a time, dip the base of the meringues into the melted chocolate, followed by the chopped hazelnuts, then place on a parchment-lined baking sheet to set. **To make the white chocolate coating,** follow the instructions for the dark chocolate topping, dipping the base into the dried strawberries instead.

Spiced praline meringues

Yotam first made these around Christmastime for his weekly column in the *Guardian*. They are intentionally oversized—just as good hung from the tree as an ornament as they are to eat—and last for ten days, so, fortunately, their use as both decoration and edible treat are not mutually exclusive options.

    If you want to make them just for the table, use the same amount of meringue mixture to produce twelve regular-sized meringues. These are great served with cream and stewed cranberries as a seasonal dessert.

MAKES 6 (EXTRA-LARGE) OR 12 (REGULAR-SIZED)

⅓ cup/50 g blanched slivered almonds
1½ cups/300 g granulated sugar
2 tbsp water
½ tsp ground cinnamon
⅛ tsp ground cloves

finely grated zest of 1 large orange (1 tbsp)
¼ tsp flaky sea salt
5¼ oz/150 g egg whites (from 4 large eggs)

If placing the meringues on the tree, use a strip of ribbon to gently wrap each one, as you would a present, creating a bow and leaving a long piece of ribbon to hang them with.

These will keep for up to 10 days. If you are not hanging them on the tree, wrap them loosely in aluminum foil and keep at room temperature.

(GF)

1   Preheat the oven to 375°F/190°C.

2   Spread the almonds out on a small rimmed baking sheet and roast in the oven for 5–7 minutes, until lightly browned. Set aside to cool. Line two large rimmed baking sheets with parchment paper and set aside.

3   Place ¼ cup/50 g of the sugar in a small saucepan with the water and stir to combine. Cook over high heat for about 4 minutes, until it has turned a light golden brown; do not stir, just gently shake the pan to help the sugar dissolve. Add the almonds and cook for 1 minute, so the nuts are coated and the caramel turns dark, without burning. Pour the mixture onto one of the lined baking sheets and set aside until cool.

4   Once cool, break the praline into smaller pieces, place in a food processor and process to form a rough powder. Remove from the machine, place in a shallow bowl and combine with the spices, orange zest and salt. Set aside.

5   Spread the remaining sugar out on the second lined baking sheet and place in the oven for 7 minutes, until the sugar is hot. Remove from the oven and lower the temperature to 275°F/130°C. As soon as the sugar is out of the oven, place the egg whites in the bowl of an electric mixer with the whisk attachment in place and beat on high speed until they begin to froth up. Carefully add the hot sugar to the egg whites, 1 tbsp at a time, and continue beating for 7–8 minutes until the mixture is completely cold. At this point it should be silky and thick and keep its shape when you lift a little bit from the bowl.

6   Line two large baking sheets with parchment paper. Use an extra-large serving spoon to scoop up some meringue, and use another large spoon to help shape it into a rough ball the size of a large apple. Sprinkle some praline over half the meringue ball, then place on the baking sheet, repeat with the rest of the mixture, spacing the balls as far apart as possible, as they will increase in size.

7   Place the meringues in the oven for 2–2½ hours. Check that they are done by lifting them from the baking sheet and gently tapping to make sure the outside is completely firm and the center is only a little soft. Remove from the oven and leave on the baking sheet to cool.

Pecan and prosecco truffles

These were made for the Christmas menu at Ottolenghi, hence their shape as little Yule logs, but you can just roll them into balls, if you prefer. Coating the truffles in a thin layer of chocolate is messy, we know, but it's worth it for the satisfaction of biting into the thin shell to reveal the rich, smooth truffle underneath.

MAKES ABOUT 35

⅓ cup/45 g pecan halves

2 oz/55 g milk chocolate, blitzed in a food processor until fine

6 oz/170 g dark chocolate (70% cocoa solids), blitzed in a food processor until fine, plus 3 oz/85 g, melted, for coating

3½ tbsp/50 ml heavy cream

2 tbsp/30 g unsalted butter

3½ tbsp/50 ml prosecco

1½ tsp brandy

⅓ cup/30 g Dutch-processed cocoa powder, for dusting

A piping bag with a ⅓-inch/1-cm tip is needed if you want to make these into log shapes.

The truffles will keep for up to 10 days in an airtight container in the fridge.

1   Preheat the oven to 350°F/180°C.

2   Spread the pecans out on a rimmed baking sheet and roast for 10 minutes. Remove from the oven, set aside for 5 minutes, then chop into very small (roughly ⅛-inch/3-mm) pieces. Set aside.

3   Place both chocolates in a large heatproof bowl and set aside. Put the cream and butter into a small saucepan and place over medium-high heat. As soon as the mixture comes to a boil, pour the cream and butter over the chocolate. Leave for a minute, then stir gently to melt. If there is any solid chocolate remaining, place the bowl over a pan of gently simmering water to help things along. Add the prosecco, brandy and pecans and fold gently to combine until a smooth ganache is formed. Set aside for the mixture to come to room temperature so that it is firm enough to pipe. It takes a long time to set at room temperature, but this is essential for the perfectly smooth and even texture needed. Give it a gentle stir from time to time so that it is malleable enough to pipe. Don't be tempted to speed up the cooling process in the fridge, as this will result in an uneven and lumpy set.

4   Transfer the mixture to a piping bag fitted with a ⅓-inch/1-cm plain tip and pipe seven 11-inch/28-cm-long logs on to a large parchment-lined baking sheet. Place in the fridge for 30 minutes to set, then cut the logs into five smaller logs, each about 2 inches/5 cm long; using a warm, dry knife will help you cut them cleanly.

5   Have the melted dark chocolate in one bowl and the cocoa powder in a separate shallow bowl or pie pan alongside. Dip one log at a time into the melted chocolate to lightly coat, then roll it in the palm of your hand to remove excess chocolate and ensure that the chocolate coating is nice and thin and sets evenly. Drop the truffle into the cocoa powder and roll gently to lightly coat. You'll need to work fast here, as the chocolate will set quickly. Get someone to help, if you can, so that one person is on the melted chocolate and the other is on the cocoa dusting; this means you won't have to keep washing your hands between coating and rolling. Once set, after about 30 minutes, lightly shake to remove any excess cocoa and serve.

Chocolate-coated ruby red grapefruit peel

Other citrus fruits can be used instead of the grapefruit, if you prefer, so long as they have a thick skin and can be peeled with the fingers; oranges also work well. Fruits with a thinner skin—lemons and limes, for example—aren't really suitable. When peeling your fruit, keep the white pith attached. Don't worry about the bitterness, most of this is removed through blanching.

We like to make these at the same time as Campari and Grapefruit Sorbet (see page 304), as you will have the peel from two large grapefruit left over from making the sorbet.

MAKES 32 PIECES

2 large ruby red grapefruit
(1 lb 8 oz/670 g)
6½ oz/180 g dark chocolate
(70% cocoa solids), roughly chopped

SUGAR SYRUP
4¼ cups/1 L water
2½ cups/500 g granulated sugar
1 cinnamon stick
1 bay leaf

When melted and used as a coating, dark chocolate can develop white streaks after a day or so. This won't affect the taste, but can be avoided by tempering the chocolate (see page 345).

Peel the fruit up to 3 days in advance and store in a ziplock bag or airtight container in the fridge.

Once coated, the peel keeps for up to 10 days in an airtight container at room temperature.

1   Slice each grapefruit into quarters and then each quarter in half lengthwise, so you have eight segments per grapefruit (sixteen total). To carefully separate the fruit from the thick peel (eat or use the flesh for the sorbet), take a small paring knife and halve each of the sixteen segments of peel lengthwise so that you have thirty-two pieces.

2   Fill a large saucepan with plenty of water and bring to a boil over high heat. Once boiling, add the pieces of grapefruit peel. Press them down lightly into the water with a large spoon and blanch for about 30 seconds, just until the water comes back to a boil. Drain the peel with a colander set over the sink. Rinse well under cold running water, then repeat the whole process once more, starting with a pan of fresh boiling water—this removes some of the bitterness from the peel. Tip the grapefruit peel onto a clean kitchen towel and leave to dry. It is important to allow the skins to dry to prevent the sugar syrup from crystallizing later.

3   **To make the sugar syrup,** place all the syrup ingredients in a medium saucepan over medium-high heat. Cook for about 2 minutes, stirring a few times, until the sugar has dissolved.

4   Bring the syrup to a boil, then add the grapefruit peel. Cover the liquid with a cartouche—a round of parchment paper—and place a plate on top to ensure the peels are fully submerged. Keep the water at a lively simmer for 60–90 minutes, until the peels are translucent and you are left with about ½ cup/120 ml of syrupy liquid. This can take up to 1½ hours.

5   Drain the grapefruit peel and, using tongs or a slotted spoon, transfer them to a wire rack. The cinnamon, bay leaf and remaining syrup can be discarded. Set the grapefruit peel aside at room temperature, uncovered, until dry. This may take 12 hours or longer, depending on the humidity of the room.

6   Once the peels are dry, place the chocolate in a heatproof bowl set over a pan of simmering water, making sure the base of the bowl is not touching the water. Stir occasionally until melted, then remove the pan from the heat but keep the bowl over the hot water so the chocolate does not cool too quickly and thicken (if it does, simply return the pan to the heat). Taking one piece of candied peel at a time—lifting them by hand here is best, rather than using tongs—dip half into the melted chocolate and shake gently to remove any excess. Transfer to a wire rack to set before serving.

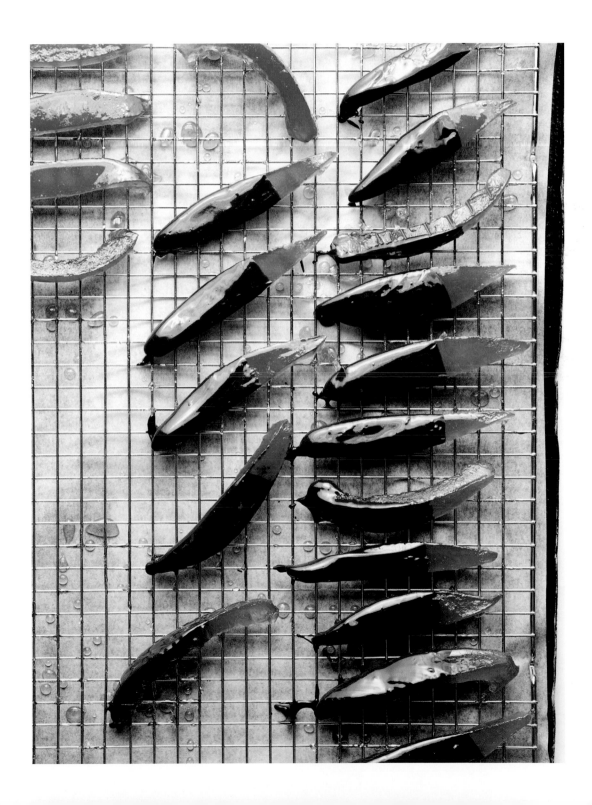

Almond and aniseed nougat

Helen learned how to make nougat from a VHS cassette she found in the 1990s! It showed the Italian mother of an Australian chef named Marco Lori making her family's famous torrone. Essentially the same thing as nougat, it's known as torrone in Italy and nougat in France. It can range in texture from soft to firm, depending on how high you take the temperature of the sugar syrup: the higher the temperature, the harder the nougat. Ours falls into the soft-but-chewy camp: it's still a little firm, but won't break your teeth. You'll know you've been on the right track when, 24 hours after it's made, your nougat has a small amount of movement when pressed. It shouldn't be too sticky and should hold its shape when cut.

Making your own nougat might seem a bit intimidating, but don't be put off: the results are hugely rewarding and (as is always the case when cooking with sugar) it's just about being organized and staying on top of temperatures and timing. The syrup needs to be at the correct temperature just as the egg whites reach soft peaks, and you'll need to work fast, as the nougat firms up quickly once it's been made.

MAKES 6 BARS OR 36 SMALLER PIECES

2 sheets (12 x 9 inches/30.5 x 23 cm) edible rice paper (or wafer paper, made from potato starch; or parchment paper)

2½ cups/400 g whole raw almonds, skin on

2 cups/260 g whole blanched hazelnuts

2 tbsp whole aniseed (optional)

1½ cups/300 g granulated sugar

¾ cup plus 2 tbsp/200 ml water

¾ cup plus 1½ tbsp/270 g light corn syrup

3 tbsp/60 g orange blossom honey (or another floral variety)

1 tbsp plus 2 tsp/25 ml Pernod or ouzo (or another aniseed liqueur)

scraped seeds of 1 vanilla pod

⅛ tsp salt

3⅛ oz/90 g egg whites (from 2½ large eggs)

A candy thermometer is a must here. We use a 9-inch/23-cm baking pan, 1½ inches/4 cm deep; alternatively, you could use two 7-inch/18-cm square pans.

Covered tightly in parchment paper and plastic wrap, the nougat will keep for up to a month in an airtight container at room temperature or in the fridge.

1   Line the base of a 9-inch/23-cm square baking pan with parchment paper and grease the edges of the pan. Lay one sheet of rice paper, smooth side down, on top of the parchment paper—the edges of the paper will rise up the sides of the pan—then set the pan aside.

2   Preheat the oven to 350°F/170°C. Spread all the nuts out on a rimmed baking sheet and roast for 18 minutes, until they are fragrant and golden brown. Lower the oven temperature to 200°F/90°C and leave the nuts in the oven until ready to fold into the nougat; the mix will seize up if the nuts are added cold.

3   Place the aniseed (if using) in a medium heavy saucepan and toast over medium heat for 2 minutes, until fragrant. Transfer to a pestle and mortar, lightly crush and set aside.

4   In a medium saucepan, combine the sugar, water, corn syrup, honey, Pernod or ouzo, vanilla seeds and salt and whisk to combine. Place over medium heat and simmer gently until the sugar has dissolved, then increase the heat to medium-high. Resisting the urge to stir, continue to cook for 15–20 minutes, until the temperature on a candy thermometer is close to reaching 244°F/118°C. At this stage, put the egg whites in the bowl of an electric mixer with the whisk attachment in place and beat on medium speed to form soft peaks. Keep an eye on the boiling syrup and, when the temperature on the thermometer registers exactly 250°F/121°C, pour half of the hot syrup into the soft peaks in a steady stream. Continue to beat on medium speed and return the remaining half of the syrup to the heat.

5   Continue to simmer the remaining syrup until the temperature reaches exactly 293°F/145°C, taking care that it does not go over 298°F/148°C. Once the temperature is reached, pour the hot syrup—it will be light golden—over the egg whites in a steady stream, whisking all the time. Continue to whisk for another 6–8 minutes, until you have a thick ribbon-like consistency. To check if it is ready, take a little of the mixture between your fingers, press together and then pull apart; the mix should stick together like chewing gum. Using a plastic spatula or large metal spoon, fold in the aniseed and warm nuts. You need to be careful here, as the bowl of the machine will still be hot. Scrape the mixture into the lined baking pan and even out with an offset or regular spatula.

6   Cover the surface with some more rice paper, smooth side up, and press down firmly to remove any air bubbles. Set aside to cool overnight, uncovered or with a clean, dry kitchen towel draped over the top. The next day, slide a hot knife around the edges to remove it from the pan. Cut into six long bars (9 x 1½ inches/ 23 x 4 cm), if giving as gifts, or into smaller squares.

ALMOND AND ANISEED NOUGAT

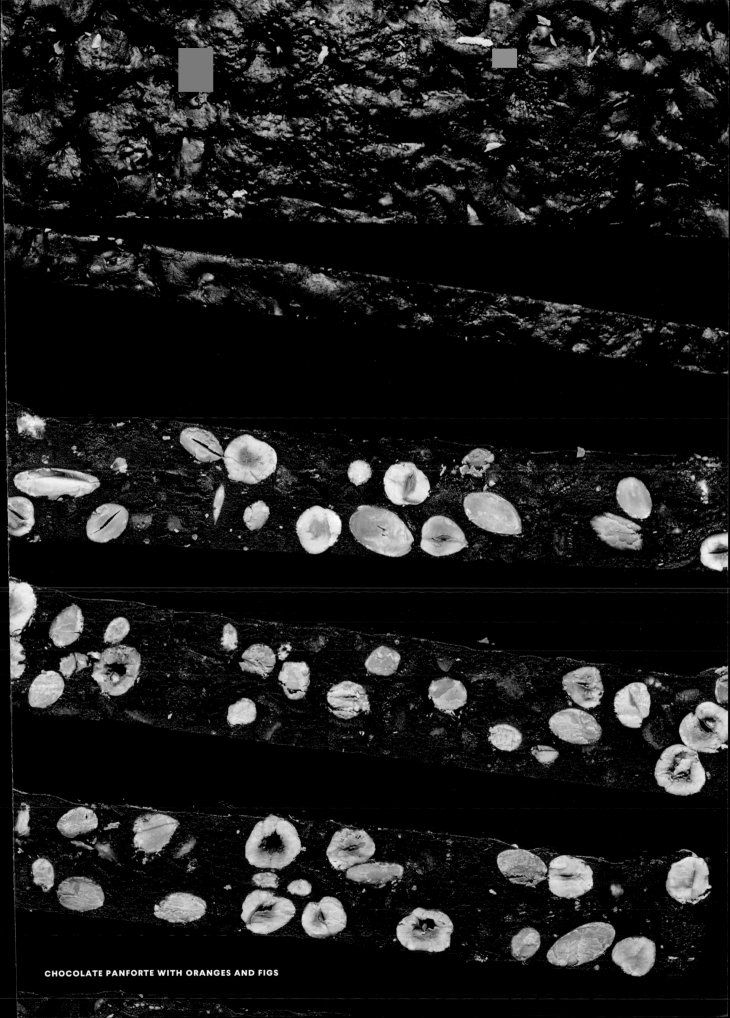

CHOCOLATE PANFORTE WITH ORANGES AND FIGS

Chocolate panforte with oranges and figs

We always love to have a wheel of panforte around. A little slice is perfect midmorning with coffee, or throughout the day whenever there is a tangy cheese on the table, looking for something sweet to complement it. It also makes for a really lovely gift, given whole or as individually wrapped segments, when you're going out to supper. The thrill of saying, "Something for the table—I made it for you!" never fails to satisfy.

Start with the best-quality dried fruit and nuts you can find, and use really fresh spices. It will make all the difference.

MAKES 10 SEGMENTS (USING A 9-INCH/23-CM ROUND PAN) **OR BARS** (USING AN 8-INCH/20-CM SQUARE PAN)

---

1 cup/150 g whole blanched hazelnuts

1 cup/150 g whole blanched almonds

7 oz/200 g candied orange peel, chopped into ⅓-inch/1-cm pieces (or whole candied oranges or clementines or mixed candied peel)

3½ oz/100 g dried figs, stemmed, chopped into ⅓-inch/1-cm pieces

finely grated zest of 1 orange (1½ tsp)

1¾ cups plus 3 tbsp/240 g all-purpose flour

1 cup/100 g Dutch-processed cocoa powder

2 tsp ground cinnamon

1 tsp ground ginger

¼ tsp ground cardamom (see page 351; increase to ½ tsp if starting with store-bought)

½ tsp ground cloves

½ tsp freshly grated nutmeg

½ tsp salt

½ tsp freshly ground black pepper

5¼ oz/150 g dark chocolate (70% cocoa solids), roughly chopped

¾ cup plus 1 tbsp/175 g granulated sugar

¾ cup/250 g honey (use whatever honey you like the taste of: orange blossom will bring a floral note; chestnut will bring an earthiness)

A candy thermometer is a must here. If you want to create a wheel shape, use a 9-inch/23-cm round cake pan; alternatively, use an 8-inch/20-cm square pan.

This keeps very well—for about 2 months—covered in parchment paper and plastic wrap and stored in a cool, dry place. You can eat it as soon as it's set, but it's actually much better left for a week so that it's had some time to sit.

1   Preheat the oven to 350°F/180°C. Grease a 9-inch/23-cm round or 8-inch/20-cm square pan and line with parchment paper, then set aside.

2   Spread the hazelnuts and almonds out on a rimmed baking sheet and roast for about 10 minutes, until they are light brown and fragrant. Lower the oven temperature to 250°F/120°C and leave in the oven until ready to use; this will make them easier to fold into the mixture, which will seize up if the nuts are added cold.

3   Place the chopped candied orange peel in a large bowl with the figs and orange zest. Combine the flour, cocoa powder, spices, salt and pepper in a small bowl and sift directly over the chopped fruit and zest. Combine with a wooden spoon or, better still, use your hands to get a more even distribution. Set aside.

4   Place the chocolate in a small heatproof bowl set over a pan of barely simmering water, making sure the base of the bowl is not touching the water. When it has nearly all melted, stir gently with a small spatula and turn off the heat, leaving the bowl over the hot water to keep the chocolate warm.

5   Place the sugar and honey in a small saucepan over low heat, stirring from time to time. As soon as the sugar has dissolved, stop stirring and increase the heat to high. Allow the mixture to simmer until the syrup has reached 237°F/114°C on a candy thermometer (the "soft boil" stage). Keep a close eye on the syrup here, as it will come to temperature very quickly. Don't panic if your batch goes above 237°F/114°C; the recipe will still work, it just means the set will be firmer.

6   Carefully pour the hot syrup over the chopped fruit, then add the warm nuts straight from the oven (increasing the oven temperature to 350°F/180°C as soon as the nuts are out). Pour the warm melted chocolate over the fruit and nuts and stir everything together with a large wooden spoon until well combined. The mixture will be very thick and will take a bit of effort to combine, but don't worry, this is normal. Use a spatula to press the mix into the prepared pan. When just cool enough to touch, wet your hands and pat the mix down so that it is even. Use a small piece of parchment paper to help flatten it, if you find it useful.

7   Bake for 18 minutes, until the panforte is set but not too hard. Remove from the oven and leave to cool completely in the pan (preferably for a few days, see Note) before slicing into ten segments or bars (around 4 x 1½ inches/10 x 4 cm).

Sesame brittle

We make large sheets of this in the Ottolenghi bakery, which are then broken into shards. Large shards are great as a garnish for all sorts of desserts—a mousse, for example, while smaller shards look great on the large or mini chocolate tarts (see pages 241 and 232). Play around with shapes and sizes and with all sorts of desserts. They're also lovely to snack on just as they are.

You can make this with white sesame seeds only, if you like, but do try and get hold of the black as well; the contrast looks fantastic.

MAKES 20 SHARDS (OR MORE OR LESS, DEPENDING ON SIZE)

¼ cup/35 g black sesame seeds
½ cup plus 1 tbsp/90 g white
    sesame seeds
½ cup/100 g granulated sugar

¼ cup plus 1 tbsp/100 g light corn syrup
3½ tbsp/50 g unsalted butter,
    at room temperature
⅛ tsp salt

These will keep for up to a week in an airtight container.

1   Preheat the oven to 375°F/190°C.

2   Spread all the sesame seeds out on a rimmed baking sheet and roast for 10 minutes, stirring halfway through, until golden brown. Keep the seeds warm in a low oven while you make the syrup.

3   Cut four pieces of parchment paper to fit on two large baking sheets. Set aside.

4   Place the sugar, corn syrup, butter and salt in a small saucepan over high heat and stir continuously until the mixture is combined and coming to a boil. Remove from the heat, add the warm sesame seeds and stir through.

5   Place two of the pieces of parchment paper on a heatproof surface and pour half of the sesame caramel onto each sheet. Cover with the other pieces of parchment paper and use a rolling pin to spread the caramel until ⅛ inch/3 mm thick.

6   Slide the paper and caramel onto the baking sheets, then remove the top layer of parchment; if any caramel sticks to the top layer of paper, just scrape it back down. Place the baking sheets in the oven and bake for 20 minutes, until golden. Remove from the oven and set aside to cool before breaking into shards.

Coconut meringue brittle

These are somewhere between a meringue and an old-fashioned coconut macaroon: as sweet as you'd want and expect, but with more of a crunch. They're informal, rustic and exceptionally more-ish.

We've offered both dark and white chocolate versions here, so either choose between the coatings or cover half the batch in one and half in the other. We've kept the dark chocolate version plain but, as with the white chocolate version, a sprinkle of freeze-dried cherries or raspberries also works well.

MAKES 12

½ cup/75 g slivered almonds

¾ cup plus 1 tbsp/100 g confectioners' sugar

½ cup/50 g finely shredded coconut

2½ oz/70 g egg whites (from 2 large eggs)

⅛ tsp salt

⅓ cup/70 g granulated sugar

½ tsp almond extract

DARK CHOCOLATE COATING
(HALVE THE QUANTITIES IF YOU ARE DOING A MIX OF DARK AND WHITE CHOCOLATE)

4¼ oz/120 g dark chocolate (70% cocoa solids), roughly chopped into ⅓-inch/1-cm pieces, to coat

WHITE CHOCOLATE COATING
(HALVE THE QUANTITIES IF YOU ARE DOING A MIX OF DARK AND WHITE CHOCOLATE)

4¼ oz/120g white chocolate, roughly chopped into ⅓-inch/1-cm pieces

¾ oz/25 g freeze-dried cherries or raspberries, minced in a food processor

When melted and used as a coating, dark chocolate can develop white streaks after a day or so. This won't affect the taste, but can be avoided by tempering the chocolate (see page 345).

These will keep for up to 1 week in an airtight container, with pieces of parchment paper between the layers of meringue.

---

1 Preheat the oven to 350°F/170°C. Spread the almonds out on a rimmed baking sheet and roast for about 5 minutes, until the nuts are starting to turn light brown. Remove from the oven and set aside to cool before roughly chopping. Keep the oven turned on.

2 Sift the confectioners' sugar into a small bowl, add the coconut and chopped almonds and set aside until ready to use. Line two large baking sheets with parchment paper and set aside.

3 Place the egg whites and salt in the bowl of an electric mixer with the whisk attachment in place. Beat on medium-high speed until soft peaks form. Gradually add the granulated sugar, 1 tbsp at a time, continuing to beat for about 5 minutes, until the mixture is thick and glossy and stiff peaks form. Stir in the almond extract, then remove the bowl from the mixer. Use a large rubber spatula to gently but thoroughly fold in the confectioners' sugar mixture.

4 Spoon twelve large spoonfuls of the mixture onto the parchment-lined sheets. Roughly spread them out with a small spatula to form shapes about 3 inches/8 cm wide and ⅓ inch/1 cm thick. Don't try for uniform shapes and sizes here; rustic is good! Place the baking sheets in the oven and immediately lower the temperature to 275°F/140°C. Bake for 1 hour, until the meringues are dry throughout but have not taken on too much color. Turn off the oven but leave the meringues inside for about 30 minutes, propping the door open with a wooden spoon, to continue to cool and dry out. Remove from the oven and set aside to cool completely.

5   **To make the dark chocolate coating,** place the chocolate in a heatproof bowl set over a pan of simmering water, making sure the base of the bowl is not touching the water. Stir occasionally until melted, then use a small metal spatula to spread the chocolate all over the base (flat side) of the meringues. **To make the white chocolate coating,** follow the instructions for the dark chocolate, sprinkling some of the cherries or raspberries on top of the chocolate after it's been brushed over the meringues.

6   Set aside for about 1 hour until the chocolate has set, then pile high on a plate, and serve.

Honey, macadamia and coconut caramels

These caramels started life as the filling to a sweet tart. Time and again, there was never quite enough to fill the tart shell. This had less to do with an issue of ratios in the recipe, however, and more to do with how hard it was to stop eating the caramel by the spoonful in the first place. The tart shell was soon dispensed with altogether so that we could concentrate on the filling alone! The resulting caramels look lovely as little bonbons. They also keep well, so make for terrific gifts, individually wrapped in parchment paper. We like them on the long side—around 3½ inches/9 cm—but you can make them shorter, if you like, in which case you'll make more. Making caramel is not difficult, but it takes practice, so don't give up if you don't perfect it first time around.

MAKES 18 (OR MORE, IF CUT INTO SMALLER PIECES)

1 cup/160 g macadamia nuts
⅔ cup/70 g unsweetened flaked
  coconut
7 tbsp/100 g unsalted butter
1 cup plus 1 tbsp/250 ml heavy cream
4½ tbsp/100 g honey

¼ cup plus 1 tbsp/100 g light corn syrup
¾ packed cup plus 1 tbsp/160 g
  light brown sugar
scraped seeds of ½ vanilla pod
¼ tsp flaky sea salt

1   Preheat the oven to 350°F/170°C. Line an 8-inch/20-cm square pan (about 1 inch/3 cm deep) with parchment paper, making sure that the paper rises 1½ inches/4 cm over the edges of the pan, and set aside.

2   Spread the nuts out on a rimmed baking sheet and roast for 7 minutes, until light golden brown. Spread the coconut out on a separate baking sheet and toast for just 2 minutes, until beginning to turn golden brown. Remove both baking sheets from the oven, lightly crushing the coconut with your fingers or a rolling pin. Place the nuts and coconut in a medium heatproof bowl and set aside.

3   Melt the butter in a medium saucepan over low heat, then add the cream, honey, corn syrup, brown sugar, vanilla seeds and salt. Stir until combined, then increase the heat to medium. Bring to a boil, resisting the urge to stir, and continue to boil until the temperature reaches 253–255°F/123–124°C on a candy thermometer (the top end of "firm ball" stage, but certainly not "hard ball" stage, which would lead to the caramels being brittle). This can take anywhere between 12 and 20 minutes. Remove from the heat immediately—move fast, as the temperature of the caramel will continue to rise—and pour over the nuts and coconut. Mix together, then pour into the lined pan, flattening the surface with a small spatula or the back of a spoon, and set aside at room temperature for an hour to firm up.

4   Cut the slab in half and then each half into nine 3½ x ¾-inch/9 x 2-cm rectangles (or 2⅓ x ¾-inch/6 x 2-cm rectangles if you want them to be more bite-sized). If not eating the same day, set aside to cool, then cover with parchment paper and plastic wrap.

A candy thermometer is a must here.

The caramels will keep for 2 weeks at room temperature, out of direct sunlight, and for 1 month stored in the fridge. Store together in an airtight container, or wrapped individually in cellophane sheets or parchment paper and plastic wrap.

SWEET

Middle Eastern millionaire's shortbread

A three-layered bar with a shortbread bottom, halva middle, and glossy tahini caramel top—this was a winning combination just waiting to happen. And happen it did, thanks to Paulina Bembel, our head pastry chef. Paulina, who comes from Poland, skillfully uses our Middle Eastern favorites—tahini and halva—to transform the famously cloying millionaire's shortbread into something so much better, with a slight bitterness and a touch of salt to offset all that sweetness.

MAKES 16

The shortbread layer can be made up to 4 days in advance and stored in an airtight container. It also freezes well.

These will keep for up to a week in an airtight container in the fridge. Remove 20 minutes before serving, to take off the chill.

SHORTBREAD

¼ cup plus 1 tbsp/40 g confectioners' sugar
3½ tbsp/35 g cornstarch
2½ tbsp/40 g granulated sugar
¾ cup/170 g unsalted butter, melted, and set aside to cool slightly
½ tsp vanilla extract
2 cups/250 g all-purpose flour
⅛ tsp salt

HALVA

7 oz/200 g halva, roughly crumbled into small pieces
⅓ cup/70 g tahini paste

TAHINI CARAMEL

1 cup/200 g granulated sugar
½ cup/120 ml water
7 tbsp/100 g unsalted butter, at room temperature, cubed
⅓ cup/80 ml heavy cream
⅓ cup/70 g tahini paste
¼ tsp flaky sea salt

1   Preheat the oven to 400°F/200°C. Line an 8-inch/20-cm square pan with parchment paper, making sure that the paper rises up over the edges of the pan.

2   **To make the shortbread,** sift the confectioners' sugar and cornstarch into the bowl of an electric mixer with the paddle attachment in place, then add the granulated sugar and mix on medium speed. With the machine still running, slowly pour in the melted butter and beat until combined. Add the vanilla extract and turn the speed to low, then sift in the flour and salt and continue to beat until the dough comes together. Tip the mixture into the pan and use your hands to pat and even out the surface. Bake for 25 minutes, or until golden brown. Remove from the oven and set aside until completely cool; this will take an hour or so, so don't start making the caramel too soon or it will have set by the time the shortbread is cool.

3   **To make the halva,** place the halva and tahini in a small bowl and mix with a wooden spoon to combine. Spread the mix over the cooled shortbread and use the back of a spoon to smooth it into an even layer.

4   **To make the tahini caramel,** combine the sugar and water in a small saucepan and place over medium-low heat. Stir occasionally, until the sugar has dissolved, then increase the heat to medium-high. Bring to a boil and cook—still at a boil—for about 12 minutes, until the sugar is a deep golden brown. Remove from the heat and add the butter and cream; take care here, as the mixture will splutter. Whisk to combine and, once the butter has melted, add the tahini and salt. Whisk to combine again, then pour evenly over the halva layer in the pan, so that all of the halva is covered.

5   Place in the fridge for 4 hours until set, before cutting into bars, about 1 x 4 inches/ 3 x 10 cm. Sprinkle a pinch of sea salt over the middle of each bar and serve.

Throughout the book there are lots of tips and notes alongside the recipes. Most are also here, for general ease of reference. It's not a comprehensive baker's bible; it's the things we think are useful and interesting to know, or which need more explanation than a recipe has the space to give.

Bain-marie

We use a bain-marie—a water bath—when baking our Hot Chocolate and Lime Puddings (see page 278), Ginger Crème Caramel (see page 279), and also for the custard in the Chai Brulée Tarts (see page 239). Although a lot of people bake their cheesecakes set inside a water bath placed in the oven—the rationale being that because the temperature of the water cannot rise above 212°F/100°C, the cheesecake will cook evenly—we are not fans. For the recipes in which we do use the technique, take care when filling your baking pan with hot water. Place the pan in the oven before pouring the water in, rather than trying to lift and move a panful of water across the kitchen, which can be both messy and dangerous.

Butter

BURNING › Burnt butter—or beurre noisette—is the process by which butter is heated on the stove for so long that it starts to foam, turn a light brown color and smell nutty. Small brown specks of sediment will form on the side of the pan, which are then removed when the butter is strained in a fine-mesh sieve. The strained butter—the burnt butter—brings a nutty caramel note (as well as a golden brown color) to your baking. We use it in our Brown Butter Almond Tuiles (see page 30).

TEMPERATURE OF › The temperature of butter when you start baking is always important. Sometimes it needs to be fridge-cold (if you are rubbing it into flour to form a crumb-like consistency for a dough, for example). Sometimes it needs to be at room temperature (if you want it to be malleable enough to be mixed with other ingredients until smooth, or if you want a batter to drop nicely and evenly into a cupcake mold). Sometimes you want it to be what we call "soft but not oily." This is where it is softer than room temperature but not so soft as to be sitting in an oily puddle (as it would be if you'd melted it for a few seconds in the microwave, for example), which would result in a dense cake. We get our butter to this point by placing it in a bowl close to the stove top while we are getting on with other bits and bobs in the kitchen. Cutting the butter into roughly 1-inch/3-cm cubes and spreading them out over the wrapper or on a plate will speed up the process further. Either way, keep an eye on it; if it's no longer solid, then you've taken it too far.

When melting butter, we also cut it into cubes, so that it melts faster and more evenly; you don't want it to boil away and reduce.

Sometimes we say that butter should be melted and then cooled to room temperature before, say, being added to a mix with lots of eggs in it. This is to prevent the eggs being cooked by the heat of the butter.

All of the butter we start with is unsalted. This then allows us to control the amount of salt used in a recipe.

Chocolate

CALLETS/CHIPS VS. BLOCK › In the shops and bakery, we use chocolate callets (or chips) in our baking. They come in a range of cocoa percentages and have the great advantage of melting evenly, which makes the chocolate less temperamental to work with. Callets or chips are available online, in chocolate shops and more generally in supermarkets, but for the ease of the home cook, we have started with blocks of chocolate that are then chopped by hand. How precise you need to be when breaking up or chopping the chocolate is indicated in each recipe. Precision will matter more in some cases than others. There are some instances where callets or chips are needed: in our Chocolate Chip and Pecan Cookies (see page 26), for example. If you started with a whole block of chocolate and cut it into uneven chunks, this would lead to an uneven bake.

MELTING › When melting chocolate, avoid the temptation to stir it too often or too vigorously, as this will cause it to seize up. It will always stiffen up a bit if another hot liquid is added to it—hot water or coffee, for example, in the flourless chocolate layer cake (see page 170)—but it will smooth out again with just a little bit of gentle stirring. If folding melted chocolate into another mixture—whisked egg yolks and sugar, for example—your melted chocolate should be slightly cooled (rather than completely cooled, which will make it too firm).

Sometimes we melt chocolate by pouring scalding milk or cream over chopped chunks of chocolate and only stirring it through once it's been left to sit. To scald milk or cream, you heat it just up to the point before it starts boiling. Once there are one or two bubbles on the surface, remove it from the heat; if it actually comes to a proper boil, you've taken it too far and the chocolate will scorch or split.

TEMPERING › When chocolate is melted and used as a coating or spread, it sometimes develops white streaks. These occur as a result of the chocolate melting and then cooling, and the cocoa butter—the fat naturally present in cocoa beans, which gives chocolate its irresistible mouth-feel—solidifying into fat crystals that all have different shapes and melting points. These white streaks—known as fat bloom—can give the chocolate a slightly dull appearance or gritty texture. The chocolate is perfectly edible, but it doesn't look great. If you want to prevent the formation of white streaks, you need to temper the chocolate. This is the process of carefully melting and cooling chocolate to ensure that the cocoa butter crystallizes properly.

There are several ways to temper chocolate, from elaborate mixing techniques with finely controlled temperatures to tempering machines that do all the work for you. The simplest way is to chop or shave the chocolate into small, even pieces, then remove about a quarter of the chocolate and set these pieces aside. Melt the remaining three-quarters of the chocolate in a bowl set over a pan of barely simmering water, making sure the base of the bowl is not touching the surface of the water. Remove the bowl from the simmering water and, when it's off the heat, add the reserved pieces of chocolate. Stir through until melted and cooled.

You don't need to temper chocolate every time you work with it. We only temper it when the chocolate is going to be used and seen as a coating: in the Coconut Meringue Brittle (see page 336) and Chocolate-Coated Ruby Red Grapefruit Peel (see page 326). You could do it for the chocolate-coated meringue in the frozen espresso parfait (see page 298), if you like, but this again is optional, as the whole thing is covered in praline before being frozen.

This might all seem like a lot of information for a process you only use a few times, but we hope it's interesting and useful, nevertheless!

CHOCOLATE (WHITE) › White chocolate can be more temperamental than other chocolate when it's being melted. If it's heated too quickly, it will seize up. To prevent this, either start with callets (or chips), shave your block of chocolate into flakes, or simply make sure you chop your block of chocolate into even pieces. If uneven, the pieces will melt at different times and will seize up when stirred. When melting, do so over low heat, either in a heatproof bowl over a pan of gently simmering water or on a low temperature in a microwave.

Citrus fruit (peeling)

When shaving peel off citrus fruit—lemons, limes, oranges—always avoid the white pith. This is bitter and can carry its bitterness through your baking (unless you are blanching the whole peel, see page 326).

Eggs

NUMBER OF › The more eggs you have in a cake batter, the closer eye you need to keep on it toward the end of baking: a relatively large number of eggs means that a cake can go from being a little bit liquid in the middle to being cooked in just a few minutes. As ever, a skewer inserted into the center of the cake will give you a good indication as to what's going on inside.

SIZE AND TEMPERATURE OF › Unless otherwise stated, we assume that eggs are large and at room temperature when you start baking. This is what our baking times are based on. For some recipes, though, the temperature of the eggs is not just important, it's crucial. In the Hot Chocolate and Lime Puddings (see page 278) or the Coffee and Cardamom Pound Cake (see page 181), which contain a lot of eggs, if you start with fridge-cold eggs then the mix won't just split; it will lead to a cold, heavy batter that has to work harder to rise in the oven. If your eggs are in the fridge and you want to start baking straightaway, bring them to room temperature by placing them in a small bowl and covering with hot tap water (not boiling water) for 5 minutes before using.

Egg whites also whisk more effectively when they are not fridge-cold, so bring these out of the fridge an hour or so before you are going to make a meringue.

FREEZING EGG WHITES › Egg whites freeze well, so always save those not used if a recipe calls for egg yolk only.

Genoise—sponge cake (making)

For all the ambitious and involved things one can do while baking, there's almost nothing more satisfying than making the perfect genoise: one that's rich and buttery, but light at the same time. There's just something a little bit magic about it! Behind the magic, there is quite a lot of method— none of it complicated, but all of it important.

› Get organized before you start. Have everything weighed out and ready for when it's needed. The sponge mixture is delicate and you don't want to lose the precious air bubbles you've worked so hard to achieve by making them wait around while you weigh things out.

› Start with eggs at room temperature (see left). Speed is important and they will whip quicker (with lighter results) than fridge-cold.

› Don't be tempted to skimp on the number of times the flour needs to be sifted. For the cake to be as light and fluffy as can be, three really is the magic number.

› Do not grease your cake rings. In order to get an even rise, you want the mixture to stick to the sides as it rises.

› Make sure the butter is fully melted but not hot. It needs to be poured into the cake mix by gently dribbling it down the sides of the bowl and folded in swiftly but gently. If the butter is too hot or poured in too quickly, it will sink to the bottom and create a dense, oily texture.

› Make sure your oven is at the correct temperature when the cakes are ready to go in. We would say this is the case for all recipes, but some cake batters are more robust than others and can afford to wait around for an oven to come to temperature if need be. The sponge is too delicate and light to sit around; it needs to go into the oven as soon as it is ready, otherwise it will deflate. Close the oven door gently and do not be tempted to open it for the first 10 minutes.

› You'll know when the cake is cooked as it will be lightly browned, the edges will have shrunk slightly away from the sides of the rings, and the center should spring back when pressed lightly.

› Once baked, the sponge is fragile, so take care when slicing it (particularly if you've made one large cake rather than several mini-cakes, which will be easier to slice). When slicing in half horizontally, we insert toothpicks around the cake to mark where to cut it, to ensure a straight line. When cutting, insert your knife, then move the cake around (rather than jiggling your knife around the cake). When lifting the top off, ready to ice, use a cake lifter or jumbo cookie spatula— or even the base of a springform pan—to help. It might crumble if you lift it with your hands.

Ice bath

An ice bath is simply a bowl filled with ice and water. It is used to quickly bring down the temperature of whatever is plunged into it (in a separate and smaller bowl). We often use ice baths when making custards for ice cream or sugar syrups for sorbets. Starting off with very cool custard or sugar syrup helps things along greatly when it is then transferred to a machine to be churned.

Meringues

There are three types of meringue: Swiss, French and Italian. They're all made in a different way and produce slightly different results.

SWISS MERINGUE › The egg whites and sugar are heated together before they are whipped. This happens when the meringue is not going to get any further cooking (when it's piped onto a cheesecake, for example). Heating it in the first instance gives it the cooking it needs to be safe to eat (it must be heated to 160°F/71°C) and makes it stable enough to hold its shape when piped onto a cake. Swiss meringue is denser than either French or Italian meringue, with a texture that's smooth, silky and marshmallow-like.

FRENCH MERINGUE › The sugar is drizzled into the egg whites as they are being beaten, creating a light and crisp meringue. French meringue always needs to be baked, to prevent the egg whites in the mixture from breaking down. This is the meringue we use for our rolled pavlova (see page 263). The reason the meringue goes into a hot oven and the temperature is turned down straightaway is to give it a nice crisp exterior and a soft and marshmallow-like interior.

ITALIAN MERINGUE › Probably the most stable of all the methods. This is the result of a very hot sugar syrup being poured into the egg whites as they are beaten. This method requires a bit more attention and patience than the other two, as the temperature of the sugar syrup needs to reach 244°F/118°C on a candy thermometer before it is poured into the egg whites. In turn, the egg whites must be beaten to a good volume without becoming grainy (overbeaten) before the sugar syrup is dribbled in. Timing is everything, as we so often say when cooking with sugar. But with all of your ingredients at the ready, and with one eye on the thermometer and the other on the whipping egg whites, you will have shiny, fluffy fabulous meringues. "I felt like I grew a foot taller," Helen says, remembering the day she mastered Italian meringue.

Moisture in a cake (oil vs. butter)

Using oil rather than butter in cakes tends to keep them moist for longer. This is because oil remains liquid at cooler temperatures, whereas butter solidifies to make cakes firm over time. The lack of butter can sometimes translate to diminished flavor, however, so this needs to be compensated for by turning up the volume on the other ingredients. In our Pineapple and Star Anise Chiffon Cake (see page 179), for example, the fresh pineapple, star anise and orange zest are there to make sure the cake delivers in all areas.

Nuts

ROASTING › Even if you start with preroasted nuts, always give your batch a quick reroast in a warm oven for 5 minutes. The success of a cookie or cake often relies on the nuts being fragrant; just 5 minutes in an oven set to 400°F/200°C will help release their oils. For our recipes, we have assumed that all nuts need roasting. Timing and temperature are given in each recipe.

When a recipe calls for toasted sliced almonds, we prefer to start with raw almonds and toast them ourselves, as we have more control over how long they are cooked for, and a fresh toasting is always good to draw out the oils. You can start with ready-toasted sliced almonds, if you prefer, however.

PROCESSING › Always wait for nuts to come to room temperature before you process them in a food processor; they'll turn to an oily paste if processed when warm.

REMOVING THE SKIN › If roasting nuts to remove their skins (as with hazelnuts, for example), transfer the nuts to a clean kitchen towel after roasting, fold in the sides of the towel and give them a vigorous rub to release from the skin.

TASTING › For notes on the importance of tasting your nuts before adding to your bake (to make sure they are not rancid), see page 354.

Oven temperature and rack positioning

Oven temperature is key to success in baking. At the same time as following our guidelines, you have to be mindful of the fact that all ovens are slightly different, so you need to use your intuition if you think something needs a few minutes more or a little less time in the oven. As well as a cooking time, visual guides are also given so that you know what to look for. The best way to get it right is to get to know your oven—you'll soon know if you consistently need to be giving things, say, 3 minutes longer than suggested—and to get to know a particular recipe really well. It's in being able to gauge for yourself whether something is ready that you'll become a really confident cook.

Unless otherwise stated, always position your racks in the middle of your oven to get an even bake (or create an even distance between your baking sheets, if you're baking with more than one). Rotating your baking sheet halfway through baking will also ensure an even bake.

If a bake starts with an initially high oven temperature that is then lowered as soon as it goes in the oven, this is often done to bring about a contrast between a brown crisp crust and a gooey, soft inside. This is a technique we employ in the friands on page 103.

Pastry

Tips and notes on the various pastries used in the book can be found at the beginning of the Tarts & Pies chapter (see page 226).

Pineapple purée (cooking of)

We always heat our pineapple purée before adding it to a cake batter. This works to intensify the flavor of the pineapple (rather than just adding more pineapple, which would make the batter too runny and prevent the cake from rising) and to destroy the enzyme bromelain, which can break down the gluten in the flour, resulting in a dense cake.

Proofing dough

The rate at which your dough will proof depends hugely on the temperature of your kitchen. You'll need to use the visual guides given in a recipe to gauge whether your dough needs more or less time to rise. The reason we keep the dough for Roma's doughnuts (see page 113) in the fridge overnight after the first proof is to decrease the amount of time spent waiting for the dough to proof for a second time on the day you want to fry and eat them. In the case of the doughnuts, the benefits of proofing the dough on individual squares of parchment paper is a baker's tip we were very happy to learn and that we're very happy to share.

Resting (the importance of)

Don't be tempted to miss out on the resting stage before a cake is baked, if it's recommended. If there is lots of almond meal in a mix, for example (as with the Flourless Chocolate "Teacakes," page 108), it's really important to allow them to fully absorb the liquids: this will make the cake as moist as can be.

Roulade "training"

In order to prepare our roulade before it's rolled, we like to "train" it by rolling it in a clean, dry kitchen towel after it's been baked. This is so it rolls seamlessly (and without breaking) once the cream filling is in place. It's a neat trick. Once you've cracked it (or not, in the case of your sponge!) you'll feel like a roulade-making pro. This also applies to the sponge in the stripe cake on page 145.

Sifting

DRY INGREDIENTS › The key to pillowy lightness is often in sifting together the dry ingredients. Not once, not twice, but sometimes (in the case of the Powder Puffs on page 82) three times! It might sound a bit much, we know, but it makes all the difference, ridding the mixture of any impurities at the same time as getting all of that aeration into the mix.

Where we have more than one dry ingredient—flour, salt, spices, confectioners' sugar, and so on—we like to sift these all together into the mixing bowl (rather than separately or in advance). This ensures that everything is evenly distributed throughout the batter or dough.

GRANULATED SUGAR › When the sugar is part of the dry ingredients (as opposed to being creamed with the butter, for example), we also tend to sift that with the flour. However, in cakes where there is a high level of liquid—in the Take-Home Chocolate Cake (see page 152) or the chocolate Guinness cake (see page 171)—the sugar is added early on, while the liquid is still warm, so that it melts into the cake batter and produces a more even texture. Since it's added at the same time as the cocoa powder, we've sifted them at the same time as it makes it easier to incorporate into the liquid. This also prevents the cocoa powder from clumping, which it can do when dumped into the liquid by itself.

CONFECTIONERS' SUGAR › With confectioners' sugar, whether or not we sift it depends on what it's used for. If it is going into a meringue, for example, it is always sifted. If mixing confectioners' sugar with water or another liquid, there is no need to sift it. If creaming with butter, whether or not we sift depends on how old the confectioners' sugar is; the older it is the lumpier it can become, from moisture in the air. Confectioners' sugar in the U.S. and U.K. usually contains cornstarch to reduce the lumpiness, but in places where pure confectioners' sugar is sold, it's often lumpy and must be sifted before using.

This might seem like a lot of information on the nature of sifting, but it does make a smoother batter—a sift in good time saves nine, and all that.

Storage

The way in which things are stored will really affect how long they last. Notes are always given as to whether things should be kept in an airtight container or wrapped loosely in foil. Again, whether they are kept at room temperature, in the fridge or in the freezer will also make a difference to whether something dries out, goes soggy or starts to weep. Do try to follow the guidelines given; it will make such a difference.

Sugar

CARAMELIZING › There are two ways to caramelize sugar: a dry method and a wet method. In the dry method the sugar is cooked, without water, in a large shallow frying pan or skillet. In the wet method, water is added to the sugar to begin the caramelizing process and the caramel is cooked in a saucepan. Wet caramel starts off as a thick sugar syrup, which begins to caramelize as the water evaporates. If there is no water, the sugar begins to caramelize faster.

The dry method produces a darker, more complex-flavored caramel in a shorter time. It's the method we use when we want a small amount of caramel, as with the spiced pineapple on our passion fruit cheesecakes (see page 207), for example. You need to be vigilant when making it and keep a very close eye on the pan—don't be tempted to move away until the caramel is all done. The wet method is useful when you need to make a large batch of caramel for a sauce, perhaps, or for the coffee praline in the frozen espresso parfait (see page 293).

CARAMEL (THE DIFFERENT STAGES OF COOKED SUGAR) › When making caramel, the cooked sugar will go through stages, from "thread stage" to "hard crack." The stages are reached at different temperatures and each results in a caramel with a very different consistency and purpose.

THREAD STAGE › The first stage of caramel, when the sugar and water have melted together and the consistency is that of sugar syrup. This stage is reached when the temperature is 230–234°F/110–112°C.

SOFT BALL › The texture here is that of a soft, sticky ball, like buttercream, fudge or fondant. This is reached when the temperature is 235–241°F/113–116°C.

FIRM BALL › This is when the caramel is firm but pliable. It is the stage you want to reach when making certain caramels or toffees. The temperature for this stage is 244–248°F/118–120°C.

HARD BALL › The consistency here is that of a harder ball, one that holds its shape. It's the stage reached by caramels, toffees and nougats with a slightly firmer texture. The temperature here should be 250–266°F/121–130°C.

SOFT CRACK › This is when the caramel has developed firm yet pliable strands. It is what you want for the making of butterscotch or firm nougat. The temperature should be 270–289°F/132–143°C.

HARD CRACK › This is the firmest stage of the caramel, almost brittle-like, where the stiff threads break easily. It is the stage you want to reach when making hard candy and spun sugar. The temperature should be 300–309°F/149–154°C.

Cooking with sugar requires a candy thermometer to take any guesswork out of the equation. It also requires the baker to be in control of timing, as the sugar syrup often needs to be at a certain stage at the exact same time that something else needs to be happening.

Temperature (of ingredients)

We have talked about the importance of eggs and butter being at the correct temperature when baking (see pages 346 and 344). In addition, the temperature of other dairy ingredients needs to be noted. In the white chocolate cheesecake (see page 203), for example, both the cream cheese and sour cream need to be fridge-cold. This allows the mix to remain cool enough for the chocolate not to melt when added. In the Coffee and Cardamom Pound Cake (see page 181), the milk and eggs need to be at room temperature, to minimize the risk of the batter splitting.

Pans

GREASING › We like to grease our baking sheets and pans with (barely) melted butter. We prefer this to cooking sprays (vegetable oils), which can affect the taste of the cake. If the molds of a pan are lined with paper liners—when making cupcakes, for example—then we are happy to use this spray, as the batter will not come into direct contact with it. In the case of muffin pans (or other pans in which the cake mixture is going to rise up and over the top rim of the mold), it's always useful to spray or grease the surface of the tray, as well as the molds, to prevent the cooked cake from sticking to the pan and crumbling when you try to remove it.

The more nooks and crannies a pan has, the more care you need to take when greasing it, to prevent the cooked cake getting stuck to the inside of the pan. Bundt pans, for example, require a lot of greasing.

If you are greasing with an oil rather than butter, always use a light sunflower oil instead of olive oil, which will be too heavy and thick.

LINING › To line our baking sheets and pans, we use nonstick parchment paper. In some cases (in the very delicate Cats' Tongues, page 27) we recommend using a nonstick silicone baking mat instead of parchment, if you have one.

CHOOSING › For more on the pans we use, along with what can be used as an alternative, see page 71. Other options and tips are given throughout the book.

MEASURING › To find the accurate width and length of a pan, always measure from inside edge to inside edge, so the measurement does not include the thickness of the pan. Fluted tart pans are measured from the inside edge of one outer curve to the inside edge of the curve directly across from it. To measure a round cake pan, measure across the top diameter of the pan, from edge to edge. If the sides are sloping, then also measure the base of the pan. To measure the pan's depth, place a ruler on the kitchen counter and measure straight up from the bottom of the pan. If the pan edge is slanted, do not slant the ruler, measure straight up.

This all sounds very prescriptive and strict, we know—we take all these details very seriously. At the same time, though, don't worry if your pan has dimensions that are slightly different to ours. As well as making recommendations for alternative shapes and sizes for pans, where we can, visual guides are given so you'll know when your cake is ready. This should give you the confidence to use a slightly different sized or shaped pan, if you need to, and then make adjustments to the baking time accordingly.

Water ganache

Water ganache sounds like a contradiction in terms—the mixing of chocolate and water doesn't feel as though it should work—but in fact it emulsifies into the smoothest of all ganaches. Using water instead of cream means that nothing distracts from the pure taste of the chocolate. It's also much more stable and easy to work with than cream-based ganaches, which (though they taste great) tend to lose their shine after an hour or two and turn a bit dull and grainy. Water ganache keeps in the fridge for days and can be reheated in either a bain-marie or in a small saucepan over low heat; you will need to stir constantly and maybe add a touch more water. For instructions on how to make the perfect water ganache, see the Flourless Chocolate "Teacakes" on page 108.

———

This is not a comprehensive list of ingredients used throughout the book. It's a list of the ingredients we think are in need of a bit of explanation: what they are, why we like them and, in some cases, what to use as an alternative.

Almond paste

Not to be confused with marzipan. While marzipan can contain as little as 10 percent almonds, almond paste is made up of 50 percent almonds. The paste contains much less sugar, as a result, and has a coarser texture. Marzipan is useful for rolling out to drape over cakes (thanks to the light corn syrup), but we use almond paste in our baking. It's available in most large supermarkets and online. Alternatively, check out the almond percentage in marzipan: the higher the better. Buy the Odense brand of marzipan if you can.

Amaretti cookies

Store-bought Amaretti cookies are either soft and pale (often individually wrapped, in a container you'll want to keep) or brown and crunchy. We use the latter to provide a distinctive crunch—not too sweet, with a bitterness from the apricot kernels in the biscuits—in the base of our Rhubarb and Blueberry Galette (see page 230). We also make our own: the Amaretti on page 38. There's more going on in these, flavor- and texture-wise, than in the simple store-bought version, so these should not be used for the base of the galette.

Aniseed

With a flavor somewhere between fennel and licorice, aniseed is a sweet and complex spice. It is most commonly associated with ouzo, raki or the French pastis, but it also works very well when ground and added to all sorts of cookies and cakes. We use it in our parsnip and pecan cake (see page 128). Alternatively, use an equal quantity of finely ground fennel seeds instead.

Apricots

Although we tend to make use of fresh, seasonal fruit, apricots have a relatively short season, so we often use canned instead. Their quality is good—and far better than unripe or out-of-season fresh apricots—so don't feel as though you're skimping on quality if you are starting with canned. If you are baking with fresh apricots and they're not as large and juicy as you'd want them to be (when roasting them for the Apricot and Amaretto Cheesecake on page 219, for example), you might need to sprinkle them with a little more water than recommended, to create some added moisture.

Bananas

When choosing bananas for baking, you want them to be ripe but not too ripe. Unripe, they'll have an astringency that will carry right through your cake or cookie. Too ripe—if they've been taken to the point of blackening—and the pH of the bananas changes from acidic to alkaline, which makes it difficult for the leavening agent to do its work. The resulting cake, though rich in flavor, will be rather heavy and dense. The perfect banana for baking is speckled or mottled; this indicates it is sweet and full of flavor.

Cardamom (ground)

Ground cardamom is not always easy to get hold of (compared with the whole green pods, which are widely available), but there are a couple of ways to grind your own. If you want to make 1½ teaspoons of ground cardamom for the coffee pound cake on page 181, you'll need to start with about 40 pods; the almond butter cake on page 176 needs ¾ tsp, so you'll need to start with about 20 pods. You can crush the whole pods with the flat side of a large knife to release the seeds and then grind the seeds in a spice grinder or pestle and mortar—this will give you the most distinctive and intense cardamom taste. Alternatively, grind the whole pod in a spice grinder and then pass the mix through a fine-mesh sieve. The second option is quicker and easier than the first, but the taste of the spice will not be nearly as intense, so you might want to add a tiny bit more than the recipe suggests.

Chocolate

All dark chocolate used in the book should contain 70 percent cocoa solids, unless otherwise stated. In terms of a specific brand, the range of chocolate on offer is absolutely huge. So long as you stick with the recommended cocoa percentage for a recipe, you can go with your preferred brand.
CHOCOLATE CALLETS/CHIPS › In the shops and bakery, we use chocolate callets (chips) in our cooking. They come in a range of cocoa percentages and have the great advantage (over starting with a whole block of chocolate and chopping it by hand) of melting evenly. Callets are widely available—they're sometimes sold as "chef's chocolate drops"—but for the most part we've specified hand chopping a block of chocolate, as bars of chocolate are readily available. The exception to the rule is with the Chocolate Chip and Pecan Cookies (see page 26), where you really need to start with chocolate chips; using chocolate with inconsistent sizing will create an uneven bake and change the consistency of the cookie.
GIANDUJA › In recipes that call for Gianduja, a particularly wonderful chocolate with about 30 percent hazelnut paste, we have provided an alternative for the home cook who can get hold of Nutella—or another chocolate hazelnut spread—more readily. Do keep an eye out for Gianjuda, though; it's really very special.

For more notes on the handling of chocolate—melting and tempering it, for example—see page 345.

Cocoa powder (Dutch-processed)

All the cocoa powder used in our recipes is Dutch-processed (as opposed to natural). The difference between Dutch-processed (also known as alkalized, European style or Dutched powder) and natural cocoa powder is that the former is treated with an alkaline, which reduces the acidity of the cocoa. This creates a smoother, milder flavor than in the more acidic natural version. Since Dutch-processed cocoa isn't acidic, it doesn't react with alkaline leaveners (like baking soda) to produce carbon dioxide. This is why recipes that contain Dutch-processed cocoa powder are usually leavened by baking powder, which has a neutral pH. The color of the Dutch-processed cocoa is also darker than the natural.

Coconut flakes

In the shops, we like to use Baker's Angel coconut flakes, which are sweet, wet and delicious. They are not easy to get hold of in the United Kingdom, though, so we have used regular flaked coconut instead. These are sold as either "unsweetened," "raw" or "plain" coconut flakes. Finely shredded unsweetened coconut can also be used as an alternative.

Coffee

We've tried to keep things simple by mainly using instant coffee granules in our recipes—we tend to use Nescafé. In some cases, though, ground coffee is called for, either for its intensity in the Frozen Espresso Parfait for a Crowd (see page 298) or for the wonderfully speckled look it brings to cakes like our Coffee and Walnut Financiers (see page 105).

Cream cheese

The texture of cream cheese can vary from brand to brand (and even from country to country, within the same brand), with one batch being much runnier than the next. In the U.K., for example, Philadelphia cream cheese is softer and more watery than the same brand version in the United States, where it's sold in blocks and is very firm. The runnier the cheese, the less time it will take to become smooth when whisked, and the quicker the mixture will come together for a dough, for example. Watch out for it while making the frosting for our beet cake (see page 130); if you beat it too much it will become too runny. The addition of cream cheese to the pastry in our rhubarb galette (see page 230) is what makes it so tender and flaky. For more on cream cheese pastry, see page 227.

Date syrup

Date syrup is the same thing as date molasses (but not the same as blackstrap molasses). Using date syrup in a cake is a great way of injecting huge amounts of rich sweetness and moisture into the mix.

Eggs

SIZE › Unless otherwise stated, eggs used in all recipes are large. Where the net weight of eggs is important, it will be given in the recipe as a guide, as large eggs can vary in size.

TEMPERATURE › Unless otherwise stated, we start our baking with eggs at room temperature. This matters more for some recipes than others. For more on the temperature of eggs when baking, see page 346.

WHITES › Several of our recipes call for egg whites only. As a general rule, 1 large egg will provide around 1⅓ oz/40 g egg white; eggs do vary in size, however, so always weigh out the egg whites where specified; it's the weight that is important. If you are not starting with a surplus of saved egg whites, you can buy cartons of egg whites from most large supermarkets. We find them really useful, as for all of our good intentions to use the yolks or whites left over, we know there is only so much mayonnaise or custard you need in your life.

Flour

RICE FLOUR › We use grainy rice flour in baking (in our orange shortbread, page 46, for example), not to be confused with the finely milled Asian variety, which you'd use to make dumpling wrappers. Bob's Red Mill is our chosen brand.

ITALIAN "00" FLOUR › The flour used in our shortbread is the "00" wheat flour (rather than the "00" semolina flour you'd use for pasta).

TAPIOCA FLOUR › We use tapioca flour, available at Asian markets or in the gluten-free section of most large supermarkets, to toss with the fruit in our Rhubarb and Strawberry Crumble Cake (see page 148). It has the capacity to thicken without leaving a floury taste. Cornstarch can be used as an alternative, if necessary. The tapioca flour also looks better—it's not opaque in the way that cornstarch is—but they function in the same way.

BUCKWHEAT FLOUR › This flour brings its distinctive nutty and slightly sour taste to baked goods; the taste is very particular and not one that can be substituted. We add a little to our Persian Love Cakes (see page 74).

SELF-RISING FLOUR › Not as readily available in some countries as in others. If you need to make your own, sift together all-purpose flour with baking powder. As a guide, use 2 tsp baking powder to every 1 cup plus 2 tbsp/150 g all-purpose flour.

Gelatin

We prefer to use gelatin leaves (rather than powder) as they are odorless, flavorless and dissolve quickly without residue. They come in three different strengths: bronze, silver and platinum. As a guide, four leaves of platinum gelatin is the equivalent of 1 envelope (or 2½ tsp) of powdered gelatin.

Ginger (stem)

If you can't get stem ginger, use the same amount of finely chopped crystallized ginger, steeped in about 1 cup/240 ml boiling water for 15 minutes, then drained. The ginger flavor won't be as intense, however, so you might want to compensate by adding a teaspoon of freshly grated ginger at the same time.

Glacé fruit

Also called candied or crystallized fruit, don't be tempted to skimp on quality when buying glacé fruit. The top-quality varieties are usually French, but you can also get a really good selection online, which is where we tend to go. You can always vary the glacé fruit you use, according to your own preference (unless a recipe states otherwise). If you can't find mixed candied peel, then candied citron or orange peel (or a combination of both) is a good alternative.

Lemon

LEMON OIL › A drop or two of lemon oil (or pure lemon extract, as it's also known) is a great way of injecting an intense citrus hit into a simple cookie or tart. It may seem extravagant to buy a small bottle when only a drop or two is asked for in a recipe, but it keeps well (stored in the fridge) and really does make a difference to the Cats' Tongues (see page 27). A drop or two is also great added to whipped cream, which is then served with fresh or roasted fruit. We use Boyajian pure lemon oil, which is top-of-the-range, but there are several other options to choose from. Steenbergs and Nielsen-Massey both do good-quality lemon extracts. Either way, do not confuse this with lemon-infused olive oil, which is commonly sold for use in savory cooking.

ZEST › Using finely grated lemon zest is another way to bring the citrus hit that we love. When grating your zest (using either a Microplane or the smaller holes of an all-purpose grater), take care to avoid the white pith: this has a strong bitterness that will carry through everything it's added to. As a rough guide, 1 regular lemon will give you 1 teaspoon of finely grated lemon zest.

Mahleb

Mahleb is a spice made from the ground seed kernel of the St. Lucie cherry. It's not widely used outside of Greece, Turkey and the Middle East, so don't worry if you can't get hold of any: a few drops of almond extract work well instead.

Marzipan

See Almond Paste (page 351) for the important difference between the two. If you do have to use marzipan (instead of almond paste), you can add a drop or two of almond extract to the mix to ramp up the flavor. Marzipan is much sweeter than almond paste, so you might want to reduce the amount of sugar a recipe calls for accordingly.

Mixed spice

Also known as quatre épices, mixed spice is a sweet blend of cinnamon, nutmeg, mace, allspice, cloves and coriander. It's similar to American pumpkin pie spice, but not to be confused with allspice, the dark berry from the pimento tree.

Nuts

Always taste your nuts before baking with them: the quality can vary hugely, from creamy and nutty on one hand, to dry and rancid on the other.

ALMONDS (SLIVERED) › The little sticks of blanched slivered almonds that we fold through our Coconut Meringue Brittle (see page 336) provide a wonderful crunch. If you want to use whole blanched almonds in place of them, roast them for 10 minutes in an oven set to 350°F/180°C, then roughly chop them—these will be fine as an alternative.

HAZELNUTS › Hazelnuts are very idiosyncratic in baking because they can cause a cake to dry out really quickly. As a result, hazelnut cakes are always best eaten on the day of baking.

PEANUTS (RAW) › Raw peanuts—unroasted, skinless and unsalted—are not always easy to find. Roasted (but still skinless and unsalted) are often easier to get hold of, so use these instead, if necessary.

PISTACHIOS › We like to garnish our cakes with slivered bright green Iranian pistachios; it's what we use in the shops, as their length and color looks great. If you are using these, be sure not to toast them, as they'll lose their color. If using regular pistachios, however, these will need a bit of toasting to really draw out their taste.

WALNUTS (QUALITY OF) › Keep a close eye on walnuts, in particular, and always taste them before adding them to your cake. They won't improve with baking, so if they taste rancid at the outset then they are not worth using.

Oats

When making the "Anzac" Biscuits (see page 52), don't start with quick-cooking or instant oats—they'll turn to mush as soon as they come into contact with liquid. You want the old-fashioned rolled oats (rather than steel cut).

Orange

BLOSSOM WATER › This is a key ingredient in various Arab and Mediterranean cuisines, used in particular to flavor baklava, as well as other sweets. Sugar syrup made with orange blossom water can be used to soak into cakes, flavor fruit salads and fold into creams as a dessert. We also use it in a savory context, where its aroma gives a wonderful exotic hue. Some brands are more concentrated than others, so have a little try before adding it; you may need to adjust the quantities accordingly.

OIL › With highly scented ingredients like orange oil (or lemon oil, almond extract, rose water, and so on), always get the best quality you can; differences from brand to brand can really affect the end result. The better the quality, the more expensive it will often be, but you really need only a drop or two in a cake, so a little bottle will go a very long way. If you can't get hold of a really good-quality oil, some finely grated zest is often a better alternative than reaching for a cheaper brand.

Pandan leaf

Often referred to as the "vanilla of the East," pandan leaves are used all over South East Asia to flavor (and color) many dishes, but predominantly cakes and sweets. The leaves look like long blades of grass and are extremely fibrous (and thus inedible), so are used instead to infuse foods. To bring out the flavor of pandan, the blades are bruised with the back of a knife, then tied into a knot and dropped into the food to be infused. They are also often blended with water or coconut milk, then strained through a fine-mesh sieve, to extract the color and flavor for cakes and puddings. If you cannot find pandan leaves (sometimes sold in the fruit and vegetable or freezer sections of Asian markets), use a quarter of a vanilla pod instead, split in half lengthwise to release the seeds.

Passion fruit pulp

We get our strained passion fruit pulp from a French company called Les vergers Boiron. It's superflavorful and tangy and comes frozen, so we can just cut off what we need and keep the remainder in the freezer for future use. Seek it out, if you can—it's readily available online. Ordering products online always feels like a bit of a hassle (until you get into the habit of it), but you can reassure yourself that the alternative is extracting the juice from about a dozen fresh passion fruit by hand!

Rice paper (edible)

Edible rice paper is a useful way to line something sticky like almond nougat (see page 328), to make it easy to handle and store. And as it's completely edible, there's no need to peel it off before eating. You can buy it in sheets, like letter-sized paper, from speciality cake shops or online. As an alternative, you could use wafer paper made from potato starch, which serves the same purpose, or just line the pan with parchment paper dusted with confectioners' sugar. The latter won't be edible, obviously, so you'll have to peel it off before eating.

Rose water

The difference between pure rose water and rose essence is huge. The ingredients in rose water are literally rose oil and water. Rose essence, on the other hand, contains ethanol as well as rose oil. Undiluted, rose essence is therefore far stronger than rose water and serves a completely different purpose; it's generally added by the drop rather than by the teaspoon or tablespoon. Adding 2 tablespoons of rose water to a cake such as our pistachio semolina cake (see page 165) may seem brazen, but it's what makes the cake both distinct and delicious. The same is true in our flourless chocolate cake (see page 170). Adding 2 tablespoons of rose essence to the same cakes, on the other hand, would make them basically inedible. Confusingly, rose essence is sometimes called rose water, so just have a look at the ingredients to double-check. We use the Lebanese Cortas brand, which we recommend. It's not necessarily the absolute best, but it's one of the good-quality brands most readily available.

Salt

We use two types of salt in the book: table salt and flaky sea salt. Table salt is what we use most for baking, as it disperses more evenly through a batter or dough. Flaky sea salt is often used as a garnish, there for its gentler flavor and more prominent texture. In certain recipes— our Chocolate and Peanut Butter S'mores (see page 48) and our Garibaldis (see page 57)— we use both types of salt.

Star anise (ground)

Ground star anise is not always as easy to find as whole star anise. To grind your own, use a spice grinder or pestle and mortar to blitz whole star anise, then pass through a fine-mesh sieve.

Sugar

We use various types of sugar throughout the book: confectioners' sugar, granulated sugar, demerara sugar, light brown sugar and dark brown sugar. There's no getting around the fact that baking requires a fair bit of sugar.

CONFECTIONERS' SUGAR › Pure confectioners' sugar is not that easy to find in the U.K. or the U.S., so we have used regular confectioners' sugar in our recipes (which has about 3 percent cornstarch in it). In some recipes—the icing for the Pineapple and Star Anise Chiffon Cake (see page 179), for example—we have mentioned pure confectioners' sugar as option one, if you can get hold of it, as it doesn't have the slightly floury taste from the cornstarch as the regular one. Don't worry if you can't find it—regular confectioners' sugar will be fine.

Treacle and molasses

For some recipes—the soft gingerbread tiles (see page 42), for example—you can use either blackstrap molasses or black treacle and you won't be able to tell the difference. While the two terms are often used interchangeably, there is a difference, in that molasses is a pure by-product of refining sugar cane into sugar crystals, while treacle is a blend of molasses with refinery syrup. Treacle (which is often paler, sweeter and more mellow than molasses) ranges in color from light gold to almost black, depending on the ratio of the blend.

Vanilla

EXTRACT › As with all extracts and oils, use the best quality you can find; it makes a huge difference. We used the Nielsen-Massey brand for the recipes in this book.

PODS › Rather than discarding vanilla pods once their seeds have been scraped and they've done their work in a recipe, always rinse and dry them, then stick them in a container of granulated sugar. It makes a lovely alternative to regular sugar in your cappuccino, and can be added to all sorts of puddings or smoothies.

Yogurt (Greek)

The rise of fat-free or low-fat (2 percent) Greek yogurt has been so great that it can sometimes be hard to find the whole-milk version; shelf space is precious in shops, we know, but it seems such a shame! You can use reduced-fat yogurt if you like—even in recipes like the yogurt panna cotta (see page 282), which needs to set—but you won't get the wonderful richness that a dessert such as this really deserves.

A

alcohol, in desserts 260
almond paste 33-4, 351
    almond butter cake with cardamom
        and baked plums 176-7
almonds 354
    almond and aniseed nougat 328-9
    almond, pistachio sour cherry wafers 23
    almond praline 108-10
    Amaretti with honey and orange
        blossom 38
    apricot and almond cake with cinnamon
        topping 156
    apricot and Amaretto cheesecake 219-20
    brown butter almond tuiles 30
    butternut, honey and almond tin can
        cake 136-7
    chocolate panforte with oranges
        and figs 332-3
    coconut, almond and blueberry cake 151
    Gevulde Speculaas 33-4
    lemon, blueberry and almond "teacakes" 88
    Persian love cakes 74
    praline cream 291-2
    saffron and almond ice cream
        sandwich 301-3
    Speculaas biscuits 37
    spiced praline meringues 323
Amaretti biscuits 351
    Amaretti with honey and orange
        blossom 38
    rhubarb and blueberry galette 230-1
Amaretto: apricot and Amaretto
        cheesecake 219-20
aniseed 351
    almond and aniseed nougat 328-9
    parsnip and pecan cake with aniseed
        and orange 128-9
"Anzac" biscuits 52
apples
    apple and olive oil cake with maple
        frosting 132-3
    gingerbread with brandy apples 266-7
    pot barley pudding with roasted apples
        and date syrup 288
    sticky fig pudding with salted caramel
        and coconut topping 287
apricots 351
    apricot and almond cake 156
    apricot and Amaretto cheesecake 219-20
    apricot and thyme galettes 253-4
Armagnac: prune cake with Armagnac
        and walnuts 126

B

baby black and orange cakes 94
Baileys Irish cream 117-18
bananas 351
    banana cakes with rum caramel 100
    banana, date and walnut tin can cake 140
    chocolate, banana and pecan cookies 29
    chocolate banana ripple
        cheesecake 216-17
beet, ginger and sour cream cake 130-1
Belinda's flourless coconut and chocolate
    cake 190-1

biscuits and cookies 16-65
    almond, pistachio sour cherry wafers 23
    Amaretti with honey and orange
        blossom 38
    "Anzac" biscuits 52
    brown butter almond tuiles 30
    cats' tongues 27
    chocolate and peanut butter s'mores 48-51
    cranberry, oat and white chocolate
        biscuits 24
    garibaldis 57-61
    Gevulde Speculaas 33-4
    orange and star anise shortbread 46-7
    soft gingerbread tiles with rum butter
        glaze 42-3
    Speculaas biscuits 37
blackberries
    blackberry and star anise friands 103-4
    celebration cake 193-4
    rolled pavlova with peaches
        and blackberries 263-4
blackcurrants: lemon and blackcurrant
        stripe cake 145-6
blueberries
    celebration cake 193-4
    coconut, almond and blueberry cake 151
    lemon, blueberry and almond "teacakes" 88
    rhubarb and blueberry galette 230-1
brandy 260
    festive fruitcake 167-8
    gingerbread with brandy apples 266-7
Brazil nuts: lime meringue cheesecakes 201-2
brittle
    coconut meringue brittle 336-7
    hazelnut crunch 241-2
    saffron and pistachio brittle 315
    sesame brittle 232-4, 334
brown butter almond tuiles 30
brownies, tahini and halva 87
brûlée tarts, chai 239-40
butter 344
    blackcurrant buttercream 145-6
    brown butter almond tuiles 30
    rum butter glaze 42-3
butternut, honey and almond tin can
        cake 136-7

C

cakes 120-95, 347, 348
    almond butter cake with cardamom
        and baked plums 176-7
    apple and olive oil cake 132-3
    apricot and almond cake 156
    beet, ginger and sour cream cake 130-1
    Belinda's flourless coconut and chocolate
        cake 190-1
    celebration cake 193-4
    Cleopatra cake 134
    coconut, almond and blueberry cake 151
    coffee and cardamom pound cake 181-2
    festive fruit cake 167-8
    flourless chocolate layer cake with coffee,
        walnuts and rose water 170-2
    grappa fruit cake 141-3
    lemon and blackcurrant stripe cake 145-6
    lemon and poppy seed cake 187
    Louise cake with plum and coconut 173-5
    Neapolitan pound cake 184-5
    parsnip and pecan cake 128-9

    pineapple and star anise chiffon
        cake 179-80
    pistachio and rose water semolina
        cake 165-6
    pistachio roulade with raspberries
        and white chocolate 159-60
    prune cake with Armagnac and walnuts 126
    rhubarb and strawberry crumble cake 148
    rum and raisin cake with rum caramel
        icing 124
    take-home chocolate cake 152-5
    Tessa's spice cake 186
    tin can cakes 136-40
    tropical fruit cake 161-3
    vineyard cake 134
    see also mini-cakes
Campari and grapefruit sorbet 304
candied pecans 247-9, 293-4
candied rose petals 165-6
cape gooseberry pavlova 274-5
caramel 349
    caramel sauce 298-300
    caramelized walnuts 170-2
    caramelizing sugar 349
    garibaldis 57-61
    honey, macadamia and coconut
        caramels 339
    rum caramel icing 100, 124
    sticky fig pudding with salted caramel
        and coconut topping 287
    tahini caramel 341
cardamom 351-2
    almond butter cake with cardamom
        and baked plums 176-7
    cardamom sugar 113-15
    chai brûlée tarts 239-40
    coffee and cardamom pound cake 181-2
cashew nuts: soft date and oat bars 45
cats' tongues 27
celebration cake 193-4
chai brûlée tarts 239-40
Chantilly cream 293-4
cheesecakes 196-223
    apricot and Amaretto cheesecake 219-20
    baked ricotta and hazelnut
        cheesecake 209-10
    chocolate banana ripple
        cheesecake 216-17
    fig, orange and mascarpone
        cheesecake 212-13
    lime meringue cheesecakes 201-2
    passion fruit cheesecake with spiced
        pineapple 207-8
    roasted strawberry and lime
        cheesecake 221-2
    white chocolate cheesecake with
        cranberry compote 203-5
cherries: almond, pistachio sour cherry
        wafers 23
chestnut spread
    chocolate and chestnut powder puffs 82-5
    Mont Blanc tarts 235-7
chiffon cake, pineapple and star anise 179-80
chocolate 344-5, 352
    baby black and orange cakes 94
    baked ricotta and hazelnut
        cheesecake 209-10
    Belinda's flourless coconut and chocolate
        cake 190-1
    celebration cake 193-4

chocolate and chestnut powder puffs **82–5**
chocolate and peanut butter s'mores **48–51**
chocolate, banana and pecan cookies **29**
chocolate banana ripple
    cheesecake **216–17**
chocolate chip and pecan cookies **26**
chocolate-coated ruby red grapefruit
    peel **326–7**
chocolate ganache **55–6, 90–3, 108–10,**
    117–18, 152–5, 190–4, 209–10, 216–17, 350
chocolate Guinness cake with Baileys
    Irish cream **117–18**
chocolate mousse **232–4**
chocolate "O" cookies **55–6**
chocolate panforte with oranges
    and figs **332–3**
chocolate, rose and walnut ice cream **308**
chocolate sauce **308**
chocolate tart with hazelnut, rosemary
    and orange **241–2**
cinnamon pavlova, praline cream
    and fresh figs **291–2**
coconut meringue brittle **336–7**
cranberry, oat and white chocolate
    biscuits **24**
flourless chocolate layer cake with coffee,
    walnuts and rose water **170–2**
flourless chocolate "teacakes" **108–10**
frozen espresso parfait for a
    crowd **298–300**
hazelnut crumble cake with Gianduja
    icing **90–3**
hot chocolate and lime puddings **278**
little baked chocolate tarts with tahini
    and sesame brittle **232–4**
Mont Blanc tarts **235–7**
Neapolitan pound cake (for the
    family) **184–5**
Nutella ganache **90–3**
pecan and Prosecco truffles **324**
pistachio roulade with raspberries
    and white chocolate **159–60**
tahini and halva brownies **87**
take-home chocolate cake **152–5**
water ganache **108–10, 190–1, 209–10, 350**
white chocolate cheesecake with
    cranberry compote **203–5**
white chocolate cream **96–9, 159–60**
white chocolate ganache **193–4**
woodland meringues **319–20**
cinnamon
    apricot and almond cake with cinnamon
        topping **156**
    chai brûlée tarts **239–40**
    cinnamon pavlova, praline cream
        and fresh figs **291–2**
    espresso cinnamon mascarpone
        cream **152–5**
Cleopatra cake **134**
coconut **352**
    "Anzac" biscuits **52**
    Belinda's flourless coconut and chocolate
        cake **190–1**
    coconut, almond and blueberry cake **151**
    coconut meringue brittle **336–7**
    honey, macadamia and coconut
        caramels **339**
    Louise cake with plum and coconut **173–5**
    sticky fig pudding with salted caramel
        and coconut topping **287**

tropical fruit cake **161–3**
coffee **352**
    coffee and cardamom pound cake **181–2**
    coffee and walnut financiers **105–7**
    coffee icing **105–7, 152–5, 181–2**
    coffee praline **298–300**
    espresso cinnamon mascarpone
        cream **152–5**
    flourless chocolate layer cake with coffee,
        walnuts and rose water **170–2**
    frozen espresso parfait for a
        crowd **298–300**
compote, cranberry **203–5**
condensed milk: lime meringue
    cheesecakes **201–2**
confectionery **310–41**
    almond and aniseed nougat **328–9**
    chocolate-coated ruby red grapefruit
        peel **326–7**
    chocolate panforte with oranges
        and figs **332–3**
    coconut meringue brittle **336–7**
    honey, macadamia and coconut
        caramels **339**
    Middle Eastern millionaire's shortbread **341**
    pecan and Prosecco truffles **324**
    raspberry lollipops **318**
    saffron and pistachio brittle **315**
    sesame brittle **334**
    spiced praline meringues **323**
    woodland meringues **319–20**
cookie cutters **228**
cookies
    chocolate, banana and pecan cookies **29**
    chocolate chip and pecan cookies **26**
    chocolate "O" cookies **55–6**
    custard yo-yos with roasted rhubarb
        icing **19–20**
    honey, oat and raisin cookies **52**
    peanut sandies **21**
    see also biscuits
cranberries
    cranberry, oat and white chocolate
        biscuits **24**
    white chocolate cheesecake with
        cranberry compote **203–5**
cream
    Baileys Irish cream **117–18**
    celebration cake **193–4**
    Chantilly cream **293–4**
    espresso cinnamon mascarpone
        cream **152–5**
    kaffir lime leaf posset with fresh papya **283**
    pastry cream **253–4**
    praline cream **291–2**
    rolled pavlova with peaches
        and blackberries **263–4**
    rose water **82–4, 170–2**
    saffron and almond ice cream
        sandwich **301–3**
    saffron custard cream **113–15**
    vanilla whipped cream **82–5, 247–9**
    white chocolate cream **96–9, 159–60**
    yogurt cream **274–5**
cream cheese **352–3**
    apricot and Amaretto cheesecake **219–20**
    chocolate banana ripple
        cheesecake **216–17**
    cream cheese frosting **128–9, 130–1, 161–3**
    cream cheese pastry **227, 230–1**

fig, orange and mascarpone
    cheesecake **212–13**
lime meringue cheesecakes **201–2**
maple frosting **132–3**
not-quite-Bonnie's rugelach **65–6**
passion fruit cheesecake with spiced
    pineapple **207–8**
ricotta crêpes with figs, honey
    and pistachio **268–9**
roasted strawberry and lime
    cheesecake **221–2**
white chocolate cheesecake with
    cranberry compote **203–5**
crème caramel, ginger **279–80**
crème fraîche, gingerbread with brandy
    apples and **266–7**
crêpes: ricotta crêpes with figs, honey
    and pistachio **268–9**
crumble cakes
    hazelnut crumble cake with Gianduja
        icing **90–3**
    prune cake with Armagnac and walnuts **126**
    rhubarb and strawberry crumble cake **148**
crystallized rosemary sprigs **241–2**
crystallized sage **245–6**
cupcakes, lemon and raspberry **79–81**
curd, lemon **79–81**
currants: pineapple, pecan and currant
    tin can cake **139**
custard
    chai brûlée tarts **239–40**
    custard yo-yos with roasted rhubarb
        icing **19–20**
    saffron custard cream **113–15**

D

date syrup **353**
    pot barley pudding with roasted apples
        and date syrup **288**
dates
    banana, date and walnut tin can cake **140**
    soft date and oat bars **45**
desserts **260–309**
doughnuts: Roma's doughnuts with saffron
    custard cream **113–15**

E

eggs **346, 353**
    apricot and Amaretto cheesecake **219–20**
    baked ricotta and hazelnut
        cheesecake **209–10**
    cape gooseberry pavlova **274–5**
    celebration cake **193–4**
    chai brûlée tarts **239–40**
    cinnamon pavlova, praline cream
        and fresh figs **291–2**
    ginger crème caramel **279–80**
    lime meringue cheesecakes **201–2**
    roasted strawberry and lime
        cheesecake **221–2**
    rolled pavlova with peaches
        and blackberries **263–4**
    spiced praline meringues **323**
equipment **261, 312, 344**
    pans **71, 123, 198, 227, 350**
espresso
    espresso cinnamon mascarpone
        cream **152–5**
    frozen espresso parfait for a
        crowd **298–300**

F

fennel seeds, schiaccata with grapes and **250**
festive fruit cake **167-8**
figs
    chocolate panforte with oranges
        and figs **332-3**
    cinnamon pavlova, praline cream
        and fresh figs **291-2**
    fig and pistachio frangipane tartlets **247-9**
    fig, orange and mascarpone
        cheesecake **212-13**
    ricotta crêpes with figs, honey
        and pistachio **268-9**
    sticky fig pudding with salted caramel
        and coconut topping **287**
financiers, coffee and walnut **105-7**
flaky pastry **226, 239-40, 245-6, 247-9**
flourless cakes
    Belinda's flourless coconut and chocolate
        cake **190-1**
    flourless chocolate layer cake with coffee,
        walnuts and rose water **170-2**
    flourless chocolate "teacakes" **108-10**
frangipane: fig and pistachio frangipane
    tartlets **247-9**
French meringues **347**
friands, blackberry and star anise **103-4**
frozen espresso parfait for a crowd **298-300**
fruit, in desserts **260**
fruit cakes
    festive fruit cake **167-8**
    grappa fruit cake **141-3**
    tropical fruit cake **161-3**

G

galettes
    apricot and thyme galettes **253-4**
    rhubarb and blueberry galette **230-1**
ganache
    chocolate ganache **55-6, 90-3, 108-10,**
        117-18, 152-5, 190-4, 209-10, 216-17, 350
    water ganache **55-6, 108-10, 190-1,**
        209-10, 350
    white chocolate ganache **193-4**
garibaldis **57-61**
Genoise sponge **346**
Gevulde Speculaas **33-4**
Gianduja ganache, hazelnut crumble cake
    with **90-3**
ginger **353**
    beet, ginger and sour cream cake **130-1**
    chai brûlée tarts **239-40**
    ginger crème caramel **279-80**
    gingerbread with brandy apples and
        crème fraîche **266-7**
    soft gingerbread tiles with rum butter
        glaze **42-3**
glacé fruit **353**
glaze, lemon **187**
gluten-free cakes
    Belinda's flourless coconut and chocolate
        cake **190-1**
    flourless chocolate layer cake with coffee,
        walnuts and rose water **170-2**
    flourless chocolate "teacakes" **108-10**
graham crackers
    apricot and Amaretto cheesecake **219-20**
    chocolate, rose and walnut ice cream **308**
    chocolate banana ripple
        cheesecake **216-17**

fig, orange and mascarpone
    cheesecake **212-13**
lime meringue cheesecakes **201-2**
passion fruit cheesecake with spiced
    pineapple **207-8**
white chocolate cheesecake with
    cranberry compote **203-5**
grapefruit
    Campari and grapefruit sorbet **304**
    chocolate-coated ruby red grapefruit
        peel **326-7**
grapes
    schiaccata with grapes and fennel
        seeds **250**
    vineyard cake **134**
grappa fruit cake **141-3**
Guinness: chocolate Guinness cakes **117-18**

H

halva
    Middle Eastern millionaire's shortbread **341**
    tahini and halva brownies **87**
hazelnuts **354**
    almond and aniseed nougat **328-9**
    baked ricotta and hazelnut
        cheesecake **209-10**
    chocolate panforte with oranges
        and figs **332-3**
    chocolate tart with hazelnut, rosemary
        and orange **241-2**
    frozen espresso parfait for a
        crowd **298-300**
    hazelnut crunch **241-2**
    hazelnut crumble cake with
        Gianduja icing **90-3**
    woodland meringues **319-20**
honey
    Amaretti with honey and orange
        blossom **38**
    butternut, honey and almond tin can
        cake **136-7**
    chocolate panforte with oranges
        and figs **332-3**
    honey, macadamia and coconut
        caramels **339**
    honey, oat and raisin cookies **52**
    honey syrup **268-9**
    ricotta crêpes with figs, honey
        and pistachio **268-9**
    saffron, orange and honey madeleines **76-8**

I

ice cream
    chocolate, rose and walnut ice cream **308**
    lemon, yogurt and juniper berry
        ice cream **307**
    saffron and almond ice cream
        sandwich **301-3**
icings and frostings
    blackberry icing **103-4**
    blackcurrant buttercream **145-6**
    chocolate ganache **55-6, 90-3, 108-10,**
        117-18, 152-5, 190-4, 209-10, 216-17, 350
    coffee icing **105-7, 152-5, 181-2**
    cream cheese frosting **128-9, 130-1,**
        132-3, 161-3
    Gianduja icing **90-3**
    lemon icing **88**
    maple frosting **132-3**

mascarpone frosting **79-81**
Nutella ganache **90-3**
pineapple icing **179-80**
roasted rhubarb icing **19-20**
rum caramel icing **124**
strawberry icing **95**
water ganache **55-6, 108-10, 190-1,**
    209-10, 350
white chocolate ganache **193-4**
ingredients **348, 351-7**
Italian meringues **347**

J

jam, pineapple **255-6**
juniper berries: lemon, yogurt and juniper
    berry ice cream **307**

K

kaffir lime leaf posset with fresh papaya **283**
knickerbocker glory **293-4**

L

lemons **345-6, 354**
    lemon and blackcurrant stripe cake **145-6**
    lemon and poppy seed cake **187**
    lemon and raspberry cupcakes **79-81**
    lemon and semolina syrup cakes **111**
    lemon, blueberry and almond "teacakes" **88**
    lemon curd **79-81**
    lemon glaze **187**
    lemon syrup **111**
    lemon, yogurt and juniper berry
        ice cream **307**
    vineyard cake **134**
limes **345-6**
    hot chocolate and lime puddings **278**
    kaffir lime leaf posset with fresh
        papaya **283**
    lime meringue cheesecakes **201-2**
    roasted strawberry and lime
        cheesecake **221-2**
lollipops, raspberry **318**
Louise cake with plum and coconut **173-5**
love cakes, Persian **74**

M

macadamia nuts: honey, macadamia
    and coconut caramels **339**
madeleines, saffron, orange and honey **76-8**
mahleb **354**
maple frosting **132-3**
marmalade
    festive fruit cake **167-8**
    little baked chocolate tarts
        with marmalade **232-4**
marron glacé: chocolate and chestnut
    powder puffs **82-5**
marshmallows: chocolate and peanut butter
    s'mores **48-51**
marzipan **351**
    festive fruit cake **167-8**
mascarpone
    Baileys Irish cream **117-18**
    espresso cinnamon mascarpone
        cream **152-5**
    fig, orange and mascarpone
        cheesecake **212-13**
    lemon and raspberry cupcakes **79-81**
    mascarpone quenelle **232-4**

Persian love cakes **74**
praline cream **291–2**
meringues **347**
  cape gooseberry pavlova **274–5**
  cinnamon pavlova, praline cream
    and fresh figs **291–2**
  coconut meringue brittle **336–7**
  frozen espresso parfait for a
    crowd **298–300**
  lime meringue cheesecakes **201–2**
  Louise cake with plum and coconut **173–5**
  rolled pavlova with peaches and
    blackberries **263–4**
  spiced praline meringues **323**
  woodland meringues **319–20**
Middle Eastern millionaire's shortbread **341**
mini-cakes **68–118**
  baby black and orange cakes **94**
  banana cakes with rum caramel **100**
  blackberry and star anise friands **103–4**
  chocolate and chestnut powder puffs **82–5**
  chocolate Guinness cakes with Baileys
    Irish cream **117–18**
  coffee and walnut financiers **105–7**
  flourless chocolate "teacakes" **108–10**
  hazelnut crumble cake with Gianduja
    icing **90–3**
  lemon and raspberry cupcakes **79–81**
  lemon and semolina syrup cakes **111**
  Persian love cakes **74**
  raspberry and rose powder puffs **82–4**
  Roma's doughnuts with saffron custard
    cream **113–15**
  saffron, orange and honey madeleines **76–8**
  strawberry and vanilla mini-cakes **95**
  tahini and halva brownies **87**
  Victoria sponge cake with strawberries
    and white chocolate cream **96–9**
molasses **356**
  gingerbread with brandy apples and
    crème fraîche **266–7**
  walnut and black treacle tarts
    with crystallized sage **245–6**
molds **71**
Mont Blanc tarts **235–7**
mousse, chocolate **232–4**
Muscat de Beaumes de Venise:
  vineyard cake **134**

N

Neapolitan pound cake (for the family) **184–5**
not-quite-Bonnie's rugelach **65**
nougat, almond and aniseed **328–9**
Nutella ganache **90–3**
nuts **347, 354–5**

O

oats **354**
  cranberry, oat and white chocolate
    biscuits **24**
  honey, oat and raisin cookies **52**
  soft date and oat bars **45**
olive oil: apple and olive oil cake **132–3**
orange blossom water **354**
  Amaretti with honey and orange
    blossom **38**
  soft date and oat bars **45**
oranges **346, 354–355**
  baby black and orange cakes **94**

chocolate panforte with oranges
  and figs **332–3**
chocolate tart with hazelnut, rosemary
  and orange **241–2**
fig, orange and mascarpone
  cheesecake **212–13**
garibaldis **57–61**
orange and star anise shortbread **46–7**
parsnip and pecan cake with aniseed
  and orange **128–9**
saffron, orange and honey madeleines **76–8**
vineyard cake **134**
oven temperatures and rack positioning **347–8**

P

pandan leaves **355**
  pineapple tartlets with pandan
    and star anise **255–6**
panforte: chocolate panforte with oranges
  and figs **332–3**
panna cotta: yogurt panna cotta with basil
  and crushed strawberries **282**
pans **71, 123, 198, 227, 350**
papaya, kaffir lime leaf posset with fresh **283**
parfait, frozen espresso **298–300**
parsnip and pecan cake with aniseed
  and orange **128–9**
passion fruit **355**
  passion fruit cheesecake with spiced
    pineapple **207–8**
pastry
  cream cheese **227, 230–1**
  docking the pastry **228**
  flaky **226, 239–40, 245–6, 247–9**
  polenta **227, 253–4**
  sweet shortcrust **226, 232–6, 241–2, 255–6**
  trimming pastry **228**
pastry cream **253–4**
pâte brisée **226**
pavlova
  cape gooseberry pavlova **274–5**
  cinnamon pavlova, praline cream
    and fresh figs **291–2**
  rolled pavlova with peaches
    and blackberries **263–4**
peanut butter: chocolate and peanut
  butter s'mores **48–51**
peanuts **354**
  peanut sandies **21**
pecans
  candied pecans **247–9, 293–4**
  chocolate, banana and pecan cookies **29**
  chocolate chip and pecan cookies **26**
  parsnip and pecan cake with aniseed
    and orange **128–9**
  pecan and prosecco truffles **324**
  pecan snowballs **63**
  pineapple, pecan and currant tin can
    cake **139**
Persian love cakes **74**
pies and tarts **224–57**
pineapple
  dried pineapple flowers **179–80**
  passion fruit cheesecake with spiced
    pineapple **207–8**
  pineapple and star anise chiffon
    cake **179–80**
  pineapple jam **255–6**
  pineapple, pecan and currant tin can
    cake **139**

pineapple purée **348**
pineapple tartlets with pandan
  and star anise **255–6**
pistachios **354**
  almond, pistachio sour cherry wafers **23**
  fig and pistachio frangipane tartlets **247–9**
  Persian love cakes **74**
  pistachio and rose water semolina
    cake **165–6**
  pistachio roulade with raspberries
    and white chocolate **159–60**
  ricotta crêpes with figs, honey
    and pistachio **268–9**
  saffron and pistachio brittle **315**
  saffron, orange and honey madeleines **76–8**
plums
  almond butter cake with cardamom
    and baked plums **176–7**
  knickerbocker glory **293–4**
  Louise cake with plum and coconut **173–5**
polenta pastry **227, 253–4**
poppy seeds: lemon and poppy seed
  cake **187**
possets: kaffir lime leaf posset with fresh
  papaya **283**
pot barley pudding with roasted apples
  and date syrup **288**
pound cake
  coffee and cardamom pound cake **181–2**
  Neapolitan pound cake (for the
    family) **184–5**
powder puffs **82–5**
  chocolate and chestnut powder puffs **82–3**
  raspberry and rose powder puffs **82–3**
praline
  almond praline **108–10**
  coffee praline **298–300**
  praline cream **291–2**
  spiced praline meringues **323**
prickly pear sorbet **306**
prosecco: pecan and prosecco truffles **324**
prunes
  festive fruit cake **167–8**
  prune cake with Armagnac and walnuts **126**
pumpkin seeds: soft date and oat bars **45**

Q

quince paste: not-quite-Bonnie's
  rugelach **65–6**

R

raisins
  apple and olive oil cake with maple
    frosting **132–3**
  butternut, honey and almond tin can
    cake **136–7**
  festive fruit cake **167–8**
  garibaldis **57–61**
  grappa fruit cake **141–3**
  honey, oat and raisin cookies **52**
  rum and raisin cake with rum caramel
    icing **124**
raspberries
  celebration cake **193–4**
  cranberry compote **203–5**
  knickerbocker glory **293–4**
  lemon and raspberry cupcakes **79–81**
  pistachio roulade with raspberries
    and white chocolate **159–60**

raspberry lollipops **318**
raspberry jam: raspberry and rose powder
    puffs **82-4**
rhubarb
    rhubarb and blueberry galette **230-1**
    rhubarb and strawberry crumble cake **148**
    rice pudding with roasted rhubarb
        and tarragon **272**
    roasted rhubarb icing **19-20**
rice pudding with roasted rhubarb
    and tarragon **272**
ricotta cheese
    baked ricotta and hazelnut
        cheesecake **209-10**
    ricotta crêpes with figs, honey
        and pistachio **268-9**
Roma's doughnuts with saffron custard
    cream **113-15**
rose petals, candied **165-6**
rose water **355**
    flourless chocolate layer cake with coffee,
        walnuts and rose water **170-2**
    pistachio and rose water semolina
        cake **165-6**
    raspberry and rose powder puffs **82-4**
    rose water cream **170-2**
rosemary
    chocolate tart with hazelnut, rosemary
        and orange **241-2**
    crystallized rosemary sprigs **241-2**
roulades
    pistachio roulade with raspberries
        and white chocolate **159-60**
    "training" roulades **348**
rugelach, not-quite-Bonnie's **65-6**
rum
    festive fruit cake **167-8**
    rum and raisin cake with rum caramel
        icing **124**
    rum butter glaze **42-3**
    rum caramel icing **100, 124**
    Speculaas biscuits **37**

S
saffron
    saffron and almond ice cream
        sandwich **301-3**
    saffron and pistachio brittle **315**
    saffron custard cream **113-15**
    saffron, orange and honey madeleines **76-8**
sage, crystallized **245-6**
salted caramel, sticky fig pudding with **287**
sandies, peanut **21**
sauce, chocolate **308**
schiacciata with grapes and fennel seeds **250**
semifreddo **293-4**
semolina
    lemon and semolina syrup cakes **111**
    pistachio and rose water semolina
        cake **165-6**
sesame seeds
    sesame brittle **232-4, 334**
    soft date and oat bars **45**
shortbread
    Middle Eastern millionaire's shortbread **341**
    orange and star anise shortbread **46-7**
shortcrust pastry, sweet **226, 232-6, 241-2,
    255-6**
s'mores, chocolate and peanut butter **48-51**
snowballs, pecan **63**

sorbet
    Campari and grapefruit sorbet **304**
    prickly pear sorbet **306**
sour cherries: almond, pistachio sour cherry
    wafers **23**
sour cream
    beet, ginger and sour cream cake **130-1**
    chocolate banana ripple cheesecake **216-17**
    white chocolate cheesecake with cranberry
        compote **203-5**
Speculaas biscuits **37**
spice **354**
    Gevulde Speculaas **33-4**
    Speculaas biscuits **37**
    spiced praline meringues **323**
    Tessa's spice cake **186**
sponge cake, Genoise **346**
star anise **356**
    blackberry and star anise friands **103-4**
    orange and star anise shortbread **46-7**
    pineapple and star anise chiffon
        cake **179-80**
    pineapple tartlets with pandan
        and star anise **255-6**
sticky fig pudding with salted caramel
    and coconut topping **287**
strawberries
    celebration cake **193-4**
    rhubarb and strawberry crumble cake **148**
    roasted strawberries **221-2**
    roasted strawberry and lime
        cheesecake **221-2**
    strawberry and vanilla mini-cakes **95**
    strawberry icing **95**
    Victoria sponge cake with strawberries
        and white chocolate cream **96-9**
    woodland meringues **319-20**
    yogurt panna cotta with basil and crushed
        strawberries **282**
sugar **356**
    caramelizing sugar **349**
    cardamom sugar **113-15**
    sifting confectioners' sugar **348-9**
    sugar syrup **326-7**
sweet shortcrust pastry **226, 232-6,
    241-2, 255-6**
Swiss meringues **347**
syrup
    honey syrup **268-9**
    lemon and semolina syrup cakes **111**
    rose water syrup **165-6**
    sugar syrup **326-7**

T
tahini
    halva **341**
    little baked chocolate tarts with tahini **232-4**
    tahini and halva brownies **07**
    tahini caramel **341**
take-home chocolate cake **152-5**
tarragon, rice pudding with roasted rhubarb
    and **272**
tarts **224-57**
    chai brûlée tarts **239-40**
    chocolate tart with hazelnut, rosemary
        and orange **241-2**
    fig and pistachio frangipane tartlets **247-9**
    little baked chocolate tarts with tahini
        and sesame brittle **232-4**
    Mont Blanc tarts **235-7**

pineapple tartlets with pandan
    and star anise **255-6**
walnut and black treacle tarts
    with crystallized sage **245-6**
teacakes
    baby black and orange cakes **94**
    flourless chocolate "teacakes" **108-10**
    lemon, blueberry and almond "teacakes" **88**
temperature
    ingredients **350**
    oven **347-8**
Tessa's spice cake **186**
thyme: apricot and thyme galettes **253-4**
tin can cakes **136-40**
    banana, date and walnut tin can cake **140**
    butternut, honey and almond tin can
        cake **136-7**
    pineapple, pecan and currant tin can
        cake **139**
toffee cape gooseberries **274-5**
tropical fruit cake **161-3**
truffles, pecan and prosecco **324**
tuiles, brown butter almond **30**
Turkish delight: chocolate, rose and walnut
    ice cream **308**

V
vanilla **356**
    strawberry and vanilla mini-cakes **95**
    vanilla whipped cream **82-5, 247-9**
Victoria sponge cake with strawberries
    and white chocolate cream **96-9**
vineyard cake **134**

W
wafers, almond, pistachio sour cherry **23**
walnuts **355**
    banana, date and walnut tin can cake **140**
    beet, ginger and sour cream cake **130-1**
    caramelized walnuts **170-2**
    chocolate banana ripple
        cheesecake **216-17**
    chocolate, rose and walnut ice cream **308**
    coffee and walnut financiers **105-7**
    fig, orange and mascarpone
        cheesecake **212-13**
    flourless chocolate layer cake with coffee,
        walnuts and rose water **170-2**
    not-quite-Bonnie's rugelach **65-6**
    prune cake with Armagnac and walnuts **126**
    walnut and black treacle tarts **245-6**
water ganache **55-6, 108-10, 190-1,
    209-10, 350**
woodland meringues **319-20**

Y
yo-yos: custard yo-yos with roasted rhubarb
    icing **19-20**
yogurt **356**
    lemon, yogurt and juniper berry
        ice cream **307**
    Persian love cakes **74**
    yogurt cream **274-5**
    yogurt panna cotta with basil and crushed
        strawberries **282**

ACKNOWLEDGMENTS

Our book has been three years in the making and involved lots of very talented people, to whom we are extremely grateful.

Two years out of the three, we've been having weekly sessions in which we would taste up to a dozen sweets in one afternoon. In charge of those marathons was one Sarah Joseph, a great cook, colleague and friend, who has dedicatedly tested all the recipes in our test kitchen, many of them several times. Sarah kept her jolly spirit in the face of many a cake adversity. For that, and for all her insights, clever contributions and very hard work, we are utterly grateful.

Tara Wigley had the impossible task of putting all this complexity in order and turning it into an actual book. Baking is already highly technical and the fact that both authors are famously fastidious didn't make it any simpler. As she always does, Tara meticulously collected recipes and information, constantly offered thoughtful suggestions and, generally, kept the ball rolling even when it was veering seriously off course. Her observations, her ability to hold the project together and her brilliant way with words were all priceless assets.

We are also totally grateful to Esme Howarth and Claudine Boulstridge, both of whom were deeply involved in the recipe testing in the United Kingdom. On the other side of the pond, Kim Laidlaw happily confirmed our inkling that we've got something good going, also by American standards.

For their part in making this book as striking as a delicious and radiant Ottolenghi meringue, we would like to thank Caz Hildebrand and Camille Blais (incredible Team Here) and Taylor Peden and Jane Munkvold (awesome Team P+M). A big thank-you is also due to Lucy Attwater and to Lindy Wiffen of Ceramica Blue.

For supporting us, trusting us and allowing us to play with our food, we are utterly grateful to our agents, publishers, editors and publicists: Felicity Rubinstein and Kim Witherspoon; Rebecca Smart, Jake Lingwood, Aaron Wehner and Hannah Rahill; Lizzy Gray, Lisa Dyer, Louise McKeever and Kaitlin Ketchum; and Mark Hutchinson, Sarah Bennie, Diana Riley, Gemma Bell and Sandi Mendelson.

We would also like to acknowledge a few colleagues and collaborators to whom we are always grateful: Jonathan Lovekin, Sanjana Lovekin, Bob Granleese, Melissa Denes, Sarah Lavelle and Fiona MacIntyre.

Throughout the book we refer to our colleagues and friends at Ottolenghi. Without them, this work would never have come to pass.

First, we should mention Noam Bar, Cornelia Staeubli and Sami Tamimi. All three of them, in their own particular ways, have contributed to shaping this book and the environment in which it has been created. Noam, Cornelia and Sami are family to us, a constant source of stimulation, support and critical thinking.

Equally important are the heads of the pastry section who worked with us over the years. Paulina Bembel, who is currently in charge, has made the Ottolenghi pastry counter her own. Her smart ideas, her practicality, her striking displays and the way she runs her team are exemplary. Her deputy, Verena Lochmuller, is equally brilliant and a privilege to have around us. Other wonderful "heads" that have been with us over the years and to whom we are utterly grateful are Savarna Paterson, Sarit Packer, Carol Brough, Jim Webb and Khalid Assyb.

At the helm of our bakery is Aaron Kossoff who, alongside Irek Krok, runs the little engine that supplies our shops and restaurants with breads, morning pastries, bagged cookies and biscuits, jams, chutneys and much, much more. Aaron and Irek's clever innovations, their willing approach and their professionalism have successfully seen us through some very busy Christmases. We'd also like to thank Faiscal Barakat, Charissa Fraser and Mariusz Uszakiewicz, all of whom have have held this ever-challenging position in the past.

Other pastry chefs and bakers, present and past, that we would like to mention here with much gratitude are Jens Klotz, Daniel Frazer, Daniel Karlsson, Przemek Lopuszynski, Brooke Gladden, Julia Frischknecht, Solvita Valaine, Celine Lecoueur, Franceska Venzon, Dan Murray, Rob Wainwright, Vita Shkilyova, Kristina Kazlauskaite, Emily Parker, Simonetta Minarelli, Giulia Bassan, Mirka Strzep, Nelson Fartouce, Daniela Silva, Carley Scheidegger, Jacopo Romagnoli, Michael Strong, Cristina Mehedinteanu, John Meechan, Lingchee Ang, Mariusz Krok, Colleen Murphy, Adam Murawski, Andrea Del Valle Garcia, Artur Matewski, Agnieszka Wozniak, Ernestas Valantinas, Carlos Prachedi Pesca, Robert Jastrzebski, Peter Polgar, Damian Zmijewski, Elimar Viale, Jared Carter, Ali Jannas, Sergio Cava, Robert Czarniak, Arkadiusz Jaroszynski, Magdalena Juhasz and Zbigniew Zubel.

More than anyone else, really, we are grateful to all the sweet-toothed customers of Ottolenghi and NOPI who have been nibbling on our brittles, chewing our biscuits, inhaling our meringues and scoffing our cakes for many, many years. Please keep on coming and let us carry on baking to our heart's delight.

Finally, we would like to acknowledge a small group of close friends and family and thank them here for being part of everything we do.

HELEN › First and foremost, David Kausman, my rock and confidante, a true mensch, and father of my beautiful children; my parents, for their examples of generosity, courage and perseverance; my siblings, Jimmy, Lucy, Lily and Margaret, for their unfailing love and support, and my precious nieces and nephews; Brendan Slater and Eng Ching Goh for their enduring loyalty to our family; Mark, Roma and the entire Kausman/Aflalo/Tauber families—the most incredible in-laws one could wish for; the Lee Family, who still loom so large and lovingly in my life—your little Ah Nung turned out all right in the end!

I am blessed and grateful to have the wonderful friendship of so many people, in London and Melbourne. There are too many to mention individually, but special thank-yous to John Redlich, Sherry Strong, Kathy Reed, Felicity Craig, Caroline Lor and Richard Ryan, Chryssa Anagnostou and Jim Tsaltis, Melly Beilby, Nicole Rudolf, Goli Nili and Ali Hazrati, Alice and James Spence, Betsy and David Gottlieb, Shehnaz Suterwalla and Azeem Azhar, and the fabulous mums at Norland Place School.

YOTAM › Karl Allen, Max and little Flynn; Michael and Ruth Ottolenghi; Tirza, Danny, Shira, Yoav and Adam Florentin; Pete and Greta Allen, Shachar Argov, Garry Chang, Alex Meitlis, Ivo Bisignano, Lulu Banquete, Tamara Meitlis, Keren Margalit, Yoram Ever-Hadani, Itzik Lederfeind, Ilana Lederfeind and Amos, Ariela and David Oppenheim.

Copyright © 2017 by Yotam Ottolenghi and Helen Goh
Photographs copyright © 2017 by Peden + Munk

All rights reserved.
Published in the United States by Ten Speed Press,
an imprint of the Crown Publishing Group, a division
of Penguin Random House LLC, New York.
www.crownpublishing.com
www.tenspeed.com

Ten Speed Press and the Ten Speed Press colophon are
registered trademarks of Penguin Random House LLC.

Originally published in Great Britain by Ebury Press, an imprint
of Ebury Publishing, Penguin Random House Ltd., London.

Library of Congress Cataloging-in-Publication Data is on
file with the publisher.

Hardcover ISBN: 978-1-60774-914-1
eBook ISBN: 978-1-60774-915-8

Printed in China

Design by Here Design

10 9 8 7 6 5 4 3 2 1

First U.S. Edition